WASHINGTON'S LADY

MARTHA WASHINGTON
Miniature painted by Charles Willson Peale around 1772
(Courtesy, the Mount Vernon Ladies' Association)

Elswyth Thane

WASHINGTON'S

LADY

DODD, MEAD & COMPANY

NEW YORK

- 973.410924
W T32w
70242
June, 1970

FOR
MARION KING

Foreword

George Washington's courtship and marriage are surrounded by a denser obscurity than any aspect of his otherwise well documented life. The lack of firsthand material is due largely to the destruction by Martha after his death, perhaps at his request, of their letters to each other. Three of his appear in his *Collected Writings*. The first of these, supposed to have been written during the 1758 campaign on the Western frontier, has now been dismissed as a forgery. Not a line from her to him has survived.

Her action, from whatever motive it arose, is a tragic loss to the historian, as they were separated during the six months which elapsed between their engagement and the wedding in January, 1759, and again from the opening session of the Continental Congress in 1774, with intervals, until the end of the war in 1783. Throughout those crowded years he wrote freely and often to his favorite brother John Augustine Washington, and to a few other trusted correspondents, who preserved at least part of the record. His letters to his wife must have been even more revealing, especially in his dark moods of discouragement and despair which were mostly hidden from the sympathetic eyes of his military family by an habitual mask of serenity.

However, a valuable characteristic emerges from a study of the remaining evidence—he usually wrote a number of letters on one day, doubtless to catch a waiting express rider, and he usually repeated himself in each, often whole sentences occurring almost verbatim several times. It is therefore likely that the letters which he wrote to Martha on the same days contained much of the same material, along with other paragraphs which were private between them. For this reason I have included in the text some of his letters which probably bear a strong resemblance to those received by her, and which should reflect her general impression of his proceedings and beliefs of a similar date.

Martha's grandson, George Washington Parke Custis, in his middle age set down his *Recollections,* and after his death they were arranged for publication by his daughter (who was Mrs. Robert E. Lee) with the assistance of that competent historian Benson Lossing, who had been a welcome guest at Arlington during Mr. Custis' lifetime. "Little Washington," as he was known in his childhood, was brought up in the Mount Vernon household as the adopted grandson of the General, his father having died in the year of his birth, and his mother having married again. His account is therefore based on the family legends which he must have heard again and again, from the Washingtons themselves and from old servants. He was twenty-one when Martha died, nearly three years after her husband, so that his memories of them both were mature. Obvious discrepancies can be traced in his narrative, due doubtless to the passing of time over his head before he wrote. But it would seem that his version of such intimate matters as the meeting at the Chamberlayne house in the spring of '58, and the ensuing rather sudden engagement, is as approximate as anything now available, since Martha herself must have been responsible for its original outline.

To avoid the continual use of *probably, possibly, apparently, presumably,* and an eternal subjunctive (especially in the early chapters) I have written a straight narrative of Martha's life, resting it on careful study of the sources and due reflection on alternative supposition and likelihood. Once the household at Mount Vernon is established and the published diaries and letters begin, less conjecture is required. Specific events emerge in chronological perspective. The whereabouts of any person at any given time can usually be determined, and their opinions, hopes, and fears lie defenseless on the printed pages of their collected writings. Sometimes without quoting I have tried to convey a frame of mind which is plainly indicated there. The personal background of unexpressed motives and reactions has not been recklessly assumed; it has been deduced. From an extended knowledge of what people actually did say and do at certain times, it becomes possible to surmise something of what they must have thought and done at other times. On this basis I must ask the reader to accept my reconstruction of Martha's unrecorded days as an educated guess. Intrinsically the whole story is there on the library shelves in yellowing volumes, and one has only to blow off the dust.

It will be observed that I have not made use in the text of the famous letter to Sally Fairfax dated from Fort Cumberland on September 12th, 1758—a letter which in its deliberately obfuscated language seems intended as a declaration of Washington's rebellious, though disciplined, love for his friend's wife. No one has seen this letter since 1877, when it is said to have turned up at an auction, and the New York *Herald* printed its alleged contents; after which it vanished again, so that no one has ever vouched for its handwriting.

A second letter to Sally from Raystown three weeks later begins with the ambiguous words: "Do we still misunderstand the true meaning of each other's letters?" and has been brought forward to support the first, assuming an obtuse reply from her in the interim. Its pedigree is less questionable, but even Fitzpatrick's text is taken from a 1927 facsimile of a privately owned original.

In view of the fact that the postal system was anything but confidential in those days, and that their correspondence was almost certain to come under her husband's eyes, if no others, and that the Fairfaxes often made joint replies, it seems unlikely that Washington would have entrusted to an express rider's pouch a rash insistence on his secret feelings. It is equally doubtful that any clandestine means of communication or connivance could have been established on the rough wilderness journey between the Fairfax home on the Potomac and the Fort.

These two letters, and a few earlier ones which cannot even be paraphrased into romance, are the foundation for the dreary sentimental fabric of his lifelong passion for Sally Fairfax, concerning which there exists no contemporary comment from a cloud of possible witnesses.

In February, 1785, when Washington had at last returned to Mount Vernon with the long war won, and the Fairfaxes had been more than ten years abroad, he looked backward, and wrote to George William Fairfax urging them, not for the first time, to return to Virginia, and inviting them in Martha's name as well as his own to consider Mount Vernon their home until their house Belvoir, which had suffered from a fire in their absence, could be rebuilt. A copy of this letter is in the Washington Papers.

In 1798, with the eight years of the Presidency behind him, and after George William's death, he wrote again to Sally, who was then ill and in reduced circumstances in Bath. The ruins of Belvoir, visible from the lawn at Mount Vernon, still made him sad. In his letter to George William more than ten years before, he said that the happiest moments of his life had been spent there, and he now repeated himself to Sally in a similar phrase. Most men at sixty-six, even without having fought a war and carried two presidential terms, recall their own relatively uncluttered twenties with rose-colored nostalgia.

Martha was almost certainly unaware of the September letters of 1758, if they were written, but the last one, to the widowed Sally at Bath, was so unclandestine that a letter-press copy was preserved among his papers, along with the draft in his handwriting of a long postscript signed by Martha and conveying the latest news of neighbors deceased and new babies born, and regretting the loss of Sally as a companion now that they were once again settled at Mount Vernon. Whatever early misgivings the bride from the Pamunkey shore may have felt as to Sally's place in Washington's regard, they would long ago have faded before the steady glow of a mutual devotion which had grown and strengthened through the anxieties of the war, the adventurous reunions at winter headquarters, and the strenuous duties of two administrations.

This is not to say that there was never an attachment, at least on his side, during his youth, for Sally must have been one of the most fascinating women he had ever seen, even in a society which included her three sisters and the three charming Fairfax girls, one of whom had married his half-brother Lawrence when George was eleven years old. It is quite possible that Sally's husband was tolerantly aware of it, and trusted wisely that it would be outgrown, as boyish infatuations for older married women usually are. George William Fairfax was anyhow a man quite capable of holding his wife's attention on his own account. He was handsome, wealthy, educated abroad, and a Burgess in the Assembly at Williamsburg when Washington was still a coltish youth with his way to make. The close friendship between the two men, Washington eight years the junior, was obvious in a hundred ways during their long correspondence, which began during Washington's early frontier days and ended only with George William's death in England in 1787.

Considering the ponderable evidence, the tendency among some of Washington's later biographers to dream up Sally Fairfax as the frustrated, tragic, and only love of his life—let alone a hidden scandal—is at least to embroider. For even if in some sudden, lonely panic at the prospect of marriage with a woman who, however desirable, was pretty much a stranger compared to anyone in his Potomac circle, he did write and send to Sally those broken, impulsive sentences just as they are cited, there is nothing in them the lasting color of scarlet, to stain the next forty years with implications.

John C. Fitzpatrick, editor of the thirty-nine-volume Bicentennial Edition of Washington's Writings, has certainly the best right to the last word. He included the September 12th letter to Sally, above a footnote full of doubt as to its status. In the single-volume by-product of his research, which he calls "A Common-sense Biography," the hard-headed Dr. Fitzpatrick puts the lid on. "It is difficult to be patient," he affirms, making the effort, "with the ideas put forth with much parade of knowledge about Sally Fairfax and George Washington. The ideas are entirely products of a type of mind."

Except for the invoice lists, I have modernized the spelling and punctuation of quoted passages, simply in order that no eighteenth century oddities of either should come between today's reader and the meaning. The sophisticated scholar also finds it hard to put up with the irrelevant amusement so often expressed at the supposed illiteracy of people who wrote long before the standardized modern rules of spelling had been invented. Until then, spelling was pretty optional and phonetic, from Chaucer right down to Dr. Johnson, reflecting the change and evolution of pronunciation, which in the case of local dialects is still variable.

Some of the letters to Washington from the Collinsesque Reverend Jonathan Boucher, who was Jacky Custis' schoolmaster for several years, have been allowed to run their ineffable course without much cutting. If there is anything left that is relatively new about Washington, it is this correspondence, buried in S. M. Hamilton's five-volume collection of letters written to him before the Revolution began, and quoted by recent writers only in fragmentary form, so that the essence of this extraordinary man's personality is lost. Yet Boucher's opinions, and his influence on her idolized son, must have bulked large in Martha's thoughts during the peaceful early years at Mount Vernon.

Wherever possible I have encouraged the story to move forward in the actual written words of the principal actors, for I am convinced that to encounter his private doubts, decisions, despairs, and occasional satisfactions, in Washington's own free-marching sentences, and to rejoice in Martha's tangled, engaging style at first hand, is more valuable to the reader now than to be fobbed off with some pale twentieth century paraphrase of their thoughts. Nothing can so quicken the Commander in Chief to life as to find a word like *rumpus* embedded in his midnight prose, without quotation marks. And bluestocking Mercy Warren's good impressions of Martha as she wrote to her friend Abigail Adams during the first winter of the war at Cambridge is worth more than any calculated estimate arrived at nearly two hundred years later.

E. T.

Contents

"Be so good as to offer my Complements in the most respectful and obliging Terms to Your Lady (a new Stile indeed) and tho' she has robbed me and many others of the greatest satisfaction we ever had or can enjoy in this Service yet none can be more sollicitous for her happiness . . ."

From Captain Robert Stewart *to* Colonel George Washington, *at the time of his retirement from the First Virginia Regiment and marriage to* Martha Custis, *January, 1759.*

WASHINGTON'S LADY

CHAPTER ONE

The Bride

1759

I T WAS NOT HER FIRST WEDDING. And in the innocent presence of her small son and daughter she could not honestly wish that it was. Married at seventeen and widowed at twenty-five, four times a mother, and two babes dead—she found it disconcerting, at her age, to be so enamored of a man. But there was no denying that the tall, diffident yet masterful soldier who was to be her bridegroom had wrought what she could only recognize as enchantment.

Not just because of the blue and scarlet regimentals, for he had laid them aside and resigned from the army. Not wealth nor dazzling prospects—he had only a small house on the Potomac and some land—a gift, a passion for acquiring land. Not social brilliance, for he was a rather silent man, who watched and listened and sometimes smiled—and never told stories about his colorful military past, in company. There was his reputation—his achievement, at twenty-six—his magnificent, heart-stirring presence, his way with a horse, his way with her children. But there was more to it than that. She was in love.

Once it had shocked her to find that everyone expected her promptly to marry again, after Daniel died so suddenly eighteen months ago; died without a will, leaving her a rich widow with full responsibility for his estate and the future of little Jack and Patsy. He had wise attorneys, a good overseer, all competent men, who made a polite comedy of consulting her. Still it was bewildering, for she had never thought to stand alone. Daniel was always there, twenty years older than she was, accustomed to his wealth and its obligations, never at a loss—never, at least, after the death of his overwhelming father in the first year of their marriage. Daniel was always so kind, capable, and careful, so—comfortable.

They had had good times together. He liked to see her wear pretty clothes from England; their plantation home, called the White House, was in New Kent County on the Pamunkey River; he kept a fine chariot and horses, and twice a year they went to Williamsburg for the public times when the Assembly met, and then they lived in the Custis mansion in the capital, with its six proud chimneys. Williamsburg was a long way from the war on the frontier, where the French were encroaching on the Ohio country, inciting Indian raids on the border settlements, massacre, scalping, and terror. A man called Braddock came out from England with a redcoated army, marched it to the Monongahela, and there was cruelly beaten in a wilderness battle. When Braddock was seen to be fatally wounded, a man called Washington, who was a Virginian, took command and brought off the survivors. Without him the remnants of Braddock's force might have been surrounded and murdered to the last panic-stricken Englishman. The Royal Governor made much of young Colonel Washington when he came to Williamsburg in the autumn of '55, and Daniel had pointed him out to her in the street—towering above his companions, with a grave, slightly pock-marked face, and the erect, straight-stepping carriage of an Indian.

Two years later, when her sister Nancy married Burwell Bassett at the Assembly time, Colonel Washington was again in Williamsburg, summoned by the ailing Governor Dinwiddie to report on the necessities of his dissatisfied forces at Fort Cumberland, such as arrearages of pay, allowances for the officers' tables, and the wisdom of securing friendly Indians with which to fight hostile ones. During the social whirl in the little capital city that May, she and Colonel Washington were introduced to each other, and exchanged a few words on several occasions. His cool blue eyes were kind and searching, his manner a trifle formal and remote. The frontier hero was shy with women. When she said so, behind his back, there was some laughter. But not blind to them, somebody said. Unlucky, though, remarked another voice. That depends, was a third opinion. Unmarried, anyway.

Soon after Nancy's wedding, when baby Jack was down with some childish complaint, Daniel was suddenly taken ill. The doctor confessed

himself baffled, and almost before she had time to be frightened Daniel
was dead. Less than ten years of marriage, and only two children living,
and it had all come to an end.

She was unprepared to find that before long several people appeared
to be more than ready to take Daniel's place, and her sister Nancy reminded her briskly that she was not a fool, not a fright, only twenty-five,
and had a fortune. Life was far from over, Nancy said, in circumstances
like hers. But she was not in any hurry to prove that. She went on from
day to day, as nearly as possible in the same familiar pattern, in the
White House in New Kent County to which she had come as Daniel's
bride. It was not far from Williamsburg, and the neighborhood was a
nest of friends and relatives; she had the children, and devoted, shelter-
ing servants, and she never lacked for company nor for invitations. She
began, rather guiltily, to miss Daniel a little less.

In the spring of '58, when she had been more than six months a widow,
she packed up the children and their nurse and went for a visit to the
Chamberlaynes nearby. It was useless to expect her to go anywhere that
Jacky, four, and Patsy, two, were not welcome. And there, captured at
the ferry by her host and brought home to dine, was the tall frontier
colonel again, wearing uniform and riding-boots and sword, his hair unpowdered; gaunt and ill after weeks of dysentery, and now on his way
to Williamsburg to consult a doctor.

They met as mere acquaintances with mutual friends and recollections.
There were other guests to dinner, and beneath the general conversation
he made an opportunity to inquire after the Bassetts and to speak gently
of Daniel and her loss. At the dinner table she noticed that he ate little,
and watching him compassionately she felt sure that he was in pain, and
she insisted with a quaint maternal authority that he drink some wine
with the food. His eyes dwelt on her as she prescribed, respectful, amused,
surprised. It came to her that he wanted looking after; men always went
a little off their heads when they were ill. The wine seemed to brighten
him a bit. That, and someone taking an interest. No women at home?
she wondered.

After dinner they all sat in the parlor for a while, and when the other
guests, who were not staying overnight as she was, rose to take their leave
and the Chamberlaynes accompanied them to the outer door, Colonel
Washington lingered, seeming on the point of departure, awaiting only
the return of his host to make his own farewells. In the hall and on the
stairs there were voices and laughter and running to and fro. Alone in

the parlor, the widow and the soldier sat down again, with only the fire between them. Making conversation to keep him at his ease, she asked the right questions, gave the right answers to his, and they found themselves on common ground. He sat facing her, his big hands clasped before him, his eyes steady and troubled, while they talked.

They did not see Mrs. Chamberlayne look in at the door and tiptoe away to intercept her husband. They forgot that his orderly waited at the gate with the horses. They forgot they were almost strangers. They were two lonely people, discovering with mutual excitement that each could succor the other. He was worn down and exhausted, he had had repeated frustrations and humiliations in his military duties, dealing with incompetent subordinates and arrogant superiors; he was on the point of resigning from the army forever, he was almost prepared for an early death like that of his half-brother Lawrence, who had returned to Virginia in '43 in broken health after serving as a captain of marines at the siege of Cartagena on the Spanish Main; and he had been since boyhood more than half in love with the brilliant, brittle wife of his closest friend and neighbor near Mount Vernon.

It was a very different type of woman who sat across the hearth rug from him now, cosy and frank and unintellectual and unflirtatious, listening without guile simply because she was kindhearted and interested and wanted to help. She warmed and soothed him like the wine, and did not go to his head like Sally Fairfax. And she, with her homely genius for cossetting, which Daniel no longer needed, saw the tall colonel as little more than a harassed boy without a woman to turn to, both proud and humble in his solitary misery. She let him discover that she too was solitary, with problems and responsibilities beyond a woman's scope, which he as a landowner himself could understand.

There had been a sort of magic about that afternoon in the Chamberlaynes' parlor, she thought later, looking back—in the flare of mutual need and mutual response. And when at last with reluctance he recollected himself and rose to take his leave, Mr. Chamberlayne blocked his way in the hall, vowing that no guest ever left his house after sunset. The horses were sent to the stables with their astonished attendant, the drawing-room candles were lighted, the children were brought in to say good night—he looked larger than ever, extending a courteous forefinger for Jacky to shake.

At supper he ate and drank what she recommended, with touching confidence and docility. As the evening drew out, the Chamberlaynes were unaccountably fatigued and retired early to bed, while their two remaining guests sat on by the fire again, and he listened, smiling, to chatter about her babies, and promptly accepted an impulsive invitation to pause at the White House when his business in Williamsburg was finished, and see Jacky ride his pony. It was only then that he recalled the grim nature of his errand in the town, and his expectation of a fatal diagnosis.

Breakfast was leisurely and talkative, and around noon he rode away, in a very different frame of mind than when he had come. He was not willing to die just yet. And there were several things he wanted to say to the Governor.

He was somewhat less incredulous than he might have been, when the dreaded interview with Dr. Anson proved reassuring. At least, he did not have Lawrence's tuberculous complaint. Irascible old Governor Dinwiddie, with whom he had been carrying on an exasperated correspondence for months, had at last departed for England, and the acting Governor, President Blair, was more tactful. There was unfinished business at Fort Loudoun, and it was no time to think of retreating from his undertaking there.

Early in April he set out from Williamsburg northward again. The White House on the Pamunkey was not much out of his way back to the bleak frontier.

In the interim she had gone to some trouble to learn more about him. The Chamberlaynes were kin to Burwell Bassett's first wife, who had died—Nancy was his second. Washington's friendship with Major Chamberlayne had begun during a frontier campaign. She needed only to show the most casual interest to set them all talking about him.

They told again the miracle of his survival on the Monongahela, the only one of Braddock's mounted officers who was not either disabled or killed, though he received four bullets through his clothes and two horses were shot under him—as if he had been preserved, the Reverend Samuel Davies of Hanover County pointed out at the time, by Providence for some further service to his country. But in the three years more or less that had passed since then, his career had been anything but triumphant, and his friends felt it was small wonder that he had become disillusioned and was even unwilling to continue his thankless effort to organize and defend the western settlements.

He had recently entertained the idea of retiring from the army altogether, and had stood for election as Burgess for Frederick County where he owned land. He was defeated—a blow at least to his pride, though his absence at his wilderness headquarters during the election campaign was reason enough. Embarrassed by the lack of the proper military authority due his rank, by lack of funds, lack of enlistments, lack of the bare necessities for feeding and housing and clothing the unruly forces he was trying to hold together, he had even journeyed to Boston to interview Governor Shirley there, in an attempt to clarify his position with the man who was Commander in Chief in America.

As for why he was still a bachelor at an age when many men could show a growing family, his life as a soldier provided little opportunity for courtship, and when he came away on leave it was usually to recover from sickness or to wrangle with the Governor and Council. His scanty leisure was spent in the lively Fairfax household at Belvoir near Mount Vernon, where George William's wife outshone all the rest. Everyone who went there was more or less in love with Sally Fairfax; slender, witty, sparkling, perhaps a bit spoilt, childless after ten years of marriage, Sally remained conspicuously devoted to her easy-going, handsome husband, who was a Burgess for the Tidewater county which bore his family name.

Martha Custis had encountered the Fairfaxes more than once during the Assembly times at Williamsburg, and was well aware of Sally's pretty figure and distinguished ways. The four Cary sisters, of whom Sally was the eldest, were all well educated and well endowed by their father, and all made suitable marriages. A man emerging into civilization after months in the wilderness would certainly be dazzled by the little balls and amateur theatricals and musical evenings and scintillating talk which enhanced Sally's world. It was a useful circle of society, too, if ever he wanted to stand another election.

The more Martha heard, the more she doubted the singular bond which had held them both that day in the Chamberlaynes' parlor. He had been at low ebb, anxious about his health, deadlocked in his army ambitions, homesick for his neglected acres, oversusceptible to family comforts and a little sympathy. The note which he dispatched to her from Williamsburg told nothing except the time of his intended arrival for the promised visit. She wondered that he had remembered to send it, even as she posted a servant to watch for him.

He was punctual to the time he set, attended as always by the faithful man Bishop, who had been a kind of legacy, along with a fine saddle horse, from the dying Braddock. She was waiting on the doorstep when they rode up to the house, and Jacky ran to meet him as he swung out of the saddle, and was tossed up on the big horse where he sat frozen with joy while she held her breath, until after a solemn parade down the drive and back he was safely removed and deposited at her feet. Jacky was now Colonel Washington's slave.

Her hand was engulfed in his as he bent above it, and even before she led the way to the parlor, where the vases stood full of spring bloom, she could see that he was greatly improved in health. It amused him to assure her that it was as much her sound advice on what to eat and drink as it was Dr. Anson's very nasty prescriptions which was hastening him to what he now believed would be full recovery. Yes, he was able to return to his post at Fort Loudoun, where he would await the arrival of the new Governor. There was nothing much to be done with the Council and the acting Governor, who preferred to temporize. Meanwhile, his men would go always a little hungry, and ragged almost to nakedness, short of ammunition, and with field equipment almost nonexistent. Always the same answer: lack of funds. But what was the Assembly at Williamsburg for, if not to grant funds for the men who risked their lives and sacrificed their daily comfort for the service of their country?

He should stand for election again, she said. Next time he would win, and then he could speak his mind from the floor of the House and demand that his soldiers be provided for. That brought him up short with a protest that he was no orator, and she smiled and said that he had been very eloquent indeed for nearly half an hour. But that was different, he explained—any man could talk to her, because she listened so well. He then apologized for imposing on her, and she set him off again with a well-placed question.

One thing was plain to her as she watched him. He said it was no use, he said he was discouraged and sick at heart for his men, he called the Council hard names—but there was no despair in him now. He was on the way back. He would go on. He was not beaten. He would never be beaten.

After dinner they walked about the grounds, accompanied by Jacky on his pony, and interviewed her steward, who was a Williamsburg man. She thought Colonel Washington's manner with her people was exactly the right blend of authority and courtesy, and he was followed by admiring glances and broad smiles. When they returned to the house baby Patsy toddled forward to offer him a limp bouquet, and he went on one knee to accept it, his face transfigured by tenderness, and she laughing up at him through her eyelashes, so that he called her a baggage and prophesied broken hearts in her wake before long.

When he rose and turned to where Patsy's mother stood looking on, their eyes met and lingered—it felt right to them both that he should be here, playing with her children, overseeing her property, dining at her table, sharing their plans and their difficulties.

His horses were waiting in the drive, the reins in Bishop's hands. Colonel Washington thanked her rather formally for a delightful afternoon, walked with her back to the doorstep, and paused there, without privacy to say good-by. The face she raised to him was full of entreaty. When the new Governor came, he said in answer to it, he would doubtless be summoned to Williamsburg again to put his case. So it would not be long, he said, looking down at her with his grave smile, before he did himself the pleasure of another visit, if she would permit.

Once more she stood and watched him ride away from her, while Patsy, responsive to every breeze that blew, burst into tears.

The next time he came she had no warning. He and Bishop rode up the drive on a hot day in May, dusty and travel-worn, bound for Williamsburg where big things were afoot, though the new Governor had not yet arrived. They had dined along the road, but the horses needed rest, and he sat down with a comfortable sigh in the shaded parlor to enjoy a cool drink and a plate of cakes fresh from the oven and doubly delicious to a man who subsisted most of the time on a soldier's rations.

He would have more time to spare on the way back, he told her. Then he would know better what was behind this summons by the Council. He hoped it meant another attempt to wrest Fort Duquesne from the French, a new campaign in which Braddock's mistakes might be avoided. Colonel Washington had waited nearly three years for a chance to take the offensive again. He believed firmly that until the French were attacked in force and thrown out of the Ohio country bodily there would be no safety for the inhabitants of the western borderland. It was an old score he longed to settle, and today he was restless and inwardly simmering at the prospect. She saw him now as a soldier, dedicated, preoccupied, in a hurry. It was disappointing. Even the children failed to catch his attention entirely. His mind had gone on ahead of him to Williamsburg, probing the odds there, devising arguments, preparing defenses, laying down stratagems.

When he rose, more abruptly than was his punctilious habit, her docile acceptance of his mood penetrated at last, and he paused with a rueful

smile. She was so small, so uncomplaining, so *good,* like one of her own
sensitive children. He held out both his big hands and hers went into them
gratefully. On the way back, he promised her, when he knew better where
he was, there would be more time. He hesitated, and then laid his lips
against her fingers before he strode out of the room.

Since he had last seen her he had had a great deal to think about besides the policy of the new Governor. He was turning twenty-seven, and
felt he had very little to show for it. His name was known throughout
Virginia, it was true, as the foremost young officer America had produced
so far. But his rank and reputation were very little good to him so long
as the King's commission outweighed a colonial one, and his hard-bought
experience and opinions could be dismissed by any commander sent out
from England to do the job he believed he had himself earned the right
to undertake.

And if he left the army, and won an election, and settled down at
Mount Vernon to become an influential planter and member of the Assembly, like George William Fairfax, for instance, then the long, sterile
devotion to George William's wife would not fill the chair on the other
side of the fire in the evenings, would not provide heirs for the estate he
cherished, nor make a gracious hostess for the guests he was bound to
entertain. His widowed mother, intransigent and arbitrary always, lived
alone near his married sister Betty Lewis at Fredericksburg. His most
congenial brother, John Augustine, who had for a while managed Mount
Vernon for him, had gone with his bride to live in Westmoreland County.
Mount Vernon required a wife. His leisure hours indoors would be cosier
for one. And if he married, who would be easier to love than the sensible
little widow at the White House, who lacked a manager for her own estate? Together they could build an establishment second to none in
Virginia.

During those long spring evenings at Fort Loudoun he had plenty
of time to think, and he recognized a crossroads. Absorbed in the dreary
daily round at the post, he had allowed himself to drift too long. If he was
to have a future, he must lay hold of it soon. Mount Vernon was his home,
and the secondhand family life he had found with the Fairfaxes at Belvoir
was not enough. Sally had told him more than once that he ought to
marry.

It was not to set someone in Sally's place, for she had no legitimate
place in his life. It was not to forget her, because they would always be
neighbors. His relationship with Sally need not change if he married, be-

cause he had nothing to lose. But let the woman he chose be as different from Sally as a woman could be, rather than some pale counterfeit who could never stand comparison with the true gold coin. Let her be small and soft, instead of tall, taut, and slender; sweet-tempered and obliging, instead of distracting and unpredictable; submissive where Sally challenged; no better read than he was, maybe; a born mother; and let her be always kind. As he totted up the total and wrote Martha's name as the sum, he failed to notice that Sally came out a bit short on wifely virtues. He was never to see Sally plain, as long as he lived, though he might have done so if he had ever got close enough to hold her in his arms.

Women, however, were secondary as he rode down from New Kent County toward Williamsburg at the end of May in 1758, and they remained banished from his thoughts during the busy days which followed. As he had suspected, Parliament was taking a hand with the French, and a man called Forbes was to lead a new assault on Fort Duquesne. Colonel Washington had been named to accompany the expedition as second in command. His immediate orders were to return at once to his post and prepare to join Forbes, who was coming down to the frontier from Philadelphia.

Now he knew where he was. He sent off a message to the White House, announcing his return in time for dinner on the 5th, and looked the thing in the face. He might be away for months. No one knew better than he the endless delay and hazard involved in the coming campaign. It was even possible that he might not come back at all. Perhaps it would be better to wait until Fort Duquesne was taken and the old score with France was settled, and then he could turn his back on soldiering forever, establish himself at Mount Vernon to grow tobacco at a profit, stand for election till he won a seat, and travel to Williamsburg twice a year when the Assembly met, with his family in a chariot with four horses, the trademark of a prosperous planter.

But when he saw her again, standing so small and straight, asking nothing of him, but so willing to give, she went to his heart, and he knew a sudden fear that he might lose her if he left it too long. A woman like that would not have to wait. He was quite sure now that since it could never be Sally it was Martha that he wanted in the chair across the hearth at Mount Vernon—as different from Sally as a woman could be, a new leaf turned, for a fair beginning.

He had not prepared a speech for it. The words came clumsily, he felt as he tried to find them, and to her the big man's lack of assurance, his innocence of all conceit or self-importance, as he made his honest offer, left no room for doubt. Besides, he was on his way to a war. If a woman's promise for his return was any sort of shield or comfort against what lay ahead of him, then he had it, with her love and her prayers.

Not until he had gone again, for no one knew how long, did she realize that it had all happened rather suddenly. Four brief meetings since her widowhood, and she had promised to be his wife, which meant she must go and live with him in Fairfax County on the Potomac, in a house she had never seen, among neighbors who, while not total strangers, were not like her lifelong friends along the James and the Pamunkey, to say nothing of her Dandridge kin at Chestnut Grove only a few miles away from the White House, and the Bassetts at Eltham. It would be a whole new world at Mount Vernon, except for Jack and Patsy. She would have the children to keep her from feeling too lonely or strange, and now there would be more. A new baby would make all the difference.

Washington's own second thoughts as he rode back toward Winchester presented some misgivings too. Now he had to tell Sally that he had taken her advice and bespoken a wife. Sally would laugh, and congratulate him. He knew her too well to suppose that she would show any regret for the loss of her exclusive empire over his private affections. Sally's discretion was such that she did not intend to have it unduly noticed and commented upon that young Colonel Washington believed himself to be in love with her. She would doubtless welcome a conventional end to that contingency, and would receive his bride cordially into the Fairfax circle, and help to make her feel at home there. It was not as though Martha Custis was unknown to the Masons and the Carlyles and the Lees and the Fairfaxes. Everyone met everyone else during the Assembly times at Williamsburg. But she had never visited among the Potomac households, and he supposed that she might feel uprooted at first. Some adjustment would be required, and he must make sure that she never was homesick. Sometimes as he rode he reflected with something like dismay that it was too late now to unsay those halting words in Martha's parlor, and then he would remind himself resolutely that marriage was a step which must be taken sooner or later.

At Winchester he announced his second candidacy as member for Frederick County, and arranged for his friends Carlyle and Fairfax to campaign for him in his absence. Then he pushed on to Fort Loudoun, where he found all the usual small army feuds and controversies grinding along. With Forbes it was the same old story too. Ignorant of the terrain, he still refused advice, and undertook to cut his own road through the forest instead of making use of Braddock's route. The extra delay and hardship caused by his obstinacy made trouble with the temperamental Indian allies and discontent among his own hard-pressed men. Forbes had become so prostrated by the bloody flux that he had to travel in a horse-litter, which partly accounted for his unreasonable state of mind.

By mid-September they had advanced only as far as Raystown on the new road, winter was threatening to overtake them along the way, and Washington knew only too well what that would mean for himself and the men. His letters were dispirited and angry. "We seem then to act under an evil geni, the conduct of our leaders (if not actuated by superior orders) is tempered with something I don't care to give a name to," he wrote, ". . . . for nothing but a miracle can bring this campaign to a happy issue."

For years he had written to the Fairfaxes out of his loneliness and discouragement in the field, and received from them enlivening accounts of Tidewater doings. Now there was another letter for him to write, to the woman who would be his wife when this campaign was over, and there were her letters back to him, full of the homely details of her placid days at the White House—comforting, unexciting letters from a woman too unaccustomed to her pen to set down her thoughts and emotions, and therefore not love letters, as they might have been, to express her devotion to him and her dreams of their future together. They were difficult letters to answer, because the acquaintance was so short, and there was so little of mutual experience to share. But he wrote conscientiously, wondering how much of the military record of delay and incompetence and hardship she could comprehend or find of interest.

Then the miracle which he had mentioned without much hope did happen. They had struggled to within a day's march of Fort Duquesne when the French suddenly set fire to the place and by the light of the flames escaped down the river, bag and baggage. The Virginians had only to take possession of the smouldering ruins.

General Forbes retired to Philadelphia in his horse-litter, and died a few weeks later. He left orders that Washington was to post a garrison at Fort Duquesne and himself ride at once to Williamsburg to persuade Governor Fauquier to make adequate provision for wintering the ragged, ill-fed troops on the frontier. Washington's horses broke down along the way, and by the time he reached the Potomac again in December he was as usual sick with the inevitable camp ailments, dysentery and fever.

A hasty inspection of Mount Vernon in June before he joined Forbes had revealed unsuspected dilapidation which must be remedied before he brought home a bride. George William Fairfax had most kindly undertaken to engage workmen and oversee the job, in addition to his efforts to secure the election of his friend to the Assembly. His letters since then had been full of knotty problems which Washington had to decide at long range on the spur of the moment, often with an express rider saddled up and waiting: Should the upstairs floors be taken up and laid new, George William inquired, or would a good planing suffice? If he wanted new flooring, then new doors would be required—the outside was suffering from need of paint, and George William had taken the liberty of hiring another man to do that—the chimneys would be better enlarged—was the landing on the stairs to be papered or stuccoed, as at Belvoir?—goods had not yet arrived from the Yorktown wharves, and nothing could be finished till the new glass went in—the work would never be done before frost . . .

Now in December Washington found the house still a confusion of carpenters and unglazed windows, though George William had himself supplied the new floor boards, as none were to be had elsewhere. He tramped unhappily through the echoing rooms, with their shrouded furniture stacked here and there, and saw no hope of inhabiting the place for months to come. The wedding would have to wait, then.

In any case, he had won the election this time, and his decision to resign from the army was taken, to the dismay of the men he commanded, who threatened right and left to follow suit. He had been five years ousting the French, and he recognized that it had been valuable experience, but the account was closed. He would now become a Burgess and a planter and a married man. He looked forward with mixed emotions to what the next five years would bring, and the White House on the Pamunkey lay between him and Williamsburg.

Six months had passed since he had last seen the woman he was going to marry, and he was wondering how to resume the mood in which they had parted. But when the door opened on rooms decked with Christmas greens and bright with log fires and the voices of children, and she gave him both her hands with simple dignity and unquestioning delight at his safe return, it all began to look much easier.

After Jack and Patsy had been taken away, protesting, by their nurse, their mother opened a locked chest and showed him, laughing and whispering like a child herself, the toys and pretty garments she had had the foresight to order months ago from England for her little family. He had seldom if ever spent a Christmas season in a household where there were children, and he had forgotten, to his chagrin, to provide any gifts of his own. It would be too late now to collect suitable trinkets even if any were to be had in Williamsburg. He put his hand to his pocket for money, and hesitated. Coins were nothing to children, it was only what the coins would fetch. Smiling, she came to his rescue, laying out a toy horse and a velvet cap trimmed with silver lace. Those could be given to the children in his name. But for her, he said, touched and awkward—he had nothing even for her. Next year, she comforted him. Next year there would be time for all that.

It was difficult then to confess the sorry state his house was in, and he discovered that the prospect of postponing the wedding, recently viewed with something like relief, was after all a depressing one—for the warm room and the tactful little woman beside him, and the indefinable holiday excitement already in the air had soothed and captivated a spirit starved of love.

Somehow it was arranged between them, to their satisfaction. He would go on at once to Williamsburg as he must do, and kiss the new Governor's hand and conclude his army business there, and attend the yearend festivities at the Palace if bidden. Early in January, all his military duties faithfully discharged, he would return to New Kent County for the wedding.

There need be no upheaval, they decided, very serious and longheaded and secretly aglow. It would be necessary for him to take his seat in the Assembly in February, for his first session as Burgess for Frederick County, and while they were in Williamsburg for that they would live in the Custis town house with the six chimneys. At the same time they could arrange for its rental to some reliable tenant, and settle all the legal formalities which would place her affairs and the children's safely in his hands. Mount Vernon could wait, and take its time, they would not be homeless. In the spring, they would go to Mount Vernon. Meanwhile they would be gay in Williamsburg. It had been too long, she told him, since he had been gay. Watching her happy face in the firelight, he perceived that he had much to learn about living with a woman, and that the lessons were going to be remarkably pleasant.

On her side, as the summer waned, she had begun to dread the day when she must leave the White House and the neighbors she was accustomed to, and set out for the Potomac with a man she was very lately acquainted with at all. Instead of being hustled, she now found herself with another Williamsburg Season ahead of her as the bride of a man everyone delighted to honor. Mount Vernon in the spring became something to look forward to, fresh with new paint and glass and timber, hers to arrange and devise and furnish like a doll's house. George drew her a floor plan, showing a central hall wtih a fine staircase between two rooms either side, upstairs and down. He made her a list of the furniture he could remember, and she began a list of the things she could not bear to leave behind. When he rode on to Williamsburg she had only a fortnight in which to deal with the Christmas holidays and her wedding preparations, both together.

She had plenty of assistance, and when the day came she was ready without any last-minute scurry or fuss. Her dress was yellow brocade, the skirt open down the front over a white and silver petticoat; her slippers were lilac silk embroidered in gold and silver, with high heels, because he was so tall. There were pearls looped through her powdered hair.

Governor Fauquier himself was coming to the wedding, in full dress, with his wife on his arm. The house was already bulging with guests, and her sister Nancy Bassett had everything in charge. The children were beside themselves with excitement and had to be restrained. It would be the same clergyman who had married her to Daniel, she would not have liked a ceremony performed by a stranger.

She sat alone in her room, waiting, a pool of quiet in the domestic vortex—resisting the temptation to peep through the curtains every time more wheels rolled up the drive, listening for the big saddle horse that had once carried Braddock in his red coat, and whose army days were over now. He must have traveled very soberly, for there was Nancy's voice outside her door, like a peal of bells—Colonel Washington had arrived.

Her heart never beat like that for Daniel.

CHAPTER TWO

The New World

1759-1765

IN FEBRUARY THEY ALL set out for Williamsburg, as she had done many times before with Daniel at her side. She and the children traveled in her coach with her servants in the Custis livery to drive it. Washington and Bishop rode escort on horseback, which Jacky thought very dashing, and Patsy wept because her new Pappa was too far out of reach to suit her infant idolatry.

Martha had watched with some anxiety to see how the big, striding man would adjust to the loving clamor of her children for his attention. They both regarded him as a new, if massive, toy, and climbed on him with shrill delight at every opportunity. He not only bore it well, he seemed to enjoy it, with never-failing patience and good nature. She could hardly have endured otherwise, but it was one of many happy portents for their future that he had already accepted the children almost as his own, and with her permission had himself taught them to address him as Pappa. Patsy could remember no other, and Jacky's impressions of his father were fading fast.

To Washington, who had moved armies, the marshaling of his domestic cavalcade to attend the Assembly presented complications undreamed of in logistics. He was more amused than anything else, to find himself at the head of a ready-made family who looked to him for direction on countless matters which were quite outside his previous experience. He learned fast, with many surprises and some laughter on both sides. And Martha, who had not really relished her brief interlude of sole responsibility, relaxed contentedly again into wifehood, and except where the children were concerned left all the decisions to him.

He discovered very soon that where the children were concerned he had no authority whatever and that very little notice was taken of his weighed opinions. Jack and Patsy Custis were hopelessly spoilt, and so charming in spite of it that one had not the heart to complain. But in view of his own rugged childhood, first under the roof of his Spartan widowed mother, and then in the adult households of his two half-brothers and the childless Fairfax establishment at Belvoir, he was bewildered by the indulgence demanded by Martha's babies. He was not satisfied that so little discipline was for the best, and there grew in him a secret resolve that his own son, when he had one, would learn what it was to obey.

The handsome Custis house in Williamsburg welcomed them with log fires and the smiling faces of Martha's well-trained servants—she did not neglect to bring up her Negro maids in the way they should go—and the little town was already bustling with the Assembly trade. George William had given up burgessing, and the Fairfaxes had not made the winter journey from the Potomac. But another near neighbor and friend from Washington's boyhood, George Mason, was taking his seat for the first time, as was Richard Henry Lee of Chantilly and his brother Francis Lightfoot Lee of Menokin, who had both grown up at Stratford near his half-brother Austin's house, Wakefield. Two Randolph brothers were there, Peyton and John, and four Carters—Landon of Sabine Hall; Charles of Cleve; and a son and a nephew, both Charles. Speaker Robinson too was an old friend—at fifty-five, old even in relative years. They all came to the Six Chimney House to pay their respects, surveying little Martha Custis with new interest now that she was Mrs. Washington.

He took the oath on his twenty-seventh birthday, and had occupied his seat only a few days when it was resolved and enthusiastically carried that George Washington, Esq., late Colonel of the First Virginia Regiment, should receive the thanks of the House for his faithful services to His Majesty, and the Colony, "and for his brave and steady behavior, from the first encroachments and hostilities of the French and their Indians, to his resignation, after the happy reduction of Fort Duquesne."

Martha was not present in the Assembly chamber, of course, but she heard more than one account of what happened then. Mason told it best, being somehow able to elongate his swarthy, robust self into a fair imitation of the tall ex-colonel while, rumbling with unmalicious mirth, he demonstrated for her in the parlor after dinner how—taken by surprise—her husband had risen in his place perforce to respond, stammered into stage fright, and sat down again, to renewed applause by his fellow Burgesses. Blushing like a virgin, said Mason, and brought down a heavy affectionate hand on the victim's shoulder. But Martha would not laugh at George, and said that anyway it was better than being too glib with his tongue, which Mason, no great orator himself, could not take amiss.

She liked Mason, in spite of the well-known cynicism of his general discourse, and his rather formidable front, and she looked forward to a better acquaintance with his wife, a Maryland girl with superb auburn hair. He had married Anne Eilbeck from across the River ten years before, and for her had built Gunston Hall on his plantation lands just below Belvoir. Mount Vernon could learn from Gunston, George told her. Mason kept some five hundred people on the place and managed it all himself with only trained slave assistants, and he was making it an almost self-contained community, even to a distillery which turned out excellent peach and apple brandy.

It was much the most social season she had known since her girlhood days under old Governor Gooch, when Daniel—among several others—was courting. The new Governor, Francis Fauquier, was friendly and hospitable and popular; her husband was a favorite at the Palace, and heads turned wherever he appeared; and she had emerged from the eclipse of mourning as a celebrated bride. Between his friends and hers, they had hardly an evening to themselves. When they did, there was always the fascinating game of planning her new home at Mount Vernon. Everything had to be ordered all the way from England, in order to get the best, and the sooner the list was sent off the less time they would have to wait for the ship to come in.

The Assembly session was not a very important one, for the war with France was thought to be almost over, and things had gone into a lull. Before the House actually adjourned, Washington received leave to depart for home in order to see about the spring planting, and they traveled northward together through the green Virginia countryside.

Impatient as she was to reach Mount Vernon now, they paused at Fredericksburg to visit his sister Betty, who was Mrs. Fielding Lewis, and from there went to call on his mother at her little house on the farm near the River. Betty was so like her brother George in petticoats it was laughable, though of course being a woman she had more to say, and she was plainly delighted with his choice of a wife. There were several children in the Lewis family, and more to come, and the Custis two were absorbed into the nursery with joyful noise. George's mother was a different matter altogether—spare, erect, hawk-eyed, her immaculate rooms a challenge to any housewife, her welcome full of reserve which amounted almost to hostility. Before long Martha found herself glancing toward her husband for a clue, and encountered there an unfamiliar mask of unsmiling courtesy. Between the two of them, Martha went on her own dignity. It was not an easy visit, and as brief as good manners would allow.

She first came to Mount Vernon on the 7th of April—and found a square, white-painted house without a porch, facing southeast across the River, which was a mile and a quarter wide. The road ran up to the west front, past the gates of Gunston and Belvoir, after it left the ferry at Occoquan. You entered a central hall from behind the stairs, which rose opposite the River door. The parlor, with its corner fireplace, was on your left, across from the stairs. If you walked straight through the hall and the east door you came out on a sweep of lawn above the shining, noble River—and downstream on a projecting point of land you could see the rosy bricks of Belvoir, where Sally Fairfax lived.

There was no stinting of welcome in that quarter, for everything in the shape of food was lavishly prepared and sent over from the Belvoir kitchen, and the most cordial messages were left, offering hospitality in case Mount Vernon proved still unready for occupancy. Martha's heartfelt thanks were accompanied by a firm declaration that Mount Vernon was entirely adequate as it stood, for nothing would have induced her to leave the house, even over night. Soon the four rooms on the lower floor were put to rights as bedrooms, dining room, and parlor, with her own favorite pieces of furniture from her home on the Pamunkey disposed among what had survived the departure of Lawrence's widow to her second marriage, and the somewhat random years since then when George or John Augustine had camped out in the house for short periods of time.

Martha gave her attention first of all to the freshly papered upstairs bedroom which would eventually be theirs. Together in the evenings they went over all the lists again, and made out the invoice to be sent off to his agents in London. Sometimes he wrote at her dictation, sometimes he interpolated his own requirements. Because the goods all had to be chosen for them by a stranger and they were at his mercy, they had to be as explicit as possible and hope that there existed somewhere in London, if he took the trouble to search, articles approximate to their desire. She had brought her own china, linen, silver, and glassware, and her pre-mourning wardrobe, in trunks from the White House, along with several of her servants. Some of her treasures got damaged on the way, and other amenities, such as fire screens, had not graced Mount Vernon since Lawrence's day.

"Invoice of Sundry Goods to be shipped by Robet. Cary, Esq., and Company, for the use of George Washington—viz:" he wrote finally in his firm hand with a new quill.

"1 Tester Bedstead 7½ feet pitch, with fashionable bleu or bleu and White curtains to suit a Room lined with the Ireland paper.

"Window Curtains of the same for two windows; with either Papier Maché Cornish to them, or Cornish covered with the Cloth.

"1 fine Bed coverlid to match the Curtains. 4 Chair bottoms of the same; that is, as much covering suited to the above furniture as will go over the seats of 4 Chairs (which I have by me) in order to make the whole furniture of this Room uniformly handsome and genteel.

"1 Fashionable Sett of Desert Glasses, and stands for Sweet Meats, Jellys, etc., together with Wash Glasses and a proper stand for these also.

"2 Setts of Chamber, or Bed Carpets—Wilton.

"4 Fashionable China Branches, and Stands, for Candles.

"2 Neat Firescreens.

"50 lbs. Spirma Citi Candles."

And then, before he forgot it in this welter of domesticity, he noted down some of his own indispensables: "A pretty large assortment of Grass Seeds—amongst which let there be a good deal of Lucerne and St. Foin, especially the former, also a good deal of English, or blue Grass; Clover seed I have."

With his uniforms laid aside and a social life before him in a hospitable neighborhood, he found himself short of such items as handkerchiefs, stock-tape, and hose in silk, thread, and worsted—"N.B. All the above stockings to be long, and tolerably large . . .

"1 Suit of Cloathes of the finest Cloth, & fashionable color, made by the enclosed Measure.

"Half a dozen pairs of Men's neatest Shoes, and Pumps, to be made on Colonel Baylor's last; but a little larger than this, and to have high heels.

"6 pr. Men's Riding Gloves, rather large than the middle size . . ."

And because he was serious about his farming now, and while in Williamsburg had taken advice from Mason and others, he made additions to his library: "Longley's *Book of Gardening;* Gibson, upon *Horses,* the latest Edition in Quarto; The newest and most approved Treatise of Agriculture—besides this, send me a small piece in octavo called *A New System of Agriculture,* or *A Speedy Way to Grow Rich.*"

And finally: "Order from the best House in Madeira a Pipe of the best Old Wine, and let it be secured from Pilferers."

Even then, they had overlooked things, and soon another list was sent off which required, in part:

"2 best Plain Beaver Hatts, at 21s.

"1 ps. black 60. Sattin Ribbon. [For his queue.]

"2 Fine flowered Lawn Aprons.

"1 pr. black, and 1 pr. white Sattan Shoes, of the smallest fives.

"6 pr. Women's best kind Gloves. 6 pr. ditto Mitts.

"6 lbs. perfumed Powder. [For their hair.]

"2 dozen packs playing Cards.

"2 Sacks of best English Oats.

"1 Mahogany Close Stool Case in the newest taste, with place for Chamber Pot etc.

"10s. worth of Toys."

And more, much more.

Their days settled into the gentle plantation routine. With her servants added to his, the house staff numbered fourteen. There were Breechy the butler, and Mulatto Jack, his assistant; Doll the cook, Beck the scullion, Jenny to wash and Mima to iron; Martha's personal maid, whose name happened to be Sally; Betty the seamstress; Jacky's boy Joe, and Patsy's Rose, and nurse Molly to oversee them all; Washington's colored body-servant, Billy; his orderly, Bishop; and John Alton, the white steward, who was soon promoted as overseer on the Dogue Run Farm. Seven more were employed outside on the home plantation, and another two dozen at the various farms; eleven worked at trades, and seven at the mill. Clothing for the slaves was mostly woven and made up on the estate; their health and their instruction in their duties, and their discipline were the daily personal concern of the master and mistress.

Sometimes there was hardly enough work to go round, except for the Colonel and Mrs. Washington. He turned surveyor again, to check his boundary lines, with a long look backward at the lad who at sixteen, with his father's old instruments, earned his first professional fee, in *cash* and not tobacco. Scarcely a year later, he had had his own warrant, and with his own earnings bought his first piece of land to the westward, outside his inheritance—his mother was still living on the farm near Fredericksburg which his father's will named as George's portion, and there was no sign then, in '49, that his half-brother Lawrence's health would fail so fast and fatally by '52, when he died, and Mount Vernon itself came into George's possession.

After an early breakfast, Washington would make his daily rides around the farms, with a raking eye on the labor going forward, while his wife took her morning hour alone in the bedchamber—an hour which even the children were forbidden to interrupt. No one knew how she spent it, and no one dared to wonder—reading her Bible, writing letters to her absent friends in New Kent County, working at her exquisite needlework, or sitting in some solitary meditation—that time belonged to her, almost the only thing about which she was inflexible. Mrs. Washington was in her room, with the door closed. Whatever came up then, it had to wait.

Dinner was at three, and he always returned in time to change out of his riding-clothes into a light suit, and put on powder, before appearing downstairs. There was usually company by then. As soon as the roads hardened and the days lengthened into summer, the neighbors came from miles around, to make their respects to the bride. Besides the Fairfaxes and the Masons, who were nearest, there were the Carlyles and the Ramsays and the Craiks from Alexandria, where the fine Carlyle house on Fairfax Street had been a sort of headquarters during the French war, when Braddock stayed there on his way to the Monongahela battlefield. Sarah Carlyle was George William Fairfax's sister, one of the handsome, intelligent young matrons of the Belvoir circle who had schooled George Washington in the social graces as he came to manhood. Dr. Craik, Scottish born and trained, had been on the frontier with him as an army physician; it was Craik who had sent him, protesting, back home to repair his health that time he rode to Williamsburg by way of the ferry which crossed the Pamunkey near the Chamberlaynes' house.

George's younger brother John Augustine Washington came up from Bushfield in Westmoreland County, with his wife Hannah; as did Austin of Wakefield, recently returned from a voyage to England undertaken for his health, most prosperous of all the Washingtons, having married one of the well-dowered Aylett girls way back in '43. The Fitzhughs came from Marmion and Ravensworth and the Eagle's Nest; the Stratford Lees, and the Johnstons of Belvale, and George's one-time playmate and present fellow Burgess, Dicky Lee from Chantilly—and if sometimes the conversation was too full of family jokes and old allusions, and the belated explanations politely entered into for Martha's benefit seemed to emphasize that she was a newcomer rather than to make her one of them, it was well-meant, she would remind herself, and everyone was being most kind.

George Washington, Esquire, the loneliness and hardships of a military life behind him, surrounded by his relatives and his friends and his beloved acres, felt sometimes like a man watching a play, it had come about so swiftly and inevitably, once it began at all. Without doubt, he knew now that he had taken the right step at the right time. Sally Fairfax was there, in his home as his guest—no less sparkling and no less beyond his dreaming than in the old days at Belvoir. But beside her now stood Martha, staunch, serene, and trustful—and his own. There would be between him and Sally no glance, no word, no silence, that could raise a question in Martha's mind.

Almost before they knew it, Christmas had come round again—their first as a family. Once more Washington looked back, as though at another man's life. Last year he had been at Williamsburg, dining at the Palace with Governor Fauquier and a brilliant company; the year before, he was alone at Mount Vernon, with only Bishop and black Billy to look after him, wretchedly ill and unable to take part in any of the neighborhood festivities, and with nothing to look forward to; in '56, at Fort Cumberland, contributing 6s. to a feeble theatrical entertainment got together by the younger officers in an effort to enliven their cheerless existence; in '55, at the Winchester post, defeated at his first election try, Braddock lately dead, desertion and discouragement eating away the hopeless men in his command.

His eyes followed Martha about the gracious rooms of Mount Vernon with gratitude, and something more, for the little miracle she was making for him—comfort, companionship, hospitality, quiet laughter, generous love; good food, willing servants, happy children—a home. He was a fortunate man. And he wondered, not for the first time, if she was ever homesick, behind her light chatter and affectionate ways.

She herself had hardly realized her nostalgia until her sister Nancy Bassett arrived from Eltham for a holiday visit. She was proud for Nancy to see Mount Vernon now—proud of her new friends in Fairfax County—and proud to produce for them an attractive member of her own family from the shores of the Pamunkey.

Nancy was still there on the first of January when a mysterious in-
disposition finally identified itself—Mrs. Washington had the measles.
The ailment had been epidemic among the plantation people during December, but no one dreamed that Martha hadn't had the measles long
ago. Nancy was sure that she herself had had them and was in no danger.
But Martha rapidly became very ill, and the doctor was sent for. Just so
long as you weren't pregnant, Nancy reassured her, asking no questions.
But in any case, measles for a woman of child-bearing age could have
serious consequences.

The children were kept from her too late, and both had mild cases.
Nancy insisted it was best for them to get it over with while they were
young, but Martha more than once struggled from her bed to see for herself that they were not dying. Washington, who was immune to smallpox
since surviving the disease during a boyhood voyage to Barbados with
Lawrence, escaped the lesser infection now. Martha was slow to recuperate, and had several alarming relapses. She was exasperated with herself,
because she was usually so well, and felt quite desolate when Nancy set
out for home again, with George as escort to Port Royal, where Mr.
Bassett would meet them and complete the return journey to Eltham with
his wife.

Sally Fairfax and her sister-in-law, Hannah, were faithful visitors,
bringing ingenious delicacies from the Belvoir kitchen to tempt her ap-
petite. Martha remained at home when George went to Williamsburg for
the Assembly in April, bracing herself to be content with secondhand
news of her old neighborhood. It was hard, as her widowed mother and
two younger sisters, Betsy and Mary, still lived at Chestnut Grove where
they had all grown up, not far from Eltham, and her brother Bartholomew and his family had leased the Six Chimney House in Williamsburg.

June found her quite recovered, and writing to Nancy, whose husband
had recently visited Mount Vernon during a journey which for an excellent reason Nancy had been obliged to forego: "I must do myself the
pleasure of congratulating you on your happy deliverance of, I wish I
could say boy, as I know how much one of that sex was desired by you
all. I am very sorry to hear of my Mamma's complaints of ill health, and
I feel the same uneasiness on the account that you are [ill] but hope
that Mr. Small's prescription will have the desired effect. The children
are now very well, and I think myself in a better state of health than I
have been in for a long time, and don't doubt but I shall present you a
fine healthy girl when I come down in the fall, which is as soon as Mr.

Washington's business will suffer him to leave home. I am very much pleased to hear Betsy continues to grow a fine hearty child . . ."

During the spring the Fairfaxes had had disturbing news from England. The death of George William's father in '57 had preceded by two years the death of his Uncle Henry the past autumn, by which George William became heir to the Fairfax estate at Towelston in Yorkshire. He had already made one voyage to England at the time of his father's death, in order to convince his uncle that although he had been born during Colonel Fairfax's Navy days in the West Indies, of a first wife some time dead, his mother was truly the daughter of an English major on duty there, and that her son was not colored. The mission was successful. His uncle was much taken with him, and made out a will in his favor. Now that the inheritance was his, it developed that Towelston was heavily mortgaged, litigation threatened, and his presence there was required. This time he planned to take Sally and his youngest sister Hannah with him for their first visit to the mother country.

Martha knew that George had a desire to see England himself, even though Austin's report on his own recent sojourn there was unfavorable. George believed that Austin was prejudiced by his bad health, which would have spoilt any pleasure to be found abroad, and when he remarked with a sigh that it was unlikely now that he would ever have an opportunity to form his own opinion she felt a stab of uneasiness. Although she had brought him a fortune, which was being laid out in manifold improvements and repairs at Mount Vernon, she and the children represented to him a tie and a responsibility which did not exist for George William. Childless, and with the Belvoir estate in good running order, the Fairfaxes were quite free to contemplate a year's absence from Virginia. But it was unthinkable that she should leave Jack and Patsy behind, and they were too small to endure the voyage. Patsy especially was delicate, so that people shook their heads and said she could never be raised.

The alternative was for George to go to England without her—and the time would be now, when he might accompany the Fairfaxes. She was determined not to try to prevent him if he wanted to go, but she lived in a private agony for some weeks, until she saw him preparing letters and invoices for George William to deliver for him in London, and could hope that he had given up any idea of it for the present.

She did not feel really safe until an August day when they watched the ship move away down the River, leaving George beside her on the dock.

It left her also with another and darker anxiety—the Fairfaxes were his oldest, dearest friends, and he was bound to feel their absence from Belvoir like an amputation. Compared to them, the Masons and the Carlyles were a little dull. Martha could see that compared to Sally everyone was a little dull, including herself. Suppose that now, in Sally's absence, he began to find his own home deficient in interest and amusement?

She watched him secretly as the summer wore on, and thought he was quieter than usual, and somewhat withdrawn into himself. Unhappy? she wondered, holding her tongue as a wise wife should. Missing the stimulus and merriment of Sally's frequent visits to Mount Vernon, and the neighborhood gaieties at Belvoir? Or did she imagine it, out of her own fear that it was so? She would probably never know.

In the autumn they all went to Williamsburg for the Assembly, traveling in style in the chariot with four horses, the servants wearing the new scarlet and white Washington livery, followed by two luggage carts full of trunks and boxes and maids. Bishop and Billy rode behind on horseback, with a led saddle-horse for the master's use when the chariot became too confining. At Williamsburg they made up for the quietness on the Potomac, and Martha cuddled Nancy's new baby girl, who should have been a boy. Martha would have been glad of either one. That was what was wanted at Mount Vernon, to fill in for the lack of Sally. A child of his own would hold George's heart at home.

They were back at Mount Vernon in time for Christmas. Belvoir stood closed and empty, but there were the usual celebrations at Alexandria with the Carlyles and the Ramsays and the Craiks, and at Gunston with the Masons and detachments of Lees. The children behaved well on the visits, and with the guest children at home, and she thought on the whole George enjoyed himself.

In January they were saddened by the sudden death of Sarah Carlyle, who left two little girls motherless. Then came the stupefying news of the King's death, and the accession of a new prince to the throne. It was unexpected, though George II had reached the age of seventy-seven. No one knew much about George III, except that he was twenty-three, unmarried, and the first Hanoverian sovereign to be born in England; but nevertheless he had been brought up in a thoroughly German household, much secluded from the world by a domineering mother.

The change of monarchs in England brought on a general election in Virginia, which required Washington to journey to Frederick County where he caught a hard cold, attending fairs and cock fights and weddings as part of the duties of his candidacy. He won by a substantial majority, but the cold lingered, stirring up old ailments and fevers. By July he was in a miserably low state of health. His friends Dr. Craik and Dr. Green seemed unable to cope with it, and muttered of consultations in Philadelphia or even in England.

A letter from George William Fairfax in London arrived just then to revive Martha's secret apprehensions. He complained of the cold weather, and of illness which had confined both him and Sally to their chambers, and remarked on the proposed marriage of the new King to the fifteen-year-old Princess of Brunswick. "Mrs. Fairfax and I, thank God, are upon the recovery," he wrote, "and hope Buxton Wells, strongly recommended, will set us both quite right, and enable us to return within the time limited, but in the meantime should be glad to know your and Dr. Green's determination about leaving that part of the world, for I assure you 'tis our greatest inducement, and will turn the scale very much whether we come back or not. Pray make my affectionate compliments etc. etc., and believe me with greatest esteem, dear sir, etc. etc. . . ."

Apparently George had at some time even discussed with the Fairfaxes and Dr. Green a permanent removal to England for all of them. Martha privately thought it a shocking idea, to leave Virginia and not come back at all, and would it ever have occurred to him without the circumstances of the Towelston inheritance which drew his friends away from Belvoir? It was a thing she could not ask. Besides, English air had not benefited Austin, as George knew very well, and now the Fairfaxes admitted to being ill there. To her unspoken relief, he decided against England once more, especially in view of their increasing concern over Patsy, who was developing some sort of occasional convulsive seizure amounting to fits.

George William's mention of the Buxton Baths started a new train of thought at Mount Vernon, however. Lawrence had failed to gain by a visit made to Berkeley Warm Springs in '51, when George had accompanied him there before their voyage to Barbados, but the necessity to attempt some further remedy in his own case now induced him to consider a trip to the mountain resort in August, when the season was almost over. Accommodations there as he recalled them were rough, and he thought best for Martha and the children to remain at home, at least until he could establish some sort of satisfactory lodgings at the Springs.

Bishop and Billy accompanied him, as always, and on the 28th he wrote back to Dr. Green, who had entertained an idea of joining him: "We found of both sexes about 200 people at this place, full of all manner of diseases and complaints: some of whom are much benefitted, while others find no relief from the waters. Two or three doctors are here, but whether attending as physicians or to drink of the waters I know not. It is thought the Springs will soon begin to lose their virtues; and the weather get too cold for people not well provided to remain here. They are situated very badly on the Eastern side of a steep mountain, and inclosed by hills on all sides, so that the afternoon's sun is hid by 4 o'clock and the fogs hang over us till 9 or 10, which occasions great damps, and the mornings and evenings to be cool. . . ."

Lodgings at the Springs were not to be had except by building them, and he lived in a tent and marquee brought in from Winchester. When he returned home in September he seemed much improved, and able to take an interest in things which earlier in the summer had seemed to him too trivial to attempt. It was time another invoice was sent off to England. The children were growing, and needed new clothes. Martha's list for Jacky named summer suits and 2 hair-bags, 4 pr. neat pumps, and a silver-laced hat; for Patsy, 2 fine cambric frocks, silver shoebuckles, a doll to cost a guinea, and a spinet. Both children were to have their own Bibles and Prayer Books with their names in gilt letters on the inside of the covers. And Jacky's personal servant, now fourteen years old, was being put into a new suit of the Custis livery. For herself, she wanted a pair of French bead earrings and a black silk apron.

The only serious disagreements between them had arisen over her indulgence to the children, and her perpetual anxiety over their health and safety. With unhappy memories of his own possessive mother, and her attempts to influence and alter his chosen course long after he considered himself a man, which in a character less firm than his might have imposed on him a leading-strings existence all his life long, he regarded Martha's everlasting supervision of her children's days and nights as a danger both to their individual development and to her own peace of mind. Children fell and hurt themselves, cried, and forgot about it. Children had harmless little illnesses, especially if allowed to stuff themselves with whatever unsuitable goodies they fancied, and recovered. Children were tough little animals like puppies, he tried to tell her, and should learn to fend for themselves as they grew older. And when, with the quick-flaring temper which was always a surprise to him because she had mastered it so well, she reminded him that he knew very little about children after all, and that these were hers, and that Patsy was so delicate they would be lucky if they raised her at all, there would fall a silence, ending in remorse on both sides, forgiveness, and another resolve on his part not to interfere again.

Christmas was quiet that year, darkened by the loss of Sarah Carlyle and the continued absence of the Fairfaxes in England.

Washington was turning thirty in 1762. While he was not conspicuous in debate, he attended the Assembly at Williamsburg conscientiously, often at some inconvenience to himself, sat on committees, and carried more weight than he knew with his colleagues. Mount Vernon was slowly shaping under his hand, but in spite of his reputation as one of the richest men in Virginia he knew himself to be in debt to his London agents for purchases, and the plantation was not yet self-supporting. The essentials were accomplished now; the fences were whole, and the roofs tight; live-stock and slaves were flourishing. The cost had been colossal, but very little of the outlay could be called extravagance. He could always find a way to keep going, somehow, in which he was more fortunate than some men he knew who had overextended themselves and in similar circum-stances were going under and having to sell out. A few bad tobacco years, a drought, a flooding rain—the margin was very narrow, even on the big estates like his.

By the spring of '62 his health was back to normal, but Austin's failed completely, and in March he died. The children of his father's first mar-riage had not the strong constitutions that Mary Ball brought to the line. Washington went to the funeral at Wakefield, where he had been born, and where Austin had lived very comfortably indeed. Austin's family was well provided for, and the estate was in order. His only son, William Augustine, was a fine lad five years old, and there were three girls.

When he returned home Martha questioned him minutely about Aus-tin's little ones, and he assured her that they were well-grown and cheerful, in the circumstances, and their mother was composed, for the thing had not happened suddenly. Austin had been ailing for years. Four children at Wakefield, and none born at Mount Vernon—she was grateful that he made no comparison in words, between his brothers' households and his own. John Augustine at Bushfield had three; her sister Nancy had now got her boy; their mother had had eight; and she herself, with Daniel, had had four, and lost the first two in babyhood. She wondered if some-thing had gone wrong at Patsy's birth, to leave her last child so frail and herself under a disability. Or was it—Nancy had thought it possible—be-cause she had had the measles nearly three years ago? Could there be some mysterious fatality in Mount Vernon itself? None of Lawrence's four babies born there had lived more than a matter of months. And if she were never to have another child, surely she was not wrong to surround little Jack and Patsy with every possible care?

The children had a tutor now. Earnest young Walter MacGowan from the Maryland shore, who had aspirations to the ministry, was much of the time resident in the house, and had undertaken to start Jacky, at eight years, on Latin and Greek, and to teach Patsy, six, the customary female accomplishments of spelling, sums, and Bible texts. It was a small beginning in Washington's cautious campaign to induce Martha to entrust them occasionally to someone else's hands besides her own, if only for their future welfare. Jacky had no objections, and was inclined to hero-worship the gentle young man who allowed himself to be tyrannized over with good grace. Patsy flirted with him beguilingly, and ran to her mother the minute lessons were done.

Under strong persuasion, and much against her wish, Martha agreed to leave Jacky at Mount Vernon with MacGowan and the colored nurse Molly, while with Patsy and a maid she accompanied Washington on a visit to John Augustine and Hannah, whose new son was to be called by his mother's family name, Bushrod. The experiment was not a success, and established no precedent, as she ruefully confessed to Nancy in a letter written after she was at home again: "I had the pleasure to receive your kind letter just as I was setting out on a visit to Mr. Washington in Westmoreland [County] where I spent a week very agreeably," she wrote. "I carried my little Pat with me and left Jacky at home for a trial to see how well I could stay without him. Though we were gone but one fortnight, I was quite impatient to get home. If I at any time heard the dogs bark, or a noise out, I thought there was a person sent for me. I often fancied he was sick or some accident had happened to him, so that I think it is impossible for me to leave him as long as Mr. Washington must stay when he comes down [to Williamsburg]. If nothing happens I promise myself the pleasure of coming down in the spring, as it will be a healthy time of the year. I am very much obliged to you for your kind invitation, and assure yourself nothing but my children's interest should prevent me the satisfaction of seeing you and my good friends I am always thinking of, and wish it were possible for me to spend more of my time amongst. . . . We all enjoy very good health at present, I think Patty seems to be quite well now, Jacky is very thin but in good health, and learn their books very fast. I am sorry to hear you are un-

well, but hope your complaint is slight. I have no news worth telling
you . . ."

The Fairfaxes, having failed to entice the Washingtons across the Atlantic, were returning to Virginia early in the new year. Martha awaited
their arrival with serenity now, secure in the benign affection of her husband and the established routine of their comfortable life together. By the
summer of '63, the old neighborly habits of borrowing, lending, and
barter and exchange between Mount Vernon and Belvoir were picked
up again as though there had been no interval. "I have not a lath in the
world, seasoned or unseasoned, or you would be heartily welcome to
them," Washington was writing to George William in July, by the hand
of a servant who had ridden over with the request.

Less well-to-do neighbors than George William Fairfax borrowed
money from him, or tried to, and though his own debts were sometimes
pressing, he found it hard to say no to an old friend, and harder to practice economy in the graces of living at Mount Vernon. He continued to
order his table wines and liveries and mantelpiece ornaments and trinkets
for the children from London. Neither could he resist buying in another
farm now and then, or a likely Negro.

Martha would watch him frowning over his books and papers as he
made up his accounts in the evenings, while she sat nearby with her
needlework. He had begun a sort of diary of his busy days, noting the
weather, the planting, the grafting, the naming of new hound puppies,
the breeding of a favorite mare, his conclusions on the agricultural ex-
periments he was always trying, the arrival of guests, and his own comings
and goings between Williamsburg, Alexandria, and home.

Sometimes if he had let it lapse too long, she was called upon to help
fill in on matters which had escaped his memory, and there would be
reminiscent smiles of mutual amusement at some past event which might
otherwise have slipped away from them; memories revived, pleasant and
unpleasant, of visits endured or enjoyed, in the unending round of hospitality which was a daily part of plantation life. Other entries, of course,
made very little sense to her. But take, for instance, the ball at Alexandria,
which Colonel Carlyle was not likely to hear the last of:

"*Friday, February 15.* Went to a ball at Alexandria, where music and
dancing was the chief entertainment. However, in a convenient room detached for the purpose, abounded great plenty of bread and butter, some
biscuits with tea, and coffee which the drinkers of could not distinguish

from hot water sweetened. Be it remembered that pocket-handkerchiefs served the purpose of tablecloths and napkins, and that no apologies were made for either.

"The proprietors of this ball were Messrs. Carlyle, Laurie, and Robert Wilson, but the Doctor [Laurie] not getting it conducted agreeable to his own taste, would claim no share of the merit of it.

"I shall therefore distinguish this ball by the style and title of the Bread and Butter Ball.

"We lodged at Col. Carlyle's.

"*Thursday, March 6.* Put the Pole end horses into the plow in the morning, and the Postillion and hand horse in, in the afternoon, but the ground being well swarded over and very heavy plowing, I repented putting them in at all, for fear it should give them a habit of stopping in the chariot.

"*Tuesday, March 25.* The wind southerly, the day changeable.

"Mrs. Possey and some young woman whose name was unknown to anybody in this family dined here.

"*Wednesday, March 26.* Spent the greatest part of the day in making a new plow of my own invention.

"Wind at N. West and very boisterous.

"*Saturday, April 5.* Planted out 20 young Pine trees at the head of my cherry walk.

"Made another plow the same as my former, excepting that it has two eyes and the other one.

"*Wednesday, April 9.* Wind at N. East, very cloudy and sometimes misty.

"Dr. Laurie came here. I may add, drunk.

"*Saturday, May 17.* Mulatto Jack returned from King William [County] with 3 yoke of oxen, and lost Punch, the horse he rid."

Washington was now convinced that tobacco would never pay at Mount Vernon, and was making a gradual change over to wheat, which grew well and was not dependent on the London market. Already flour made at his mill had a local reputation and brought good prices. Martha was a good listener, and learned to take an intelligent interest in his problems, but she thought it an excellent idea when he engaged one of the Chotank Washingtons from down the River, a vaguely related cousin named Lund, to come and live at Mount Vernon as a manager and general assistant. Lund's chief duty was to take over a part of the estate business, which was becoming too much for one man to handle alone, and do some of the traveling which the purchase of additional western land entailed. He was twenty-eight, and had had some experience as overseer at Ravensworth, one of the Fitzhugh plantations. He was a sober, industrious, agreeable man, and soon fitted in very well, so that George had more time for fox-hunting with his guests, and the enjoyment of his own hospitality.

Rumors of a new tax were coming out of England—a stamp which must be affixed to all legal papers and newsprint. The autumn Assembly at Williamsburg voted a formal remonstrance to the mother Parliament, mentioning firmly the colonial right to self-government, which had always obtained hitherto. The New England states were said to be all in a ferment about it. Sally Fairfax understood what they were talking about, apparently, being lately returned from London, and she took an active part in the fireside discussions, which sometimes became heated. Sally was furious if anyone hinted that the young King was a little mad. The King was ill, but any other word was rude.

Washington attended the spring session briefly in '65, alone. There was some ordinary dull business about the Tobacco Bill, and no mention of a reply from London to the Burgesses' protest against the proposed tax. With his mind on the grafting of his cherry trees, he left Williamsburg before the adjournment, and so was not present when a new member named Patrick Henry took the roof off the Capitol building with his Five Resolutions on the Stamp Act, addressed to the Ministry in London.

They heard about it secondhand at Mount Vernon, from their neighbor George Johnston of Belvale, who had brought Henry to the floor of the House and turned him loose there to challenge the tax again. The conservatives in the Assembly thought that Henry's Resolutions went much too far. Peyton Randolph, Pendleton, Wythe, and the rest attempted to vote them down, and then Henry boiled over. The chamber was half empty when he began his speech, Johnston related, but those who heard him were spellbound. It was the old, old principle which went all the way back to Runnymede—the Englishman's right to his privileges and immunities. Henry argued that the Virginia Assembly had the sole and exclusive right to lay taxes on the inhabitants of the colony, and that the Stamp Act was a flagrant violation of that right—the Stamp Act was no less than tyranny. His voice rose, his eyes flashed, his gestures broadened—until the Speaker belatedly pulled himself together and ruled against talking treason in the very chamber of the House. "And if this be treason make the most of it!" cried Patrick Henry, and sat down amid his stunned colleagues.

And who had seconded the Resolutions? None other than their humble servant, George Johnston, seated there in their midst at Mount Vernon, and proud of it. What's more, the Resolutions were passed, by a narrow margin, after being fought over one by one, but when Henry had ridden back to his country law practice they were well watered down by the Randolph faction before being entered in the Journal of the House. Even so, Governor Fauquier was outraged by their intransigent tone, and dissolved the Assembly abruptly without the usual amenities of adjournment. That meant another election. Johnston of Belvale predicted that there would be trouble when the stamps arrived in America and the agents tried to enforce their use.

Martha could not understand why George looked so grave, why Johnston was so aflame, why the Fairfaxes argued so passionately on the side of the London Parliament, why the Governor had taken offense, or what sort of trouble they anticipated. A penny on the newspapers, a few shillings on a court judgment—nobody was so poor as all that. It was unconstitutional, Johnston said. Ill-judged, was as far as George would go just then.

There was something else on Martha's mind, as she sat among them with her needlework, silent but aware. Randolph, Robinson, Wythe, Pendleton, Bland—all familiar names, all people she had known and respected for years. But who was Patrick Henry? It seemed better not to ask.

CHAPTER THREE

The Small Cloud

1766–1773

TROUBLE MEANT FIRST that the colonies undertook not to engage in any transactions where the stamps were required—might even mean that the stamps when they arrived would be seized and destroyed. Business would come to a standstill, they said, and the English tradesmen would suffer too. Most of the bare necessities of life could be grown or procured in America. There would be no new silk dresses, of course, no English shoes and saddles, no fanciful toys, no replacements for tools that were lost or broken—because the manifests all had to have the stamp attached before the ships could sail.

Meanwhile discussions went on in London with regard to a repeal of the Stamp Act. Benjamin Franklin represented the colonies there, and he was reported to have declared at the Bar of the House of Commons that it would be the pride of Americans to wear their old clothes till they could themselves make new ones, rather than import any cloth from England so long as the Act was in force. *Homespun?* Martha wondered. How seriously they took things. Well, at least the clothes they already had would last quite a while. She accompanied George to the weaving house, to consider what sort of materials might be made there, and how the output might be increased at need.

But it blew over, after all, largely thanks to Pitt in Parliament. The Stamp Act was repealed in the spring of '66. See what firm resistance in

America could accomplish, said George Johnston. See how magnanimous are Parliament and the King, said the Fairfaxes. In the midst of general rejoicing, Governor Fauquier made a formal announcement of the repeal in June. Washington thought it a narrow escape from chaos, and took the whole family to Williamsburg for the November session. The Six Chimney House was leased, so Martha and the children stayed with the Bassetts at Eltham and Washington lived at one of the taverns in the capital. It was not too far for her to drive into town to attend a ball or a play, or to dine at the Palace. Relief made everyone very gay.

By '67, Washington had begun slowly to pull ahead on his farming, growing wheat, corn, and hemp in place of tobacco, besides selling the flour from his mill. He was still short of ready cash, and was deeply involved in some of his impecunious neighbors' tangled financial affairs. But he was proving that Mount Vernon could be made to pay. Martha's money had not been wasted, it would all come back home, and with Lund's help he was enjoying more leisure for fox-hunting, visiting and entertainment. Long invoices went off to England again, perhaps with an eye to future shortages.

The lull ended when Pitt retired to the country in ill health. England's new Chancellor Townshend slapped an import duty on a dozen articles more or less essential to the colonies—paint materials, glass, paper, and even tea—for the support, he announced with what looked like willful provocation, of additional British troops which were being sent out to maintain order in New England. To make things still more difficult in Virginia, amiable Governor Fauquier succumbed to illness in the spring of '68, and was buried with ceremony and sorrow in Bruton Church at Williamsburg.

Fauquier's tenure had just begun when he attended the wedding in New Kent County, and his death marked the end of a chapter for the Washingtons. They paused in dismay to take stock of the passing of time outside their little Arcady on the Potomac. Austin Washington, Speaker Robinson, Dr. Green, George Johnston, Martha's youngest sister Mary, and now the Governor—their friends were slipping away. And those who were left were all a little older. They drew closer together for comfort, and instinctively they looked with love and anxiety at Patsy, so pretty with a ribbon in her dark curls, so easily diverted and made happy—so delicately balanced between health and the prostrating attacks of her mysterious affliction.

Everyone worried and wondered about what the new Governor would be like when he came, for a great deal would depend on his attitude and personality. Meanwhile the Williamsburg Assembly composed another address to the King and a remonstrance to his Ministers, in terms even stronger than Patrick Henry's debated Resolutions on the Stamp Act. There was no longer any opposition, although conservative Peyton Randolph was now in the Speaker's chair. Less than four years since that stormy session of '65, the viewpoint had changed.

The Washingtons on a round of family visits during the summer heard persistent rumors of clashes between the soldiery from England and the colonists in Boston and New York. No one quite understood why the southern colonies were spared this additional exasperation of an insolent occupying force, and they all felt it might begin at any time in Virginia as in Massachusetts, where the colonists had formed associations binding their members not to import anything from England but absolute necessities. There was a general disposition to back up Massachusetts in a united opposition to the Townshend taxes. United, north and south. One colony alone could be terrorized and overborne. But if all the colonies stood together, it would take an army to break their resistance.

Martha listened in her accustomed serene silence, but inwardly she was disturbed. When England sent an army against the French out on the Ohio, George had been one of its officers. But this was not the French. This was Massachusetts. A British army against British subjects? Which side would George be on, if it came to that? To hear him now, he stood up for Massachusetts. But Massachusetts had no army. She supposed that eventually she would understand.

When they reached home again a new domestic problem awaited them. Jacky's tutor, young Mr. MacGowan, was departing for England to enter Holy Orders. And although he meant to return soon to Maryland and hoped for a living in the near neighborhood, some other arrangement must be made for the education of Jacky, who was now fourteen and well out of hand, charming, willful, pampered, and pretty ignorant. While in Williamsburg they had heard of a school for boys in Caroline County below Fredericksburg, kept by a Reverend Jonathan Boucher, who had come out from England as a young man some ten years back. The Lewises had heard the school well spoken of, and Washington's old frontier comrade, Dr. Hugh Mercer, also of Fredericksburg, had more than once been called in to attend one or another of the boys there, which indicated on Mr. Boucher's part a due concern for their welfare. Washington finally convinced Jacky's unwilling mother that a few terms of school discipline, among other boys of his age, would do more for him than tutoring at home, where he could always coax or wriggle out of unwelcome assignments.

As soon as he had won her consent, which was accompanied by tears and misgivings, Washington sat down to compose a letter to Mr. Boucher before she could change her mind. When he had finished, Martha asked to see it and insisted on certain additions and amendments, so that he had to write it out all over again. He was not entirely satisfied with the result, but sent it off quickly in order to avoid further discussion, aware that his wife's influence must be clearly traceable in its pages.

Mr. Boucher's reply when it arrived was scrutinized and commented upon at great length. Martha thought he sounded most thoughtful and kind, and was encouraged by the tone of his letter almost to cheerfulness. Washington contemplated it in the light of his experience of men, and thought it would do; a bit long-winded, perhaps, but that was doubtless the parson in him. And so, after the exchange of further correspondence in which the final arrangements were made, at the end of June Martha saw them set out for the school together, like true father and son, accompanied by the indispensable Bishop and Jacky's colored boy servant, who wore the Custis livery. Jacky was too excited at the prospect of the adventure ahead of him to feel the parting from his mother and sister as she had feared he might, but for a child brought up as he had been it was inevitable that homesickness would overtake him when he at last found himself left alone among strangers.

The luxury of a good cry was denied his mother when the travelers had ridden out of sight down the western avenue, for Patsy, always too emotional and too easily upset, was already in tears and must be gently diverted before she could develop one of the dreaded seizures which were coming more frequently and with greater violence as she grew older.

While Martha played with Jacky's sister she strove against a double grief. Ten years of her second marriage lay behind her and there was no child of Washington's. She was thirty-seven, and hope diminished fast at that age. He was devoted to Daniel's children, thoughtful of their interests and their future, and she knew even while she often held out against it that his judgment on their upbringing was more sound than her own. Now that she had yielded to him on this matter of Jacky's schooling, she must stifle daily panic that if anything went wrong at the school, if Jacky were taken ill away from home, if any accident happened to him and she was not there. . . . She closed her mind firmly on the ungracious corollary that it would be George's fault.

Boys no older than Jacky were sent as far as England for their education, and at least George had not suggested that. She knew it was foolish of her to feel so bereft, and Jacky was bound to enjoy himself among the other boys, once he got used to it, and he would soon endear himself to Mr. Boucher—he was so gay and wheedling he could melt a heart of stone. He was the last of his line and must have the best of everything, as became the only Custis son. If he had been a Washington he would have had to go to school now just the same. But there were other Washington sons; Austin, John Augustine, Samuel and Charles all had sons. . . . Clasping poor Patsy in her arms, she wept in spite of herself because George, the best of all the Washington brothers, was the only one to be childless.

She had not, of course, expected that he would relent and bring Jacky back home in any case, but when George and Bishop rode in without him a fresh realization of her fledgling's absence reduced her welcome to a cross-examination on the accommodations and surroundings of the school. George answered her patiently, though a dozen matters outside the house awaited his attention.

Mr. Boucher had a small plantation, he told her, with cattle, slaves, and a little farm where some of the food was grown. Jacky would have plenty of fresh milk and eggs and butter. The house stood in a glebe some distance from the church, and was run by the clergyman and his sister, both of whom were unmarried, and Miss Boucher seemed a sensible, capable woman. There were perhaps two dozen boys, and among them two sons of their friend Addison, and Addison as she knew was an educated man and could afford the best, and would be particular. Boucher's connections could hardly be better. As for the man himself, he was perhaps about Washington's age, George thought, a bit run to fat, but he set a good table and enjoyed his food and drink. He was quite a jolly fellow, not one of your hell-fire parsons, and the boys seemed a healthy, lively lot, and it would do Jacky a world of good to knock about with people his own age. No, he had not felt of the bed, but it looked comfortable—no, he had not asked about the water, but it was bound to be all right. . . .

A good wheat crop, and the unexpected payment of an old debt eased the pressure on Mount Vernon economy that summer, and Washington's London invoices were more extravagant than they had been for several years. The most they could do for Patsy, so pretty and so frail, and helpless before her encroaching malady, was to shower her with gifts and deny her nothing that would give her pleasure. Martha's lists for Patsy always cramped his heart as he wrote them out—a smelling-bottle, a very handsome and fashionable lady's saddle with bridle and everything complete, for the little mare he had given her, a riding hat with a white feather, a neat pocket looking-glass, a book with the new version of Psalms and Hymns set for the spinet. Patsy was twelve, and almost a young lady, and gave promise of great beauty.

For themselves, there was the momentous purchase of a new chariot, the most ambitious outlay since the original furnishing of the house at the time of their marriage. His letter to his London agents on this matter was the result of much thought and observation and inquiry, and it incorporated both a woman's whims concerning what met the eye, and a masculine knowledge of value and construction: ". . . in the newest taste, handsome, genteel, and light; yet not slight and consequently unserviceable," he specified. "To be made of the best seasoned wood, and by a celebrated workman. The last importation which I have seen, besides the customary steel springs have others that play in a brass barrel, and contribute at one and the same time to the ease and ornament of the carriage; one of this kind, therefore, would be my choice; and green being a color little apt, as I apprehend, to fade, and grateful to the eye, I would give it the preference, unless any other color more in vogue and equally lasting is entitled to precedency, in that case I would be governed by fashion. . . . A light gilding on the mouldings, that is round the panels, and any other ornaments that may not have a heavy and tawdry look (together with my arms agreeable to the impression here sent) might be added, by way of decoration. A lining of a handsome, lively colored leather of good quality, I should also prefer; such as green, blue, or etc. as may best suit the color of the outside. Let the box that slips under the seat be as large as it conveniently can be made (for the benefit of storage upon a journey) and to have a pole (not shafts) for the wheel horses to draw by; together with a handsome set of harness for four middle-sized horses ordered in such a manner as to suit either two postilions (without a box) or a box and one postilion. The box being made to fix on, and take off occasionally, with a hammel cloth etc. suitable to the lining. On the harness let my crest be engraved. . . ."

But for the worry about Patsy's health, life was easier than it had ever been at Mount Vernon as '68 drew to its close. Washington went alone to Williamsburg for the autumn session, and brought back Martha's niece Betsy, William Dandridge's daughter, for a long visit. The new Governor, Lord Botetourt, proved to be a very imposing man, who kept great state at the Palace, and whose title instead of Your Honor was required to be Your Excellency. His mood was on the whole conciliatory. He promised amendment of the Townshend Acts, and at the same time promptly dissolved the Assembly, which did not endear him to the Burgesses.

Jacky arrived home from school in mid-December for the Christmas holidays, in high spirits, and was allowed to accompany his elders out hunting. Poor Patsy had a seizure in the carriage on the way to a dinner party, and they had to turn back. A man named Evans charged £1.10 for an iron ring which was supposed capable of relieving spasms like hers, but she showed no benefit from it, to no one's great surprise. Usually by the time a doctor could be summoned to her aid, the fit had passed and she was herself again. Betsy Dandridge was still there and Sally Carlyle, whose father had married again, joined the party for a few days at Christmastime and the house was full of youth and laughter.

A proposed visit from Boucher, who was to escort Jacky back to school, was canceled by an illness which confined him to his bed till the other boys began to return from their holidays, and Jacky was sent back under Bishop's convoy at the end of January. It was noticeable that he went willingly enough, and to Martha's astonishment if not relief, he appeared to have adapted himself to his exile with much less repining than might have been expected. It did not occur to his mother yet that a broadening horizon held certain new attractions for Jacky as time went on.

A British garrison had moved into Boston, where there had been speech-making and riots against the importation of British goods, and Massachusetts was calling for a united resistance to the Ministry's policy of coercion.

Preoccupied as she was with her daily anxiety about Patsy, Martha took less notice of what she secretly considered long faces, as the menfolk prepared to encounter Governor Botetourt again at the spring Assembly, than she would have done if all had been well at Mount Vernon. She had already given up going to Williamsburg with George, even though the new chariot had arrived in a splendor of gilded scrolls, diamond-cut glass, painted panels, and green morocco. Excitement in any form was thought to be bad for Patsy, and they agreed that she had better stay quietly at home with her mother, during what promised to be an exacting time for the members of the Assembly.

Martha knew that George Mason, who was tormented by gout, had given up his seat in the House in order to devote himself to Gunston and his growing family, although in place of attending the session he had prepared a list of the articles which he considered that Virginia should refuse to buy from England. He had even written out Resolutions for a sort of intercolonial agreement binding all the colonies in one association to resist the Townshend duties, and to enforce non-importation on such colonial merchants as thought more of their pockets than of their rights as free men. But loving finery as Martha did, and delighting to indulge her afflicted child with trinkets and pretty clothes, she thought they were carrying it a bit far when George read out to her some items from a packet of documents he received on the eve of his departure for Williamsburg. It seemed to her that Mason only began where the others had left off several years ago, and unless Lord Botetourt tried some different approach than any former Governor had so far devised, another dissolution was inevitable.

Spirits and wine came first on Mason's proscribed list, but there were distilleries at most of the big houses in Virginia, and no one would suffer much from that. Beef, pork, butter, cheese, candles—they could manage all those. But the list got worse as it went on. Confectionery, pewter, watches, clocks, looking-glasses, joiners and cabinet work of all sorts, carriages (theirs had arrived just in time), upholstery of all sorts, trinkets and jewelry, gold and silversmiths' work of all sorts, India goods of all sorts (except spices) silks of all sorts (except sewing silk), cambrics, lawn, muslin, gauze (except boulting cloths) calico or cotton stuffs of more than 2s a yard, stockings, shoes, saddles—and more, much more, the colonies undertook to do without "until the late acts of Parliament imposing duties on tea, paper, glass, etc., for the purpose of raising any revenue in America are repealed."

George seemed to feel that she did not fully appreciate the obligation of personal sacrifice in the united effort to bring the British Parliament to its senses. He paused to read aloud to her from the letter he was writing to accompany the papers which he was sending on to Gunston: "At a time when our lordly masters in Great Britain will be satisfied with nothing less than the deprication of American freedom, it seems highly necessary that something should be done to avert the stroke and maintain the liberty which we have derived from our ancestors," he had written. "But the manner of doing it to answer the purpose effectually is the point in question. That no man should scruple or hesitate to use a-ms in defense of so valuable a blessing, on which all the good and evil of life depend is clearly my opinion—"

She made a little sound, half gasp, half cry, and he looked up across the paper to see her sitting, needle poised, gazing at him in dismay. A-r-m-s? she repeated, as though she could not have heard him aright. But that meant *war!* War with *London?* How could there be war with London, when they were all British subjects? Addresses to the Throne, he reminded her, and remonstrances to Parliament were equally without result. The next step was to try to starve out England's trade with her colonies. If that failed . . . He picked up his pen, and bent his head again above the paper.

Long after George's letter was on its way to Gunston, she sat bemused and frowning. She had no idea that things had got so bad; she had not been paying enough attention to what she assumed was just the same sort of talk which went on before the Stamp Act was repealed—as of course this new trouble would in time resolve itself. Anything else was inconceivable. No one went to war against the King any more. . . . She felt as though she had come suddenly upon the brink of a chasm.

Washington returned from Williamsburg at the end of May, and now his wife was alert to the crisis and impatient to hear about the session he had attended. He found Mount Vernon full of guests, and the guests were full of questions. His cousin Warner Washington, who had married Hannah Fairfax as his second wife, and lived along the road to Winchester, was there with his family; Jacky Custis had come on a holiday accompanied by the indulgent Mr. Boucher; Walter MacGowan was back from England and in possession of a Maryland living which Mr. Boucher had hoped for himself, and suspected was had by influence. They had all heard a fast rumor that Lord Botetourt had dissolved the Assembly again, but they wanted to hear what had happened first.

It was not so much what happened first as afterward, George suggested, and Martha put a glass of wine into his hand and they begged him to begin at the beginning. Well, there were a few new members since the last election, he began; an odd-looking, scholarly youngster from Albemarle County named Thomas Jefferson, for one, whom Patrick Henry thought very promising; and most of the old guard were still there, like Peyton Randolph, Pendleton, Richard Bland, and the Carters. You never saw such style as Governor Botetourt put on, his servants wore green and scarlet and gold livery; his coach was regal and carried the arms of Virginia on its panels, and was drawn by six magnificent cream-white horses—Hanoverian horses, said to be a gift, like the coach, from the Royal Duke of Cumberland—you never saw such horses—the Governor was a bachelor and gave most impressive parties, and cut quite a figure with the ladies—in fact, he made rather a point of being pleasant and hospitable, but—oh, yes, indeed, he had dissolved them, no doubt about that.

It was of course not unexpected, George reminded his anxious listeners. The members had simply collected their hats and belongings from the chambers, and reassembled in the Apollo Room at the Raleigh Tavern—the supper room hitherto identified with balls and dance music and concerts, jewels, lace, and candlelight, syllabub and cakes and wine—a room which carried over its mantelpiece a Latin tag about Laughter and Good Living. Everyone in the parlor at Mount Vernon could visualize the gathering of the gravely disturbed Burgesses in those incongruous surroundings, of so many frivolous memories. Peyton Randolph was put in the chair, and Washington laid before them Mason's non-importation plan, which had been prepared and entrusted to him by its author for their consideration in just such circumstances as these.

To be brief, he said, and drained his glass, they had adopted Mason's plan almost intact, effective September 1st. No more tea, he said, with an amused glance round at the aghast faces of the ladies, after September 1st. They had all signed, the veterans and the new men, side by side; those present numbering nearly a hundred made a three-fourths majority. Common cause. United resistance to the tyranny of arbitrary taxation. Peyton Randolph was the first to write his name; then Robert Carter Nicholas (who had married Sally Fairfax's sister Anne), Richard Bland, Dicky Lee. Washington had signed just below Charles Carter, and the next hand to take the pen was Thomas Jefferson's.

Virginia now stood committed beside Massachusetts, and that might make them think, in London. In any case, it was dry work, and an order went out from the Apollo Room for wine and glasses. The first toast drunk was quite properly *"The King,"* and later they all drank to *"The constitutional British liberty in America."* The following night most of them, including himself, had attended the ball given at the Palace by the Governor in honor of the Queen's birthday. They were dissolved, very well, but there was no need to be discourteous. The day after that he had started home, and here he was.

What next? They would know that when the King had had time to receive and act upon the result of this most momentous session at Williamsburg. Meanwhile, Washington had never seen his wheat growing thicker, or broader in the blade.

A few days later he set out in the new coach with Martha and Patsy for Towelston above Alexandria, the Virginia house named for the Fairfax ancestral estate in England, where Bryan, half-brother of George William Fairfax and husband of Sally's sister Betsy, had a new son, to whom Washington was to stand godfather.

All that summer of '69, when they made up the diary together in the evenings, sometimes after a week's lapse of time, the items were pleasant ones to recall—welcome visitors, and little excursions when Patsy felt well, and nothing about when she didn't.

"*June 5*. Dined at Belvoir. Mrs. Washington and Patsy Custis going with me.

"*June 6*. At home all day. Mrs. Fairfax, Col. Fairfax, and Mr. Wormeley the elder dining here and returning in the afternoon.

"*July 3*. Rid round to my harvest field in the Neck, with Mrs. Washington, Patsy, and Milly Posey. Returned to dinner.

"*July 13*. Mrs. Ramsay and Sally Carlyle went away. I rid to the mill, where I was cutting of wheat, and returned to dinner where I found Mr. Francis Thornton and my brother Charles and his son, with whom rid out after dinner."

Because Martha had heard of a new doctor at Williamsburg who must be consulted about Patsy, the whole family drove down to the capital in the green chariot, at the end of November. The prospect of a visit with Nancy and her children always raised Martha's spirits. As Jacky's school lay between Mount Vernon and Williamsburg it was inevitable that he should be swept up into the party on the way, for yet another unscheduled holiday, bought with passionate promises of double effort to make up for lost time when he returned to his lessons.

Jacky was turning sixteen, and nearly two years' attendance at Mr. Boucher's school, however much interrupted by diversion, had wrought in him changes which both enchanted and dismayed his mother. Her cherished baby was gone forever. In his place she found an elegant young gentleman whose remarkable good looks and self-possession were adequate to any society in which he was placed. Washington's gift of getting on with young people had earned and kept the devoted admiration of his stepson, who was now old enough to appreciate the affectionate esteem all Williamsburg felt for the man he still called Pappa.

Martha watched with rueful pride the growing companionship between them, as Jacky unconsciously assumed the prerogatives of the son and heir which George might never have. Jacky was taken to dine at the Palace and behaved with the utmost propriety. His often neglected dancing school had nevertheless made him sufficiently adept to take his place on the floor at the Assembly balls, whose splendor was not yet affected by the non-importation restrictions on fine dress and lavish entertainment, just as political bitterness had not yet impinged on the cordial social relations in the miniature court which surrounded the complaisant Governor.

They were in another of those periods of illusive colonial calm, based this time on an unaggressive opening speech by Lord Botetourt which indicated that most of the recent Townshend duties would soon be removed "in the interest of commerce." The address of the Burgesses in reply tacitly recognized a truce. There was no mention on either side of the word *tea,* yet tea was to remain subject to tax in any case, even after other articles were freed from it, as a reminder to the colonists that Parliament maintained its arrogant authority to tax where and what it pleased. People like Patrick Henry pointed out that the Governor's glossy words were only wind, that the principle did indeed remain the same, and the circumstances were unaltered.

Martha did not have to ask now who Patrick Henry was—she had met him—a johnny-come-lately from Hanover County in a parson's coat, who chose to speak with an ostentatious up-country twang which he had had plenty of time to unlearn through association with his betters. He was accepted everywhere, and was particularly the friend of young Thomas Jefferson, who was at least a gentleman, although not a Tidewater one, and whose lodgings Henry was welcome to share when he could not afford to pay his way elsewhere. She wondered why they thought so much of the man. He had married an innkeeper's daughter who stayed at home with the children. He had no chariot, and at Assembly times he rode into town alone on a bony hack with his belongings in the saddlebags. But they said when he got up to speak no one breathed. With that accent? she wondered. In that coat?

It was a remarkably gay and polite session, concerned largely with legislation on the western boundaries and the bounties for the veterans of the French and Indian War, an old debate which had been running on for years to her certain knowledge. The Washingtons left Williamsburg several days before the ball, which was being given at the Capitol for the Governor by the Speaker and Burgesses and their wives—a ball at which the ladies had bound themselves to wear homespun instead of silks and satins, in order to demonstrate their willingness to do without fripperies imported from England. It was a gesture which seemed excessive to Martha, especially in view of the Governor's diplomatic speech and generous hospitality. She would not be so tactless as to appear at the ball in one of her usual rich imported dresses when the others had chosen to do differently, but she had nothing made up, naturally, in Mount Vernon homespun. Anyway, she considered the idea theatrical and uncalled for. Everyone still had plenty of good English clothes which would last for some time to come. It was rude to underline controversy at the Governor's ball. It was provincial. The Governor would not be favorably impressed with such behavior. Washington heard her with a smile.

They set out for Mount Vernon on the 21st of December, having received no encouragement from any doctor available to Patsy in Williamsburg. They paid an overnight visit to George's mother, and spent Christmas Day with his sister Betty and her family at Fredericksburg. Betty and Fielding Lewis now had four boys and a girl and, among the Washington brothers, Samuel had two children, John Augustine, five, and Charles, two. None of his family could be compared to George for looks or accomplishment or future prospects of prosperity, Martha thought. In fact, the Lewises were frankly disappointed in their eldest, Fielding, Jr., a headstrong boy who had just married at eighteen and would take advice from nobody, by his own father's testimony. Martha's Jacky was easily the handsomest of the younger generation. Things went so well, life was so good, except that there were no babies at Mount Vernon.

New Year's Day saw them at home again, and the weather throughout January was so severe that Jacky could not get back to school, though it did not interfere with his hunting. The year 1770 started quietly on the Potomac, with family visits, friends coming back to dinner after church on Sundays, meetings of the neighborhood dancing school, of which Patsy was an accomplished member. Washington would sometimes stand in the parlor doorway and watch the children turning and dipping to the tinkle of the spinet, until they caught sight of him, faltered in their steps, and were either overcome with embarrassment or, following Patsy's lead, broke ranks and ran to surround him, chattering like birds, with small, warm, tugging hands which he felt obliged to put from him in a hasty retreat so as not to interfere with the lesson. His

new mill, the smithy, the weaving house, all flourished, and the fishing
even showed a profit in shining herring and shad from the River. He
was now a justice of the Alexandria court, which meant pleasant jaunts
into town with an opportunity of attending theaters and balls where one
encountered both old and new acquaintances, and justified the erection
of a small house there for the family's use.

Once more the prophesied trouble with England had not materialized.
And yet March brought the incredible report of a riot in Boston during
which British soldiers in red coats had fired into the crowd, leaving three
citizens dead of bullet wounds. Everyone was horrified, for this was not
bloodshed by the French or the Indians, this was English against English, this was the King's men shooting down unarmed townspeople, this
was massacre. The Assembly would have something to say to this.

The main concern of the Assembly session that spring—besides Boston—was the unwilling realization that Mason's non-importation plan
had had very little effect in England, while the colonial merchants found
it a serious handicap, and some revisions downward were voted in its
requirements. On the way home the Washingtons made the usual round
of visits, and George's old friend, Dr. Hugh Mercer at Fredericksburg,
in his turn admitted that he knew of no remedy for Patsy's complaint.

Meanwhile Jacky continued to present problems on his own account.
Mr. Boucher had put forward a suggestion—at some length—that an extended trip abroad might assist to cultivate the boy's mind and improve
his manners, though Colonel Washington must not, the clergyman insisted, conceive that his own personal inclination to travel, and inciden-
tally to visit his native England, had anything to do with this inspiration.
In any case, the question arose of Jacky's inoculation for smallpox, which
was now quite a general practice, especially before a journey on the European continent. Several of the boys at the school had recently undergone it, with no ill effects.

The necessity for these vital decisions affecting Jacky's whole future
threw Martha into a melancholy mood, for she was already worn down
and anxious over Patsy's condition. It did not seem right to Washington
that she should be pressed further at the present time, as she had got
herself into a state of mind where the prospect of having Jacky inoculated
loomed nearly as large in her apprehensions as the proposed voyage itself. And while Jacky's opportunities for education and a knowledge of
the world beyond a Virginia plantation had always seemed enviable to
Washington, after his own Spartan youth, he undertook compassionately

to spare his wife any further strain just then. He wrote to Boucher post-poning the matter of the European tour indefinitely, and at the same time acknowledged the advisability of getting the inoculation, whether or not Jacky traveled abroad. But complications and anxieties persisted.

During the summer of 1770 Mr. Boucher achieved a long coveted Annapolis living, which carried with it the post of chaplain to the Lower House, a close association with Governor Eden of Maryland, and more fashionable surroundings than the rural parish of St. Mary's. He sold out his farm and cattle and moved to a house near Annapolis with his sister and servants and three of his pupils besides Jacky Custis—Master Overton, Master Carr, and Master Benedict Calvert, Jr. The new loca-tion created new dilemmas with regard to Jacky, for Annapolis was a lively, sophisticated town, the seat of the Maryland government, and of-fered a variety of entertainment and temptation to an adventuresome boy with money to spend. After observing his ward during an autumn holi-day at Mount Vernon Washington found himself writing to Boucher at a time when Martha would not be looking over his shoulder: "Accord-ing to appointment, Jacky Custis now returns to Annapolis," he wrote slowly, after much thought. "His mind is a good deal released from study, and more than ever turned to dogs and horses and guns; indeed, upon dress and equipment, which till of late he has discovered little inclination of giving in to. I must beg the favor of you, therefore, to keep him closer to those useful branches of learning which he ought now to be acquainted with, and as much as possible under your own eye. Without these, I fear he will too soon think himself above control, and be not much the better for the extraordinary expenses attending his living in An-napolis. . . ."

He got a little more than he had bargained for in Boucher's reply, and was thankful that Martha had not observed its arrival, so that he was able to assimilate its contents in private: "It is not without much concern I own to you that your sentiments of this young gentleman have for some time been my own," Boucher began with his usual flourish, and went on to discuss the system "of tender persuasion" which he con-sidered the most suitable discipline for a boy of Jacky's temperament. ". . . . There are but two cases in which I can foresee much real danger to this young gentleman; and if he can be preserved from these I shall not be greatly apprehensive as to others," he conceded then. "I mean his love of ease, and love of pleasure—pleasure of a kind exceedingly uncommon at his years. I must confess to you I never did in my life

know a youth so exceedingly indolent, or so surprisingly voluptuous; one
would suppose Nature had intended him for some Asiatic prince. Against
these two insinuating and most dangerous foes to all that is truly valuable
in a character, I have exerted all my opposition, and I trust not altogether without success. . . . It could not be but that at one time or another Mr. Custis must have been introduced to Life, as 'tis called; and
is it not almost too much to expect from one brought up in so very
guarded a manner as he has, that he should pass the fiery trial unhurt?
. . . Unluckily, too, there lodged with us a youth of a character exactly
calculated to spoil such a lad as Custis. You will know that I allude to
a son of Mr. Samuel Galloway's. . . . You cannot conceive with what
delight Custis would listen to his droll tales and accounts of his pranks
at school in England. . . ."

Endless as Mr. Boucher's letter promised to be, he had now succeeded
in riveting Washington's attention beyond any danger of skipping, or
laying it aside for a more leisurely moment. With a glance at the door
which he had taken the precaution to close behind him, Jacky's stepfather read on apprehensively. "There is another particular too which
perhaps discretion would bid me suppress, but which I think I cannot
honestly conceal from you," Boucher's next paragraph began in an ominous way. "Samuel Galloway has also a daughter, young and pretty. Out
of respect to you, as I supposed, he frequently invited young Custis to
his house; it was disagreeable to me to be obliged to refuse him, because
it gave offense. But I believe he was never with them but twice—once
when I was, and once when I was not. It was about the time of the
Players being here. Miss Galloway came to town. Jack has a propensity
to the Sex, which I am at a loss to judge of, much more to describe. I
observed somewhat of a particular attention, exceeding bare civility, to
this young lady. I took such steps as I judged most likely to wean him
in time—and it was done, I believe, effectually. . . . I am ashamed to
add, because it is but a mere conjecture of my own, and imparted to
you in great confidence, that I could not help thinking this gave some
disquiet to the family. I would not willingly suspect people without cause;
but however absurd and foolish such a project may have been, were I
to give you a detail of all my reasons, I am inclined to believe you would
think as I do. I am mistaken, if you or Mrs. Washington have not also
had an opportunity given you of penetrating through such a design; there
are here, besides me, who think them capable of it, though I do not
know that there are any besides myself who have suspected them in
this instance. . . ."

When he had done reeling from the bludgeon of Boucher's rhetoric, Washington stowed the letter away in his desk for more than one troubled rereading. He had another chance for observation during the Christmas holidays, when Jacky was again at Mount Vernon. He found the boy grown, and remarkably handsome in the brunette Parke style, and it was not at all improbable that the wild Parke blood, which had skipped Jacky's father, should show itself again in Daniel's son. At the same time, his unfailing sweetness of temper with his mother and sister at once relieved his guardian's worst fears. Basically, Jacky had not changed. A passion for dress, horseflesh, fox-hunting, guns—surely that was pretty normal at Jacky's age. But this matter of the Galloway girl, who according to Boucher had been encouraged by her family to involve Jacky in a love affair—the first, no doubt, of a flock of young women with an eye to the Custis estate. Galloway was a man one saw at the races— owned a fine brick house on the West River called Tulip Hill—had married a Chew—the implication of fortune-hunting seemed unlikely.

The more he saw of Boucher, who had by now paid several visits to Mount Vernon, and the more letters he received from him, the more Washington wondered. On at least one occasion, he had noticed a tendency toward tipsiness after dinner. Overtalkative, certainly, at the table as well as on paper, and overanxious to please, neither fault unusual among the clergy. He was not satisfied with Boucher, but he knew of no one better.

A little to his stepfather's surprise, Jacky had put no insistence on the European tour, though not from any apparent fear of separation from his Mamma. He seemed merely to have a happy faculty of being content where he was, and a disposition to allow events to shape themselves around him while he amused himself from day to day with whatever came to hand.

Even in the matter of inoculation, Jacky was docile. He recognized the need, and it was understood that if he undertook it himself the colored boy Joe who always attended him was to have it too. He minimized the risk and discomfort which so agitated his mother, he named friends of his who had undergone it and so achieved a certain prestige among their contemporaries. But he seemed easily to accede to Martha's unwillingness to have it done away from home, which she felt would increase her suspense as to the outcome, at the same time that she expressed an inconsistent wish that she need not know about it until it was safely over and done with.

Happily the next communication from Boucher was placed in Washington's hand while Martha was preoccupied with preparations for a trip to Williamsburg to consult a Dr. Carter, who was said to be using ether with some success in the treatment of seizures like Patsy's—for the letter announced that Jacky had already received the inoculation at Baltimore in the household of a doctor who specialized in performing it. Apparently Jacky was supposed to have written his mother to tell her of the appointment, and had either forgotten or intended not to do so. Washington's protective impulse not to worry her about it prevailed, and he regarded Jacky's oversight as all for the best. "Jacky left this place with so many doubts and difficulties about going to Baltimore to be inoculated with the small-pox that we all concluded nothing was more foreign to his intention," he wrote hastily to Boucher behind a closed door. "Mrs. Washington having fully adopted this opinion, I have withheld from her the information you gave me in respect to his undertaking, and purpose, if possible, to keep her in total ignorance of his having been there till I hear of his return, or perfect recovery. As one step towards this, I should be obliged to you to address any letter you may write to me under cover to Lund Washington, and in a hand not your own; for notwithstanding it is believed that Jack was resolved to postpone this business, yet her anxiety and uneasiness is so great that I am sure she could not rest satisfied without knowing the contents of any letter to this family of your writing. . . ."

The next letter from Boucher, which duly reached him through Lund, justified his deception and allowed him to set out for Williamsburg with Martha and Patsy, and a clear conscience. "I feel much heartfelt satisfaction," Boucher wrote, "in having it in my power to inform you that Mr. Custis is now out of all danger of the small-pox; in Dr. Stephenson's own phrase, He cannot now die if he would. . . . His fevers began on Monday, and were sometimes pretty high; yet never so much as to confine him above now and then an hour or so to his bed. In short, I think I have now seen better authority than ever to say that the small-pox, in this artificial manner, is really nothing; its virulence is so abated and subdued that I now no longer wonder to find men think so little about it as they do in Baltimore. And to me, the whole secret seems to be in keeping them cool; Custis, I believe, has not been within five yards of a fire since he went to Baltimore. I should wrong him not to add that he has been exceedingly manageable, and always in spirits. . . ."

Williamsburg was again in a quiet interval between Governors, as Lord Botetourt had died the previous autumn, just when they had all begun to get along with him very well. As usual, the Washingtons enjoyed the Bassetts' hospitality, and George made an inspection tour around the prosperous farms of the Custis estate. Also, he succumbed to temptation in horse trading, for the superb cream-white animals which had drawn the dead Governor's coach came up for sale while he was in town. He did a quick deal with his brother-in-law for his own two chariot teams, and bought four of the Hanoverian horses for £130. You never saw such horses. . . .

Patsy was taken to consult Dr. Carter, who prescribed four boxes of fit-drops as a new remedy. She was nearly sixteen now, and a real beauty —very dark, like the Parkes, and greatly beloved for her sweet-tempered ways. They bought her a blue necklace, a book of songs, and a parrot, and she sat to have her miniature painted. On the way home they dined with Mrs. Chamberlayne, who was now a widow. It was thirteen years almost to the day, since Colonel Washington and Mrs. Custis had met in the same parlor. When they reached Mount Vernon again, there was Jacky, lively and well and unmarked, come to demonstrate to his Mamma that the inoculation was really nothing at all.

That September Washington made his first visit to the Annapolis races, lodged at the school overnight, and took Jacky with him to the track. They dined with Governor Eden and went to see the play at the new theater on East Street, which was followed by a ball. Later in the autumn, when the Governor brought a party across the River to dine at Mount Vernon and Belvoir, Boucher was included in his suite, along with George and William Digges and a Mr. Benedict Calvert, whose son was a pupil at the school. The grave colonel from Virginia was a little surprised at the way Governor Eden encouraged Boucher's sallies, and at the headway the ambitious clergyman had already made in Maryland society.

In November, Virginia's new Governor arrived at Williamsburg, and at once dissolved the Assembly, so there could be no session till the spring of '72, after another election, which Washington won without opposition. He went down to the capital alone, attended the theater to his heart's content, and dined and supped with Governor Dunmore, who was being compared unfavorably with his predecessor. His lordship was an arrogant, pompous man, with a surface affability. It was a routine session entirely without fireworks, and when Washington returned to Mount Vernon, after a painful visit to the Williamsburg dentist, the Bassetts and their four children accompanied him for a visit.

Jacky arrived home in May, towing a portrait artist whom he had engaged to paint the whole family. Charles Willson Peale was an attractive young man who had studied in London under Benjamin West, and was fast acquiring a reputation since his return to America. Martha was delighted with him, and set him to work to do miniatures of her children and herself. Washington at first refused to entertain the idea of sitting for his portrait, but was overruled, and Peale embarked on a large three-quarter length canvas. Washington wore—after some discussion—the blue and scarlet uniform of a Virginia colonel, in which he still appeared on full-dress occasions at the Palace in Williamsburg, but which he never expected to wear again in the field. His sash was purple and his gorget was gold, and Martha herself rubbed up the hilt of his sword after black Billy had done his best with it. He looked very grand, she thought, as she always did when he put it on, and very much as she could still see him in the fond eye of her memory on that first afternoon in the Chamberlaynes' parlor. Mr. Peale persuaded her to sit to him for her miniature without a cap or powder, as he saw her about the house in the mornings, and George was so pleased with the result that he at once took possession of it, and bought a frame and a long gold chain, and thenceforth wore it round his neck hidden between his shirt and his coat. She was as touched and flattered as a girl, at the sentimental gesture. But to George Mr. Peale had done a small miracle in transferring to a slip of ivory the slight curving smile and steady, friendly eyes of the woman who had made Mount Vernon a home.

Since the removal of Jacky's school to Annapolis the entries in Washington's diary were becoming quite eventful, as the friendships on the Maryland Shore multiplied and flourished, while the usual neighborhood social round in Virginia continued.

"*Jan. 14.* Went to Belvoir with Mrs. Washington, Miss Custis, and Mr. MacGowan, and stayed all night.

"*May 12.* Went up to Alexandria with Mrs. Washington and Miss Custis to see Capt. Wood's ship launched. Returned in the afternoon.

"*August 7.* At home all day, writing, and posting my books.

"*August 8.* Ditto—ditto.

"*September 4.* Set out with Mrs. Washington and Miss Custis (attended by Mr. Custis) on a visit to Mr. Boucher, etc. Breakfasted at

Mr. William Digges's (the horses and carriage being got over the day before) and dined at Mr. Boucher's with Governor Eden and Mr. Calvert and his two daughters.

"*September 8*. At Mr. Calvert's all day and night. (To cash won at cards at Mr. Calvert's, 10s.)

"*September 11*. Returned home by way of Mr. Wm. Digges's, where we dined, and where my boats met us."

Thus casually, in the midst of a family gathering, screened by an equally pretty sister, Nelly Calvert had been introduced to Jacky's people. Washington did notice that the two girls appeared to be not unacquainted with Jacky from former visits, but when he and Martha tried to look back on that autumn sojourn in Maryland, nothing remarkable stood out which might have warned them. Benedict Calvert of Mount Airy was an acknowledged natural son of the fifth Lord Baltimore, and therefore was related left-handedly to Governor Eden's wife. Perhaps because of the peerage, the accident of his birth was never held against him. He was a member of the Governor's Council, he married a legitimate Calvert cousin, and had ten charming children.

November of '72 found the Washingtons in Williamsburg again. They dined at the Governor's Palace, and thought Virginia very unlucky to have Dunmore instead of the handsome and popular Eden of Maryland. They attended a ball in the Apollo Room at the Raleigh, where only a couple of years before, that solemn session of dismissed members of the Virginia Assembly had determined upon non-importation. (Very little was said about that any more, but patriotic families still abstained from tea, which was still taxed.) They took Patsy to see the waxworks and a puppet show, and bought her two bottles of a new medicine called Norris's Drops.

Governor Eden and the father of the pretty Calvert girls paid a visit to Mount Vernon at the end of the year, accompanied by Jack, and George William Fairfax joined them for hunting. Local society was lively that winter, with a great deal of entertaining and traveling to and fro from the Maryland Shore.

As Jacky's European tour had pretty well died of inanition, the next problem was his promotion from Boucher's school to attendance at some American college. Washington understood the College of William and Mary at Williamsburg to be in the doldrums, mismanaged by its current faculty and no longer first class. For the very obvious reason that he considered its atmosphere disloyal to the King, Boucher objected to Princeton. Neither did he recommend Philadelphia, but the President of King's College at New York he allowed to be as sound and sensible a man and a scholar as any in America. In fact, King's College had recently conferred on the rector of St. Anne's, Annapolis, a quite unsolicited honorary M.A.

Reluctantly, Martha consented to Jacky's further removal to a school from which it would not be possible for him to escape at such frequent intervals as from Boucher's establishment, and Washington prepared to accompany him to New York. It was seventeen years since he had last seen that city, in the course of his journey to Boston to consult Governor Shirley on the touchy question of rank in the First Virginia Regiment, and he found himself regarding the prospect with genuine pleasure. But whether in a deliberate attempt to forestall his exile to King's College, or whether merely by one of his happy-go-lucky accidents, Jacky created new complications by announcing that he and Nelly Calvert considered themselves engaged to be married. He was eighteen, she was not yet sixteen.

Martha was less horrified in a way than Washington was, for she had first married at seventeen herself, although Daniel Custis had been some twenty years her senior. Nelly was a delightful girl, and if Jacky married young and settled down it would put an end to all this talk about traveling abroad, and to Mr. Boucher's veiled insinuations about his moral character. Of course he and Nelly would live nearby, if not actually at Mount Vernon, and it would add another bright young face to the family and, in the course of time, more babies. When Jacky came into his inheritance on his majority, which was after all not far off, there would be plenty for them to live on, and take it all in all, it might not be such a bad idea. . . .

For once, Washington set himself firmly against her fatal inclination to let her children do whatever they wanted to do so long as it made them happy, and he insisted that Jacky should acquire more education, if not more experience of the world, before he married anybody. He could not imagine what Boucher had been about, that the thing had progressed so far under his very nose, except that he had allowed himself to be much taken up with the patronage of the Governor and his friends, and had been dabbling in politics, along with the inevitable domestic distractions of his own recent marriage. The young people had broken all the rules by settling it between themselves before consulting their parents. And while Jacky's fortune would be adequate, Nelly as one of a large family could hardly expect to be well dowered.

Chided by his stepfather with more than usual severity, Jacky took refuge with his mother, and after a long and sometimes stormy family discussion, Washington undertook a difficult letter to Nelly's father. He was well aware when it was finished that as often happened under stress his sentences were a trifle labored and involved, and Martha thought he had borne down a little too hard in the matter of Nelly's dower. His main object was to secure a reasonable amount of delay, and he refused to alter a line. Jacky set off with the letter in his pocket the same afternoon, bound for Mount Airy and doubtless another wigging there.

In a few days he was back again, somewhat cocky, for it had not been as bad as he expected, with Mr. Calvert's reply: "I entirely agree with you that it is, as yet, too early in life for Mr. Custis to enter upon the matrimonial state," Nelly's father had written, "and hope his being placed at New York may be attended with every advantage to him which you and Mrs. Washington can, at present, desire, or I could hope for, in the future happiness which I sincerely wish him and my daughter long to enjoy; to which that must, as you observe, greatly contribute. Permit me at the same time to hope with you, that this separation will only delay, not break off, the match. . . ."

Washington liked Mr. Calvert well enough, and he liked pretty Nelly. Nevertheless, it looked very much to him like the story of the Galloway girl all over again, on a slightly higher level. To a man with ten children, a daughter who had caught John Parke Custis was indeed a blessing. No doubt at all that Nelly was in love, but Washington perceived that he was going to get no encouragement from her father in any effort to disentangle Jack.

Resigned, but not happy, he rode with his elated ward to Annapolis, where he dined with Boucher, who was in a state of guilty optimism, and with Governor Eden, who agreed with him that Jack's commitment so young was a great pity, but she *was* a dashed pretty girl. He then proceeded to Mount Airy and bore with supreme politeness the exclamations and apologies and triumph of the Calvert family, before conducting Jacky on to New York and the supervision of the benevolent Dr. Cooper of King's College.

He had just returned to Mount Vernon when Nelly Calvert arrived with a friend for a visit; and then his brother John Augustine and Hannah drove in, with their daughter Jane, who was Patsy's age, and their youngest, called Billy. In the midst of this happy but unexciting family party Patsy's final and fatal attack occurred. "She rose from dinner about four o'clock in better health and spirits than she appeared to have been in for some time," Washington wrote to his brother-in-law Burwell Bassett on the 20th of June, "soon after which she was seized with one of her usual fits, and expired in it, in less than two minutes, without uttering a word, a groan, or scarce a sigh. This sudden and unexpected blow, I scarce need add, has reduced my poor wife to the lowest ebb of misery; which is increased by the absence of her son (whom I have just fixed at the College in New York, from whence I returned on the 8th) and want of the balmy consolations of her relations . . ."

He intended to have the news of Patsy's death broken to her brother by Dr. Cooper at King's College, but it went wrong as the letter happened to be handed first to Jacky himself, who recognized its source before anyone knew its contents, and so received them unprepared. The letter which he then wrote to his mother had obviously been labored over —first shirking the issue entirely, and then falling back on a self-conscious parody of the consolation undoubtedly voiced to him by the kindly clergyman in an attempt to ease the first shock of grief. Washington thought it a rather poor effort for a boy nearly come of age, but it was soon stained with Martha's tears in countless rereadings, and seemed to bring her comfort.

The Fairfaxes, the Calverts, and the Washington brothers all closed ranks around her, arriving to dine quietly at Mount Vernon, or coaxing her out as far as Belvoir for the afternoon. But loss and change and grief were in the air of Fairfax County that summer. The Bassetts lost a young daughter, and George Mason's lovely Anne died of a slow fever, leaving nine children, and a husband utterly distraught who could only pace her empty room in silent agony.

Sally Fairfax had been mysteriously ailing, and George William's gout was growing worse, and the Yorkshire inheritance was still entangled. They had determined to sail again to England, in the hope that English doctors and English spas might restore them, and their friends in Virginia dreaded that they might not return. Now the parting would be a wrench for Martha as well as for her husband. She had grown to love Belvoir hospitality, and the return visits to Mount Vernon. She enjoyed Sally's stimulating presence, and did not know how to do without such fond and helpful companionship as theirs had been for nearly fifteen years.

The Washingtons went with Dr. Craik to Belvoir to see the Fairfaxes take shipping in mid-July, and watched through a mist as the boat slid away down the broad stream. Martha groped for George's arm as they turned back toward the carriage, and felt the quick answering pressure against his side. The last time the Fairfaxes sailed, she could be philosophical and comforting to him. Now they were all older. This time, though his own heart was aching, George was resolutely cheerful above their mutual apprehension that they would never see Sally Fairfax again.

By a previous arrangement, the Calverts and the Diggeses were arriving at Mount Vernon the next day in a jolly family party which would deposit Nelly and her sister Betsy there for another visit. For that one evening he and Martha were alone together—much more alone, and closer together than they had ever been, each with a separate as well as a mutual sorrow.

It was perhaps fortunate that Nelly Calvert had been in the house the day that Patsy died, making it quite natural that she should step innocently into the empty place where Martha's daughter should be. Before long, they had asked for her back again, and Betsy too, so that the house would be less silent all day long—wisely, it turned out, for with Belvoir deserted and closed, their little world was full of echoes. The Calverts had eight more, and the loan of two girls was no hardship at Mount Airy.

Nelly and her sister did their youthful best for Martha, with instinctive tact and honestly loving ways, during that bewildering summer when without Patsy there seemed to be so little for her to do. She made an effort to respond, and went with them to church, and even allowed herself to be persuaded up to Alexandria and over to Mount Airy. She rode out with George around the farms in the usual way—but Patsy was not there beside them on her little mare, with the white feather in her riding hat. All that summer Martha was brave, and good, but heartbroken. Unwillingly Washington recognized the inevitable remedy, which was the presence of Jacky.

Early in October he went alone to Annapolis for the races, dined with Governor Eden, and went to the play. He had written to Jacky to join him there, and they returned to Mount Vernon together. On December 15th he acknowledged defeat, and wrote to Dr. Cooper in New York withdrawing Jacky from the College and requesting his bill: "At length I have yielded, contrary to my judgment and much against my wishes, to his quitting college in order that he may enter into a new scene of life which I think he would be much fitter for some years hence," he confided. "But having his own inclination, the desire of his mother, and the acquiescence of almost all his relatives to encounter, I did not care, as he is the last of the family, to push my opposition too far; and therefore have submitted to a kind of necessity. . . ."

It was the first Christmas without Patsy, and the gifts which had been ordered for her were given to Nelly in her involuntary usurpment of a daughter's place, which brought a measure of comfort to Martha. George Mason in his own loneliness rode over from Gunston for dinner, and Dr. Craik looked in from Alexandria, with a professional eye on Martha's resolute composure. Young Mr. Peale came back to Mount Vernon to paint another miniature of Jacky as a present for his bride, and the men did a little hunting, and discussed with other visitors a new rumor from Massachusetts—for Boston was in trouble again.

It made no sense to Martha, about Boston. There had been a tax on tea since '67, but people had half forgotten about it, and tea had quietly reappeared on many tables in the colonies. Now Boston had suddenly gone mad and dumped a cargo of tea casks into the harbor and raised another howl about representation and monopoly. Lord North's Ministry, instead of letting well enough alone, had pressed home some stupidity about the East India Company—everybody knew there was smuggling at New York and Philadelphia—but now they were taking it so seriously again. Those were not the serious things, not like children who were gone forever, and only sons getting married. Threepence a pound on the price of tea—what did it matter, when Patsy could not see her brother married? Patsy would have loved the wedding. Patsy would have been a beautiful bridesmaid. Patsy could never be a bride. . . .

Tears stung her tired eyelids again, and fortitude deserted her again, and again she wept, and refused to face the prolonged festivities of a wedding. George would have to go to Maryland without her. George and Lund could go and see Jacky married, she would cry and spoil the whole thing, because Patsy was not there to enjoy it too. There should not be tears and mourning at a wedding. She only hoped George and the rest of them would have the good sense to spare Nelly all this long-faced mumbling about Massachusetts and a man named Sam Adams, who did not belong at a wedding either.

CHAPTER FOUR

The Rising Wind

1774–1775

OUTWARDLY, the spring of 1774 passed at Mount Vernon much as other springs had done, with visits made and received, rides around the farms, a day's hunting for the men followed by cards and neighborly talk over the punch bowl. But now the talk was less of foxes treed or gone to earth, the killing frost, the renewed threat of Indian warfare in the West, the planting of peach kernels and Mississippi nuts, than it was of the latest rumor from the North, where suspense grew daily as the time drew near for the arrival of Britain's reaction to the reckless gesture of dumping the tea at Boston. There was no doubt that some punitive action would be taken. When, and on whom, would the ax fall?

Moreover, the Fairfaxes were not there, and Patsy was not there, and when Jacky came home for a few days he was usually knee-deep in Calverts. He and Nelly were spending most of the time in Maryland, instead of taking up permanent residence at Mount Vernon as Martha had hoped, but they talked of establishing themselves in a house of their own somewhere in the neighborhood of Alexandria.

In May George and Martha drove to Williamsburg for the session which would await the news from England and the answer to the question at the back of everyone's mind. They dined at Speaker Randolph's on the 17th and on the 19th they heard about the Boston Port Bill.

"The Parliament of England," said Landon Carter, "has declared war against the town of Boston, and rather worse."

The inner faction of the House, led by Patrick Henry and Thomas Jefferson, were known to have their heads together, which was quite enough to make Martha uneasy. Why, she wanted to know reasonably enough, did it matter so much in Virginia about Boston? Because, they explained, if Boston's wharves could be completely closed and paralyzed at the whim of the King, so could those of Alexandria, Yorktown, and Norfolk—it was coercion, it was tyranny, and it must not be put up with, in Boston or anywhere else. She wondered what they could do about it. There was only one army, and that was the King's.

When George returned from the House on the 24th he told her what they were going to do about it. The Assembly had resolved that on the day that Boston's port was to be sealed, a week hence, Virginia would observe a day of fasting, humiliation, and prayer, to implore divine interposition to avert the evils of civil war. There was to be a procession, with the Speaker and the mace, from the House to the church, for special prayers and a sermon. The public was invited to share in the services and the fast. The Washingtons dined with Peyton Randolph again that night, and it was as though someone dear to them all lay critically ill.

Two days later, while proceeding with their business as usual, the Burgesses were summoned to the Council Chamber by an angry Governor and dissolved in a single sentence, because the resolutions of the 24th had "reflected" upon his Majesty and the Parliament of Great Britain. And as he might have anticipated, they simply adjourned to the Raleigh's Apollo Room, where they had reconvened in '69, and continued their session there. Landon Carter said it was the first time he knew of that praying for the King and his Parliament to be inspired with wisdom from above was ever thought derogatory to the honor of either of them.

But as in the time of Botetourt, the social amenities of the Governor's little court were maintained. On the very night of the dissolution, Washington dined at the Palace wearing powder and his militia colonel's blue and scarlet uniform, and the next night they all attended a ball in honor of the Governor's wife, who had recently arrived in Williamsburg from New York with his children. Yet on the Sunday set aside for interposition services the only entry in Washington's diary read: "Went to church and fasted all day."

Now that neither her son nor the ailing Patsy presented a continual distraction, Martha regarded the alarming developments with undivided attention, and began to see more clearly and to realize the extent of Washington's preoccupation with the cause of justice in the colonies. George William Fairfax and Sally were in England, but Bryan Fairfax and his wife, who was Sally's sister Betsy, still lived at their place called Towelston above Alexandria, and maintained a viewpoint obstinately loyal to the King. Many old friendships like this one were feeling the strain of differing opinions, and even families like the Randolphs were split asunder as the rift widened between the colonies and the home Government.

Washington's old comrade at arms, General Gage, who shared with him the memory of that terrible day with Braddock on the Monongahela, had been sent out by Parliament to Boston as its military Governor, with troops to enforce the closing of the port. The scarlet British uniform which had once meant protection from their enemies the French and the Indians, now stood for oppression and tyranny.

While he was still at Williamsburg in June, Washington rendered a conscientious personal accounting to his absent neighbors, during the course of a report on his management of affairs at Belvoir, which had been left in his hands and which now included the melancholy duty of renting the house and putting its contents up for sale. The Fairfaxes had decided to remain indefinitely abroad. It was only what their Virginian friends had feared all along, but the final realization nevertheless came hard at Mount Vernon.

At the end of July Jacky brought his wife to visit at his old home. Nelly and Martha remained behind while Jacky accompanied his Pappa when Washington went back to Williamsburg for the special August 1st Convention which met to choose the delegates to the Continental Congress to convene at Philadelphia in September. Jacky had hopes of seeing some political fireworks, but it was a quiet, orderly meeting, held in the Apollo Room since the House was not open to them for this extraordinary session. Peyton Randolph, Richard Henry Lee, Patrick Henry, Richard Bland, Benjamin Harrison, Edmund Pendleton, and George Washington were named to represent Virginia in the Congress. Thomas Jefferson would doubtless have been one of them, but he had been overtaken by illness on the way from Albemarle County to Williamsburg, and was forced to turn back. He sent them a paper called "A Summary View of the Rights of British America, Set Forth in Some Resolutions Intended for the Inspection of the Present Delegates of the People of

Virginia Now in Convention." It was soon published in pamphlet form, and Washington bought a copy for 3/9 to take home with him.

Martha had anticipated, if he had not, that his name would appear on the list of delegates, and she watched with dismay this steady encroachment of what she still vaguely termed "politics" on his time and interest. For Martha an era had ended. Within one year she had parted with both her children, her nearest neighbors, her comfortable days of established habit and the whole secure routine of her second marriage. Now she was reminded of that time when General Forbes was on the way from Philadelphia to the frontier—George was again preoccupied in his own mind, thinking ominous, unpredictable things, withdrawn into a masculine world where there loomed some menacing unknown factor.

Reading the letters he wrote and rewrote when he had discussed them with her, listening to the talk around her dinner table, she realized with a fatalistic clarity that there would be no resisting his absorption in the relentless trend of events, even if she had been foolish enough to try. She might not understand, but she must at least fall in behind him and tread in his footsteps wherever they might lead. He had enough to worry about without encountering argument and despair on his own hearth. He believed that the government of England was wrong. He believed that the colonies had a cause. That other time fifteen years ago, when he believed that the French should be driven out of the Ohio country, he had led British troops into the wilderness and done it. She could not contemplate the present corollary without wincing, but she knew, she felt it in her bones, that the domestic idyl at Mount Vernon was over.

Militia companies were forming in all the counties, as though the Indians were coming again. George had ordered a new uniform, blue with the buff facings which Fairfax County had adopted, in place of the scarlet facings he had worn under the British command. Once they had both been so sure he had done with soldiering. And so he had—for the King. It was a frightening unvoiced idea—that if George went back to the army now he would not be fighting for the King, but against him. Another army was forming under their very noses—an American army.

Washington returned from Williamsburg to Mount Vernon in time for the Belvoir sale, which took place on August 15th. Martha would not face it, but Colonel Carlyle, Dr. Craik, and Jacky went with him to see the familiar articles dispersed by auction. He bought in a card table, a Wilton carpet, the dining-room chairs and window curtains, a looking-glass which had often reflected Sally's face. . . . Sadly they closed the book. Sally was gone and Belvoir was empty. A grim new chapter was about to begin at Philadelphia.

The first test of Martha's secret resolve to uphold George in every possible way was his invitation to Patrick Henry to spend the night at Mount Vernon and accompany him to Philadelphia for the September Congress. Try as she might, she did not like the man, whose persistently back-country ways and speech she considered far more of an affectation than a little superficial polish would have been. "Naiteral parts is better than all the larnin' upon the yearth," he was fond of asserting defensively. She had heard it said that he had gone so far in private talk as to declare that the only course left to the colonies was to break away from Great Britain entirely and establish an independent government in America. Not even George Mason thought it would ever come to that.

With Henry there arrived Edmund Pendleton, serene, conservative, and scholarly, an example of what a man not born to a Tidewater fortune could make of himself with a little effort. A protégé of Washington's old friend Speaker Robinson, by diligent study and observation Pendleton had become one of the best lawyers in Virginia, with a silver voice of great persuasiveness and a knowledge of his profession which Henry, who had never been able to master the black-letter texts, could not hope to attain. In appearance, manners, and speech, he and Henry made an odd pair, and they had been joined on the way by George Mason, who continued to take a quiet but active part in Virginia affairs from his self-imposed retreat at Gunston. He had recently drawn up another paper for the guidance of the Virginia delegates to Congress, and these Fairfax Resolves of Mason's were to have a lasting influence on the procedure at Philadelphia.

The dinner table at Mount Vernon was a sober one, that evening of August 30th, but in no way depressed. Patrick Henry's twanging tones were a trifle subdued by the company in which he found himself, and he behaved better than Martha had anticipated, dressed in a new gray coat of clerical severity. As usual George said less than anybody; the perfect host, inclined to question and listen rather than to expand. Silent and tranquil at the other end of the table, she heard for the first time, quoted by Pendleton, the dynamic two dozen words which had been uttered by her husband at the August 1st Williamsburg Convention: "I will raise one thousand men, subsist them at my own expense, and march myself at their head for the relief of Boston," he had said in his cool, unexcitable way, to their astonishment, for this was action and not oratory. Not one of them doubted that he had the means and the ability to back up his offer, and he was the only one among them qualified to make such a statement.

In the dining room at Mount Vernon a month later, Martha was no less stirred, secondhand, than his original hearers had been. Her quick glance sought his face, though she gave no other sign that it was the first she had heard of the matter, and his eyes met hers briefly—his wise, deeply cut eyes, lean-lidded, with the glint of inward amusement she was often at a loss to account for. There was in them now a flash of gratitude, and compassion, for her good manners in allowing no hint of surprise or alarm to escape her. The speech, if it could be called one, had been one of his rare impulses, utterly sincere, but he had since been thankful that he was not at once required to act upon it. He had not mentioned it at home because he saw that it would not become an immediate issue, and would only make her apprehensive and unhappy. But she played up to it now, after Pendleton's innocent revelation, as Washington had been sure she would respond to any sudden call on her composure and courage. A stupid woman, a thoughtless woman, would have turned to him before them all for enlightenment. Martha only smiled, and caught his eyes, and withheld comment, and Pendleton never knew he had blundered.

Her fortitude was quicker and came harder than Washington suspected, for he had now in his own words, so lightly repeated to her in the peaceful room, given substance to her most secret fears, and she was from that moment convinced that he was caught up in something he himself could no longer control or deflect—that he was moving with a destiny against which there was no appeal. They were all brave, clever, and dedicated men at that table. But only the host possessed the single extra factor which already marked him for the greatest hazard—he was the soldier.

None of them saw the little shiver which ran through her before she rose, with unruffled grace and charm, and left them to their wine and their endless, patient, informed discussion of the dilemma they would ride out tomorrow to meet, and to deal with according to their lights. Supper came and went in the same fashion before at last they separated for the night, Mason having arranged to sleep at the house so that there would be time for another low-voiced conference in the morning. After a leisurely dinner on the 31st, he rode back to Gunston alone, and George set out with Pendleton and Henry, intending to spend the first night at Marlborough in Maryland, across the River.

Martha would have been surprised at the reference to herself in a letter Pendleton wrote about his visit: "I was much pleased with Mrs. Washington and her spirit," it read in part. "She seemed ready to make any sacrifice and was very cheerful, though I know she felt anxious. She talked like a Spartan mother to her son going into battle. 'I hope you will stand firm—I know George will,' she said. The dear little woman was busy from morning till night with domestic duties, but she gave us much time in conversation and affording us entertainment. When we set off she stood in the door and cheered us with the good words, God be with you, gentlemen!"

They could not see her later in the blue and white bedroom she and George had shared for fifteen years, with its eastward window looking toward the River and away from the avenue where the three men had ridden out of sight, followed by their mounted servants and led horses. They did not know how long she sat there, in his chair by the cold hearth, listening to the empty house—empty of the voices of her children, and now empty of her husband's firm, quiet footfall and the familiar clean smell of a well-groomed horse which so much of the time clung to his clothing. She sat without moving, her hands idle in her lap, her eyes fixed on space, gathering strength for a loneliness and a resignation too deep for tears.

She watched for his letters hungrily, and searched each one for any hint of an early return, even while she tried to school herself to patience. He knew the kind of news she liked, and he wrote freely and with deep affection to his "dear Patsy," using the little name for Martha which had always until recently been doubled at Mount Vernon, the younger one having never been known by any other. Peyton Randolph had been unanimously elected President of the Congress, he wrote, with a Charles Thomson of Philadelphia as Clerk. The Psalm chosen to be read at the opening ceremonies was the Thirty-fifth—he knew better than to write out for her the ominous words which at once came tramping through her memory: *Plead my cause, O Lord, with them that strive with me: fight against them that fight against me. Take hold of shield and buckler, and stand up for mine help. Draw out also the spear, and stop the way against them that persecute me: say unto my soul, I am thy salvation. . . .*

Nearly sixty delegates were present at the Congress, most of them strangers to all but the representatives of their own colony, and it was often difficult, he confessed, to find common ground, so that a good deal of fencing and jockeying went on at first. The sittings began at 9 A.M. in Carpenters' Hall, and continued till 3 P.M., when the hungry, weary delegates were free to dine where they pleased, discuss the day's oratory, play cards, and get acquainted. As he had not been appointed to one of the committees, he was able to be a frequent guest of the first citizens of Philadelphia, who were very hospitable to the visiting members, and he made new friends every day—Joseph Reed, a young lawyer who had studied in England and married a charming English wife and had a baby son; Thomas Mifflin, a Quaker of the "gay" kind, wealthy, good-looking, something of a dandy, and with a remarkably pretty wife; while among George's fellow delegates the names of John and Sam Adams of Massachusetts, Silas Deane of Connecticut, the Rutledges of South Carolina, William Livingston of New Jersey, and his brother Philip Livingston and John Jay of New York occurred most often. Their own Patrick Henry had caused one of his usual sensations on the first day, during a debate on the number of votes due each colony. He had made an eloquent appeal for unity and the burying of local differences, winding up with an already much-quoted cry; "I am not a Virginian, I am an American!" Since then, he had been remarkably quiet—for him.

She could well imagine George moving with his habitual untalkative dignity through the crowded days of the session, which was probably not unlike what he had encountered as a Burgess, although at Williamsburg everyone knew everyone else, and he, with fifteen years of uninterrupted membership, had become a respected landmark in the House. He was of course no stranger in Philadelphia, and had passed through the city only the year before with Jacky on the way to New York. It would not take long, she thought, for his tall figure and military carriage to make an impression in his new surroundings—she had often watched with affectionate pride the mysterious magic of his personality, which drew attention and admiration like a magnet. It was his complete unawareness of his own impact on the beholder which was so disarming. There was never a man of less pretension, who wore powder, velvet, silk stockings, and a dress sword as easily as he wore uniform or riding clothes, and took the floor for a minuet with the same unself-conscious grace that he sat a restive horse.

She would have enjoyed the comments written by his new acquaintances, such as Silas Deane's letter to his wife; "Colonel Washington is nearly as tall a man as Colonel Fitch, and almost as hard a countenance; yet with a very young look, and an easy, soldierlike air and gesture. He does not appear above forty-five, yet was in the first actions in 1753 and 1754 on the Ohio, and in 1755 was with Braddock, and was the means of saving the remains of that unfortunate army. It is said that in the House of Burgesses in Virginia, on hearing of the Boston Port Bill, he offered to raise and arm and lead one thousand men himself at his own expense, for the defense of the country, were there need of it. His fortune is said to be equal to such an undertaking." Already the legend was forming around him.

The session dragged on until some of the Virginia members went home to be in time for the November meeting of the Burgesses at Williamsburg. Washington and Richard Henry Lee were the last to leave Philadelphia, after signing for their absent colleagues on October 26th, when the address to the King was finally approved and adopted. He brought Martha a present of a handsome pocketbook. The next day he rode out as usual to have a look at the mill.

Even when he gave a firsthand account of all those weeks of talk and argument at Philadelphia, it seemed to her that very little that was new had been accomplished there. The grievances of the colonies and their right to self-government had all been set out again. A united association against the importation of luxuries from England had been reaffirmed on a continental scale. Massachusetts had been promised united support and encouragement, as the most heavily oppressed community so far. Any threat of transporting any citizen of the colonies to London for trial was to be met by united resistance by all the colonies. United—that was the word. They had pledged themselves to act together, and even the Southern colonies, which had not as yet been occupied by the King's troops, would go to the defense of Boston if need be. There was to be another Congress at Philadelphia in the spring, unless the situation had improved.

Martha listened in her attentive silence, without looking up from her needlework, or raising awkward questions. But what did they mean by resistance and defense? she was thinking. Surely they did not expect the King's troops to give way as the French had done on the Ohio? Surely they had no idea that the gawky county militia companies which were drilling with new colors and uniforms, and with arms scraped together wherever they could be found, could stand up against the fire of British regulars? They wanted George to join the militia boys, to drill them, to lead them in the field. Commander in Chief of the volunteer Virginia forces—*again?* Much of his time was spent watching these earnest boys march and wheel and halt and present arms; in correspondence about ammunition and colors and drums; in interviews with eager young patriots who were ready to start for Boston tomorrow. There were other veterans of the French and Indian wars living in Virginia, but it was Colonel Washington everyone turned to first. It made his wife both proud and sad.

Early in the year the King was known to have expressed himself furiously to Lord North: "The New England governments are in a state of rebellion, and blows must decide whether they are to be subject to this country or independent," he was supposed to have said. Independent. It was Patrick Henry's word. Now it came from the Throne.

In February at a meeting in Alexandria Washington was named a delegate for Fairfax County to the Convention which was to meet in Richmond on the 20th of March to choose the Virginia members of the Second Continental Congress, which was to convene at Philadelphia in May. There was little doubt of the result, and he was not blind to Martha's effort to accept the prospect cheerfully. He would not be long at Richmond, he reminded her—it was no different from a session of the House at Williamsburg. And even if he was chosen to go to Philadelphia he would have some time at home first. She tried to smile away his concern for her personal happiness when so much was at stake.

To her relief, he was back at Mount Vernon after only a fortnight's absence at Richmond, where Patrick Henry had raised the echoes again with a speech on the necessity of putting the colony of Virginia in what he called "a posture of defense." Petitions and addresses, he said, were futile. Washington had long held that opinion himself, but he admitted ruefully that Henry was spoiling for a fight. Martha, being a woman, was not too gallant to mention tartly that Mr. Henry's experience of combat was exactly the same as her own. With the spark of laughter in his eyes which she so often set there, Washington conceded the point, and added that Mr. Henry had now committed himself to liberty or death, and anyway it was a great speech and had left them all in a sweat.—Yes, he had to go to Philadelphia again.

April, 1775—the sixteenth anniversary of her first homecoming to Mount Vernon—passed in a cloud of visitors. All the regulars came, to hear about Richmond and speculate about Philadelphia—Walter MacGowan, Dr. Craik, Jacky and his wife, George Mason, John Augustine Washington and his little son Billy, two of the Lewis nephews from Fredericksburg, Bryan Fairfax, a couple of Carters, and that European oddity whom Washington had already encountered at Philadelphia, Charles Lee, in company with young Harry Lee of Leesylvania, who was in no way related but being nineteen and not long out of Princeton had a fine case of hero-worship for the swaggering soldier of fortune. Charles Lee held a lieutenant-colonel's commission in the British army, but professed himself devoted to the cause of the colonies and ready to fight for it. Washington, who was always put off by flamboyance in any form, treated him with cautious courtesy and listened to his tales of wars in Portugal and Poland with honest respect. But Martha noticed that his linen was dirty, his table manners atrocious, and his language unfit for her parlor, and her politeness was stiff as icicles. Major Horatio Gates, another British officer who had survived the French and Indian war after a serious wound, had since married an heiress and bought an estate in Berkeley County which he called Traveller's Rest, and was a close friend and neighbor of Washington's brother Samuel. He now appeared at Mount Vernon and was exceedingly pleasant to everybody, while expressing his intention of joining the colonial army as soon as there was one. Washington received him cordially, and promised to bear it in mind.

Just before George's departure for Philadelphia came a letter from George William Fairfax in Yorkshire, with directions about the upkeep of Belvoir and the payment of some accounts he was shocked to find he had left outstanding. He concluded with a discreet comment on the current situation: "It is reported in London that you are training the people of Virginia to the use of arms; I hope you do not find those of your own county the most deficient, or that they misbecome their new uniform. They are going to have a general Review of all the Military here, but for what I know not as it's not customary. Time only will show the event of all things, and God grant you your privileges and a happy and speedy reconciliation upon constitutional principles, is the daily prayer of, Dear Sir, your affectionate and most obliged humble servant. . . ."

There came also an express from Hugh Mercer at Fredericksburg, who had just heard that Governor Dunmore had ordered the seizure of the powder from the town magazine at Williamsburg, which the citizens regarded as a public insult. It was proposed to send light horsemen into the capital to support the honor of Virginia, and they were awaiting Colonel Washington's instructions and assistance. Peyton Randolph and Robert Carter Nicholas had narrowly averted a riot in front of the Palace.

Almost simultaneously arrived still more alarming news from the North. There had been a similar attempt by General Gage at Boston to secure arms belonging to Massachusetts, which resulted in a skirmish between British soldiers and colonial militia at a bridge near Concord, and a running fight ensued as the regulars retreated into Boston, leaving dead and wounded. The whole city was now said to be besieged by an excited colonial force which was encamped across Boston Neck.

Between Williamsburg and Boston, Washington's departure for the Congress hung in the balance. The wind was rising. If Dunmore was going to behave like Gage, with actual bloodshed, the Virginia colonel's presence would be required nearer home. But Dunmore, who had had a thorough fright in his barricaded Palace at the end of the Green in the capital, agreed to pay for the powder, and as the Virginia companies disbanded to their homes it seemed that Washington would be able after all to keep his obligations in Philadelphia. Martha had never doubted it, for Virginians did not behave like the inhabitants of Massachusetts.

All George's recent absences from home were most inopportune, when their cherished plans for building an addition on either end of the house were just getting under way. There were not enough rooms at Mount Vernon, nor enough privacy for the owners. At the south end Washington had designed a spacious library beyond the dining room on the ground floor, into which he could retire with his correspondence and his account books; and above it, to provide sanctuary for himself and Martha, there was to be a bedroom with two windows looking down the River and two large lighted closets as dressing-rooms. There was even a little private stair leading up to it from the library. At the other end, he had drawn up a room for entertaining, two stories high and long enough for a banqueting table or a ball. Their new quarters on the south were enclosed and glazed, but not finished on the inside, when it came time for him to go, and a new chimney piece for the dining room had just arrived. She knew his intentions—they had been over it many times in detail—and Lund had the specifications all written out, so the work would proceed without him. The new dining hall could be raised and enclosed at some later time.

She could see how he hated to leave the job midway, and she knew how he had looked forward to occupying with her the rooms they had planned for their own convenience and comfort in the midst of so much enforced hospitality. She hoped that by the time he came back from Philadelphia she and Lund could have the upstairs part all arranged and ready for him, with the carpet down and the new curtains hung and their furniture from the old bedroom installed—though half the satisfaction to her would be lost if he was not there while that was being done.

The library below, which was to have bookshelves built all around the walls, could await his supervision.

He was often in uniform now, with so many calls to review and drill the independent companies of three or four counties, but she had not expected to see him set out for Philadelphia wearing buff facings and a sword, and her breath caught in her throat as he stooped to kiss her good-by. He had to travel by way of Baltimore, in order to review some companies there and attend an entertainment in his honor, he reminded her, and it seemed to him the proper garb. He was still wearing it when he reached Philadelphia, and he continued to wear it at the daily sessions of the Congress, apparently unconscious or indifferent that he was the only member there so dressed. He was, of course, the only member so qualified.

Once again at Mount Vernon she awaited his letters. The Concord affair was very serious in its implications, he found, though it had its encouraging aspects. "I believe that if the retreat [of the British] had not been as precipitate as it was—and God knows it could not well have been more so—the Ministerial troops must have surrendered or been totally cut off," he wrote. Partly because of Concord, and partly because they were no longer strangers in the Congress, the members greeted each other cordially in the hot, tree-lined streets of the tidy Quaker city. Their arrival had amounted to a parade. They sat now in the State House instead of in Carpenters' Hall, and Peyton Randolph was again placed in the chair, though his presence would shortly be required in Williamsburg as Speaker of the Assembly there. The beloved Dr. Franklin had come home after ten years in England, just in time to be unanimously elected to the Congress by the Pennsylvania Assembly.

Then George wrote that he had been named to a committee to consider the proper procedure for New York City, which was soon to receive an increased garrison like Boston. A fellow named Ethan Allen had captured a place called Ticonderoga in New York State, where a small British garrison had surrendered—it was on the line of British communication to Canada, and might be important. When Peyton Randolph returned to Williamsburg in June, John Hancock of Massachusetts was named to succeed him as President of the Congress. He was the wealthiest man in New England, they said—elegant, slender, irritable, and proud, often in delicate health. George dined again with the Reeds and the Mifflins, and made the acquaintance of Schuyler the Indian fighter, who owned a fine house in Albany and had put the fear of God into the Six

Nations. After the muddling about of last year's session, Washington was impressed by the unanimity of this one. The colonial troops besieging Boston were short of ammunition and provisions, which the Congress undertook to forward as soon as possible, though it had no funds for such a purpose. . . .

But gradually as the first warmth of reunion wore off, a note of discouragement and doubt invaded the sittings. Even Patrick Henry produced no enlivening oratory, and accompanied Randolph back to Virginia. When Congress authorized the raising of ten companies of riflemen to march to Boston and "act under the command of the chief officer of that army," they were well aware that there was, at present, no such man. A leader for the combined colonial forces which were to reinforce the half-trained militia outside Boston must be chosen in Philadelphia.

Something came between Martha and the page of that letter. She had accepted the idea that George would be drawn into the conflict if it came, but as a Virginian. He had never had anything to do with Massachusetts. Surely he would not undertake to go to *Boston*. Hadn't New England any officers of their own? There was Schuyler, George thought well of Schuyler. Or else there was Horatio Gates, he wasn't a native Virginian, he wouldn't mind going to Boston. And there was that odious Charles Lee from England, who had no roots at all. Let him take charge of the New England army.

But she knew it was no use. When George's next letter came, she was braced for the news it contained.

"My Dearest [he had written]:

"I am now set down to write you on a subject which fills me with inexpressible concern, and this concern is greatly aggravated and increased when I reflect upon the uneasiness I know it will cause you. It has been determined in Congress that the whole army raised for the defense of the American cause shall be put under my care, and that it is necessary for me to proceed immediately to Boston to take upon me the command of it.

"You may believe me, my dear Patsy, when I assure you in the most solemn manner that, so far from seeking this appointment, I have used every endeavor in my power to avoid it, not only from my unwillingness to part with you and the family, but from a consciousness of its being a trust too great for my capacity, and that I should enjoy more real happiness in one month with you at home than I have the most distant prospect of finding abroad, if my stay were to be seven times seven years. But as it has been a kind of destiny that has thrown me upon this service, I shall hope that my undertaking it is designed to answer some good purpose.

"You might, and I suppose did perceive, from the tenor of my letters, that I was apprehensive I could not avoid this appointment, as I did not pretend to intimate when I should return. That was the case. It was utterly out of my power to refuse this appointment, without exposing my character to such censure as would have reflected dishonor upon myself and have given pain to my friends. This, I am sure, could not, and ought not to be pleasing to you, and must have lessened me considerably in my own esteem. I shall rely, therefore, confidently on that Providence which has heretofore preserved and been bountiful to me, not doubting but that I shall return safe to you in the fall. I shall feel no pain from the toil or the danger of the campaign; my unhappiness will flow from the uneasiness I know you will feel from being left alone. I therefore beg that you will summon your whole fortitude and pass your time as agreeably as possible. Nothing will give me so much sincere satisfaction as to hear this, and to hear it from your own pen.

"If it should be your desire to remove into Alexandria (as you once mentioned upon an occasion of this sort) I am quite pleased that you should put it into practice, and Lund Washington may be directed by you to build a kitchen and other houses there proper for your reception. If on the other hand you should rather incline to spend a good part of your time among your friends below, I wish you to do so. In short, my earnest and ardent desire is that you will pursue any plan that is most likely to produce content, and a tolerable degree of tranquility; as it must add greatly to my uneasy feelings to hear that you are dissatisfied or complaining at what I really could not avoid.

"As life is always uncertain, and common prudence dictates to every man the necessity of settling his temporal concerns while it is in his power, and while the mind is calm and undisturbed, I have, since I came to this place (for I had not time to do it before I left home) got Colonel Pendleton to draft a will for me, by the directions I gave him, which will I now enclose. The provisions made for you in case of my death will, I hope, be agreeable. I have included the money for which I sold my land (to Doctor Mercer) in the sum given you as also all my other debts. What I owe myself is very trifling, Cary's debt excepted, and this would not have been much if the bank stock had been applied without such difficulties as he made in the transference.

"I shall add nothing more at present as I have several letters to write, but to desire that you will remember me to Milly and all friends, and to assure you that I am, with the most unfeigned regard, my dear Patsy, your affectionate,

GEORGE WASHINGTON

"P.S. Since writing the above, I have received your letter of the 15th, and have got two suits of what I was told was the prettiest muslin. I wish it may please you. It cost 50/ a suit, that is 20/ a yard."

More than once as she read, the lines had blurred and run together, and at the end she dissolved into rueful tears. He was taking command of the colonial army, as she had feared—but first he had bought her the prettiest muslin. He was bound for heaven knew what at Boston, but he worried about how and where she would spend her time while he was away. He had drawn up a will for her protection, and enclosed the solemn evidence in his letter. But what made her cry was the vivid picture in her mind's eye of the big earnest man setting aside the time to go and buy her the muslin they told him was the prettiest, and because he knew she would ask, relating to her the price per yard. *I wish it may please you. . . .*

His thoughtfulness for her was revealed by the arrival of Jack and Nelly for a visit, as the result of a letter they had received from him. Compassionate of her hungry questions, Jack allowed her to read it for herself: "My great concern upon this occasion is the thought of leaving your mother under the uneasiness which I fear this affair will throw her into," he wrote to Jack. ". . . . At any time, I hope it is unnecessary for me to say that I am always pleased with yours and Nelly's abidance at Mount Vernon; much less upon this occasion, when I think it absolutely necessary for the peace and satisfaction of your mother; a consideration which I have no doubt will have due weight with you both, and require no further arguments to enforce. . . ."

Within the week another letter from George brought his best-loved brother John Augustine from Bushfield with his wife Hannah, to urge Martha to join their household in Westmoreland County if ever she was lonely, or even if she wasn't. The Bassetts then sent to invite her to stay with them at Eltham while he was away, expressing sympathy for her anxiety at his present occupation. She was grateful to them all for their kindness and prompt response to his appeals, but she was determined to remain at Mount Vernon at least until the autumn, when they were all quite sure that he would return.

One campaign, John Augustine agreed with her confidently, just to show the King that his American colonies meant what they said, and there would be a new Minister in London, one more disposed to common sense. The red-coated regulars had retreated at Concord, hadn't they? It would be the Braddock story all over again. The British regulars didn't know how to shoot, they were taught to point the gun forward and fire, hoping the bullet would carry and would hit something. The colonial riflemen, on the other hand, aimed at the crossbelt and the bullet got home. Those riflemen could shoot out a squirrel's eye, John Augustine reminded her. The British couldn't stand up to shooting like that. They ran.

It was all very reassuring. Everyone thought the Concord affair would have blown over by Christmas. The John Augustines went home, and Jack and Nelly settled in at Mount Vernon to keep her company. George wrote to her once more from Philadelphia, on the 23d of June.

"My Dearest:

"As I am within a few minutes of leaving this city, I could not think of departing from it without dropping you a line, especially as I do not know whether it may be in my power to write again till I get to the camp at Boston. I go fully trusting in that Providence which has been more bountiful to me than I deserve, and in full confidence of a happy meeting with you some time in the fall. I have no time to add more, as I am surrounded with company to take leave of me. I return an unalterable affection for you which neither time nor distance can change.

"My best love to Jack and Nelly, and regard for the rest of the family; conclude me with the utmost truth and sincerity, your entire

GEORGE WASHINGTON"

With the letter in her hand, she climbed the stairs to the new bedroom and felt her way to the chair she had placed by one of the windows which looked down the River toward deserted Belvoir. She sat there a long time, in unaccustomed idleness, alone.

CHAPTER FIVE

The Soldier's Wife

1775-1776

SHE WAS IN LOVE WITH HIM, but not yet his wife, when he had set out in June of '58 to join General Forbes in the march on Fort Duquesne, and her two children were small and comforting. Now, for all their good intentions, Jack and Nelly were absorbed in each other, and while Lund was good—everyone was good—there were no babies, and not enough companionship. She told herself she must not expect George to write to her very often, with what he had on his hands at Boston, but all those full and rewarding years at Mount Vernon, their contentment and adjustment and accomplishment, and the sorrow shared and so divided, had forged memories which could only bind closer during the separation and anxiety which were beginning.

There was no difficulty any more about what to write in their letters. Martha, who was never handy with her pen, as with necessity he had become, knew that he hungered for the small daily news of the place he loved best, and she strove to write down for him the sort of thing she had always chattered about so easily on his return from brief absences in Williamsburg and Maryland. He had never been so far away since their marriage. There had never been a time, except at Philadelphia last year, when she did not know when to look for him home again.

He had bought saddle horses and a phaeton and team at Philadelphia, and sent home the green chariot and four for her use, so that she might make her usual visits in the usual comfort. Faithful Billy was with him, of course, as his body-servant, but Bishop was getting old and had acquired a family, and remained in his cottage at Mount Vernon.

George had refused to take any pay as Commander in Chief, asking only his expenses in return for the sacrifice of his home life in Virginia. It was a noble idea, but she worried about it. Lund might be wise and careful, and for years he had carried his share of responsibility, but it stood to reason that Mount Vernon would not do as well in the master's absence. The building program which was moving forward without stint represented a heavy outlay. If the situation at Boston turned into a real war, and George did not come home by Christmas as they hoped, she dreaded that their recent prosperity after years of debt and planning, might evaporate again. If the colonial army was beaten and had to surrender, his wealth and his lands and his house would all be subject to confiscation—even his life might be forfeit if he was taken by the British.

This was her nightmare—this was what stretched her fortitude beyond the demands made upon it by her loneliness and the unforeseen daily problems which arose on the estate and must be settled by her or by Lund without George's advice and support—the dark foreboding of his defeat and capture, which was almost sure to bring him to the hangman's noose. This was what set her palms to sweating and drove her about the house on endless tasks devised to keep herself busy, made her sharp with the servants and exacting with Lund—gave her sleepless hours and hidden tears. And always the lack of him, the empty chair, the silent rooms, could be felt like an actual ache.

He did write, though, and told her the things she wanted to know. His headquarters were at Cambridge, where Harvard College was located; a charming town, he said, and the weather had mostly been fine. After a crowded week in the home of Harvard's President, inconvenient to everybody, and embarrassing to Washington as Dr. Langley was allowed to retain only one room for his private use, they had set up a new headquarters in a house belonging to a loyalist named Vassall who had deserted it, leaving its furniture intact, and fled into Boston when the colonial army first appeared. It was a handsome dwelling, with paneled rooms on either side of a central hall, and space enough for the aides and secretaries to work there—so she need have no fear for his health or comfort, as he was at least not compelled to live in a tent.

Besides Billy, he had his military "Family"; the officers who made up the Headquarters personnel and ate at the General's table. She was glad to hear that the two young Philadelphians he had liked best, Joseph Reed and Thomas Mifflin, had ridden with him to Cambridge, to act as secretary and aide. Both were experienced men of the world, and would be companionable as well as useful. The adventurer, Charles Lee, with a new major general's commission in the American army, was already unpopular and difficult, being touchy about his rank and privileges, and had promptly demanded of Congress a financial guarantee for his services. Schuyler, a landowner and Indian War veteran himself, who would have been a congenial friend, had been detached at New York for duty along the Canadian route, on the borders of Lake George and Lake Champlain. Gates, recommended by his past military experience with Braddock and Governor Shirley, was the Adjutant-General.

There were new names now in George's letters—Nathanael Greene of Rhode Island, another Quaker who had nevertheless joined the army; John Sullivan from New Hampshire, who had left the Congress to take the field as a soldier, a wild Irishman, proud, impulsive, hard to handle, but always ready to fight; Henry Knox, a young Boston bookseller whose hobby was military history and engineering, with a natural love of big guns, hearty, noisy, and efficient. There were no uniforms, so they had worked out a system of colored ribbons—light blue for the Commander in Chief, worn diagonally across his breast between his coat and waistcoat; the Brigadiers wore pink ribbons, the Major Generals purple, and the Staff green. The field and company officers had colored cockades and shoulder knots. It sounded rather gay.

For some reason the British did not come out and attack, no one knew why, though reinforcements were known to have arrived from overseas under Generals Howe, Burgoyne, and Clinton, before the fight at Bunker Hill, which Washington had missed by only a matter of days. The British had paid a terrible price there for what they chose to call a victory. It was said that at one time General Howe was left quite alone on the field, with every man on his Staff disabled, and that his white buckskin breeches and silk stockings were stained with their blood, as though it were his own. If the Colonists had not run out of ammunition the battle might have turned in their favor. In any case, the British were now sitting tight in the town, as though they did not know that the patriot army was still perilously short of powder.

Washington had written to George William Fairfax that he would no longer be able to handle the affairs of Belvoir, at a distance of six hundred miles, and advised that some other arrangement must be made, as he could only direct his own Mount Vernon business now at second hand, through Lund. Before June was out Martha had something more than the peaceful round on the Potomac to discuss in her letters to George. During the stormy session of the Williamsburg Assembly which had recalled Peyton Randolph from Philadelphia, Governor Dunmore made an angry retreat with his family on board a British man-o'-war, after which the Burgesses simply proceeded without him, as though the Royal rule was at an end in the colony. The Governor then collected a rabble of loyalists and runaway servants and slaves on the lower James, and threatened fire and destruction to the great houses along the Tidewater river banks. Some alarm was being expressed for the home of the American Commander in Chief, and even for the safety of his wife.

Martha thought that was nonsense, and said so. A man who took up arms against his King and failed might well be tried for treason and hanged, but to suggest that the Royal Governor would harm a middle-aged American lady in her own home was ridiculous. She was not afraid of Dunmore. He was, after all, a Scottish lord, not an Indian.

George held somewhat the same view. Late in August Lund received a letter from Cambridge: "I can hardly think that Lord Dunmore can act so low and unmanly a part as to think of seizing Mrs. Washington by way of revenge on me," Washington wrote coolly. "However, as I suppose she is by this time gone over to Mr. Calvert's, and will soon after returning go down to New Kent, she will be out of his reach for two or three months to come, in which time matters may, and probably will, take such a turn as to render her removal either absolutely necessary or quite useless. . . . Our lines of defense are now completed, as near so at least as they can be; we now wish them to come out, as soon as they please, but they (that is, the enemy) discover no inclination to quit their own works of defense; and as it is almost impossible for us to get to them, we do nothing but watch each other's motions all day at the distance of about a mile, every now and then picking off a straggler when we can catch them without their entrenchments. In return, they often attempt to cannonade our lines to no other purpose than the waste of a considerable quantity of powder to themselves which we should be very glad to get. . . . I wish you would quicken Lanphire [the carpenter] and Sears about the dining-room chimney-piece (to be executed as mentioned in one of my last letters) as I could wish to have that end of the house completely finished before I return. I wish you had done the end of the new kitchen next the garden as also the old kitchen with rusticated boards; however, as it is not, I would have the corners done so in the manner of our new church; (those two which front the quarter). What have you done with the well?—is that walled up?—have you any accounts of the painter? . . ."

At first they both broke their hearts because of the homesickness in his letters; then they realized that it was a form of escape from the heavy reality of his present task to sit alone at his desk, probably late at night, and find his way back on paper to the simpler problems he had left behind him. The new mantelpiece for the dining room would be installed by the time he returned. The new bedroom would be finished too, and the library below it was ready for his final instructions. They still hoped that he would be home for Christmas.

In the meantime Lund sent off a reassuring reply: " 'Tis true that many people have made a stir about Mrs. Washington's continuing at Mount Vernon, but I cannot think her in any sort of danger. The thought, I believe, originated in Alexandria. From thence it got to Loudoun. I am told the people of Loudoun talked of setting a guard to conduct her into Berkeley, with some of their principal men to persuade her to leave this and accept their offer. Mr. John Augustine Washington wrote to her pressing her to leave Mount Vernon. She does not believe herself in danger, nor do I. Without they attempt to take her in the dead of night, they would fail, for ten minutes notice would be sufficient for her to get out of the way. Lord Dunmore will hardly venture himself up this River, nor can I think he will send up on that errand. Surely her old acquaintance, the Attorney [John Randolph] who with his family are aboard his ship, would put him off doing an act of that kind. I have never advised her to stay, nor indeed to go. Colonel Bassett thinks her in no danger. She sets off next week with her son and daughter down the country. . . . I proposed to her to put whatever she thought most valuable into trunks, and should there be a necessity to move them, it will be sooner done. . . . Your papers are among the things which will be put up. . . ."

Jack and Nelly were at Mount Vernon, prepared to make the journey to Eltham with her, and they gave earnest advice as to what it was most important to preserve from Dunmore. On her own decision, Washington's account books and diaries, and bundles of his private papers were packed before the silver and trinkets which were dearest to her own heart. Then they set out for New Kent County in the chariot. Nancy had lost her four eldest children by now, but Burwell II was eleven, John was ten, and Fanny eight—just the ages which children born at Mount Vernon might have been, and Martha watched their development with something more than the usual affection of a devoted aunt.

She was at Eltham with the Custises and the Bassetts in November, when Washington's saddle-sore express rider, forwarded by Lund from Mount Vernon, arrived to set off twice as much excitement as Dunmore's appearance in the River would ever have done. George wanted her to join him—at Cambridge—at once—she could be there in time for Christmas. *He wanted her.*

Seventeen years fell off her age in as many seconds, and her heart was beating like a bride's again. Jacky . . . Nelly . . . Nancy . . . Sally, the maid . . . the trunks . . . the coachman and postillion . . . the chariot and horses . . . her voice rang through the house, and they all stared at her in amazement amounting to paralysis. But it was a *thousand miles* to Boston, said Nancy—she would be all winter on the road. But not *today,* said Jacky—Nelly had to pack. Besides, the servants had not had their dinner.

They caught her like a bird in mid-flight, reasoned, pleaded, commanded, and prevailed. She would wait till tomorrow morning, then. No longer. From Eltham to Mount Vernon by chariot was five days—from Mount Vernon to Philadelphia, she was not sure—from Philadelphia to New York, she did not care—from New York to Cambridge, what did it *matter,* how many days—at Cambridge he would be waiting. He wrote that he would arrange for the stages, lodging, and escort, if she gave the word. *If!* Joseph Reed was back at Philadelphia, and he would see to everything. An aide would join them along the way to bring them past the pickets to Headquarters. Jack and Nelly were to come too if she liked, that also would be provided for. And so, by the same express rider who took back her happy scrawl to Cambridge, a message must go to Lund at Mount Vernon to pack hampers of food and extras for the table at Headquarters—hams, and useful things like that—food from home. Christmas presents, little things that would go in the corners of the trunks, yarn for knitting, sewing-thread, needles, there would be mending to do. . . .

They looked on with compassion and love while she wrote out her list of things to take to him. The length of the journey, the winter weather through which she must travel, the inconveniences and discomforts to be encountered did not occur to her. She had never in her life been north of Alexandria, Virginia, but she was already on her way to

Cambridge, Massachusetts. They admired her courage, when courage was a word which never crossed her mind.

Except for her impatience, the drive back to Mount Vernon was much as usual. At Fredericksburg, where they always halted for the night, George's sister Betty Lewis worried about the danger of smallpox in the Cambridge camp, and Martha replied stoutly that if George advised it she would take the inoculation. Betty stared as if the fireside puss had turned into a tigress, and Jacky told them all over again how the inoculation was nothing at all, as he had himself demonstrated years ago at Baltimore.

Lund was not surprised. He had more than once heard her utter the wish that if George could not come home soon, she might go to him, and unlike some of the others he believed her. He undertook to pack the chariot with their necessities for a journey which, while a bit short of Nancy's horrified thousand-mile guess, would consume something like three weeks without allowing for stopovers along the way which break-downs or fatigue might require; and in whatever space was left he stowed the hams, bacon, nuts, and dried fruit for pies which would enhance the Christmas dinner at Headquarters.

With Martha, Jack, Nelly, and the colored maid Sally, a colored coach-man and postillion in the white and scarlet Washington livery, and Jack's body-servant in the Custis livery riding Jack's saddle horse and leading another, the chariot with its four white horses got under way for Philadel-phia, crossing the Potomac at Alexandria, and passing through all those towns which had been to her only names mentioned by George on his return, or words scarcely glanced at before she read on into the hasty letters which had come back to her each time the distance between them widened as he rode northward.

On the 21st of November they reached the ferry on the Schuylkill River which would carry them over to Philadelphia, where they would be welcomed by people who, because George knew and liked them, were already her friends. Awaiting her on the farther shore was a polished escort of horsemen in smart brown uniforms with peaked caps and shiny boots, ranks of Pennsylvania militia infantry, a gay cluster of gold-epauletted officers, and handsome young Joseph Reed himself, with an invitation from his wife to lodge at their house in the city, which Martha gratefully accepted. Lovely, fragile Esther Reed, heroine of a transatlantic romance during his law student days at the Middle Temple in London, was a gracious hostess, and there were three small children.

As she sank into slumber that night after a week on the road from Mount Vernon, Martha could admit to herself that she was tired beyond all imagining. She was forty-four, and she had traveled nearly five hundred miles, and had as many again to go before she came to the doubtful comforts of the Headquarters house at Cambridge. She was willing to draw breath now, in the luxury of the Reeds' hospitality, while the horses rested too.

The next day the new wife of Mr. Hancock, President of the Congress, came to call, as did the wife of Mr. Duché, the clergyman who had chosen to read the prophetic Thirty-fifth Psalm at the opening of the first Congress. They showed Martha the notice of her reception, printed in the Pennsylvania *Gazette:*

"Yesterday the Lady of His Excellency General Washington arrived here, on her way to New England. She was met at the Lower Ferry by the officers of the different battalions, the troop of Light Horse, and the Light Infantry of the 2d battalion, who escorted her into the city."

She was sufficiently impressed—not for herself, but for his Excellency, whom they honored by honoring her. She felt an additional responsibility in bearing his name. She would feel it always, even if in the end he should fail, for it would be a glorious failure now, in a great cause. She was dumbfounded—and furious—to learn that malicious rumors had been spread about that her sentiments were unalterably Tory, and that she had chosen to live apart from the Commander in Chief because of the difference in their views. At least her arrival at Cambridge would put a stop to that. And she would have joined him sooner, she explained anxiously, except for their obstinate hope that a settlement would be reached, and that the first campaign at Boston would be the last. . . . Philadelphia smiled at her indignation, and reminded her that they all knew that, and told how he often spoke of her with affection in other family circles.

The patriot society of Philadelphia proposed to give a ball in her honor at the City Tavern. Flattered and excited at the prospect, she and Nelly got out their best gowns for the maid to freshen, and sent for a hairdresser. But Sam Adams interfered, on the grounds that the Congress had requested the people to refrain from "vain amusement," and a committee waited upon her at the Reed house, respectfully to urge her not to attend the ball. Her native tact rose up quickly to meet politeness with courtesy, and she assured them that she quite agreed that the entertainment was an extravagance which might be dispensed with. The committee retired like clumsy schoolboys, disarmed, confused, enchanted by the little woman's dignity and unruffled good humor. Plans for the ball were abandoned. His Excellency's wife, a little disappointed, perhaps, but vaguely conscious of having scored, enjoyed a restful evening at home with the Reeds.

The Virginia delegates to the Congress called to pay their respects to her, though none of their wives had gone to the expense and inconvenience of accompanying them to Philadelphia. The sudden death of Peyton Randolph from an apoplexy had left John Hancock in the President's chair. Peyton's nephew Edmund, a recent and welcome addition to the Headquarters Staff at Cambridge, at once returned to Virginia to assume control of the Randolph inheritance, which was complicated by the absence of his Tory father as one of Dunmore's adherents.

On the 27th of November, escorted by the Philadelphia Light Horse, the Infantry, and the mounted officers in their privately purchased finery, Martha's chariot took the road for Trenton, from where the Elizabethtown troop would accompany it to Newark, which greeted the arrival of the General's lady with pealing bells and cheering townsfolk, who waved and called encouragement from the roadside. She was delighted to see how popular George was—and never guessed that some of the enthusiasm might be for the smiling, rosy-faced woman who had had the pluck to leave a comfortable Southern home and join her husband for the rigors of a New England winter within sight of the enemy.

After Newark the towns crawled by day after day till she lost track of them. A mounted escort took her across the Hudson at King's Ferry above New York, where loyalist feeling ran high. There was a place called New Rochelle—New Haven, Wethersfield, Springfield—it got confusing. Sometimes they outran the local preparations for their reception, sometimes they missed the next posted escort or the road itself. Springfield, Brookfield, Worcester—now they were in Massachusetts, she was told— Marlborough, Watertown. Two weeks of it—strange beds, strange food (she would not touch the precious delicacies from Mount Vernon, destined for the Headquarters dinner table), jolting, rutted, frozen roads, and jaded horses—even Jacky was lost, once New York lay behind them.

At a dreary crossroads inn they were joined by a single aide accompanied by an orderly, who proved to be Colonel George Baylor from Virginia, and whose father was an old friend—he had been waiting there for several days, he told her, on the General's orders to meet and guide Mrs. Washington's party through the lines to Headquarters. As near as that, at last? She was at once less tired. She gave young Colonel Baylor her hand, and her warm, curving smile. With his own smile still on his lips in the afterglow of her pleasure, Baylor mounted and rode out ahead; the orderly fell in behind, and the travel-worn chariot drawn by its four weary horses rolled on.

Washington had known and loved her for nearly twenty years, and he had still to discover her capacity for devotion. At the same time he sent off the letter which followed her to Eltham, he had written to his brother John Augustine: "Nothing new has happened since my last worth communicating; since finishing off our own lines of defense we, as well as the enemy, have been busily employed putting our men under cover for the winter. Our advanced works and theirs are within musket shot of each other; we are obliged to submit to an almost daily cannonade without returning a shot, from our scarcity of powder, which we are necessitated to keep for closer work than cannon distance, whenever the red-coat gentry pleases to step out of their entrenchments. . . . Seeing no great prospect of returning to my family and friends this winter, I have sent an invitation to Mrs. Washington to come to me, although I fear the season is too far advanced (especially if she should, when my letters get home, be in New Kent, as I believe the case will be) to admit this with any tolerable degree of convenience. I have laid a state of the difficulties which must attend the journey before her, and left it to her own choice. . . ."

He had not allowed himself to count on it, guarding against disappointment, reminding himself of the enormity of the adventure for her. She might not be well, Jack or Nelly might be ill and need her, bad weather might already have set in, or she might simply think it was too far. . . . When he received her message that she was coming, *instantly,* as fast as the horses could bring her, he was almost surprised, and he was touched, and perhaps a little apprehensive.

Orders flew right and left at Headquarters. General Washington's lady would arrive within a month's time—a Virginia lady. At once a universal garnishing began. Other officers' wives were spending the winter at Cambridge, of course—General Greene's Kitty from Rhode Island, and Mifflin's pretty Quakeress from Philadelphia among them—but this was the wife of the Commander in Chief, all the way from Mount Vernon.

She was drowsing against Nelly's shoulder when they passed the pickets without a halt, and in the cold twilight of that gray December day came to a large gracious house painted yellow, with white pilasters in front and a porch at each side, standing above a double flight of steps in the middle of a broad snowy lawn much trampled by horses' feet. There was no welcome prepared because no one knew when to expect them. Sentries walked their bleak rounds, looking pinched and frozen; an officer's mount waited, tail to the wind, at the hitching bar. The windows were already lighted from within, where the overworked secretary-aide, Colonel Harrison, labored at his writing-table, and the General himself was pushing a dogged quill across the pages of a long, confidential letter to Reed in Philadelphia: "I am much obliged to you for the hints contained in both of the above letters, respecting the jealousies which you say are gone abroad. . . . I cannot charge myself with incivility, or what in my opinion is tantamount, ceremonious civility, to the gentlemen of this colony; but if such my conduct appears, I will endeavor at a reformation, as I can assure you my dear Reed, that I wish to walk in such a line as will give the most general satisfaction. . . . With respect to what you have said of yourself and situation, to what I have said on this subject I can only add that whilst you leave the door open to my expectation of your return, I shall not think of supplying your place. . . ."

Outside in the dusk the riding-aide, Colonel Baylor, dismounted somewhat stiffly and opened the door of the chariot, while his orderly passed the word into the house. Martha was still standing beside the mud-encrusted vehicle, dazed with fatigue, waiting for Jack to hand Nelly down, when George's arms closed around her from behind. No one paused to stare, and the sentries stood tactfully blind and turned to stone, while she clung to him and wept, and he, half laughing and very much moved, held and soothed her. The General's wife had come to Cambridge.

They had not seen each other for seven months. But time to talk and listen and ask questions, and above all, time to be quiet together, as they had learned to do during the years at Mount Vernon, was hard to come by now. Washington was always either pinned down at his desk by the contents of the post-bag, or riding out to survey the new works at Lechmere Point, or making an inspection of the barracks and kitchens which were still under construction for the wintering of the troops, or watching evolutions and maneuvers of the new companies which came in so slowly, or receiving with patience and courtesy countless callers, committees, and would-be helpers of no particular qualifications. His days began before dawn and ended long after dark, with only the brief interlude of the dinner table to relax his constant concern for his army.

His office was the room on the right of the door on the ground floor, and Martha was given one of the paneled, handsomely furnished parlors on the left of the hall. Here she received her own callers with her natural cordiality and charm. Transplanted into a neighborhood of strangers, whose very accent in speech marked the distance she had come from home, and whose curiosity was sometimes ill-concealed, she might have felt shy except for her sense of responsibility to George. She was the General's wife, and from his stature she took confidence and a determination to do her share of his work, which was to greet all comers graciously, bear with them amiably, entertain them as best she could with a glass of wine and a bit of cake, since it was no longer proper to serve tea, and make sure they would go away with nothing but praise for her hospitality.

The officers' wives were friendly and anxious for her good opinion, and were soon at their ease in her company. Mrs. Gates, a somewhat overpowering woman who had arrived at Cambridge just behind Martha, already considered herself, as a fellow Virginian, an old friend. Young Mrs. Mifflin was among the first of the Headquarters wives to wish her welcome, along with the wife of Dr. Morgan, the Philadelphian who had been appointed Director-General to the army hospitals. The Morgans shared lodgings with their friends the Mifflins. Dr. Morgan had studied medicine in London, where he had enjoyed the acquaintance of Dr. Franklin, and in Edinburgh and Paris. He had improvised a hospital in a house opposite Headquarters, which was also requisitioned Tory property, and without adequate supplies or equipment was doing his best there for the sick soldiers who far outnumbered the few wounded from the desultory daily fire out of Boston. General Greene's Kitty drove over from his headquarters two miles distant at Prospect Hill on the left of the American lines, to introduce to the Commander in Chief's wife the baby son who had been recently christened George Washington Greene.

Martha soon developed a particular fondness for Mrs. Greene, who was the niece of the Governor of Rhode Island. Kitty had lost her heart to the downright, fresh-faced Quaker when Nat Greene was drilling his first militia company in his home town of Coventry. He had a stiff knee which made him limp increasingly with fatigue, a humiliation to him on parade, and war was against the religion in which he had been reared, and which he never renounced when he became a soldier, relapsing still into the Quaker "thee" at times of stress or emotion. Yet already he had become one of the mainstays of the fledgling army, and held a profound admiration for Washington, who returned in full measure an affection and trust which was never abused. In contrast to some of the other brigade encampments, Prospect Hill was a model of military tidiness and sanitation achieved by no other officer.

Martha's news from home was supplemented by Washington's own from Southern sources since she began her journey. She brought him the sad story of Mr. Boucher's increasing aggressiveness and unpopularity at Annapolis, which had occasioned a near riot in his church and led to a theatrical situation when he preached a final, furious Tory sermon with loaded horse-pistols displayed on the pulpit cushion beside him. He had then sailed for England with his devoted American wife, though his sister chose to remain in Maryland. Washington produced for Martha a letter written to him not long before Boucher's departure, in which with typical grandiloquence the clergyman-schoolmaster foreswore his former admiration for the American Commander in Chief. "You are no longer worthy of my friendship," he wound up after several turgid pages. "A man of honor can no longer without dishonor be connected with you. With your cause I renounce you; and now, for the last time, subscribe myself, Sir, your humble servant, J.B." Martha shook her head with a tolerant sigh. His poor wife, she said.

She brought also the latest details from Lund Washington on the building operations at Mount Vernon. Their bedroom was furnished and waiting, with George's favorite chair by the hearth, and a new coverlet on the fourposter, and the fire screen she had started to work last summer finished and mounted; two more spinning wheels had been added in the weaving-house, and the girls were learning to make attractive new materials, with stripes, in place of the drab homespun; a new litter of hound puppies had arrived, and Lund submitted a list of proposed names. . . .

Meanwhile, there was another Christmas to celebrate, and soon after that, the seventeenth anniversary of their marriage. At first George seemed reluctant to indulge in festivities at Headquarters, as a distraction they could not afford. But he soon recognized the value of the change which had come over the household and his military Family with the arrival of his wife and the young Custises.

It had not taken long for the homesick, overworked boys who were his Staff officers to discover that Mrs. Washington was not as formidable as might be expected. Robert Hanson Harrison, the writing-aide, who spent his life at a cluttered table in a room on the right of the hall behind the General's study, was anyway a friend from Alexandria, and had visited Mount Vernon and done small legal chores for George ever since '69. Colonel Baylor, who had joined her on the road and witnessed the meeting between her and the General, was also a Virginian, and not

much in awe of the sweet creature he knew her to be. Nearly of an age
with Jacky Custis, Baylor was on an almost filial footing in the Commander in Chief's household, and was glad of Jack's eagerness to share
in the aides' military duties, which had not been simplified by Edmund
Randolph's abrupt departure and present intention to serve henceforth
in a political capacity in the Virginia Convention instead of returning to
Headquarters. The Family missed Randolph's social grace and strong
back, but promised themselves that he would be equally valuable in Congress, where he was sure to wind up. The Greenes had demonstrated
Martha's weakness for small children, and her genius for housekeeping
at once showed itself in the very food which came to the General's table.
To be invited to dine at Headquarters was a coveted privilege among the
officers and the Massachusetts neighbors, and a sewing and knitting circle
was formed to meet in Mrs. Washington's parlor to do mending for the
bachelors, and provide comforts as well as bandages for the hospital
across the road.

Without the presence of the ladies, the year's end might have been
overlaid with military gloom, for besides the everlasting shortage of powder, the term of enlistment for the militia was running out, and a new
army must be built under the very noses of the enemy, with recruits who
were slow and unwilling to join. Nevertheless, the Christmas dinner was
a cheerful occasion, lighted by many additional candles, adorned by the
hoarded goodies from Mount Vernon, and with enough wine for all the
usual toasts. The aides had hung the rooms with Christmas greens and
garlanded the staircase, and there was mistletoe on the overhead lamp
in the front hall. Everyone wore powder, and the wives got out their best
gowns and bits of jewelry, and even the weather obliged with a fresh
snowfall on Christmas Eve, which was clean and sparkling on the
twenty-fifth under a bright sun. Not a shot was fired on either side all
day, and the Christmas bonfires burned high in the American camp that
night, deriding the lack of firewood in Boston town.

Martha was accustomed to attend church, particularly at such times
as holidays, and was disturbed to learn that Christ Church in Cambridge
had been deserted by its largely Tory membership when they removed
into Boston before the colonial troops took possession of the ground. It
was used as a barracks for a time, and since then had stood boarded up
and forlorn. At the request of the General's wife, the little white building
was ordered to be cleaned and put to rights for a service on New Year's
Day, which fell on Sunday.

One of the ladies who was present then wrote to a friend in Philadel-

phia: "The Sexton took us to Mr. Henry Vassall's pew, No. 3, he said,
but I could see no number. All have been taken off by the soldiers who
used the place as a barracks. Soon after, Mrs. Washington, Mrs. Gates,
and Mrs. Custis entered together and were shown to a seat in front of
us, the Royal pew, Welch said. Do you think the name prophetic? Our
Queen looked very well in peach-colored satin which is worn on all State
occasions, and she glanced most kindly upon us, wishing us 'the compliments of the season' in quite an audible tone.

"Soon we heard the sound of fife and drum and knew that the Commander in Chief was approaching. The two vestrymen or wardens whom
I have mentioned before stood facing the middle door, with wands of
office in hand, crossed, ready to escort General Washington to his place.
As he entered they each made a most stately bow, which was returned
with his usual courtesy. They preceded him up the east aisle to a pew
within two of the vestry door. Major Mifflin walked by his side as had
been arranged and took the seat of honor next him; then followed a long
row of officers in their best uniforms, for everyone who could be spared
from duty had been requested to be present. The bodyguard of our chief
stood around him and threw their shakos rather irreverently, we thought,
on the window sills.

"The soldiers, a company of whom were present, grounded their arms
and nothing was heard save the shuffling feet of the Negroes in the background, the former slaves of the Tories who had often come here with
their masters in days gone by. The clerk brought out the huge prayer-
books given by the Honorable Thomas Lechmere and found the places,
putting in long purple and gold markers, and Mr. Palfrey, the chaplain,
read service. He had composed a prayer instead of that in use for the
King, and we thought it very good. The townspeople wondered if King
George would be prayed for as usual. Unfortunately the organ could not
be used. Some of the leaden pipes had been taken out to furnish ammunition for our men at the fight in Charlestown last June, and it was quite
out of order, but a bass viola and clarionet played by some musical soldiers led the singing, which was very good. The strong voices of the
many men who thronged the Church made fine music for my ears, and
when part of Psalm CXVIII and a verse from Psalm CXIX was rolled
out I saw some tearful eyes. . . ."

Considering that young Colonel Palfrey of Boston was no chaplain
whatever, but had been chosen by Martha from among the General's
Staff officers to devise the service—having doubtless been recommended

to her notice by his friends the Hancocks in Philadelphia—he had done rather well: *"The Lord taketh my part with them that help me: therefore shall I see my desire upon them that hate me. . . . It is better to trust in the Lord than to put confidence in princes. . . ."*

At the end of the month Martha found time to send off a letter to her young friend Betty Ramsay at Alexandria: "I now set down to tell you that I arrived here safe, and our party all well. We were fortunate in our time of setting out, as the weather proved fine all the time we were on the road. I did not reach Philadelphia till the Tuesday after I left home. We were so attended and the gentlemen so kind, that I am under obligations to them that I shall not forget soon. I don't doubt but you have seen the figure our arrival made in that Philadelphia paper—and I left it in as great pomp as if I had been a very great somebody.

"I have waited some days to collect something to tell, but alas, there is nothing but what you will find in the papers. Every person seems to be cheerful and happy here. Some days we have a number of cannon and shells from Boston and Bunkers Hill, but it does not seem to surprise anyone but me; I confess I shudder every time I hear the sound of a gun. I have been to dinner with two of the generals, Lee and Putnam, and I just took a look at poor Boston and Charlestown from Prospect Hill. Charlestown has only a few chimneys standing in it; there seems to be a number of very fine buildings in Boston, but God knows how long they will stand; they are pulling up all the wharfs for firewood. To me that never see anything of war, the preparations are very terrible indeed, but I endeavor to keep my fears to myself as well as I can.

"Your friends Mr. Harrison and Henly are both very well, and I think they are fatter than they were when they came to the camp—and Captain Baylor is a lusty man to what he was when you see him. The girls may rest satisfied on Mr. Harrison's account, for he seems too fond of his country to give his heart to any but one of his Virginia friends. There are but two young ladies in Cambridge, and a very great number of gentlemen so you may guess how much is made of them; but neither of them is pretty, I think.

"This is a beautiful country, and we had a very pleasant journey through New England, and had the pleasure to find the General very well. We came within the month from home to the camp. . . . Please to give my love and good wishes to your mamma and grandmamma. . . ."

No one was more astonished than the General himself to find his wife seated at the end of the secretary's table with a quill pen in her hand,

making a copy of his New Year's General Orders under Colonel Harrison's benevolent eye. They looked up at him blandly when he paused
on the threshold. The Orders for that day were so long, she explained,
with a compassionate glance at the aide, and there had to be so many
copies of them, and besides there were letters to get ready for the express-
bag; they thought her handwriting would be good enough for the Brigade-
majors to make out. Nothing confidential, of course, like the regimental
returns, said Harrison with a cocked eyebrow—just routine, like the Orders and the letter-book entries of letters to Congress and General
Schuyler and the Provincial Governors.

They waited like polite children, their pens hovering, till he laughed.
She wrote a better hand than Baylor any day, he said. And as long as
she did not tire herself he saw no objection to her employment as assistant secretary, provided she could come to terms with Congress on the
matter of pay. He passed on into his private room, and she bent her
head again above the page.

GENERAL ORDERS [she had written]
Headquarters, Cambridge, January 1, 1776.
Parole *Congress*   Countersign *America*
"This day giving commencement to the new army, which in every point
of view is entirely continental, the General flatters himself that a laudable
spirit of emulation will now take place, and pervade the whole of it;
without such a spirit, few officers have ever arrived to any degree of
reputation, nor did any army ever become formidable; His Excellency
hopes that the importance of the great cause we are engaged in will be
deeply impressed upon every man's mind, and wishes it to be considered
that an army without order, regularity, and discipline is no better than a
commissioned mob. Let us therefore, when everything dear and valuable
to free men is at stake; when our unnatural parent is threatening us with
destruction from every quarter, endeavor by all the skill and discipline in
our power to acquire that knowledge and conduct which is necessary in
war. . . ."

After that, when she had time to spare from her visitors and her return
calls and her housekeeping, she often joined Colonel Harrison at his
writing-table, and learned to keep her pen moving even while the General was dictating another letter a few feet away. Sometimes he only laid
some notes before Harrison and requested him to say so and so, and left
the aide to wrestle out the wording himself. Sometimes he brought back

an interlined and rewritten draft for a fair copy. Sometimes he strode up and down in the narrow space and composed aloud as he went. As the days passed, she overheard and transcribed many things she only half understood, and while they tried not to impose on what they called her good nature, her essential trustworthiness made her more valuable than she knew.

But the letters Washington wrote to Reed in Philadelphia went out in his own hand, and not through the secretary's room, and it was probable that even Martha remained unaware of the depths of discouragement he allowed himself to express to the man whose absence he felt most keenly, and whose complete loyalty he had come so quickly to depend on for bad news as well as good. "The reflections on my situation and that of this army produces many an uneasy hour when all around me are wrapped in sleep," he confessed to Reed during January. "Few people know the predicament we are in on a thousand counts; fewer still will believe if any disaster happens to these lines from what cause it flows. I have often thought how much happier I should have been if, instead of accepting of a command under such circumstances, I had taken my musket on my shoulder and entered the ranks; or if I could have justified the measure to posterity and my own conscience, had retired to the back country and lived in a wigwam. If I shall be able to rise superior to these and many other difficulties which might be enumerated, I shall most religiously believe that the finger of Providence is in it, to blind the eyes of our enemies; for surely if we get well through this month, it must be for want of their knowing the disadvantages we labor under. . . ."

Later that month Reed sent to Martha as a joke one of the highly imaginative portraits of Washington which were being manufactured abroad and offered for sale as a likeness of the American rebel general. The copy which Reed had somehow secured for their amusement at Headquarters was a mezzotint signed by one Campbell, and represented Washington in full uniform and cocked hat, mounted on a fat horse, with a drawn sword, and a battle going on in the background. The aides pretended to be impressed by the grandeur of the subject, and Martha set it up in her parlor, where it caused considerable merriment. "Mrs. Washington desires I will thank you for the picture sent her," Washington wrote to Reed. "Mr. Campbell, whom I never saw to my knowledge, has made a very formidable figure of the Commander in Chief, giving him a sufficient portion of terror in his countenance. Mrs. Washington also desires her compliments to Mrs. Reed. . . ."

Headquarters was in need of a good laugh just then. An American expedition into Canada had failed at Quebec, and while leading the gallant fight outside the city General Benedict Arnold was severely wounded. In the South Lord Dunmore had laid Norfolk in ashes on New Year's Day, bombarding the blazing town from his ships off shore. No one along the Tidewater rivers knew where he might strike next, and anxiety spread up the shore as far as Alexandria.

Martha did not need to transcribe his midnight meditations to Reed to know that George was not as confident as he managed to appear, and that he nevertheless had arrived in his own mind at the idea which only a short time ago had seemed in Patrick Henry's utterance so reprehensible —a final severance from the home Government—independence. And she did not have to be told that that would mean a long and bitter struggle, with the outcome much in doubt.

Better than anyone else, she could trace in his face and bearing the almost superhuman self-control which enabled him to sit at the dinner table cracking nuts and drinking little toasts in apparent serenity, for the sake of maintaining the spirits of the men who depended on him for guidance and support, and for the deception of the watchful guests who were always eager for his hospitality. She did not suspect the sleight of hand he performed with the returns on enlistment, desertion, and sick, so that no one officer, not even Harrison, ever saw the whole dreadful situation at any one time. She could guess at his hours of discouragement and despair, spent alone at his desk behind a closed door when other weary men had gone to bed. And she could see him aging day by day under the crushing load he had set himself to carry alone—in the tightening lips and jawline, in the hooded ice-blue gaze, the enigmatic drop of the lean eyelids, the deliberate levelness of tone when he spoke.

The leisurely fox-hunting planter, making his rather stately jokes with the worshiping young people of his Virginia neighborhood, enjoying a mild gamble at cards with old cronies, unbending at an election ball, had changed back into a dedicated soldier, as when she first knew him. And how the story repeated itself, she thought, on a larger scale. Ammunition, clothing, food, equipment, all in short supply—the wherewithal to do the thing required of him denied—the decencies, the mere necessities for the men who looked to him and who would risk their lives at his command, all lacking. He had been through it before with the Williamsburg Assembly under Dinwiddie and Fauquier, and now the Congress at Philadelphia was no better. It must seem to him like one of those dreams, she would think, marveling at his patience and unflagging effort—where you feel you are reliving an experience which you know has already transpired. He must sometimes wonder if he had ever been anything but a soldier. Perhaps it was Mount Vernon that now seemed to him the dream.

In spite of the new friends she had made, Martha watched anxiously for news from Virginia, especially with Dunmore at large in the rivers. Lund's faithful accounts of the building, the horses, the hounds, the slaves, the visitors, were reassuring. But letters from New Kent County were scarce, or went astray. She got quite vexed with Nancy about it, by the end of January: "I have wrote to you several times in hopes that would put you in mind of me," she complained, "but I find it has not had its intended effect, and I am really very uneasy at not hearing from you, and have made all the excuses for you that I can think of. But it will not do much longer, and if I do not get a letter by this night's post, I shall think myself quite forgot by all my friends. The distance is great, yet the post comes regularly every week. The General, myself, and Jacky are very well. Nelly Custis is I hope getting well again, and I believe is with child, I hope no accident will happen to her in going back. I have not thought much about it yet. God knows where we shall be. I suppose there will be a change soon, but how I cannot pretend to say. A few days ago General Clinton, with several companies, sailed out of Boston Harbor, to what place distant for we cannot find out. Some think it is to Virginia he has gone, others to New York—they have been kept in Boston so long that I suppose they will be glad to seek for a place where they have more room, as they cannot get out any way here but by water. Our navy has been very successful in taking their vessels. Two was taken last week loaded with coals and potatoes, wines, and several other articles for the use of the troops. If General Clinton is gone to New York, General [Charles] Lee is there before him, and I hope will give him a very warm reception—was sent there some time ago to have matters put in proper order in case any disturbance should happen, as there are many Tories in that part of the world, or at least many are suspected there to be very unfriendly to our cause at this time. Winter here has been remarkably mild. The river has never been froze hard enough to walk upon the ice since I came here. My dear sister, be so good as to remember me to all enquiring friends—give my duty to my mamma, and love to my brothers and sisters, Mr. Bassett, your dear children, and self—in which the General, Jack, and Nelly join me. . . ."

The change which Martha sensed in the air, as well as in the letters and orders she transcribed at Colonel Harrison's elbow, had begun with the return to camp in January of General Knox, bringing the cannon from Fort Ticonderoga. The big hearty man, as tall as Washington and weighing half again as much, had a natural affinity for artillery which had enabled him to perform a small miracle. In the dead of winter he had ridden on horseback from Cambridge to Lake Champlain and there collected some fifty pieces of heavy ordnance, idle since the capture of the fort by Ethan Allen the previous May—mortars, howitzers, and a quantity of lead and flints, more than sixty tons of iron and brass—and transported them on sledges drawn by eighty yoke of oxen, three hundred epic miles to the lines at Cambridge.

They never thought he could do it. Even when he wrote from Albany to explain that he was only detained there by a thaw, it did not seem possible that he would actually produce those cannon in front of Boston. When he rode in on the 24th at the head of the column, burly and bellowing and triumphant, the camp tossed its hats in the air and cheered till the British in Boston must have wondered what was up. Washington came out from Headquarters to see, and found the troops gathered round gaping at the guns, and caressing them as though they had been warm flesh and blood like the faithful, stolid oxen which had struggled through snow and ice and mud to get them there. The oxen too were heroes, Knox reminded his audience. Horses panicked in deep snow, and damaged themselves on the harness. Oxen didn't care, they would break a road for horses any day. So everyone patted the oxen, worn and weary and benign.

The biggest guns had been left at Framingham temporarily, but even so it made quite a show. And early next morning Knox was at work arranging his artillery parks on the Roxbury front near Dorchester, and at Prospect, Winter, and Cobble Hills, overlooking the town. They now had the range of Boston, its wharves and harbor, and the British were soon to be very uncomfortable there—if only Washington could scrape together enough powder for a respectable bombardment. More *noise,* sighed the wives. But none of them wished to retire from earshot.

There were other signs that the war was stirring again after the winter lull. Drilling and discipline were tightened up, and the men were required to overhaul their equipment and clean their guns. In obvious anticipation of bloodshed to come, Dr. Morgan sent out a request to the ladies for an increased supply of bandages and hospital shirts and blankets, and there was a thorough turnout of his medical chests, and a call for experi-

enced male nurses. His requirements were strict, and a man had to know
his way about with tourniquets and cauterization before he was accepted
for duty. Much of the work on bandages was done in Martha's parlor,
with the assistance of the neighborhood women, who willingly gave their
time in the company of the Commander in Chief's wife.

A letter from Lund written at the end of January revealed the extent
of Dunmore's growing reputation for old-fashioned piracy: "Alexandria
is much alarmed, and indeed the whole neighborhood," he wrote. "A
report prevails that there are 5 large ships lying off the mouth of the
Cone River. . . . The women and children are leaving Alexandria
and stowing themselves into every little hut they can get, out of the reach
of the enemy's cannon as they think; every wagon, cart, and pack-horse
that can be got are employed in moving the goods out of town. The
militia are all up (but not in arms, for indeed they have none, or at least
very few). . . . They say they are determined to fight, although they
move out their effects; I hope they will.

"I am about packing up your china, glass, etc., in barrels . . . and
other things into chests, trunks, bundles, etc., and I shall then be able
at the shortest notice to move your things out of harm's way (at least
for a while) some to Mrs. Barnes, and the rest into Morris's barn; and if
they are found not to be safe there, move them further. . . . I fear the
destruction will be great, although the greatest care will be taken; Mr.
McCarthy has offered me his cellar to put your wine, rum, etc., in. I shall
either send it there or to Mrs. Barnes. . . . As yet I have moved nothing
except your papers. Everybody tells me that if they could have notice
they would come and defend your property so long as they had life.
From Loudoun, Prince William, Fauquier, and this county, 100 men in
my opinion could prevent 1000 from landing here to do mischief. . . ."

The idea of Mount Vernon becoming a battlefield was horrifying to
them both, but since Norfolk not even Martha's common sense could
identify her one-time crotchety, quick-tempered, but well-born host at the
Governor's Palace on many a civilized formal occasion with the ruthless
vandal who was threatening pillage and even death to people who were
known to him by long acquaintance. She realized what it would mean
to George in loss and grief if the home he loved and had labored over
so long should be destroyed, and in this rage of revenge which had gripped
him, the Royal Governor was apparently capable of burning Mount Vernon to the ground. They could only hope at Cambridge that Lund's usual
discretion and foresight could mitigate disaster if it came, and that none

of their devoted neighbors would come to any harm by some hot-headed act of defiance. Eltham, though nearer the present scene of Dunmore's raids, was not after all a Washington possession, and might escape his attention.

To Washington's disappointment, his Council of general officers had not supported his suggestion that an attack on Boston might be made across the ice. It was objected that the British were too strongly entrenched and the Americans' stock of powder might run out before a decisive action could be completed. But at the Council a new idea had been conceived; if the little hills on Dorchester could be occupied and some of Knox's artillery set up there, they could fire into the town from redoubts without exposing the men or requiring them to make a frontal attack—and the British would have to come out themselves in order to try to take or silence the guns. It sounded simple enough. But the ground was frozen too hard to dig entrenchments on Dorchester, so behind the lines construction was begun of hurdles and fascines and hay bundles to be used as traverses against enemy fire while the works were being prepared, and barrels were to be filled with earth and stone and rolled down hill into a British assault. Wagons and carts were assembled to transport the materials at the last possible moment beyond the Roxbury lines, which rested toward the Heights. Leaves were stopped, and militia ordered up. There was a new bustle and smartness to the aides, who sniffed action. Washington worked later and later at his desk. The wives exchanged knowing glances, and tried not to ask questions of the harried men they so seldom saw. Nerves stiffened daily, as February wore on.

Each morning Martha woke wondering: will it start today? Each time the wives sat rolling bandages, stitching, knitting, in the parlor at Headquarters, hearing the jangle of spurs and sword belts and the tramp of riding-boots in the hall as the low-voiced, bright-eyed, keyed-up officers came and went, the same question waited behind their quiet talk of babies and housekeeping and letters from home: when will they be ready? Will it start tomorrow?

At midnight on March 2d, lying awake in their room above the office waiting for George to come to bed, she heard the now familiar boom of a cannon somewhere on the right—Roxbury, maybe, where several of Knox's big ones had come to roost—and another, and a third. The answer came back promptly from across the water. The British were awake too, and at their posts. There was a pause—she was getting used to cannon, she thought, and dozed a little.

Next time it came from the left, where Greene was, at Prospect Hill. They would wake the baby. What a beginning for the Commander in Chief's little namesake—a lullaby of gunfire. Children didn't seem to mind. Kitty said he showed no fear, when the guns began.

Seven, eight, nine. She was suddenly wide awake, on the realization that this was no ordinary exchange of discourtesies; this was a purposeful bombardment. It was not like George to spend so much powder at one time. Was this the overture? No one had warned her. The windows rattled, and the British fire came back like an echo, round for round. George always said they hadn't got the range to hit Cambridge, their guns could barely reach the lines in front of it. Poor Nelly was nervous about gunfire, and Jacky would have a bad night. She wondered if George was still at his desk, or if he had gone down to the lines, and she resisted the impulse to get up and see. She was determined not to go clucking after him like a mother hen. He was a soldier. She was a soldier's wife. She lay still, tense and listening.

Footsteps approached her threshold along the upper hall outside the room—she knew that light, firm tread among a hundred. A candle showed in the widening crack of the door, illumining a schoolboy levity on the weather-beaten face above it. With a gasp of relief, she raised herself on one elbow and spoke his name, and he came on into the room as another round shook the window frames. He lighted the bedside candle from the one he carried. He knew that she hated gunfire in the dark, though she had never told him so. It was nothing, he said—not tonight—wouldn't last long. No, he was not going out. Knox was there. Just a bit of practice. Nothing to worry about. He patted her pillow, pulled up the coverlet, and went away with his candle—back to his desk where there lay an unfinished letter to Reed about the camp furniture and marquee which Reed had undertaken to purchase for him in Philadelphia and which did not arrive.

She had lost count now. It was like him, to come and reassure her, and she was comforted. But she suspected that he was up to something, all the same.

The Cambridge guns did stop pretty soon, but the British continued their fire, now and then, till dawn, and it was Sunday. They hit nothing of consequence, George remarked at breakfast. And during the day nothing unusual occurred that she could see. Sunday night, however, was like Saturday, the guns on the American side going off just often enough to keep the British—and everyone else—awake. On Monday, Martha noticed extra activity around the hospital opposite Headquarters. Hand-barrows and litters were collecting for the removal of wounded from the lines, and the men assigned to carry them stood about in little knots surveying the preparations. There were no wounded—yet. Except for a good deal of running to and fro, the day again passed much as usual. The real activity, she gathered from what she overheard, was down at the Roxbury end, next to Dorchester. A steady stream of carts and wagons moved in that direction, loaded with tools and hurdles and barrels. She stood at the window more than once, a hand at her throat, which was afflicted with an aching tightness. No one had to tell her it would be tonight.

The guns began earlier, at twilight of the 4th, and fired faster, and the British kept pace with them, until it was reported that once there were as many as seven shells in the air at the same time. The moon rose through a haze, and even at Headquarters the sound of rolling wheels and marching feet was audible between the salvos during the night, as fresh infantry moved quietly toward their posts, relieving the men who had been at work with spades and pick axes since dusk. From end to end of the rough semicircle of the American lines men stood to arms, awaiting daylight and the inevitable British sortie out of Boston.

When the dawn fog over the city shifted, there was no apparent damage in the streets, and no unusual activity. Then the astonished British were seen suddenly to discover the change in the landscape of Dorchester Heights, and a furious cannonade began against the new American works, which set the aides all laughing because the British guns could not be sufficiently elevated to reach the hilltop batteries. Then British troops began to embark like scarlet ants in small boats for the transports in the bay. But they had missed the tide. All Headquarters was agrin.

Washington had been out most of that night in the lines, returning for a brief breakfast, and again to eat a belated dinner. By then the wind had changed, and a sudden storm was lashing in with driving rain. There could be no night attack by the British in flat-bottomed landing boats, and he was persuaded to sleep awhile. At candlelighting time he went out again, making sure that no powder was wasted in reckless firing at a weatherbound enemy. He came back in the small hours, shivering and soaked, drank a hot toddy, and went to bed till dawn.

Bloodshed had so far been at a minimum—two killed in the American lines, and half a dozen wounded—but the wives waited warily, not daring to count on such good fortune. The question now was what the British would do to retaliate. Conditions in Boston were known to be frightful.

Added to the smallpox in the town, there was scurvy, for want of fruit and vegetables. The shortage of firewood was acute, so that undefended property was ruthlessly appropriated in the search for something to burn.

General Gage had been recalled to London to report on the unsatisfactory state of affairs in Massachusetts, and General Howe was now in command. Perhaps he had not forgotten Bunker Hill. At any rate, he showed no impulsive desire to encounter entrenched American troops again. Clinton had sailed for that still unknown destination. Burgoyne, they said, had returned to England on furlough. But surely the British were not just going to sit there and allow themselves to be shelled into the harbor. They must either counterattack or evacuate.

On the 7th Washington sent off his modest account of that busy week to Reed: "The rumpus which everybody expected to see between the Ministerialists in Boston and our troops has detained the bearer until this time," he wrote. "On Monday night I took possession of the Heights of Dorchester with 2000 men under the command of General Thomas. . . ."

The next day a merchant sea captain who had slipped out of Boston under darkness appeared at Headquarters with an astonishing report that the British were going, and the Tories were embarking with them, in crowded transports or in ships hired by themselves, in a wholesale confusion amounting to panic. Their destination, like Clinton's, was anybody's guess—Halifax, New York, even the Carolinas had been suggested. Those citizens who planned to remain in Boston had cause for some uneasiness, lest the British undertake to destroy the town before they left it. "It is given out that they are bound to Halifax," Washington reported to Congress, "but I am of the opinion that New York is their place of destination. It is the object worthy of their attention; and it is the place that we must use every endeavor to keep from them. For should they get that town and the command of the North River, they can stop the intercourse between the Northern and Southern colonies upon which depends the safety of America. . . ."

Watching through his glass, he could see everything from cannon to tables and chairs being carried aboard the British ships still lying alongside the wharves. Looting and destruction were visible in the streets. Refugees began to stream out toward the Cambridge camp, as the British picketing relaxed, and they brought exaggerated stories of the bombardment. Their presence represented a new hazard of infection.

Meanwhile Washington extended his fortifications on the Heights overlooking the harbor, but did not fire into the overcrowded ships. If the British were actually leaving the town undefended he would occupy it at once, post a garrison to clean it up, and move his main force to New York as fast as possible to defend the mouth of the Hudson. It would be a long march through spring mud, and the ships could travel faster. By the 15th of March the first rifle companies got under way, though the Royal standard was still flying in Boston, and the British military music could still be heard there as the guard changed. The wind was wrong for sailing until the 17th, when suddenly the wharves were full of marching redcoats, who loaded themselves into small boats and pulled away to the anchored transports in the bay.

On Dorchester Heights and at Lechmere Point at the other end of the lines, exuberant Continentals watched that superb target for hours without firing a round, on a tacit agreement that if the embarkation was unmolested the town would be left standing. Only when the canvas was spread and the ships were in motion could they really believe that it was evacuation and not attack, and a scattered cheering ran along the lines.

On the 18th Washington rode into Boston to take formal possession, and found the town had not suffered as much as he had feared. He went first to the elegant house owned by the President of Congress, expecting that it would have been stripped of its valuables. To his surprise, although it had served as General Clinton's headquarters, even the pictures on the walls remained undamaged, and he hastened to reassure Mr. Hancock in a letter written the same day, after his return to Cambridge.

As Howe's intentions were unknown, though he was believed to have made for Halifax, and as Clinton seemed to have disappeared southward along the coast, General Charles Lee had been dispatched from his post at New York to Charleston, to organize defenses in the Carolinas, and General Stirling took command at New York. Sullivan would march at once to join Stirling, Greene would follow, and Washington promised to be not far behind. General Ward would be left in charge at Boston. Faithful Colonel Harrison, seated at his writing-table morning, noon, and night, grateful for volunteer assistance but cheerful without it, seemed to Martha the only immovable rock in a sea of change.

It was a time of partings, at Headquarters. Kitty Greene and the baby were seen off home to Coventry in Rhode Island. General Knox's plump and talkative Lucy, having joined her husband soon after his return from Ticonderoga, was now awaiting his marching orders, which would send her under protest back to friends at Fairfield. Mrs. Gates, whose mannish riding-dress had caused some unfavorable comment in New England, had started for New York, and the Philadelphia wives would soon be on the way to Pennsylvania. Dr. Morgan prepared to move his hospital back to New York, and Mifflin as Quartermaster-General was already there.

The universal uprooting and bustle brought some anxiety to Martha for Nelly, whose first child would be born late in the summer. As Washington's route would lead roundabout through Providence and Norwich, it was decided that the young Custises and Martha should take a more leisurely course in the chariot by way of Hartford, arriving in New York after the establishment of Headquarters there, for which a suitable house was being sought.

One of the lasting friendships which Martha formed at Cambridge that winter was with Mercy Warren, wife of the Massachusetts merchant who was President of the Provincial Congress now sitting at Watertown. The Warrens lived at Plymouth with their five sons, the youngest ten years old, and were close friends of the John Adamses at Braintree, which lay on the south side of Boston between Plymouth and Cambridge. During January Mrs. Warren had written to Headquarters offering the Commander in Chief's wife a refuge in her household at Plymouth in the event of any emergency nearer Boston; a thoughtful suggestion which, though never taken advantage of, was much appreciated by the Washingtons.

Whenever Mercy visited her husband at Watertown she spent a night with Abigail Adams on the way, and they kept up a brisk correspondence between meetings. Both were highly intelligent, educated women, and Mercy wrote poetry and metered drama, which sometimes affected her daily style. As Abigail's husband was at the Philadelphia Congress, she had no occasion to go into Cambridge or Watertown, and was always anxious to hear her friend's impressions.

In April, after the British had left Boston, Mercy wrote to her from Watertown: "I arrived at my lodgings before dinner the day I left you—found an obliging family, and in the main an agreeable set of lodgers. The next morning I took a ride to Cambridge and waited on Mrs. Washington at 11 o'clock, where I was received with that politeness and respect shown in a first interview among the well-bred, and with the ease and cordiality of friendship of a much earlier date. If you wish to hear more of this lady's character, I will tell you I think the complacency of her manners speaks at once the benevolence of her heart, and her affability, candor, and gentleness qualify her to soften the hours of private

life, or to sweeten the cares of the hero, and smooth the rugged paths
of war. I did not dine with her, though much urged. She desired me to
name an early hour in the morning, when she would send her chariot
and accompany me to see the deserted lines of the enemy, and the ruins
of Charlestown. A melancholy sight, the last, which evinces the barbarity
of the foe, and leaves a deep impression of the suffering of that unhappy
town.

"Mr. Custis is the only son of the lady above described—a sensible,
modest, agreeable young man. His lady, a daughter of Colonel Calvert
of Maryland, appears to be of an engaging disposition, but of so ex-
tremely delicate a constitution that it deprives her as well as her friends,
of part of the pleasure which I am sure would result from her conversation, did she enjoy a more perfect state of health. She is pretty, genteel,
easy, and agreeable, but a kind of languor about her prevents her being
sociable as some ladies. Yet it is evident it is not owing to a want of that
vivacity which renders youth agreeable, but to a want of health which a
little clouds her spirits. . . ."

Boston was in such a condition of dilapidation and smallpox infection
that Washington had ordered all the occupying forces to be men who
had already experienced the disease and become immune. When Martha
arrived at New York early in May, after having been delayed on the
road by an illness of Jacky's, the situation there was equally bad, because
of the infection among the troops returning from Canada, and the question of her inoculation became imperative. She declared herself willing,
but as Dr. Morgan had not yet arrived in the city there was again a delay.

Headquarters in New York were set up in a pleasant house called
Mortier's which had belonged to the Paymaster-General of the British
army. It stood in a rural setting known as Lispenard's Meadow with a
garden overlooking the Hudson to the Jersey shore, and was all of two
miles from the fort at the Battery, so that Washington had for convenience
an office at the bottom of Broadway. Due doubtless to this division of
the household, and to the quickening tempo everywhere, the old easy
atmosphere which had prevailed at Cambridge was never recaptured. The
Custises would soon depart for Maryland, in order that Nelly's baby
might arrive safely at Mount Airy, but Martha insisted on remaining in
New York as long as George would allow her to risk some sudden action
by the enemy.

One of his sister Betty's sons, named for his uncle, arrived in a zealous
lather to join both the secretarial staff and the newly formed Lifeguard.

But still Joseph Reed did not return, being preoccupied in establishing his little family outside Philadelphia at Burlington for the summer. Esther was pregnant again, and did not want him to leave her at all. Washington was aware that with growing responsibilities at home, Reed actually could not afford to give up his lawyer's fees for the $66 a month which was all the secretaries received, and undertook to let daylight into the Congressional mind on the subject of aides-de-camp: "It requires men of abilities to execute the duties with propriety and dispatch, where there is such a multiplicity of business as must attend the Commander in Chief of such an army as ours; and persuaded I am, that nothing but the zeal of those gentlemen who live with me and act in this capacity, for the great American cause and personal attachment to me, has induced them to undergo the trouble and confinement they have experienced since they became members of my Family. . . ."

Late in May he was writing to his brother John Augustine from New York: "We have already gone great lengths in fortifying this city and the Hudson River; a fortnight more will put us in a very respectable posture of defense . . . Mrs. Washington is still here, and talks of taking the smallpox [inoculation] but I doubt her resolution. Mr. and Mrs. Custis will set out in a few days for Maryland. . . ."

Bad news was pouring in from everywhere, during that first month in New York, though nothing could quite rob them of the satisfaction they had left behind in Boston. There were further disasters in Canada, and Washington was forced to divide his tiny army and to part with Sullivan, who was sent to Arnold's aid.

Then Charles Lee wrote from Williamsburg, where he had lodged himself in the Governor's Palace, to the displeased surprise of the citizens, that an express from North Carolina had brought word of a large fleet of British transports sighted off Cape Fear, confirming the suspicion that the next attack might be on Charleston—whither Lee intended to continue on his way at once to train the local militia and set up defenses. His letter ended with characteristic Lee impertinence: "My love to Mrs. Washington, Gates, and her bad half, and to Moylan; but Palfrey is a scoundrel for not writing. Adieu, my dear General. Yours most entirely, CHARLES LEE." Martha made a little face above her knitting when it was read aloud to her. He was too glib, he thought himself too charming—and he was not clean.

An escaped prisoner of war brought proof to Headquarters that the British government had entered into treaties with three German princelings to hire some 17,000 German troops to supplement the British forces in America. This had been suspected as far back as March, when Stirling, after his transfer to New York, reported a rumor that the Home Government saw fit to employ foreign mercenaries in what was after all a family quarrel among people of the same blood and language. With the arrival in America of troops from Hesse-Kassel and Hanau would go the last obstinate hope of any reconciliation with the present Ministry in London; and a struggle for an independent government was sure to mean a long and bitter war on the colonists' own ground, with unthinkable consequences in the event of defeat.

Washington felt too long out of touch with the powers at Philadelphia, and wished for an opportunity to explain to Congress more fully and more privately than was possible in letters, the situation in which he found himself, menaced from the North, East, and South; by the Canadian force under Carleton; by Clinton and Howe somewhere up and down the coast at sea; and by the German reinforcements which were said to have sailed from England with General Howe's brother the Admiral during April. Until he knew the destination of at least one out of three British fleets he felt compelled to remain at his New York post, and sent Gates, as his Adjutant-General, to report to Congress in his place.

Gates had been only a few hours on the road when an invitation arrived for Washington from President Hancock to visit Philadelphia for consultation and a brief rest, which he was obliged to accept. It also seemed a good time for Martha to accompany him and receive the inoculation. To everyone's admiration she underwent the ordeal with spirit and fortitude. Washington at the same time was experiencing an ordeal of his own, appearing before the Congress to answer questions and explain his position and future prospects. Gates was now promoted by Congress to take command of the desperate situation in Canada, which made it possible to offer the Adjutant-Generalship, with its pay of $125 a month, to Reed. Mifflin was made a brigadier with a field command at New York, and the aide Stephen Moylan, a Philadelphia Irishman of lively ability, moved up to Quartermaster-General.

Other Virginians in Philadelphia that May of 1776 gathered round Washington's dinner table to exchange their news from home for the inspiriting details of the British flight from Boston, and speculation as to Howe's next move. And it was news indeed, for Thomas Nelson, Jr., had just ridden up from Williamsburg with the momentous Resolution which had been passed by the Fifth Virginia Convention, and which Mason,

Pendleton, and Patrick Henry had had a part in forming, though Jefferson had again been detained by illness and only reached Philadelphia simultaneously with the incendiary paper carried by Nelson. The Virginia men already at Philadelphia read it with varying emotions, for events were moving a little fast for some of them: *"Resolved unanimously that the delegates appointed to represent this colony in General Congress be instructed to propose to that respectable body to declare the United Colonies free and independent States. . . ."*

Lying in bed with the inoculation fever in their Philadelphia lodgings, Martha heard the same solemn drone of voices in the next room which had gone on at Mount Vernon before ever the First Congress had met, and knew the same uneasy apprehension of impending change which she had learned several years before. Independence. The word was no longer an indiscretion of Patrick Henry's. Now they were all talking about it. There was no holding back since Boston; they were all committed to it now. To back down now would only mean humiliation and reprisals. They would have the redcoats everywhere in no time, and there would be treason trials and hangings. It was too late to do anything but go on. Even a woman could see that.

But still they talked around Washington's dinner table, over the nuts and wine; Dicky Lee of Chantilly, who had shared George's first session at Williamsburg eighteen years before and was still a Burgess and leader of the Virginia delegation—tall, spare, cerebral, with a profile which belonged on a Roman coin, and the brilliant dark eyes which all the Lees inherited, his crippled hand in its neat black silk bandage; Francis Lightfoot Lee, more genial, more charming, more popular in a quiet way than his elder brother; George Wythe of Williamsburg, courtly and kindly, the legal mind at its best and sharpest; Thomas Jefferson, lean and sandy-haired, with his light, boyish voice which failed him in debate; Falstaffian Benjamin Harrison, with his broad jokes and fat laughter, who could never get along with New Englanders; Thomas Nelson, massive, ardent, and confident, owner of a fine brick house at Yorktown and famous for his horses, ready to stake it all on the cause of freedom from British rule; and at the head of the table, the Commander in Chief, cracking nuts in his powerful fingers, watching, listening, egging them on —with his head in the noose.

The contents of the paper which Thomas Nelson had brought to Philadelphia soon leaked out in the Congress, and while the Virginians consulted among themselves tension began to rise among the other delegates. On the 27th, in response to pressure, Richard Henry Lee read out to Congress the Resolution as he had received it and after a few stormy minutes it was tabled for ten days to allow other immediate business to be cleared away. But they all knew now, and the factions began to form, and the private committees to meet, as the opposition gathered its forces.

"I am very glad to find that the Virginia Convention have passed so noble a vote, and with such unanimity," Washington wrote to John Augustine, sitting by Martha's bedside on a night when Philadelphia's muggy heat made sleep difficult. "Things have come to that pass now as to convince us that we have nothing more to expect from the justice of Great Britain. . . . Mrs. Washington is now under inoculation in this city; and will, I expect, have the smallpox favorably, as this is the 13th day and she has very few pustules; she would have wrote to my sister, but thought it prudent not to do so, notwithstanding there could be but little danger in conveying the infection in this manner. She joins me in love to you, her, and all the little ones. . . ."

Martha was at no time really very ill, and once the pustules appeared the worst was supposed to be over. They lived in daily expectation of a dusty express rider from New York with a report from General Putnam, who had been left in command there, that British sail had been sighted. None came, and the matters of promotion and enlistment and supply which required Washington's presence proceeded in the Congress without haste or interruption, while the Virginia Resolution lay waiting, like an unexploded shell, on the table.

He was able also to settle personally to his satisfaction the final details of his camp equipment, at a modest cost of £51.6, for a large dining marquee, a living tent with an arched chamber, a baggage tent, and various stools, furniture, and utensils. On the 3d of June he received the formal thanks of the Congress and its permission to return to New York whenever he chose. It was a little soon for Martha to travel, and he was in a hurry. She had many friends in Philadelphia, and they all promised to see that she did not lack for company. She and George agreed that if the British remained invisible after he arrived in New York, she should follow him at a comfortable pace in the chariot, and he set out on horseback the next day.

Each time it was harder to see him go, as his hazard increased. She knew that if when he got to New York he found the British coming in from the sea, she would not be allowed to go to him, in case they shelled the town and set it on fire, as Dunmore had done at Norfolk. If she were already there when they appeared, she hoped to find lodgings out of range but much nearer than Philadelphia.

Meanwhile everyone was most kind, and brought her all the news as fast as it happened—such as on June 7th, when Dicky Lee stood up in Congress, tall and elegant in his light summer suit, and read out his Resolution, drawn from the one prepared by the Virginia Convention three weeks earlier: *"Resolved, that these United Colonies are, and of Right ought to be Free and Independent States; that they are Absolved from all Allegiance to the British Crown, and that all political connection between them and the State of Great Britain, is and ought to be totally dissolved."* John Adams of Massachusetts leaped to his feet and seconded. A raging debate ensued. A committee was named to prepare a Declaration of Independence, while the vote on the Resolution was postponed until July 1st, another three weeks distant. Martha tried to write it all down for George the way she heard it, and Mr. Hancock was most obliging about forwarding their letters by Congressional riders.

She got back to New York before the British came, after all, on the 16th of June. There was nothing but gloomy news from Canada, where the British general Carleton had received reinforcements from England, and Sullivan was falling back toward the Lakes in what amounted to evacuation. Gates, on his way to Sullivan, could accomplish little now without substantial reinforcements of his own. The powder situation at New York had improved, and Knox's artillery had been augmented by a company of ninety-three gunners under the command of a young captain not yet twenty years old named Alexander Hamilton, who was until recently a student at King's College.

On the 29th the long expected signal flags went up in the Bay. The British ships were sighted.

Headquarters was abustle as never at Cambridge. More new aides were appointed to the Staff—in particular, Samuel Webb of Connecticut, nephew to Silas Deane who was at present one of the American agents at Paris; and Tench Tilghman of Maryland, who came in as a volunteer aide from the Flying Camp, and instantly took hold of anything that wanted doing, no matter how tedious or difficult, and usually succeeded at it. Small boats were being secured in the rivers; arms were being inspected; sentries were cautioned; strangers were warned off the works; provisions for detached posts were ordered for several days ahead. And the wives were told to pack.

Kitty Greene had just arrived in New York, and was determined to remain, since she had left the baby safe at home in Rhode Island. Lucy Knox had established herself rather grandly at her husband's headquarters in lower Broadway, and was also reluctant to be banished. But New

York was vulnerable from the sea and down the Hudson. The wives must go, and New Jersey was not thought safe enough. The wives must go home.

For Martha, Philadelphia lay along her way, and because of Dunmore she was to remain there until the news from Virginia was more satisfactory. Hancock would know how long Philadelphia was tenable. If the worst happened, and Howe descended on Philadelphia, Congress would move out in time and she must go with it. The wife of the Commander in Chief would have been a prize of some consequence in British hands.

It was an idea that she could not easily entertain, that her personal whereabouts and freedom were a part of the war. At first she maintained stoutly that it was nonsense, and that she would go home to Mount Vernon like any other wife, and wait till she could return to Headquarters with the rest. So then, just like anybody else, she got her marching orders. Philadelphia. With an escort. Tomorrow.

She was cross about it, but when the time came she clung to him, and wept. No tears, he told her kindly. She was a soldier now. No one must see the General's wife in tears, or they would think the war was lost for sure. She straightened at that, and her sobs stopped with a jerk. How could the war be lost, when they had got Boston back again? But now it was a matter of hanging on to New York, he reminded her. That would take him all his time. And to give his whole mind to it, he must know that she was safely stowed away in Hancock's pocket, with her friends all around her.

She saw the point then, and put away her handkerchief and her heroism. The next day, wearing powder in her hair, and a fresh lace cap and a sober traveling gown, she set out in the chariot, accompanied by her faithful colored maid, with the colored coachman and postillion in their scarlet and white liveries, followed by a clattering mounted escort which could ill be spared from the lines of defense around New York. The road to Philadelphia was becoming familiar to her now, as were the coach and liveries to the countryside. People ran to see her pass—the General's wife —Lady Washington's coach—she was on her way to Philadelphia—then the British were really coming to New York—he had sent her away before the fighting started—look, the General's wife. . . .

Smiling and serene, she bowed to them through the open window of the coach, and waved her hand to the children. Her chin was high, and there were no signs of her growing anxiety for the General. She was a veteran now herself. Now she had heard the guns.

CHAPTER SIX

The General's Lady

1776–1780

PHILADELPHIA WAS TENSE and watchful when Martha arrived there, and it was not just because of the British at New York. Suspense resided also in the State House, where Jefferson's Declaration of Independence had been read to the assembled Congress and was now under debate. Big Benjamin Harrison came to call as soon as he learned of her presence at the lodgings in Chestnut Street, and from him she heard, with Harrisonian embellishments and some confidential asides, punctuated by his subterranean laughter, how it had fallen to him, as chairman of the Committee of the Whole, to read aloud that first draft of Tom Jefferson's composition. Dicky Lee, as she probably knew, had been called home to Virginia in mid-June by the illness of his wife, and President Hancock had stepped down to sit among the Massachusetts delegates while a Virginian pronounced the momentous words his fellow-countryman, in committee with Dr. Franklin, John Adams, Roger Sherman, and Philip Livingston, had set down.

There was no doubt, Harrison added, that it would stand pretty much as it had left Jefferson's pen—independence was already a fact by the July 2d vote on Lee's Resolution—but this document which was designed to expound to the whole world the rights and wrongs of the matter had set Congress to splitting hairs, page by page, sentence by sentence, while Jefferson sat there squirming, without once lifting his voice in the argument. The weather was very hot, and horseflies from the stable next door to the State House were tormenting the silk-stockinged legs of the delegates. What did it say, in the Declaration? Well, it said that a man had a right to his own life, liberty, and pursuit of happiness, and that no thundering foreigner was going to coerce him from any thundering throne with a lot of thundering hirelings from across that thundering ocean.

Early on the afternoon of the 4th, the bell in the State House steeple suddenly began to peal, and the crowd of citizens waiting in the streets roundabout broke into cheers. Martha had gone to call on Mrs. Hancock, who was expecting her first child in the autumn, and their quiet talk of family affairs broke off while eyes met eyes. The bell would signal the signing, as they were both aware. John Hancock's name was therefore written; the thing was done; and now the whole resounding text would be entered in the Congressional Journal and engrossed on parchment, and dozens of printed copies would be struck off for distribution to each of the colonies and the army.

Those United Colonies were by that signature proclaimed to be the United States of America, and between the two women the specter of the gallows was very plain—the wife of the man whose pen endorsed the treason, who was already proscribed in London for his record in the Massachusetts Provincial Assembly; and the wife of the man who wore sword and spurs even at his writing-desk, and opposed the King's troops in the field. The shouting, excited citizens in the State House yard, already embarking on bonfires and potations, did not stop to think what failure now would mean. But Martha Washington, simple and loving and wise, and Dolly Hancock, beautiful, spirited, and clever, sat looking at each other in the gracious parlor of the President's house in Arch Street, without the need for words to share their mutual apprehensions. The thing was not done at all, it was only begun.

The official public reading and grand demonstration in Philadelphia took place on the 8th of July—followed by a salute of cannon, burning of the King's arms torn down from the courtroom, more bonfires, illuminations, and general carnival which was viewed with sour disapproval by the Quakers and the Tories. The delegates gave dinner parties and there were toasts and confident laughter and wholesale optimism, and the General's wife was made much of, and she smiled serenely through it all, until late that evening she regained the sanctuary of her lodgings, while a sharp summer storm drove the last noisy revelers indoors and quenched the bonfires. The roll and crash of the thunder sounded like the guns at Cambridge, but no one came with a candle to reassure her.

Tomorrow the printed copies of the Declaration would reach New York, and she wished that she could be there when George first read it. It seemed to her not very dissimilar from the other resolutions and representations which Dicky Lee and George Mason had been writing for months, but Mr. Jefferson had a special knack. Phrases rang out. It was the best of all the colonial addresses and protests, even she could see that. In her heart, she followed the express rider pounding through the storm toward New York with Hancock's urgent packet in his saddlebag. She knew the road—she could almost have found her way along it alone —back to the army camp and the morning and evening drums, and the clank of sword belts and spurs, and the young voices of the aides calling for their horses—the bustle and tension and stretch of Headquarters— and before long again, the guns.

Mount Vernon seemed very remote, as she sat listening to the storm, too weary and disturbed to make ready for bed. Even here at Philadelphia she felt cut off and out of things, and Mount Vernon was hundreds of miles further away from New York. Nelly's baby would be born soon, and they expected her to return to Virginia in time. She wondered a little that she was not impatient to be on her way. It was not Dunmore in the Chesapeake, nor the British ships off the mouth of the Hudson that made her unwilling to continue her journey southward. It was the tall, tired general at New York who held her where she was. Once she would not have dreamed of missing the arrival of her first grandchild. Now there were things that mattered more. Her center of gravity had shifted. The needle of her emotional compass pointed north, where George was.

She sat alone in her room while the storm died away and the candles burned down, contemplating her own private, personal domestic revolution. For years she had allowed the children to rule and absorb her life. George was always there when she wanted him, steady and kind and patient. The children were demanding and helpless—Patsy was so often ill, and after Patsy died there was still Jacky, entering the difficult years, creating uneasiness, making mistakes, not using good judgment. Now Jacky too was gone, into his own life, heedless, not heartless, but with no further need of her. Jacky was fledged. And all those years at Mount Vernon, the peaceful years, when George must often have felt that she put her children first—they were gone.

But he did not hold it against her, that was the miracle. He still needed her, of that she had had proof in a hundred ways at Cambridge and New York. Even in the middle of a war, he turned to her with relief and confidence, and took comfort and pride in her company—as though she had never failed him. She would wait awhile in Philadelphia; the baby would not care. The British under Howe might be beaten off in one decisive engagement, or they might go on to the Carolinas. Wait and see. Perhaps she would be allowed to go back to Headquarters in a matter of days or weeks.

It was General Clinton who got beaten off, down at Charleston at the end of June, and that was a feather in General Lee's hat, for he had arrived in time to conduct the defense. Then Clinton's ships came limping north to add his battered force to General Howe's from Halifax, who were encamped on Staten Island. Then Howe's brother the Admiral arrived with some Hessians. And still there was no battle. Late in August she was writing from Philadelphia to Nancy at Eltham: "I am still in this town and no prospect at present of leaving it. The General is at New York; he is well, and wrote to me yesterday that Lord Dunmore with part of his fleet was come to General Howe at Staten Island; that another division of Hessians is expected before the regulars will begin their attack on us. Some here begin to think there will be no battle after all. . . . I do, my dear sister, most religiously wish there was an end to the war, that we might have the pleasure of meeting again. My duty to very dear Mamma, and tell her I am very well. I don't hear from you so often as I used to do at Cambridge. . . . I hope Mr. Bassett has got the better of his cough long ago. Please to present my love to him, my brothers and sisters, my dear Fanny, and the boy, and accept the same yourself. . . ."

Only a week later President Hancock forwarded to her lodgings the grim news that Washington's army had met the combined forces of Howe, Clinton, and the new British general Cornwallis on Long Island, and had been defeated and forced to withdraw across the East River, abandoning the Brooklyn fortifications. The first hurried report had come from Colonel Harrison, whose especial job it was to conduct the correspondence between Headquarters and Congress, and had been written at New York while the Commander in Chief was still on the field. Washington's letter when it arrived did nothing to contradict the impression of almost total failure in the first engagement with the British. General Sullivan had been outflanked and captured, and Stirling also was a prisoner of war, while General Greene had been kept out of the action with a prostrating fever which confined him to his quarters in New York.

The American troops were exhausted and dispirited, and had begun to desert in shoals. "Since Monday we have scarce any of us been out of the lines, till our passage across the East River was effected yesterday morning," Washington had written, "and for the forty-eight hours preceding that I had hardly been off my horse and had never closed my eyes, so that I was quite unfit to write or dictate till this morning."

The hasty note which he had enclosed for Martha told her very little more. Now that the campaign had opened, there would be no hope of rejoining him before winter, when the fighting would stop for a while again. Everyone advised her to go home. Dunmore was now accounted for and Lund was writing to her from Mount Vernon of perplexities she might be able to help him unravel if she were there. Still she lingered, unwilling to lose touch with President Hancock, who always got the news first. There was talk of evacuating New York entirely. Would they have to retreat on Philadelphia, then, with the enemy in pursuit?

She had begun to pack when word of the Kip's Bay fight came to Hancock's hand. The British had landed on New York Island, and to his rage and humiliation Washington's men had broken and fled in a wild panic. His own account was restrained as usual, but hair-raising rumors soon filtered into Philadelphia. The General himself had nearly been taken by the British—the General had ridden furiously among his men with the flat of his sword, and his language had been a lesson in invective—if the General's aide had not caught his bridle he would have charged alone straight into the whole British army. . . .

Martha listened with a white face. She knew his rare, tremendous rages, his fierce zeal for the honor and reputation of his troops. He would have been beside himself at cowardice. Which aide had saved him? No one knew. What now? Where would he make the next stand? There was a river at his back.

Hancock tried to reassure her. Headquarters were established in the Roger Morris house on Harlem Heights, a defensible position. Washington could hold out there indefinitely and reorganize. The troops were already rallying. Kip's Bay was an accident which might never happen again—there was no accounting for panic.

Martha smiled politely and made her own reservations. Mr. Hancock was not a soldier, beyond a little drilling with the Boston militia before the Concord Bridge affair. He had no idea of what it required to command in the field. He sat here, in Philadelphia, with his wife—they dined in comfort, slept in their own house every night, they had never heard a real cannonade. Quite suddenly she wanted to go home. She was of no earthly use here, while at Mount Vernon she and Lund could work together to carry out George's wishes for the place he would one day return to.

Congress gave her an escort as far as Baltimore, and there the Calverts sent to meet her. She paused at Mount Airy to rest the horses and admire Nelly's baby, a healthy girl who was to be called Eliza Parke Custis. Jacky accompanied her the rest of the way to Mount Vernon, where she inspected and praised Lund's accomplishment during her absence. At his request she read through the letters he had received from George since she left New York, and together they strove to comprehend and act upon the sometimes complicated instructions entailed.

With the British encamped in plain sight of Headquarters, and the Hessians arriving by the boatload, George had taken time in mid-August to describe his position in detail to Lund, and then relaxed into the less ephemeral subject of hedges and ornamental trees to be planted at Mount Vernon, and the more immediate question of a bay horse which Jacky Custis aspired to.

He seemed to carry a large-scale map of his property in his head, and knew to the fraction of a foot where every tree and small outbuilding stood. He wanted a grove of trees started at each end of the house, "extending as low as a line from the stables to the dry well," but leaving a lane for the carriages to pass to and from the stables to the wharf, "all the clever kind of trees, especially flowering ones," to be interspersed with evergreens. "It will not do to plant the locust trees at the north end of the house till the framing is up, covered in, and the chimney built," he reminded them, "otherwise it will be labor lost, as they will get broke down, defaced and spoilt . . . Before I conclude, I must beg of you to hasten Lanphire [the carpenter] about the addition to the north end of the house, otherwise you will have it open, I fear, in the cold and wet weather, and the brick work to do at improper season, neither of which I shall be at all desirous of . . ." This was the two-story addition designed as a dining hall and ballroom, at the opposite end from the new library and master bedroom on the south. And as for the horse, Jacky might buy it and have the use of it, if he and Lund could come to terms, on condition that Washington could buy it back at the end of the war if he so desired.

Within a few days of Martha's return she and Lund had brought each other up to date on mutual friends. She knew that Patrick Henry had left the Philadelphia Congress, where since the first session he had cut no particular figure. After a brief excursion into the military life, which everyone agreed was not a success, he had resumed his seat in the Virginia Convention at Williamsburg, and helped to draft the famous Resolutions of last May. His wife had died, leaving six children. In July, while Jefferson was sweating out his Declaration in Philadelphia, Henry had got elected the first Governor of Virginia; whereupon, said Lund, he had gone to the best tailor and was now dressed in handsome black, with a scarlet lining to his cloak; had taken to wearing a powdered wig; had acquired a coach and horses, and was living in style in the Governor's Palace in Williamsburg. Martha at this point accused Lund of exaggerating, and when he swore he was not, she made no further comment. After all, the Governor ought to make a good appearance. Mr. Henry was quite bald, and a wig was the only way he could wear powder. He would have to marry again, too, with all those poor children, and he was now in a position to make someone a good offer. She wondered if he still talked with that maddening upcountry twang. A second wife who was not afraid of him would be a good thing.

In answer to her queries about Gunston, Lund said that George Mason was going on much as usual, exercising his quiet influence at Williamsburg though refusing to venture as far as the Philadelphia Congress, where many people thought he was badly needed—nursing his gout, rearing his children, performing his neighborhood duties as justice, trustee, and vestryman, tending his prosperous acres. Hugh Mercer, who was some ten years older than George and had got a wound in the Braddock campaign, was smelling gunpowder again, Lund said. He had left his physician's practice at Fredericksburg and gone to drilling militia, till Congress made him a colonel in command of the Flying Camp in Jersey.

Martha settled into the familiar routine of Mount Vernon, and found some refuge from anxiety in the daily rounds of kitchen and weaving-house and gardens. Everyone beamed to see her home again, everyone within a day's ride came to call or to spend the night, everyone wanted to hear all about her experiences at Boston and Philadelphia, and begged for her opinion on the present crisis at New York.

John Augustine had received a letter from George, written at the Harlem Headquarters, which so alarmed him that he came posting to Mount Vernon to hear her own account, and arrived just in time for the latest letter to Lund. Things looked very bad indeed, owing chiefly to the evil consequences of the short enlistment system, against which Washington had repeatedly warned the Congress from the beginning. "In short, such is my situation that if I were to wish the bitterest curse to an enemy this side of the grave, I should put him in my stead with my feelings," he had written Lund, in one of his overwhelming midnight necessities for a confidant. "But I will be done with the subject, with the precautions to you that it is not a fit one to be publicly known or discussed. . . . With respect to the chimney, I would not have you for the sake of a little work spoil the look of the fireplaces, though that in the parlor must, I should think, stand as it does; not so much on account of the wainscoting . . . as on account of the chimney-piece and the manner of its fronting into the room. . . . Remember me to all our neighbors and friends, particularly to Colonel Mason, to whom I would write if I had time to do it fully and satisfactorily. . . ."

By common endeavor at Mount Vernon gloom was held at bay throughout dinner. He was tired that night when he wrote, they told each other, and no doubt things looked worse to him than they really were. After all, they reminded each other, he had despaired at Cambridge too, and look how well that turned out.

There was a lull at Harlem during October, which raised their spirits again in Virginia, and then the bad news never stopped coming in as Washington's desperate, discouraged army went reeling back across the Hudson and down through New Jersey—White Plains, Fort Washington, Fort Lee, Hackensack, Newark, Brunswick, Princeton, Trenton, and finally across the Delaware into Pennsylvania—would they never stand again? Baggage, equipment, even entrenching tools and camp kettles were left behind in a retreat which only the determined man on the big bay horse somehow prevented from becoming headlong flight. It was not a panic, like Kip's Bay, and they were not having to fight as they went. Under Washington's firm hand, it was a deliberate withdrawal, a calculated maneuver to avoid a general engagement with superior numbers and discipline.

His letters home reiterated the hopelessness of the militia system, and the daily mortification of seeing his army melt away without new enlistments to fill up the thinning ranks. And always they ended on a touching note of affection and homesickness: "I am glad to find by your last letter that your family are tolerably well recovered from the indispositions they labored under," he wrote to John Augustine in November. "God grant you all health and happiness; nothing in this world would contribute so much to mine as to be once more fixed among you in the peaceable enjoyment of my own vine and fig-tree. . . ."

The final humiliation in his position, they felt at Mount Vernon, had been the return of Charles Lee, haloed by his recent spectacular success at Charleston, to assist the Commander in Chief to stave off the ultimate disaster which threatened the whole American army. Lee passed through Philadelphia in a blaze of glory to receive a generous welcome at the Headquarters camp then still on the Hudson, where he was at once given the responsibility of guarding the rear. Since that assignment, all during the retreat through Jersey, Lee's operations and whereabouts had become increasingly obscure.

"I tremble for Philadelphia," Washington wrote to Lund from the lower bank of the Delaware on December 10th. "Nothing, in my opinion, but General Lee's speedy arrival, who has long been expected, though still at a distance (with about 3000 men) can save it." Philadelphia was trembling too, and on December 12th Congress adjourned hastily to Baltimore, bag and baggage, and set up shop there at considerable inconvenience to themselves. It was very alarming to the country to learn that Congress did not feel sufficiently secure to remain at its post. Maryland and Virginia began to wonder. Dunmore was no longer raiding the river banks. But if Howe took Philadelphia the whole British army would be not far north of Baltimore—Alexandria—Mount Vernon.

And so it was Christmas again, the worst Christmas ever, worse than the one after Patsy died, so much worse than last year at Cambridge, when the guns fell silent all day, and the gracious yellow and white house overlooking the Charles River was full of callers and the cheerful voices of the aides, and the smiling, affectionate officers' wives. Martha's mind went back to the green-decked rooms, the extra candles, the fragrant Mount Vernon hams and pies on the long table, the toasts, the impromptu entertainment, the ease and security and goodwill of the Cambridge Headquarters. Where were they all now, she wondered—Harrison and Baylor and Palfrey, and the new boys who had joined the Family at New York. How about enormous Knox with his beloved guns, and Quaker Greene, whose Kitty at home in Rhode Island would be thinking of Cambridge too? Joseph Reed was at Headquarters again, as Adjutant-General, and handsome Mifflin, and tempestuous Irish Sullivan who had been exchanged, along with Stirling, after their capture at Long Island, and returned to duty. There would be no exchange for the Commander in Chief if ever he were taken by the enemy. . . .

And there was her nightmare again, dampening her palms, tightening her throat. They would transport him to England for trial, the charge would be treason, it would mean the Tower. Would they let her go with him?

She would sit staring at the fire, her knitting lying idle in her lap, trying to prepare herself for what might come. If they would not allow a prisoner's wife to accompany him, she must slip aboard a vessel at Yorktown or Alexandria—she had friends who would help her to elude the British and get passage on something bound for London. She must go alone, for Jack could not leave Nelly and the baby. There was no son of George's to go with her. And now, in this extremity, she could bear to leave Daniel's son behind, and cleave only unto George, who must never again go short because of a child of hers. When she got to England she must find the Fairfaxes—they would tell her what to do, whom to see, they would know the people who might save George from hanging. . . .

These were the thoughts that drove her from the fire and up to the new bedroom which he had never shared, where she could close the door behind her and in solitude strive again for composure equal to his, which was an example to them all—drying her eyes, pinching her cheeks to their accustomed pinkness lest Lund should notice and think she was moping or afraid. Afraid? This was terror, a thing she had never known before; not for Jacky, ill at school, not for poor Patsy in her seizures; not when Dunmore might come up the River, not when the guns boomed at Cambridge; terror for a soldier's life, for a man's last dignity in death—and for her love.

She would sit down at her desk to write to him, aware that the letter might never find him, but out of her loneliness and anxiety impelled to try to reach him somehow, even on paper—tearing up the page because it sounded unhappy or complaining and would distress him; or too fond, which she could not trust to the public conveyance, for letters had been intercepted and published with ridicule before now—none of hers, but you could not be sure; or too impersonal, which was worse. She would reread his letters to her, already knowing them by heart, with their occasional flaring passion of anger or homesickness, and their colossal patience in adversity—reading, writing, blotting the tears before they splashed on the paper under her hand.

The campaign would be over soon. It was time for winter quarters again. They said Howe meant to winter in Philadelphia. If Philadelphia were taken would it mean the end of the war? Christmas, '77—where would they all be then? Would the war be won or lost, a year from now? And would they at least be together again?

The family and neighbors did what they could to cheer her at the holidays, though she refused to go to Mount Airy to join the Calvert Christmas, and remained at home to receive her callers and serve the usual collation. At the end of the month John Augustine Washington arrived for a visit, accompanied by his wife Hannah, his daughter Jane, and his eldest son Bushrod, who at fifteen was studying law at William and Mary College—a mild, delicate-seeming youth who was always reading.

After dinner that day John Augustine took from his pocket a letter he had received from George, in camp on the south bank of the Delaware. By his account of it during the meal it was apparently a near counterpart of those which Martha and Lund had shared a few days before. She asked if she might read it, and as he was aware that George had not attempted to conceal from her the disastrous course of events, John Augustine handed the folded sheets across the table to her. With a swift glance which asked their permission, she lost herself at once in the clear, familiar handwriting. "I have no doubt but that General Howe will still make an attempt upon Philadelphia this winter," she read. ". . . . In a word, my dear sir, if every nerve is not strained to recruit the new army with all possible expedition, I think the game is pretty near up. . . ."

He had said that in Lund's letter too, though he had tried to put a little better face on it for her, and there was no secret about the army's extremity. But the letter continued. "Before this reaches you, you will have heard of the captivity of General Lee. This is an additional misfortune, and the more vexatious as it was by his own folly and imprudence . . . he was taken. . . . You can form no idea of the perplexity of my situation. No man, I believe, ever had a greater choice of difficulties and less means to extricate himself from them. However, under a full persuasion of the justice of our cause, I cannot entertain an idea that it will finally sink, though it may remain for some time under a cloud. . . ."

Martha was sorry about General Lee only as far as his absence inconvenienced George. He should have caught up to the main army days ago, from what George had written. It almost looked as though . . . But no man would deliberately allow himself to be taken by the British. The conditions in the prison ships were said to be frightful, and even for an officer of Lee's rank—besides, he would run the additional risk of being tried as a deserter from the British army. Still, one wondered about Lee.

John Augustine was still at Mount Vernon a few days later when a letter from George arrived to say that he had turned the tables on the British at Trenton on Christmas night—recrossed the Delaware in a snowstorm, captured the Hessian garrison there, and got away again to his Pennsylvania Headquarters, with a loss of only two men, who had frozen to death. The troops had behaved splendidly this time. In fact, they had so enjoyed themselves in the captured town that it was difficult to round them up for the return march. Restrained as his report contrived to be, it was plain that a great stroke had been made, and his reputation as Commander in Chief was reestablished and enhanced.

The atmosphere at Mount Vernon brightened like magic, and there were modest celebrations as the news spread and the neighborhood arrived with congratulations to his wife. Congratulations were still going on when another letter from the North announced his further success at Princeton, which had been accomplished by a brilliant all-night flanking maneuver that compelled the confused and mortified British to withdraw their garrisons from the whole of Jersey as far as Brunswick and Amboy. This second triumph was dimmed in Virginia by the fact that Hugh Mercer had been mortally wounded during the Princeton engagement and died a prisoner in the British camp—an old friend, and a dear friend, lost.

But the militia were "taking spirit" now, and began to come in, even during the hardships of winter quarters, established at Morristown in the Jersey hills. Howe had settled down to the diversions of captive New York, and Cornwallis was believed to have resumed his plans for a voyage to England on leave which had been interrupted by Washington's descent on the Hessians. The fighting was over, at least for a while, with the situation entirely reversed, almost overnight, in favor of the Americans. Martha began to make preparations to travel to Headquarters.

Washington wrote that he was living in the Morristown tavern which had long been a meeting place for patriots and the Masonic Lodge. It was by no means as commodious as the house at Cambridge, though he had for his own use two upstairs rooms over the bar, as office and bedroom, and the Lifeguards were encamped around the building. Some of the officers, like General Greene whom he had grown to love as a friend, had lodgings in nearby houses, and some were quartered in the Tavern itself. Smallpox was already a menace, and he had ordered a general inoculation including the civilian population. Both churches in the town were being used as hospitals, so that the services were held out of doors, and some private houses were taking in patients. There was also a great deal of putrid sore throat and dysentery, against which there was no inoculation. Changes had occurred in his Family, owing to promotions and transfers, with considerable resulting confusion. He had been separated from his luggage during the move on Princeton, and it was not yet recovered from the old Headquarters at Newtown, where Colonel Harrison had been left in charge and had fallen ill. Moylan, after a brief unhappy tenure in the Quartermaster Department, which Mifflin had resumed in January, was back in the Family as a writing-aide, for George was short-handed as always with the post-bag.

The war was confined to skirmishes between scouting and foraging parties, in which the British usually came off second best. But the note of renewed confidence, even optimism, which had followed the Princeton advantage soon gave way to all the same old worries which had beset him at Cambridge, along with some new ones. Provisions for the troops were short, and the men suffered from the want of warm clothing, shoes, and blankets. Enlistments were not holding up after the first enthusiasm, winter weather and the smallpox and the inoculation rule being inevitable deterrents, while the Tory element in the countryside was very strong and active in intimidation and persuasion. Before February was out, his brief expectation of an augmented force had faded, the treasury was empty, to the embarrassment of Colonel Palfrey, who was now the Paymaster—and they were back in the old necessity of deceiving their friends in order not to reveal their weakness to the enemy. There was some mystery, Martha felt, about Colonel Reed, who appeared to have resigned suddenly from the Adjutant-Generalship, though he had not left the army. While she awaited the summons at Mount Vernon, there were several false alarms that Howe might move on Philadelphia without waiting for spring weather—enough to make George doubt the wisdom of her presence at Headquarters in case of a surprise attack. It was not until early in March that he allowed her to set out.

Jacky rode with her as far as Baltimore, where she called on Mrs. Hancock, who had remained there with her baby girl after Congress returned to Philadelphia. Dolly Hancock seemed in no hurry to rejoin her husband, who was living in lodgings and complaining about it. Martha thought it rather odd, and pressed on to Philadelphia herself, where an escort from Headquarters was to meet her. The city had exploded into gaiety again after what was now considered either a false alarm or a narrow escape in the past December.

George Lewis, son of Washington's sister Betty, was the aide who had been sent this time with a few dragoons to ride behind Martha's coach to Morristown, and he brought news of the General's illness there; a quinsy sore throat, they said, a high fever, great discomfort, and—with respect and affection, it was admitted—an unusual shortness of temper. Martha dispensed with Philadelphia hospitality and hurried on. By the time she reached the friendly village in the Jersey hills, George was on his feet to welcome her, but she found him thin, older, tireder, worn down.

She heard with outward composure the Family's dismal story of the night when his breathing was so bad, and they all got frightened and gathered round him, tiptoeing into the bedroom, bareheaded, apprehensive, all of them weighed down by the same dread—what would become of them, and of the Cause, if he died now? Finally someone asked him —whom could they turn to, who was there to shoulder the burden if he was forced to lay it down? His throat was closed with phlegm and pus, his eyes burned deep and bright with fever. He made no attempt to speak, but as it were almost against his will his gaze wandered among them until it came to rest with affection and relief, on Nathanael Greene. Greene made a sound, half laugh, half sob, and caught the hot dry hand on the coverlet in his, and made a lame, brotherly jest at which they could all try to smile. Next day the Commander in Chief was better, but no one had forgotten, least of all Quaker Greene, that an almost involuntary choice of an heir apparent had been indicated.

Martha liked Greene, whose wife was at home awaiting the birth of her second child, and she was sure that there would be no self-importance in such a man, but she thought it unlikely that he would be called upon to run the war. She knew George's rare, brief, but total collapses, and his miraculous recoveries. He had made a superhuman effort at Trenton —the tremendous, lonely decision to cross the half-frozen river with his ill-clad, exhausted men in open boats—the physical endurance and spiritual strength to see it through, after those punishing weeks of defeat and fatigue—a reaction was inevitable. She put on an apron and went down to the kitchen, which was soon fragrant with a mysterious brew of onions and molasses which always stopped his cough. There was Mount Vernon ham for dinner, and a fruit cake. Everyone's step was a little brisker, everyone looked a little spruced up—Mrs. Washington had taken charge of the General.

Even the *Continental Journal* recognized the change: "His Excellency had been ill for some days, but is now perfectly recovered and has the satisfaction of his amiable lady's company, who arrived here this day in good health," it recorded on the 15th of March.

It did him good to hear her gentle chatter of Virginia affairs. He took

an interest in Nelly's baby, and in Martha's own detailed accounts of
Lund's progress with the work at Mount Vernon. He heard with indulgent laughter her private commentary on Patrick Henry's gubernatorial
goings-on in the Palace at Williamsburg. They grieved together over the
death of Hugh Mercer at Princeton, and the final departure for England
of John Randolph, Tory brother of the late Peyton. His son Edmund,
once a member of the Cambridge Headquarters Family, had lately married his childhood playmate, Betty Nicholas. Martha thought her an odd,
unfriendly sort of girl for a highly strung man like Edmund Randolph
to choose. He was eking out an uncertain income in Williamsburg as
Attorney-General for the Tidewater district. Belvoir had at last been
rented, to a clergyman named Morton.

Gradually she caught up on the checkered Headquarters history since
her departure from New York nearly ten months before. At first George
was reluctant to account for Joseph Reed's absence, and she saw that
somehow he had been deeply hurt by the man in whom he had reposed
the utmost confidence. When she was finally able to get the facts from
him, it was difficult for her to contain her indignation. Reed had incon-
ceivably been taken in by Charles Lee's romanticized opinion of himself,
added to the spectacular defeat of the British fleet at Charleston which
was credited to Lee's presence there at the time. During the long retreat
across Jersey, when Washington was under the hard necessity of conceal-
ing even from his own Family his paralyzing handicaps, and while Lee
with the rear guard had hung back, delayed, lost touch, and generally
failed to be of any support, Reed had written to Lee a letter which ex-
ceeded indiscretion and amounted to flagrant disloyalty to the Commander in Chief. In it he spoke of a want of decision at Headquarters,
and stressed the confidence which everyone there felt in Lee, to whom
he attributed the army's escape from New York without a wholesale surrender. Lee's inflated reply had arrived at Headquarters on a day when
Reed was absent on detached duty, and it was innocently opened by
Washington in the natural supposition that it pertained to Lee's whereabouts and intentions, which were then vitally important. "—received
your most flattering and obliging letter—lament with you that fatal in-
decision of mind which in war is a much greater disqualification than
stupidity, or even want of personal courage . . ." he read before he even
began to comprehend. "—eternal defeat and miscarriage—for to confess
a truth, I really think my Chief will do better with me than without
me . . ."

This was at Brunswick, on the 30th of November, when Fort Washington had been lately lost, and the army had fallen back through Hackensack and Newark. Retreat had been agreed on in a general Council of officers, which recognized that their force was insufficient to make a stand. The chase was so close that they had heard the British drums most of the way, and the British advanced guard entered Newark as the American rear had left it.

In the little bedroom at Morristown, as he tried to tell her of his chagrin and disappointment over Reed's treachery, George paced the floor with unaccustomed gesture and vehemence in words, and she saw how deep the dagger had gone, how bitter even now was his sense of betrayal by a beloved member of the Family. There was no question of "decision" at Newark, he cried out, the British were making all the decisions. If he had not kept going, kept on the run, the pitiful remnants of his army would have been enveloped in a total catastrophe. And Reed had been there at Newark, he knew as well as anyone that they had nothing then with which to face the British onslaught. No, he had never seen Reed's letter to Lee; there was no need, it was plain enough from the reply to what he had written. And when she asked George what he had done about it he turned to face her with hopeless, outflung hands—what was there to do? He had simply enclosed Lee's letter to Reed at Burlington, with an apology for having inadvertently seen the contents of what he had not suspected was a private correspondence.

An *apology*—to *Reed*. He waited patiently in the middle of the floor while she had her say about Joseph Reed, until she went to lay her arms around him where he stood, and pointed out to him passionately that when the right time came, and he was able to gather his men together and drive the British almost out of Jersey, the indispensable General Lee had been for two weeks a prisoner of war; and where was Joseph Reed that bitter night they crossed the Delaware to Trenton? Not with the army which made the crossing, he admitted. And where was the infamous Reed now? In Philadelphia. He had made an effort to explain, when he received Washington's letter with the enclosure. They had tried to go on as before and ignore the whole thing, but it was too embarrassing, and Washington had finally accepted Reed's resignation from the Adjutant-Generalship—which in itself was a vast inconvenience—and recommended him to the command of a regiment of cavalry. Well, it was hard to know whom to trust these days. His clasp tightened briefly before he released her with a grateful sigh.

At least they were well rid of General Lee, she said, returning to her chair and her knitting. And she had heard since she came here that there were some other generals at Charleston who had had something to do with driving off the British there. Word had seeped back from the Carolinas through their delegates at Philadelphia of a man named Moultrie and a man named Marion; Carolinians, both, who without benefit of Lee's assistance had built a fort of palmetto logs which proved well-nigh impervious to the British shot and shell. Was there anything to that story, she wondered now, above her busy needles. And with the old, familiar glint behind his hooded gaze, he conceded that there was, indeed, some truth in it.

She missed Colonel Baylor from the Staff, one of her favorites, and learned that he was off raising his own regiment of Virginia Horse. No treachery there, George assured her cheerfully. He had chosen Baylor for the honor of carrying to Congress at its Baltimore roost the glorious news of the Trenton surprise, along with a captured Hessian flag and his particular recommendation of Baylor's spirited behavior throughout the campaign. Congress had voted the aide a new horse, caparisoned; and had promoted him to the command of a regiment of dragoons, which he was at this moment trying to recruit and train in his home county. Colonel Moylan also was to have a cavalry command now, and Colonel Sammy Webb, nicknamed the Unlucky because of his minor wounds and narrow escapes, had left the Staff in his turn to raise a regiment in his native Connecticut. All these transfers and promotions required some reorganization at Headquarters.

With the light-hearted, cultured Palfrey as Paymaster, they were hoping to get Gates back into his old post where he had begun the war, as Adjutant-General, which had been vacated by Reed's recent resignation. But Gates eluded the appointment with his usual serpentine ability not to offend anyone, and remained in Philadelphia as senior officer in charge of the incoming militia reserve. He continued to ingratiate himself with the New England delegates to Congress, as he had done the previous winter with the Massachusetts Assembly, and in a letter to President Hancock admitted that he had no wish to "dwindle again into the Adjutant-General" after having had command of the Northern Department, adding that he must insist on retaining his present rank, pay, and staff *if,* at the Commander in Chief's personal request, he should consent to return to Headquarters. As a soldier who had once been very sensitive about matters of rank himself, Washington could recognize an unwillingness to step down, and he was so in need of Gates's army experience that he passed over the ungracious insistence on prerogative, which might have warned him about Gates's future conduct. When even an urgent letter from him failed to bring Gates to an acceptance of his obligations, a narrow-faced, near-sighted New Englander named Pickering unwillingly undertook the difficult post.

Martha asked who wrote the letters now, besides dear old Harrison, who had returned from sick leave as a married man and was again nailed to a writing-table set up at the Tavern in a room on the ground floor across from the bar. But they were not doing so badly about that any more. Tench Tilghman, the obliging Marylander who had been a lawyer in Philadelphia and then a captain in the Flying Camp under Mercer, till he came to Headquarters last summer at New York, had served faithfully right through the worst of it in Jersey, and meant to stay on forever, without bothering about rank or pay; a New York ex-merchant named Benjamin Walker with some knowledge of French, and Harrison's young brother-in-law George Johnston, Jr., of Belvale, were useful at copying; and two more Virginians were settling down to Staff work very handily—Colonel Fitzgerald, who at Princeton as a newcomer to the Family was seen to cover his face in horror as the Commander in Chief rode through murderous point-blank fire from the British ranks; and Dick Meade, whose specialty was hard riding. The most recent appointment, a young captain of artillery whom Greene had discovered at New York, was a lad from the West Indies who could speak and write French, named Alexander Hamilton.

Martha had noticed young Colonel Hamilton at once on her arrival at Morristown—no older than Jacky, slender, graceful, boyish, very charming, and just a bit above himself. He had come to America from St. Croix before the war began, with letters of introduction from his island tutor to the Livingstons and the Boudinots in the neighborhood around Princeton. Both families had young people of Hamilton's age, and received him cordially into their circle. Princeton had not suited Hamilton, or the other way round, and he had gone on to King's College in New York, the same year that Jacky Custis was enrolled so briefly, and had joined the artillery from there in time for the Jersey retreat and the fight at Trenton. The women spoiled him, Martha suspected, till now he had almost the air of expecting it, which left her unresponsive. She observed the affectionate indulgence he received from her friend Colonel Harrison, and even from George, whose attitude was almost paternal.

Not that the lad did not work hard—he took his duties very seriously, and his French was better than Walker's, for he had spoken it as a child with his mother, and this made him particularly useful in handling the European adventurers who were beginning to be a nuisance with their demands for rank and pay in the American army, which most of them nevertheless affected to patronize. She also observed that while Colonel Hamilton's conversation sparkled with a kind of wit, he had trouble to see the simple type of Headquarters joke that set all the others laughing. She was perhaps the only person at Morristown that spring who had any reservations about Alexander Hamilton, and as usual she kept her opinions to herself.

William Livingston was now Governor of New Jersey, and his fine house, Liberty Hall, like Elias Boudinot's, was in the near vicinity of the present Headquarters. His two beautiful daughters, Susan and Sarah, and Sarah Boudinot were frequent visitors there, as part of the local society which always gathered around the General's Family. Sarah Livingston was married to Chief Justice John Jay of New York, but often lived at home with her parents during his absences at Philadelphia or Kingston where the state Legislature was. Her cousins, Kitty and Mary Stirling, whose mother was Governor Livingston's sister, usually joined them in their visits, as General Stirling's house at Baskingridge was also nearby, and he was confined there during the winter by a severe bout of rheumatism.

Another knitting and sewing circle was soon established under Martha's supervision, after a rather comic beginning. "I was never so ashamed in my life," a Morristown matron recorded. "[We] thought we would visit Lady Washington, and as she was said to be so grand a lady, we thought we must put on our best bibs and bands. So we dressed ourselves in our most elegant ruffles and silks, and were introduced to her ladyship. And don't you think we found her *knitting and with a specked* [*checked*] *apron on!* She received us very graciously, but after the compliments were over, she resumed her knitting. There we were without a stitch of work, and sitting in state, but General Washington's lady with her own hands was knitting stockings for herself and husband. . . . She seems very wise in experience, kind-hearted and winning in all her ways. She talked much of the poor soldiers, especially the sick ones. Her heart seems to be full of compassion for them. . . ."

Kitty Greene had been seriously ill after the birth of her second child in March—a girl who was to be called Martha Washington Greene—and

did not arrive at Morristown until the army was about to move out on
its summer campaign, when she took lodgings with friends in the Jersey
countryside. Lucy Knox likewise was kept at home by the birth of a son,
who did not long survive.

In May Mrs. Theodorick Bland, wife to the nephew of that Richard
Bland who had attended the First Congress with Washington, became a
member of their community when Colonel Bland brought his Virginia
cavalry to Morristown. The lively Mrs. Bland was a welcome addition,
and her letters to her husband's sister, who had married a Randolph,
were full of camp news: "I left Philadelphia last month and came to
Morristown where General Washington keeps Headquarters," she wrote
to Fanny Randolph. "Mrs. Washington had arrived three weeks before
me, so that I could with a good face make a visit to camp. . . . I found
Morris a very clever little village, situated in a most beautiful valley at
the foot of five mountains. It has three churches with steeples which give
it a consequential look—and is something larger than Blandfield. It has
two families, refugees from New York, in it, otherwise it is inhabited by
the errantest rustics you ever beheld. You cannot travel three miles without passing through one of these villages, all of them having meeting-
houses and courthouses etc., decorated with steeples which gives them a
pretty, airy look, and the farms between the mountains are the most rural
sweet spots in nature, their meadows of a fine, luxuriant grass which
looks like a bed of velvet interspersed with yellow, blue, and white
flowers. . . .

"Now let me speak of our noble and agreeable Commander (for he
commands both sexes) one by his excellent skill in military matters, the
other by his ability, politeness, and attention. We visit them twice or
three times a week by particular invitation—every day frequently from
inclination. He is generally busy in the forenoon—but from dinner till
night he is free for all company. His worthy lady seems to be in perfect
felicity while she is by the side of her *Old Man,* as she calls him. We often
make parties on horseback—the General, his lady, Miss Livingston, and
his aides-de-camp, who are Colonel Fitzgerald, an agreeable, broad-
shouldered Irishman; . . . Colonel Johnson, who is exceedingly witty
at everybody's expense, but can't allow other people to be so at his own,
though they often take the liberty; Colonel Hamilton, a sensible, genteel,
polite young fellow, a West Indian; Colonel Meade; Colonel Tilghman,
a modest, worthy man who from his attachment to the General volun-
tarily lives in his Family and acts in any capacity that is uppermost with-

out fee or reward; Colonel Harrison, brother of Billy Harrison that kept store in Petersburg, and as much like him as possible; a worthy man; Captain Gibbs of the General's Guard, a good-natured Yankee who makes a thousand blunders in the Yankee style and keeps the dinner table in a constant laugh. These are the General's Family, all polite, sociable gentlemen, who make the day pass with a great deal of satisfaction to the visitors.

"But I had forgot my subject, almost, this is our riding party generally—at which time General Washington throws off the hero, and takes on the chatty agreeable companion. He can be downright impudent sometimes—such impudence, Fanny, as you and I like—and really, I have often wished for you. It is a life that is calculated for one of your temper. . . ."

It did not disturb Martha that most of the young women who set eyes on the General fell a little in love with him, for that had happened before at Alexandria and Williamsburg, as the member for Fairfax County moved in his tall dignity through the election balls and Assembly times. He liked to dance, and made a magnificent partner. He enjoyed a picnic, and appreciated an attractive woman who could sit a horse beside him on these excursions. With impenetrable courtesy and amusement he had allowed himself to be flirted with and teased by admiring young females for years. Now the prestige of his command was added to the splendor of his booted, spurred, and uniformed presence, and he seemed to grow daily in stature and personal magnetism with the responsibility of his position. The modest, soft-spoken, but authoritative Virginia Burgess had become a superlative figure as the Commander in Chief of the American army—still without a trace of self-importance or vanity, still listening with grave attention to the opinions of anyone who chose to present them, still unconsciously irresistible to the ladies.

Martha could smile over her knitting, well knowing that the time would come at the end of the day when they escaped at last into their scanty privacy upstairs, and the boots would be eased off into Billy's waiting hands, the sword belt and epauletted coat laid aside, and he would relax with a sigh and sometimes a rueful glance at her, which acknowledged heartfelt relief at refuge from their recent company, to hear the latest letter from Jack or Nancy, to discuss the weekly report from Lund at Mount Vernon, and to anticipate the time when he could once more ride out in the early morning to see for himself what was being done at the mill and the brick barn, and to supervise the building and planting at the Home House.

As the spring went on, the British remained ominously quiet around Brunswick, and preparations to meet their next move went forward on the American side. The European soldiers of fortune continued to arrive in shoals, with letters of introduction from the Congressional commissioners at Paris, who had recently been augmented by Dr. Franklin in the hope of arranging for quick and substantial aid from England's old enemy, France.

One of the overconfident strangers was an Irishman named Conway, whose chief recommendation was that he at least spoke English, though his allegedly distinguished military service had all been done for France. Congress was impressed, and without further ado, made him a brigadier of an as yet nonexistent brigade.

The old threat of a junction of British forces from Canada with Howe's New York army, via the Lakes and the Hudson River, revived as the roads hardened and the time for the new campaign drew near, and Burgoyne returned from England to Quebec to conduct the enterprise. Recruitment in the American army continued to lag, and desertion was a major problem. The first signs of activity on the part of the British in Canada and Jersey brought about a sort of general post among the American officers—Putnam to Peekskill, Sullivan to Princeton, Gates and Arnold to the North again, where Schuyler was thought (in Philadelphia) to be inadequate. By the end of May the British transports at New York were seen to be loading, and the odds were on Philadelphia as their objective. Headquarters prepared to break up for a move into tents at Bound Brook nearer Brunswick, and the wives began reluctantly to pack for the journey home.

Early in June Jacky Custis came to Morristown, traveling somewhat roundabout to the west of Princeton by Washington's orders, to make the journey back to Mount Vernon with his mother. Washington wanted her to be well past Philadelphia before the British could move on the city, and so Jacky's visit at the camp was brief. Quartermaster Mifflin was directed to provide them with an escort on a safe route between Philadelphia and Baltimore.

She was pleased to see how Jacky had matured and steadied, and she gave Nelly credit for the gratifying change in him. His manner toward herself was as always devoted and charming, and the aides welcomed him as one of themselves, so that an old dread stirred within her—would Jacky

fall in love with the military life and want to take the field himself? There
was little doubt that the Commander in Chief's stepson would be granted
a commission and a place on the Staff if he wished it. But Jacky had
plans for entering the Virginia Legislature, and was taking seriously the
administration of his considerable estate. Another child was expected
during the winter, and Nelly's health was a constant uncertainty. It made
the parting from George and all her friends at Morristown more sup-
portable when she could drive away with Jacky in the coach beside her,
holding her hand very tight out of sight on the seat between them, to help
her master tears.

The summer of '77 was full of alarums and excursions, marching and
countermarching, which wore out the soldiers' shoes and accomplished
very little else, until the two armies under Howe and Washington finally
confronted each other on the Brandywine in September. Sullivan made
the same mistake he had made on Long Island the year before, and was
again outflanked. Again the Americans broke and again were withdrawn
from the field. Again Congress fled from Philadelphia, westward through
Pennsylvania this time to Lancaster and then on to York. And just in
time. The American rally and counterattack a few days later was caught
in a drenching downpour of rain, with forty rounds of ammunition per
man distributed in leaky cartouche boxes, where it was nearly all ruined.
Neither side could fire a shot, but it was all that Washington's troops had
on hand. He retired toward Reading to await supplies, and the British
occupied Philadelphia at their leisure on the 26th of September.

A little to everyone's surprise, the sky did not fall when Philadelphia
was lost to Howe at last. Still more surprising to Washington at least, the
men's spirits did not evaporate. Perhaps during the long hot summer,
tramping up and down in the desperate attempt to defend both the city
and the Hudson River line to Canada where Burgoyne was, they had got
used to the idea that Philadelphia could not be held. Some people
thought there was no sense in trying to cover both, and that Washington
should have pulled all his forces into the campaign for Philadelphia.
Mifflin, whose home was there, was one of those who deplored the effort
to maintain the Hudson River defense at the expense of Philadelphia. He
accompanied the Congress to York where he remained, threatening to
resign because of alleged ill health, while his Quartermaster department,
which was already in a bad way, deteriorated still further. The army was
in desperate need of shoes, blankets, and tents, with cold weather near.

From Mount Vernon George's situation looked quite as hopeless as it had done before the Trenton miracle, and it was necessary for his anxious relatives there to remind themselves frequently of his incredible resilience in defeat. His failure at Philadelphia was bracketed by two encouraging events in the North—General Stark's victory at Bennington in August over a detachment of Burgoyne's army, and a successful engagement against Burgoyne himself by the troops under Gates's command, at Bemis Heights near Saratoga on October 7th. When Washington attacked Howe's main encampment at Germantown on October 4th everything went wrong in a fog, and confusion reigned until the Americans fired into, and fled from, each other. Washington gathered them up somehow and retired to Whitemarsh to recoup. Ten days later Burgoyne's entire army surrendered to Gates at Saratoga.

Toward the end of October when George's niece, John Augustine's oldest daughter Jane, married her cousin William Augustine Washington of Wakefield, Martha went down to Bushfield for the wedding, and John Augustine showed her a letter from George written on the 18th—she already had its news, but she always liked to read anything that came from Headquarters, where they were still trying to determine what had happened at Germantown.

George's account of Gates's triumph at Saratoga was enthusiastic and without reservations. They knew very well at Bushfield what his generous rejoicing over the northern victory would have cost a lesser man. They knew that to George, so long as the battle was won, it mattered not who got the glory; but it was the disastrous pattern of 1776 all over again, when Lee had saved Charleston and Washington lost New York. Now Gates took Burgoyne, and Washington lost Philadelphia. And there were so many little, officious people who could not see the difference in the circumstances of the Commander in Chief and a detached field maneuver, and who conceived that it was only necessary to attack in order to win a battle.

Nelly's second daughter was born early in December, and was named for her grandmother Martha. Soon after that the news reached Mount Vernon that Nancy Bassett had died at Eltham. She was only thirty-eight, and left three children surviving. The youngest, Martha's favorite niece Fanny, was ten years old. It was a bad time to lose gay, loving, beloved Nancy, lifelong confidante and closest friend among her sisters. There were only four of them left now, in the devoted Dandridge family. Their mother still lived at Chestnut Grove, their old home in New Kent County. Bartholomew was married and had children. Betsy, who had married an Aylett, was already a widow at twenty-eight. And Martha, childless except for Jacky, was alone at Mount Vernon. Change and loss —change and gain—but change alone was constant. She longed for the comfort of George's mere presence in the next room.

It was another dreary Christmas, empty and anxious and obstinate, like last year—the second the war had robbed them of. And this time there was no last-minute miracle. Thanks as much to the growing deficiencies of its own Quartermaster and Commissary departments as to the fog at Germantown, the American army could do no more at the end of 1777 than dig itself in for the winter in what poor comfort it could contrive out of nothing, within a bleak circle of windswept Pennsylvania hills at a place called Valley Forge.

Even from a distance of several hundred miles, Martha was sure that something was very wrong at Headquarters. The reasons for delaying her arrival there sounded logical enough as George set them down. Farmhouses which could be used as living quarters were few in that part of the state, and the men must build their own huts out of logs, even for some of the officers. Until then, they were under canvas in a Pennsylvania winter, and as the General refused to take better shelter than was available to his troops, he was living in his marquee tent, and would continue to do so until the men's huts were completed, when he would take possession of a stone dwelling at the upper end of the valley which belonged to a Mrs. Hewes. Provisions were so short that the men were sometimes on the point of mutiny, and horses were dying on their feet for want of forage. Instead of a hard freeze or snow, the winter began with perpetual rains, which in some ways was worse, as everything got soaking wet and stayed that way. The house which Headquarters would eventually occupy was small and inadequate—less comfortable than the tavern at Morristown, nothing like the place at Cambridge. So the excuses and explanations ran.

Although Jack and Nelly had brought the babies and come to stay at Mount Vernon as soon as they heard about Nancy's death, Martha was packed and ready to start northward at a day's notice. The chariot would be weighted with sound Mount Vernon food which was badly needed at camp—hams, cheeses, dried fruits, and nuts. Nelly was frail since the birth of the new little Patty, and they were all very careful of her. When the summons came for Martha, Mrs. Lund would take charge of the Custises, for there was no question where the General's wife belonged.

But something was wrong at Valley Forge besides starvation and the weather. She remembered the mysterious absence of Joseph Reed's name from George's letters last year, and the unhappy story of duplicity and backstairs criticism which then unfolded. She searched his closely written pages anxiously during the present winter, looking for clues. Who now, she wondered. Charles Lee was still a prisoner. Reed—what had become of Reed, then? Mifflin was not mentioned either. Baylor? Ah, no, Baylor was a rock, it was just his promotion that removed him from the Family. Moylan? Wild Irish, but loyal to the bone, she could swear. Hamilton? He was too clever. The foreigners—the Germans and the Poles and the French—a man named Conway, a man named Lafayette, Pulaski, De-Kalb—whose dagger now? Harrison would know. She could always get it out of dear, faithful Harrison.

By mid-January George wrote that the troops were tolerably housed in log huts of their own construction, and he was about to occupy the stone farmhouse which had been made ready for his use, with a log dining room built on. With misgivings he consented that Martha should set out whenever it was convenient to her, and sent one of his Virginia aides, Colonel Meade, to meet her on the road below Wilmington, where General Smallwood was stationed to watch the river mouth.

She arrived at Valley Forge at twilight on a raw, icy day early in February. The road from Philadelphia ran through the whole length of the camp before it came to Headquarters, and as the coach rolled in she had seen from its windows the rows of snow-capped log huts facing each other in streets like little towns, and the smoky, green-wood fires, and the shivering sentries with their feet bound in rags and their heads tied up in scarves over their hats and under their chins to keep their ears from freezing. She had seen the poor horses, mere skeletons covered with shaggy hair, stumbling with weakness against the weight of the sleds full of firewood, while the ragged men in charge of them added their feeble strength to push the load from behind, and paused in their tracks to stare at the coach drawn by its own near-foundered horses, its scarlet and white liveries hidden by greatcoats. Some of them recognized it, and saluted or waved as it went by, and once they raised a sort of cheer, and she let down the glass to the bitter wind and waved back to them—so they saw her face, rosy and smiling, and the word passed quickly that the General's lady had come to camp, and everyone felt better for his Excellency's good fortune.

They did not minimize the journey she had made to share the bleak, cramped quarters allotted to the Commander in Chief and his Family. There were bigger houses round about the countryside, more suitable for his accommodation, where his wife could have lived quite comfortably. Greene had one of them, and Knox also was better off than the Washingtons, in a nice place down by the covered bridge, and Stirling too, nearby—but these houses lay exposed at the outer rim of the camp, some of them beyond its limits. For security General Washington had to live entrenched at the head of the Valley, with the whole army and its fortifications between him and the British at Philadelphia. It left him no choice of houses, the Engineers under General Duportail who had designed the defenses saw to that. But the men in the huts, their eyes smarting and streaming from the ill-ventilated fires on the primitive hearths, turning themselves like fowls on a spit to warm their backs, bragged to each other that Lady Washington, having come all that way to winter with her man, would not complain.

Once more the coach drew up before the lighted windows of an unfamiliar house with sentries outside, and she stepped down stiffly, holding to Meade's bent arm. They had cleared a path to the door, but the snow banked either side of it rose as high as her waist, and the wind whirled it higher, to sting her cheeks. She gasped as the wind caught her, and Meade held her up, while the door opened before them into a narrow hall with a stairway, where a tall man seized and held her a long moment without regard to onlookers. Each time she came to him, so small and resolute and faithful, so dauntless and so dear, he was swept by an almost uncontrollable emotion of which sheer gratitude was a large part—he knew so well what she had left behind and what she so cheerfully endured just for the sake of keeping him company at camp, and what an example she set to the selfish and the faint-hearted. What he did not suspect was how little any of that meant to her, beside the single daily privilege of living in the light of his countenance.

The little sitting room on the right of the hall welcomed her with a blazing log fire, and her outdoor things were carried away by the colored maid Oney who always traveled with her, and she heard her trunks and boxes coming in and going up the stairs. The social amenities duly observed, with a glass of wine to warm the travelers, Meade melted tactfully away, doubtless to the kitchen across the hall, and George conducted her up to the front bedroom on the second floor. The tip of his scabbard caught the wall on the landing with a remembered sound as they went, and the epaulettes on his shoulders were cold and hard under her hands when they embraced in a moment's privacy. Then Oney arrived at the door with a jug of hot water and towels, and he left them while Martha changed out of her traveling dress into a soft homespun gown and house shoes, and Oney produced a fresh frilled cap and a silk apron.

Downstairs, the front door opened and closed more than once, and voices drifted up to her—the young, uninhibited voices of the aides, assembling for a special supper in her honor. Oney found the fruitcake they had packed ready for immediate consumption, and with it in her hands Martha descended again to the sitting room which the Staff at enormous inconvenience had set aside for her use.

They too had made preparations. They had collected a couple of bottles of good wine, a pound of tea, a hard lump of cheese, fresh-baked bread, and nuts to be cracked and every crumb picked from the shell. As the evening went on she encountered the still unfathomable Valley Forge jokes, and heard again the well-worn reminiscences of Morristown and Cambridge. It was like a homecoming, she thought, touched and proud, glancing round at the lean, fine-drawn faces in the merciful candlelight. No matter that she had never seen this crowded and stuffy room before, or that they were not all old friends of hers like Harrison. They were a Family, and she was a part of it, and they were glad to have her among them again.

George was not so short of help as he had been when the war was young. Besides his nephew George Lewis, the Staff still included the devoted Tilghman and Harrison; Hamilton was there, brilliant and handsome and efficient, as at Morristown last year. Big Colonel Fitzgerald was in Virginia on well-earned leave, they told her. Baylor and Moylan were as far away as Trenton in the hard necessity of finding forage for their cavalry horses. Unlucky Sammy Webb, on the business of raising his Connecticut regiment, had contrived to get himself captured by the British while crossing Long Island Sound, and was a prisoner of war. Colonel Meade did most of the riding jobs, on his cherished black mare, and a new secretary-aide had joined them last summer—John Laurens of South Carolina, whose father had succeeded John Hancock as President of the Congress, and had stood behind George during the recent difficulties more firmly than Hancock might have done. She at once thought young Laurens an asset; quick and keen and affectionate, educated and polished abroad, and tuned at Geneva. The acid, hypercritical Pickering had gone to York to take his seat on the new Board of War, and jolly Scammell of Massachusetts was now Adjutant-General, trading drolleries with Yankee Captain Gibbs of the Lifeguard and sunny Palfrey the Paymaster.

Valley Forge, they explained with some regret, was not a populous neighborhood like those of the past two winters, and there would not be much society this year besides the army's own. All the old-timers among the officers from Cambridge and Morristown were eager to welcome her back, and had all left the most cordial messages to be delivered to her on her arrival. She could depend on it they would soon call to pay their respects, some of them riding in from their posts outside the Valley as far away as Haddonfield and Trenton.

Kitty Greene was already there, they said, having stowed the two babies safely away with friends at home. Lucy Knox was still at Boston, where her General was bound on artillery business to visit the New England foundries and the arsenal at Springfield—he would doubtless bring her back with him. It was their second Christmas apart, and Lucy was complaining, having been kept away from Morristown last winter by the birth of the son who had not lived. Stirling's wife and daughters were expected to join him any day now. Sullivan, who had a wife in New Hampshire whom he never saw, and Wayne, whose wife always pleaded ill health and never came to camp, although their home was only a few miles away from Valley Forge, were both in bachelor quarters and not pining, so far as anyone could see. Young Harry Lee had arrived with Colonel Bland's Virginia cavalry at Morristown the previous spring, and had turned his body of Light Horse into such a scourge of the British foraging and scouting parties from Philadelphia that he was promoted to command an independent company of irregular cavalry and infantry known as Lee's Legion.

She listened with her usual smiling attention to their first flow of camp news, dispensing cups of the precious tea, while George looked on indulgently and the fruitcake disappeared piece by piece from the plate— a meager treat, sliced small to go round, and received with the respect it deserved, but filling a vast void—until suddenly someone remembered that she was tired, and they all rose, clanking, scraping, and apologetic, enormous men wearing swords and spurs in a small square room, bowing over her hand again, wishing her a good night.

She woke at daybreak to the drum-rolls running from right to left along the front line in the distance, and back again, more plainly heard, from left to right, through the second line, and on to the reserve and the Lifeguards nearest the house. The reveille beat was a familiar sound to her ears now. George had already left the bed, and she could hear him moving about, shaving, no doubt, in the candlelighted closet which opened off the bedroom and through to the room behind it. Then came Billy's voice, as he brought in the polished boots. Yes, she had been tired, to sleep like that, till the whole house was stirring. It was not an easy journey, ever, and this year the weather was the worst she had seen, and the coach was clumsy with its load of provisions. Colonel Meade was a miracle of efficiency and good humor, but more than once along the way she had been near to tears of weariness and despair at this endless war, which was robbing them of privacy and comfort and a home. It was not that she ever thought of turning back. She only longed for George to make an end of it, so they could live at Mount Vernon.

There was a knock on the bedroom door, and a voice asked permission to come in and make up the fire.

When she had dressed she stood at the window in the dawn of that first morning at Valley Forge, to get her bearings. The house faced away from the camp, and from the front bedroom she looked out across a little icebound stream which lay between the road and the snowy slope beyond, where the huts of the French engineer Duportail's artificers corps were set. Already there was activity around the forges and cook fires, and soon the ring of iron on iron would begin as the blacksmiths and gunsmiths set to work. Except for that huddle of huts in the snow, and the shapeless, bundled-up figures which moved among them, it was a surprisingly tranquil scene. Most of the trees had been cut for logs, and their dark stumps showed. But the squalor and misery and ugliness of the company streets, the artillery park, the earthworks and the abatis, lay behind the house. A window on the staircase landing looked that way, toward the Lifeguards' camp a stone's throw from the back door, on the near slope of another little hill. The air was smudged and acrid with the smoke from hundreds of green-wood fires, but apart from the Lifeguards and the artificers, to anyone inside the Headquarters house the army might not have been there at all.

Martha wondered about the hospitals, which never bore thinking of, and the other officers' quarters. Her own house was indeed small, but it was snug and well-furnished. The sitting room, with the General's office (which had been the dining room) behind it on the right of the stairs, made up the ground floor, besides the kitchen across the hall—a good kitchen, with a red brick floor. The log room, which they had added to dine in, served also as a reception and orderly room between meals. Upstairs there were two good bedrooms and a small one over the hall, another over the kitchen, and a frigid third floor full of cots, its only heat coming from the warm chimney of the fireplaces below.

As the days went on, many old friends dropped in to bid her welcome —Weedon, the innkeeper from Fredericksburg, a brigadier now, and touchy about his rank—the poor man never knew how to get along with people, though he yearned for popularity; Muhlenberg, the Virginia pastor who had gone straight from the pulpit to the recruiting drum; Woodford, who had been in the war ever since he beat Dunmore at the Great Bridge below Norfolk in '75; Scott, who swore incorrigibly with every other breath he drew, but had been at the Trenton crossing and was therefore of the first fraternity; Varnum of Rhode Island, whom she knew from the early days at Cambridge, supposed to be the handsomest officer in the army; Stirling, red-faced and smelling of liquor as usual, but a great soldier, greatly loved; and humorless James Monroe, Stirling's aide—an odd pair but apparently quite compatible; Wayne, with his bold dark gaze and gallant manner, and what was his idiot of a wife thinking of to leave him to himself like this; Irish Moylan, ordered in from the outskirts to receive a fatherly reprimand from the General for his perpetual feud with the Polish brigadier Pulaski, who was a genius with cavalry, however difficult with men—a feud which had recently boiled up into an ungentlemanly brawl during which Moylan had struck a Mr. Zielinski who was in the Polish service, and had then given "irritating language" to General Pulaski. The resulting court-martial having acquitted Moylan and discharged him from arrest, a sobering interview with the Commander in Chief was in order, after which Martha kept her face straight and poured out tea for both of them.

Clement Biddle, one of the wealthy fighting Quakers of Philadelphia who had begun the war in the old Flying Camp was now appointed to the almost hopeless post of Commissary-General of forage for the Continental Army. His quarters were at Moore Hall, a mansion on the Pottstown road outside the Valley which had been considered adequate even for the comfort of General Cornwallis. The Congressmen who ventured into camp to criticize or give advice all preferred to lodge at Moore Hall, where Biddle's private resources provided comparative luxury, and his wife made a charming hostess. Rebecca Biddle soon came to call at Headquarters, for she and Martha had been friends since the exciting summer of '76. There were many more visitors, some of whom Martha could hardly remember having seen before, though they never guessed that—all of them anxious for a sight of her, which was for some reason reassuring to them, and they all felt a little less dreary when they went away again.

There was no need to pump Colonel Harrison about what had been going on behind the scenes at Valley Forge—and who was to blame this time—for Conway's Cabal was on everyone's tongue. *Gates.* She might have thought of Gates. For it was that smooth and slippery man who had armed the Irish-French adventurer with the dagger. A small conspiracy to undermine the Commander in Chief by a whispering campaign aimed at destroying confidence in him, so that he could be forced to resign or could be arbitrarily replaced by a more successful man—such as the victor of Saratoga—had been uncovered and firmly dealt with just before Christmas, although it had involved even a faction within the Congress at York. The aides at Headquarters were still dancing with rage, and yearned for Conway's blood, and Mifflin's, to say nothing of Gates's. Washington's only comment was a rueful smile.

Martha had not been sure what a cabal was, but she understood that George had been betrayed again by men he had trusted, and that they had made use of an outsider who disliked and resented him for standing in the way of personal ambition and vanity—Conway had encountered at Headquarters some of that ceremonious civility which Washington himself had once acknowledged to be worse than outright rudeness. This time George had defended himself vigorously, not because the burden of the command was dear to him, but because he considered it beneath his duty and honor to be driven from office by the burrowings of little men with little grudges. On the very day that Martha arrived at Valley Forge, he had been closeted with Hamilton devising the final, crushing unanswerable letter which with scrupulous courtesy and almost legal clarity would point out to Gates that he lied. The thing was finished now—there was nothing more to be said. But a stink still rose from its ashes, which were still warm.

Martha got out her mending basket and performed wonders of patching and stitching and darning for the bachelors; listened to letters and news from families at home; asked after babies by their names; brewed the treasured tea or coffee in her little sitting room, and stretched the Mount Vernon delicacies as far as they could go. The tired, tense faces of the lonely men brightened into smiles in her company, but she saw with pity and concern the threadbare coats and ragged breeches and stockings, the weather-stained buckskin and broadcloth worn by the officers, not one of whom had been able to renew his kit since the summer fighting. She pitied too the gaunt, heavy-footed saddle horses, whose well-polished equipment and loving grooming could not hide their bones. The want of forage was heartbreaking, and Knox suffered acutely for his Artillery animals, which were useless from hunger, while the wagon-teams were literally starving to death and dropping where they stood. As for the men in the huts, they often went for days together without a mouthful of meat, and their clothes were indecent rags. Many were barefoot, and for lack of blankets they sat up around the fires all night to keep from freezing. The hospitals—inevitably—were the worst of all, and everyone did his best to keep out of them.

When Martha asked why, and who was to blame, the answer seemed to be the Quartermaster Department—which was Mifflin, sulking in comfortable domesticity at Reading—and the Commissary, which was Joseph Trumbull, who had for weeks been ill at home in Connecticut. When she wanted to know why these men had not been replaced by more efficient people, it appeared that Congress had objections, and that an army could not be run that way. But an army could not be run as it was now, she cried. Driven into a corner by feminine logic, someone would then try to divert her with a story, like the one about the dog which had turned up in the American lines after Brandywine, wagging and fraternizing, with the name of its owner engraved on its collar. Colonel Hamilton penned the note which accompanied the special white flag of truce sent to escort the visitor past the pickets on its way home: "General Washington's compliments to General Howe. He does himself the pleasure to return him a dog which accidentally fell into our hands, and by the inscription on the collar appears to belong to General Howe."

Another old friend was Charles Willson Peale, who had been a welcome guest at Mount Vernon in '72. He had joined the army as a volunteer just before Trenton, and had now formed a grand design of collecting a portrait gallery of the leading figures in the war, painted wherever and whenever he could find the time and a subject who could be persuaded to sit to him. Serving as a captain of the Pennsylvania militia at Valley Forge, his precious paints and brushes traveling with him in his saddle-bags, he had set up an easel in a wretched earth-floored hut which he called his studio. The furniture consisted of a derelict bedstead and a three-legged chair, and the smoky fire had so little effect on the temperature that every few minutes he must stop to warm his hands close to it in order to wield his tools.

Washington posed patiently, seated in discomfort on the creaking bed-stead, while Peale balanced on the uncertain chair. Having run out of canvas, Peale had stretched a piece of blue and white striped bedticking, on which he was executing a fine likeness of the General to add to the unfinished portraits of his officers which were accumulating against the walls. Martha gave it her instant approval, for it seemed to her that George's affectionate indulgence for the amusing artist who could recall to him the good days at Mount Vernon six long years ago was visible in the attentive eyes and half-smile of the painted face.

The Staff also enjoyed Peale's ability to evoke a time before their ac-quaintance with the Commander in Chief began, and often lingered in the cheerless hut to gather stories from him—like the one about the warm afternoon in '72 when Peale and some other young visitors at Mount Vernon were out in their shirtsleeves getting some competitive exercise at pitching the bar. Washington watched for a while and gravely noted the pegs which marked the furthest distance achieved by his juniors. Then, without removing his coat, he held out his hand for the bar—which, Peale would say with a long arcing wave of his brush, at once lost the power of gravitation entirely and whizzed through the air to make its mark far beyond their best efforts. Beat the pitch, said their host with a modest smile, and he would try again. He never had to.

With Gates as President of the new Board of War, and Pickering and Mifflin as members, they soon hatched another scheme, designed to se-duce the young Marquis de Lafayette from Washington's side by offering him a gilded command in a proposed expedition against the British in Canada. When the Marquis arrived at York from Headquarters to receive his instructions from Congress, he found Conway there, behaving, said Lafayette, like a man sent from heaven, and he refused to accept the flashy Irishman as his second in command. In their eagerness to annex the Marquis and, with him, the whole European element in Washington's army, the conspirators hastily agreed to the substitution of Lafayette's friend and traveling companion on his voyage to America, the Baron DeKalb.

Headquarters lamented that Martha had missed the Marquis by only a matter of days. When she arrived at the camp he was already on his way to Albany to take charge of the new Canadian venture, which no one at Valley Forge viewed with any enthusiasm, and which Washing-ton had privately described as a child of folly. They claimed to be very dull without him, and she could see that the young French nobleman had won a firm place in their hearts. Unlike the other European adventurers, the Marquis had plenty of money and rank in his own right, and asked only to serve under Washington as a volunteer, without any inconvenient pretensions. "I have come to learn, and not to teach," he had told them. After taking a nasty wound in the leg at Brandywine, he had recovered at Bethlehem in the care of the Moravians there, and rejoined the Family, limping a bit, just before the news of Saratoga was received. His absence now was going to be keenly felt.

Because Lafayette was considered indescribable, George gave her some of his letters to read, and they brought a smile for their boyish spontaneity, their occasional oddities of phrase, and their extravagant devotion: "Could I believe for one single instant that this pompous command of a *northern army* will let your Excellency forget a little us absent friends, then I would send the project to the place it comes from," the Marquis had written the day after he left camp. "But I dare hope you will remember me sometimes. I wish you very honestly the greatest public and private happiness and success. It is a very melancholy idea for me that I cannot follow your fortunes as near your person as I could wish; but my heart will take very sincerely its part of everything that can happen to you, and I am already thinking of the agreeable moment when I may come down to assure your Excellency of the most tender affection and highest respect. . . ."

It seemed to Martha that after each separation she found an alarming change in the man she knew so well—each time he seemed older, harder, grimmer, wearier, and yet strangely stronger than when she saw him last. After a few days this first impression faded and he was just the same again—or was it that when she came she brought back to him something he lost in her absence? In the late evenings, when the door of the upstairs bedroom closed on the tramping boots and clinking spurs and occasionally unguarded laughter and voices of the Family—when the drums were still for the night, and the candles had all burnt low, and the wind howled down the Valley—they would sit together in their room, grateful for a brief privacy, and singularly at peace, and exchange their eight months' news. Hancock's baby daughter had died during the summer, and he had gone home to Boston with Mrs. Hancock to nurse his gout. George's brother Samuel was taking very much to heart the death of his wife, which had followed a smallpox inoculation—Sam's son Thornton by an earlier marriage had joined the army, and there were younger children whose upbringing would be a problem—Sam had bad luck with his wives, poor Anne was the fourth to die, and her three little boys were all under five years of age. John Augustine's wife Hannah had sent George a present of some stockings, beautifully knitted, but not as good a fit as the ones Martha made. And then in their rambling talk they would come to her sister Nancy, and how queer it felt not to write to her any more—she always wanted to hear about life at the camp—and Martha would wipe her eyes on her mending and snatch up a hasty new topic.

Patrick Henry was into his second term as Governor of Virginia and had taken a second wife who was (Martha had to laugh at this) a Dandridge and a distant connection of hers. She was not to belittle the man, George would remind her, having preserved his own gravity with a visible effort, and to prove what he said he brought out a letter from Henry which had enclosed an anonymous communication received by him at Williamsburg attacking Washington's abilities as Commander in Chief. "I am sorry there should be a man who counts himself my friend who is not yours," Henry had written. Martha agreed that was very handsomely put, and thought it no more than was due. Yes, George had recognized the handwriting on Henry's enclosure—Dr. Rush of Philadelphia, the Surgeon-General of the Middle Department, who had never betrayed animosity face to face.

It was frightening, she said, and infuriating, how the Cabal had thrown its poisoned darts even as far as Virginia—to no avail, he assured her calmly. His last letter to Gates, composed in consultation with Hamilton the day of her arrival at camp, had done the job. Gates had climbed down most abjectly, and asked only that bygones be bygones. A close relationship with him would be impossible henceforth, of course, as it had been with Reed, but some sort of command must be found for him —perhaps on the Hudson; and for Mifflin, who now maintained that he had never harbored anything but the highest regard for the Commander in Chief, but only (splitting a hair) deprecated the General's amiable tendency to listen to bad advice from his subordinates instead of exercising his own excellent judgment. Here George had the effrontery to meet her incredulous gaze without blinking. And Conway? At Albany. Lafayette detested the sight of him, and he couldn't be having a very good time.

The 1776 pattern continued to repeat itself. When Lafayette reached Albany, still reluctant to leave Washington's immediate Family even for an independent command, he had learned that there were several other generals concerned in the victory at Saratoga, just as Lee had not been alone at Charleston when the British fleet was sent limping northward. Benedict Arnold and Benjamin Lincoln had both been wounded in the Saratoga action, and Dan Morgan too had taken part, with his famous Virginia riflemen. It appeared now that Gates had not come under fire at all, on the day that Burgoyne was beaten. Then how, Lafayette inquired with indignant Gallicisms, had Gates come to be acclaimed the victor? No one seemed to know. He said he was. Lafayette was simmering, and desired only to return to Valley Forge.

A month after her arrival, Martha sat down to answer a letter from Mercy Warren at Boston, who being a friend of John Adams in the Congress might conceivably have got some wrong ideas about the situation at Headquarters: "I came to this place some time about the first of February, where I found the General very well," she wrote. "I left my children at our house—Mrs. Custis has lately had a fine girl, which makes the second since she left Cambridge. She is so much confined with her children that she stays altogether with them. . . . The General is encamped on what is called the great valley on the banks of the Schuylkill. Officers and men are chiefly in huts which they say is tolerably comfortable; the army are as healthy as can be expected in general. The General's apartment is very small, he has had a log cabin built to dine in, which has made our quarters much more tolerable than they were at first. It would give me great pleasure to deliver your compliments to Mrs. Gates, but she lives at so great a distance from me that I have not seen her since we parted at New York two years ago. . . . The General joins me in offering our respectful compliments to General Warren and yourself. . . ."

Tolerably comfortable—as healthy as can be expected—no word from the General's loyal, discreet wife to reveal the shocking sights and sounds which assailed her compassionate heart whenever she ventured down the road beyond the nearest line of entrenchments which lay between the Headquarters house and the rest of the camp; the sentries standing with their shoeless, rag-bound feet in their hats to stave off frostbite; the bloody tracks left in the snow around the smoky, comfortless huts; the amputations made necessary by feet which had frozen black; the dying men without even clean straw to lie on; the horses idle and groaning with hunger, while men scantily clothed in pieces of blanket and in remnants of half a dozen garments stitched together to form one, yoked themselves with grape-vine harnesses to rough sledges to draw firewood and whatever provisions could be issued; the unburied carcasses of animals, so difficult to dispose of in the frozen landscape; the pitiful efforts at decency and cleanliness by the inhabitants of the log villages; and the intermittent, tuneless chant of feeble, hopeless men in the last extremity of want: "No meat—no food—no rum—no meat. . . ."

By the third week in February it seemed impossible that the situation could endure. "For some days past there has been little less than a famine in camp," Washington wrote on the 16th. "A part of the army has been a week without any kind of flesh, and the rest three or four days. Naked and starving as they are, we cannot enough admire the incomparable patience and fidelity of the soldiery, that they have not been ere this excited by their sufferings to a general mutiny and dispersion. Strong symptoms, however, of discontent have appeared in particular instances; and nothing but the most active efforts everywhere can long avert so shocking a catastrophe. . . ."

But even the Commander in Chief underestimated the fidelity of his soldiers, and on the 22d they contrived a surprise for his birthday. The cook at Headquarters managed some fowls and some boiled parsnips for dinner, and there was rum and water in which to drink his health, and one of the assistant commissaries sent in a package of tea, at £5 a pound. During dinner Knox's artillery band paraded to Headquarters and played the "Old Continental March," standing in the snow and biting wind— after which they were invited inside and given a present of hard money and a gill each of something warmer, and made their bows to his smiling lady.

Because the Tory population persisted in its preference for the profitable Philadelphia market for its produce, Washington was forced to use his ultimate power of seizing forage, food, and blankets where they could be found, which was accomplished with as little hard feelings as was possible in the circumstances, and matters began slowly to improve. Colonels Bland and Baylor were sent off to Virginia to buy horses to replace some of those which had died of privation. A visiting committee from Congress was convinced on the spot that something must be done about the neglected post of Quartermaster, and they nominated General Greene for the thankless duty.

Only his love for the harassed Commander in Chief induced Nat Greene to quit his place in the Line for the semicivilian kind of drudgery entailed in supplying the army with clothing and provisions. "No one ever heard of a quartermaster in history," he complained in a letter to his brother. But he agreed to accept the post for one year on condition that he might appoint his own subordinates, retain his major-general's rank and pay, and not have to do the accounts. Within a remarkably short time he had established a chain of depots, and cloth, canvas, cattle, and grain began to trickle in. The absent Mifflin, who had been displaced entirely by Greene's appointment, tried to play up an already existing jealousy of the close friendship between Greene and Washington, and was heard to imply that General Greene was glad to be out of the way of bullets—which of course came back to Greene, who used Washington's tactics with Gates, and sent Mifflin a written request for an explanation—whereupon Mifflin denied that he had ever said any such thing, and the matter was allowed to drop. By now even some of his fellow troublemakers had to perceive that Mifflin's record as Quartermaster was a disgraceful one.

Except for Lafayette, who was still at Albany awaiting recall after the collapse of the Canadian venture, and Louis Duportail, the capable, unsociable French engineer who had laid out the encampment at Valley Forge, they had long since had enough of foreigners at Headquarters. When Baron Friedrich Wilhelm Augustin von Steuben, Knight of the Order of Fidelity, former aide-de-camp to Frederick the Great, arrived with recommendations from the American commissioners at Paris and from Congress, he came, like Lafayette, with an adequate amount of rank and pay behind him. Unlike Conway and the rest, he possessed a lovable warmth and modesty behind his rather formal Prussian style exterior. But he had come to teach, with an appointment as Inspector-General which Conway had once demanded for himself.

No one was more aware of the army's need for a competent drillmaster and a book of rules than the Commander in Chief. The sight of the earnest, impressive Baron, wearing the jeweled star of his European Order and handling the musket himself like a sergeant as he tramped tirelessly up and down with his harried companies, was an engaging one. In the beginning he had not a word of English with which to make himself understood by his amused or infuriated pupils. Traveling with him was his very articulate secretary, Pierre Etienne Duponceau, who could translate the Baron's German into French. Assigned to them was the American aide, Benjamin Walker, who could translate Duponceau's French into English. When the Baron swore at the awkward squad, as he constantly did, he called upon them both and upon his God in the frenzied effort to express himself in the right language. Somewhat to their own surprise, they all began to love him.

"We dined twice or thrice a week with General Washington," Duponceau recorded in his journal. "We visited him also in the evening, when Mrs. Washington was at Headquarters. We were in a manner domesticated in the family. As to the situation of our army, suffice it to say that we were in want of provisions, of clothing, of fodder for our horses, in short, of everything. . . . We who lived in good quarters did not feel the miseries of the times so much as the common soldier and the subaltern officers; yet we had more than once to share our rations with the sentry at the door. We put the best face we could upon the matter. Once, with the Baron's permission, his aides invited a number of young officers to dine at our quarters on condition that none should be admitted that had on a whole pair of breeches . . . and in this the guests were very sure not to fail.

"The dinner took place. The guests clubbed their rations, and we feasted sumptuously on tough beefsteak and potatoes, with hickory nuts for our dessert. Instead of wine we had some kind of spirits, with which we made 'salamanders,' that is to say, after filling our glasses we set the liquor on fire and drank it up, flame and all. Such a set of ragged and at the same time merry fellows were never brought together. The Baron loved to speak of that dinner, and of his *sans-culottes,* as he called us.

"In the midst of all our distress there were some bright sides of the picture which Valley Forge exhibited at that time. Mrs. Washington had the courage to follow her husband to that dismal abode, and other ladies also graced the scene. Among them was the lady of General Greene, a handsome, elegant, and accomplished woman. Her dwelling was the resort of foreign officers because she spoke the French language and was well versed in French literature. They often met at each other's quarters, and sometimes at General Washington's, where the evenings were spent over a cup of tea or coffee. There were no levees, or formal soirees, no dancing or playing, or amusement of any kind except singing. Every gentleman or lady who could sing was called upon in turn for a song. . . ."

The Cabal had barely sunk into limbo when an unexpected attack came from a new quarter, with the publication of a collection of personal letters alleged to have been written by Washington to his family and friends in '76, and presumed damaging to him by revealing that he had not been in favor of independence at first, and had privately criticized the very people who turned to him for leadership. Clever and well-timed as the forgeries were, they could do him very little harm, as everyone associated with him was well aware that he had never held radical views, but had come reluctantly with his more conservative colleagues like Peyton Randolph and Mason to the conclusion that separation from the mother country was inevitable.

What hurt and disturbed both Martha and himself was that the spurious letters had been composed in England by someone who had at one time been acquainted with his family and home life, though many small errors did brand them as obvious fabrications. They were believed to be the invention of Peyton Randolph's brother John, Edmund's father, who before he accompanied Dunmore to England in '77 had often been host, guest, and friend to the Washingtons at the Assembly times in Williamsburg during the '60's. Martha wept at such perfidy, until anger came to her rescue—for this latest betrayal touched herself and Mount Vernon as well as the Commander in Chief, and went deeper than any political controversy over his record as a soldier since the war began. She was learning the cost of greatness, and she liked it less and less, after a sheltered lifetime in dignified seclusion.

Lafayette returned to Valley Forge early in April, seeming to bring springtime in his saddlebags. It did not take him long to captivate Martha, though she had never seen anything like him before—tall and slender, with a conqueror's carriage, and a long, aristocratic profile, his hair showing reddish through the powder, speaking remarkably fluent English with a French accent; the cut and materials of his uniform surpassing all the others, the epaulettes more elaborate than Washington's own, and worn with such an air; yet he was unself-conscious and unconceited, lighthearted, and sincerely devoted to his General, able and willing to put his affection and his anxiety to please into words and action. He adorned the rather sober evening entertainments they put together in Martha's little sitting room, where there was no room for dancing, and cards were forbidden (as an example) and refreshments were scarce, so that about all there was left to do was sing songs and tell puzzles and stories. The Marquis had plenty of stories to tell, if only of his recent travels, and sometimes it was as good as a play to hear him.

A less welcome return to the Family was that of Charles Lee, whose exchange Washington had labored to effect, and himself appeared to regard with satisfaction. George rode out with an escort to meet Lee the day he arrived, and Martha presided with unblemished courtesy at a dinner in Lee's honor at Headquarters. She found him quite as impudent as she recalled, still lacking in respect, and still not clean. His undisciplined, short-tempered dogs came with him, and were fed from the table, as was his habit. Captivity with the British had not improved either his manners or his appearance. She fancied that the new men on the Staff were not favorably impressed. But nothing of this showed in her usual curving smile, her cool, kind eyes, her polite response to the conversation. Washington watched her with inward amusement and approval, for he knew very well that his Patsy was anything but pleased.

While Lee's arrival may have caused private misgivings, they could at least agree at Headquarters in the hope that they had seen the last of Conway. After fretting at Albany for a time he sent in his resignation to Congress, expecting to bring them to heel again by threatening to remove his invaluable presence from their councils. To his furious surprise, President Laurens saw to it that the resignation was snapped up without delay, and Conway found himself out of a job. He rushed down to York to explain that he didn't speak English very well, owing to having lived so long in France, and that he must have expressed himself badly and been misunderstood. But nobody was interested any longer. The unmoved, immovable man at Valley Forge had sat it out.

Meanwhile the life of the camp went on around the General's wife, with its customary daily sounds and smells and sights to which she and the others had become almost inured. Steuben's eternal drilling began soon after breakfast, in a rasp of shouted commands and a dogged shuffle and tramp of marching feet, interrupted at intervals by motionless silence beneath a flood of trilingual invective at which no one in the ranks dared to grin. And there were the eternal drums, which like the cricket's song finally staled by custom into oblivion. Because the drums were relied on to give notice in case of a sudden alarm, which might come at any time, an order prevailed against random beating by idle drummer boys. But two authorized practice hours from 5 to 6 A.M. and from 4 to 5 P.M. were added to the regular camp beats which began with the reveille at daybreak and ended with the tattoo at 9 P.M.

As the warmer weather arrived a general housecleaning of the whole encampment was explicitly ordered by the Commander in Chief; bedding was aired, clothing was laundered, the streets between the log huts were tidied, dirty straw and rags and refuse were burnt with a fine, smoky stench which drifted from one end of the Valley to the other, mingling with the older, even less pleasant odors which the fires were designed to eradicate, and causing turned-up noses among the ladies. Fresh boughs and hurdles were placed to screen the necessaries, and at least two windows were required to be let into every hut. Bathing parties, supervised by a sergeant, watch in hand, swarmed into the streams, limited to ten minutes each in the water, as if anyone was hardy enough to last so long. Soap, vinegar, shirts, and even shoes were coming under Greene's competent quartermastering. A run of shining shad up the Schuylkill was chased into nets by sending the cavalry into the water to drive the fish, which provided days of wholesome feasting, and plenty more to be salted down for the future. Fresh vegetables began to appear in the rations, and small garden plots were optimistically laid out by the country lads. Dogwood flowered into a spring fairyland on the hillsides, wild flowers gleamed in the grass, and there was an individual feeling of survival, of something accomplished merely by being still alive, now that the worst was over for another year.

The universal sprucing up came just in time for the mammoth picnic which celebrated the French Alliance on the 6th of May. Most of the Pennsylvania countryside came in to see the troops parade and hear the cannon salutes and the running fire of musketry from right to left and left to right in the *feu de joie,* and to join in the huzzas for the King of France and the American States.

It was Steuben's hour. With his jeweled star flashing on his breast in the sunshine, his hair powdered and dressed Prussian style, he led the inspection of the ranks assembled under arms, and pronounced them ready. Washington and his Staff moved into their appointed position on the slope, the ladies clustered under a marquee of tent cloth, the signal gun boomed, the fifes and drums struck up, and the whole American army, Stirling commanding on the right, Lafayette (wearing a dramatic white scarf) on the left, and DeKalb in the second line, swept forward to perform the drill they had so laboriously learned under Steuben's exasperated but fatherly guidance.

To Martha, who stood watching surrounded by the stout-hearted wives who like herself had weathered the winter with their men, the spectacle was enchanting almost beyond belief. These were the ragged, groaning, cursing human skeletons who not long ago had huddled in their murky huts coughing up their hearts—these washed and mended and self-respecting soldiers, stepping out with their heads up and their accouterment rustless and sparkling. This pulsing, exciting music to which their swinging tread was so expertly timed came from the same instruments which had for weeks past squeaked and clattered in what only seemed like childish noise. Now she saw an army which George could be proud of, and with which he could win the war. She raised one hand to the ache in her throat and glanced toward him—and saw by his rigid face and statuelike stillness in the saddle that he too was gripped by an emotion almost too deep to bear.

But later, when they adjourned to the tables which had been set in a grassy amphitheater in the center of the encampment, for a cold collation and toasts while the band played everything it knew and began all over again, Washington was radiant and merry, and received the congratulations of his many guests with obvious delight. At the end of the meal the Headquarters party rose to go, and the whole company, several hundred strong, came to their feet, clapping and cheering and tossing up their hats, and among the huzzas for the King of France and the Commander in Chief and the Thirteen States, she heard—more than once—some voice which cried, "Long live Lady Washington!" It was a great day, a day to remember—as they were all to do, ruefully, many times over while they awaited the slow fulfillment of its promise.

They hoped too much too fast, of course. From having been so low, they bounced too high too soon, except for a few farsighted sages like President Laurens, who wrote cautiously: "It is my opinion that we are not to roll down a green bank and toy away the ensuing summer. There is blood, much blood, in our prospect, and in my view there will be opportunity and incitement to unsheath your sword. Britain will not be hummed by a stroke of policy; she will be angry, and if she is to fall, her fall will be glorious. We, who know her, ought to be prepared. . . ." France had undertaken to come to America's aid, it was true, and the French navy would be of immediate value against the strangling British fleet. But it would take time for French supplies and reinforcements to arrive. The ragged Continentals had still a long way to go alone, and with all the same old vexations. What would the British do now? At a Council of War on the 8th of May the officers decided to remain at the Valley Forge encampment and await the next British move. There were still too many sick, and too many shortages, to risk any decisive action.

Before long an exhilarating rumor went round that the British were preparing to evacuate Philadelphia. Without a fight? Washington thought it unlikely. But General Howe had been recalled to London to defend his inactivity, and Clinton was now in charge at Philadelphia, uneasy at the prospect of French ships in the Delaware below the city. If he tried to withdraw his forces in order to consolidate at New York it might be possible to catch him on the wrong foot.

Once again Martha watched the ominous conferences and dispatches which always preceded the new campaign. The secretary-aides were swamped with table-work, so that the scratch of pens and the drone of dictation went on till the small hours in the office behind her sitting room, and outside the house there was always the sound of hoofs and spurs as the riding-aides came and went on their endless errands. They were calling in the cavalry commanders; writing out the foot-regiment returns; totting up the tragic demand for more hospital stores—hog-lard and sulphur were available again; attempting to organize the camp women, many of whom were honest and capable, as extra nurses; laying out the marching order for each brigade in the event of the expected sudden move, assembling the wagons, teams, tents, and boats, taking inventory of forage and stores as far away as Albany and Wilmington, reporting on the overhaul of the big guns and the ammunition supply. And always there was the urgent petition for more firelocks, more shirts, more shoes, more blankets, and more horses.

Meanwhile, among the wives the familiar reluctant preparations began also, for it was time to go home again. Kitty Greene had been too long away from her two small children, even for such a lighthearted—some said lightheaded—creature as had married Quaker Nat, and she set off for Rhode Island among the first. There would be another child in the summer. Lucy Knox, having lost her second, had only little Lucy, now nearly three and thriving on Headquarters life. Lucy announced her firm intention of remaining with the army till the British left Philadelphia, and there was only Washington to forbid her, and he only smiled. The camp was much gayer since stout, busybody Lucy had come to the big house by the covered bridge, and her sitting room was large enough to contain the sewing parties where the wives made bandages and shirts and socks, or the evening parties with charades and songs which both husbands and wives enjoyed. The Knoxes always managed somehow to serve refreshments, and both of them were unfailingly jolly and happy in each other's company.

But Philadelphia lay between Martha and Mount Vernon, and as usual George wanted to know that she was safely past it before the trouble began. She said good-by on the 8th of June, a little comforted by the French, a little homesick for the Custis babies, but rent asunder all the same by her growing comprehension of the lonely anxieties George must still endure in the rooms they had shared.

As anticipated, Clinton felt obliged by the French to give up Philadelphia and make a run for New York. Washington lay in wait for him along the road, and there was a battle at Monmouth Courthouse late in June, on a day of paralyzing heat. When George's letters and the gazettes came to Martha at Mount Vernon it seemed to her that she had still not got the whole story, but plainly it was something to do with Charles Lee again, who was understood to have begun a retreat without firing a shot, and whose conduct this time led to his arrest and court-martial. Washington himself had saved the day at Monmouth, the public gossip ran; Washington at a racking gallop on a great white horse, everywhere at once, heartening and rallying the men, riding between them and the British bullets unscathed, agonizing the aides as he had done at Princeton by the reckless way he exposed himself to point-blank fire. But his troops had turned and stood and held the field, thanks partly to the discipline and training of their implacable, affectionate drillmaster, General Steuben. The British left their dead behind, and rolled on toward New York.

Not a word appeared in Washington's letters at that time of the duel fought at Philadelphia between his friend General Cadwallader of the Pennsylvania Line and the still arrogant Conway, but Martha heard about it with a shudder. Cadwallader was not hit, but his ball went through Conway's mouth, inflicting a nearly fatal wound.

In July a French fleet under Admiral D'Estaing raised the most extravagant prospect of cooperation against the British at Newport, and Lafayette, John Laurens, Hamilton, and Greene were all sent off to join Sullivan who was already in Rhode Island. But Sullivan's bad luck held, along with his natural tactlessness and some adverse weather, and the whole thing came to nothing but hard feelings which involved even the amiable Lafayette, with Greene as peacemaker to all. D'Estaing sailed away to his West Indies base, leaving the British just about as he found them.

Washington too remained in a position of status quo at White Plains, from where he had begun the long retreat into Jersey in the dreadful autumn of '76. "It is not a little pleasing . . . to contemplate that after two years of maneuvering and undergoing the strangest vicissitudes that perhaps ever attended anyone since the creation, both armies are brought back to the very point they set out from," he wrote to his old friend Colonel Nelson of Yorktown, who had recently insisted on making him a present of a fine saddle horse from the famous Nelson stables. He went on to point out with some satisfaction that this time it was the British who were using spades and pickaxes for defensive works, as they settled in for another cosy winter in New York.

Martha could read the signs now, and in November, writing from Mount Vernon to her brother Bartholomew in New Kent County about the illness of their mother, she added: "I am very uneasy at this time— I have some reason to expect that I shall make another trip to the north- ward—the pore General is not likely to come to see us from what I can see here—I expect to hear by the next post. If I do I shall write to inform you and my friends. If I am so happy [as] to stay at home, I shall hope to see you and my sisters here as soon as you are at leisure. Please to give little Patty a kiss for me. I have sent her a pair of shoes—there was not a doll to be got in the City of Philadelphia, or I would have sent her one. The shoes are in a bundle for my Mamma. I am very glad to hear that you and your family are well. I cannot tell you more news than I can. I have had no letter since he came from the camp. By some neglect my letters do not come regularly to hand. . . ."

She was disappointed but not surprised when George wrote that he had given up all hope, for the fourth winter, of coming home at Christ- mas time, and that Headquarters would be established at Middlebrook in New Jersey, with the army posted in a wide arc from there to Danbury in Connecticut. The French alliance had worked no overnight miracle. He must prepare during the coming winter for the campaign of 1779. There was of course no question in her mind of remaining at Mount Vernon if he could not join her there.

Early in December she set out again toward Philadelphia, which since the evacuation was said to be as scandalously gay under its American com- mandant, Benedict Arnold, as it had been when the British were in pos- session. When she arrived there on the 17th, she was conducted to the residence of Henry Laurens, who had recently succeeded in turning over his Presidential duties in Congress to John Jay in order to conserve his health.

The Congress had invited General Washington to come to Philadel- phia for a conference during the Christmas holidays, and Colonel John Laurens at Headquarters had persuaded his chief to accept the hospitality of Laurens, Senior, for himself and Martha during their stay in the city. She had to wait for him five days, before he rode in from Middlebrook, accompanied by his aides Laurens, Tilghman, and Hamilton, and Gen- eral Greene. General Stirling had been left in charge at Middlebrook. Charles Lee was in Philadelphia, still snarling at the verdict of the court- martial, which, with Stirling presiding, had imposed on him a year's sus- pension from the army—for disobedience to orders in not attacking the enemy at Monmouth, agreeably to repeated instructions, and for disrespect to the Commander in Chief.

Like Conway before him, Charles Lee could not stop trying to vindicate himself by disparaging General Washington—implying publicly that thanks to Lee's wisdom and valor at Monmouth there had remained little for the Commander in Chief to do but strip the dead—remarking in company that he meant to retire to Virginia and learn to hoe tobacco, which appeared to him to be the best school to form a consummate general. Unpopular as Lee had made himself in Philadelphia, there were still people to snigger at and repeat his satanic jibes and, as in Conway's case, there were other people who longed to silence him forever. Steuben had already sent him a challenge on his own account, but Lee managed to convince him that there was nothing personal to the Baron in his remarks at the court-martial about "distant spectators."

John Laurens and Hamilton arrived in town seething over a published article of Lee's supposedly written to justify his conduct at Monmouth, but which in reality was only a spiteful rehearsal of Washington's past defeats and alleged mistakes. Their General had forbidden Hamilton to reply in the press, but he apparently overlooked the alternative, which Laurens seized by demanding satisfaction from Lee on behalf of his chief. When Lee replied to the challenge with another slurring comment on Washington's need of a champion, he was in for it. Somehow the duel took place before Washington got wind of it, on the 23d of December in a wood outside Philadelphia. Hamilton acted as Laurens' second and it was Lee who fell, his own shot going wild. The wound was not mortal, though blood flowed freely. Like Conway, Lee had to learn at considerable expense to himself that it did not pay to slander the Commander in Chief.

Rumors of the encounter ran ahead of the two aides to the Laurens residence, and Washington's rare anger flared, that any of his own Family should indulge in the irresponsible, forbidden escapade of dueling. Returning home, they entered an atmosphere thick with anxiety and disapproval. Martha had to make sure first of all that they were both whole, and that poor General Lee, reprehensible as he was, would not die of his bloodletting. Then they took their wigging from the General with becoming meekness, and accepted stimulants from Laurens *père,* who had long since had enough of Lee.

It occurred to Martha that their lively Philadelphia Christmas might have been a very different affair at the home of the ex-President of the

Congress, if the outcome of John Laurens' reckless gesture had been fatal —on either side. By good fortune, the opposition had been set down again —including Sam Adams, Dr. Rush, Mifflin, and company. Joseph Reed was now President of the Pennsylvania Council, which was equivalent to being Governor, and there was great politeness exercised all round; Reed's unlucky '76 letter was still in Charles Lee's possession. General Arnold as Commandant of the city was popular with all the wrong people, criticized by the rest of his extravagant style of living, his ostentatious coach and horses, his servants in livery, his banquets and drinking parties, his apparent Loyalist bias, and his conquests among the ladies—in particular his attention to the pretty Tory Peggy Shippen, who had been such a belle among the English officers, and whose name had been openly linked with that of the British Major André. Not even Reed could quite stomach Arnold. Where did he get the money? But Washington knew him for a fine fighting man when his blood was up, and had given him the Philadelphia appointment because his honorable Saratoga wound kept him still a cripple, unable to stand alone, and useless in the field.

The Commander in Chief was formally honored by a reception on the floor of the Congress on the 24th, and later he entertained them all at dinner at the City Tavern. He had prepared a paper for their consideration, on the army's immediate necessities and prospects, and he took it up with them point by point—and came away profoundly disturbed by the party factions and personal enmities he discerned among them. Most of the current members were strangers to him. His old colleagues from '74 and '75 were scattered by private emergency, state elections, and precarious health, so that Congress had become a commonplace body of politicians, where graft and high living were nullifying the effort of the few noble exceptions like Henry Laurens and John Jay and the two Morrises, Robert and Gouverneur, who were in no way related to each other. With a new campaign ahead of him, a depreciated currency, and divided councils, Washington felt only dismay and discouragement amid the elaborate festivities organized in his honor.

Tench Tilghman summed it up in a letter to Colonel MacHenry of Maryland, one of the bachelor officers who had joined the Staff at Valley Forge and was soon absorbed into the inner circle, and who had been left behind at the new Headquarters. "I suppose you think we must be by this time so wedded to sweet Philadelphia that it will break our hearts to leave it," Tilghman wrote his fellow-aide. "Far from it, I assure you, my friend, I can speak for myself when I say that we anxiously wait for the moment that gives us liberty to return to humble Middlebrook. Philadelphia may answer very well for a man with his pockets well lined, whose pursuit is idleness and dissipation. But to us, it is intolerable. A morning visit, a dinner at 5 o'clock, tea at 8 or 9, supper, up all night, is the round, *die in diem.* Does not the Republic go on charmingly? By the body of my father, as honest Sancho used to swear, we have advanced as far in luxury in the 3d year of our independency as the old musty Republics of Greece and Rome did in twice as many hundred. . . ."

Nevertheless, it was the Washingtons' first social fling together since the carefree family jaunts to Alexandria and Annapolis had come to an end four years ago, and Martha, with her hair dressed and powdered and a new gown to wear, took a secret satisfaction in the deference paid the Commander in Chief and the honors at his disposal. She enjoyed having time to visit the Biddles again, the Morgans, and the Powells (Samuel Powell had been the mayor in '75, and his wife was one of the beautiful Willing girls) and the Shippens—the *right* Shippens, cousins to the notorious Peggy—and the Robert Morrises. She also made the acquaintance of M. Gérard, the first French Minister Plenipotentiary to the United States, who had arrived in D'Estaing's flagship last summer.

But by the time they escaped the Philadelphia fleshpots early in February Martha was not unwilling to resume the crowded, noisy, informal, strenuous life at Headquarters. Greene as Quartermaster had chosen the Washingtons' house this time, and George had seen and approved it before he came to Philadelphia. Built by a man named Wallace, it was still so new that they had left carpenters at work, and the General's wife was anyway assured of more space and comfort than she had had last winter. They even promised her a little sitting room entirely her own, with blue and white tiles let into the chimneypiece, and she could do exactly as she liked with it, as there was another reception room across the hall where all the official visitors could come and go without intruding on her.

The white clapboard house at Middlebrook, with its green shutters and columned porch, was not imposing from the outside, but it was surprisingly roomy when you entered the wide central hall which had a door at each end and the stairs built in. There were three good rooms downstairs, besides the little back parlor which was to be hers. Since the workmen were still about, and were anxious to oblige, she had them build cupboards with glass doors either side of the fireplace, where she could keep some china for serving tea, some simple refreshments, and her books and needlework and mending basket. The General's office was the other side of the wall, its fireplace sharing the same chimney with hers, and across from him was the dining room with an ample kitchen beyond, both connecting with the reception room opposite her parlor. The wide upper hall, well lighted with a window at each end, made another sitting room for the guests and aides, and there were four bedrooms. One of these on the front, twin to that used by the Washingtons, was still called Lafayette's, because it had been set aside for him before he departed for France on a mission to speed up the promised aid to America. They all missed his ebullient presence, and looked forward to his return. Meanwhile his quarters were occupied by several of the aides, who had not seen such accommodations since the war began, and frequently had to surrender them to guests of importance.

Kitty Greene was installed with all three babies in a house built of Holland brick on the Raritan shore. Last summer's infant newcomer was named Cornelia, after one of her Jersey friends. The Knoxes too had a recent baby, another girl, Julia, and were living at Pluckemin where the Artillery Park was. General Wayne lodged nearby, as did Sullivan, both men philosophically wifeless as usual, and Baron Steuben, equally footloose and almost as popular with the local ladies. The Stirlings' Baskingridge home again was not too far away for the General to live there *en famille,* which was easier on his rheumatism. A group of bachelor officers, including Moylan and Harry Lee, were so fortunate as to be quartered in the Van Horne house, whose wide roof also sheltered five accomplished Van Horne daughters. There were many of the same neighbors, like the Livingstons, who had come to Morristown in '77. After Valley Forge, Middlebrook was a paradise.

In the long evenings there, the Washingtons at last found time to talk at their leisure, and Martha could tell him the news which had had to wait at Philadelphia. The son born to Jane and William Augustine Washington at Wakefield had been named for his grandfather, who was always called Austin; Jacky had completed the purchase of the Abingdon estate a few miles from Alexandria, as a home for his growing family—another child was expected in March—preferring the Potomac neighborhood near his mother and Nelly's to New Kent County and Williamsburg where most of his Custis inheritance lay. George had been giving long-distance advice on the transaction and was gratified to hear that Jacky was settling down to his responsibilities and a happy domestic life. Poor Nancy's daughter, Fanny Bassett, now twelve, was a charming girl, and a great comfort to her father, who apparently had no intention of marrying

again. Bartholomew's Patty was a true Dandridge, and very like her Aunt
Martha, so they said, and the boy was a fine lad. And then, because
they were all other people's children, after all, she hurried on about the
depreciation in money, on account of which Lund found himself rather
hard up at Mount Vernon, and should be allowed some kind of raise.
Even old Bishop was complaining that he could not make ends meet on
his present allowance, and there were only himself and his wife and one
daughter—and the liquor.

Martha in her turn heard about George Baylor, caught off guard in
camp with his cavalry at Tappan last September, and half his men mas-
sacred by British bayonets while unarmed and crying quarter. Baylor had
got a wound through the lung, and was left for dead at Orange, on parole,
but it looked now as though he might recover, even if he never led a
troop again. A great pity if the thing was mortal, as he had married
Lucy Page only last summer when he was in Virginia buying horses for
the army. George's distant kinsman, William Washington of Stafford
County, had been given command of the remnants of Baylor's corps,
who had lost most of their mounts in the Tappan affair. Martha spent
some time working out again William's complicated relationship to
George—their grandfathers, or was it great-grandfathers, had been
brothers.

The weather continued mild, and some well-made uniforms were arriving in the French ships—the French shoes were flimsy. The men's huts
were better than those at Valley Forge, and the British remained inactive
around New York. But there was still and always the problem of food,
because money wouldn't buy enough any more, even when it was there
to be bought, and Congress seemed unable to cope with the financial
situation. George remained depressed by what he had seen of the frivolous, spendthrift atmosphere of Philadelphia. Where were all the able
and patriotic men who belonged in Congress, he wondered—in their
home legislatures, on their home acres, practicing law, raising families.
He composed long, careful, urgent letters to Benjamin Harrison and
George Mason and the Carters in his own hand, late at night, after the
day's work was done, while Martha sat nearby with her knitting, silent
and companionable, sharing the low-burning candles—letters which insisted that the States must send better delegates to Congress, that people
at home must not think that because the French had signed a treaty of
alliance the war was already won.

And what about the French? A British detachment had gone down the coast from New York and taken Savannah and was now in a position to come at Charleston from behind. General Lincoln, still lame from his Saratoga wound which kept reopening, had gone after them overland, but he could not hold them off with the small force which could be spared to him. The South must raise its own army for its own defense. George had had to let young Laurens go—the boy wanted to defend his native Charleston single-handed—and it left a vacancy in the Family. Where was the French fleet? Could D'Estaing be persuaded to come back and try again, this time at Savannah? It was one more question for the Commander in Chief to answer, one more burden on his mind, on top of the do-nothing sort of plan which was all the Congress had allowed him for the summer of '79. There was no money to do anything with. The soldiers had not been paid for months, and their families at home were suffering. The soldiers were not even properly fed.

Martha had an anxiety of her own. "My dear children," she wrote, at the end of her patience, "I hear from you so seldom that I don't know where you are or whether you intend to come to Alexandria to live this spring or when. The last letter from Nelly she says both the children have been very ill; they were, she hoped, getting better. If you don't write to me I will not write to you again, or till I get a letter from you. Let me know how all friends below are; they have forgot to write to me, I believe. . . . Give the dear little girls a kiss for me, and tell Bett I have got a pretty new doll for her, but don't know how to send it to her. The General joins me in love to you both and begs to be remembered to all our friends that inquire after us. . . ."

The Middlebrook camp in its happy reunion of old neighbors started a subscription dance assembly, to which Washington contributed, and seized upon every excuse for a party. The first anniversary of the French Alliance was celebrated by the Knoxes with a ball at Pluckemin which the whole countryside attended, taking over the Academy building and riding-school where Knox taught military science. "We had on the 18th a most genteel entertainment given by self and officers," he wrote his brother with visible satisfaction. "Everybody allowed it to be the first of the kind ever exhibited in this State at least. We had above seventy ladies, all of the first *ton* in the State, and between three and four hundred gentlemen. We danced all night—an elegant room. . . ." On this evening Washington unbent, as he sometimes did most surprisingly, and opened the ball with Lucy Knox, who in spite of her increasing girth was a graceful and tireless dancer. General Greene's gay Kitty was not to be outdone as a hostess. A short time later the Greenes sent out invitations to a dance at the brick house on the Raritan, where if the drawing room was cleared of furniture, six couples could take the floor in a minuet, and more for the country dances.

No one stepped a minuet with more grace and finish than his Excellency, and Kitty, a little heady with excitement, slim and well again after the birth of Cornelia, declared recklessly that she could dance forever without once sitting down. General Washington ventured a conservative opinion that forever was a long time, and she flung out a dare. She would dance as long as he could, without sitting down, she said. Smiling, he made her a bow, and caught the fiddler's eye, and led her out again. At his cordial gesture, other couples fell in behind them, laughing, vowing to outlast them. Greene, who was always hampered by his stiff knee and asthma, sat down beside Martha, who very seldom danced at all, and took out his watch. Someone laid a jesting wager. It was all in the family, and his Excellency had been heard to complain of too little exercise. He was not even winded when Kitty gave in, a good two hours later, flushed and breathless, with a stitch in her side. Another camp legend had been born.

It was Kitty who laughed like a clown when she learned that Martha had named a handsome cat with a ringed tail Hamilton, having adopted it as a pet. Martha asked her what was so funny, and Kitty said it was a tom, and a great fellow with the lady cats of the neighborhood. No doubt it was, Martha agreed, and did not change its name. After all, it had followed Hamilton in at an open door the first time she saw it, and so christened itself. The presumably involuntary joke—but you could never be sure with Madam Washington—circulated among the knowing aides. George gave her one of his long, amused looks, and made no comment. Spoilt, popular "Hammy" ignored the cat, with his customary self-possession.

Spring came early to Middlebrook, after an open winter, and the fruit blossom had never been lovelier. In May the whole camp turned out for a military review to honor the visit of the French Minister, M. Gérard, who was accompanied by the mysterious Spanish grandee from Cuba, Miralles. It was Steuben's day again. A stage was erected with seats for the ladies, and Major Harry Lee's Light Horse, clothed in smart short-coated green uniforms, made a sensational display in the maneuvers. The diplomatic guests were suitably impressed, and sent back gifts of wine, chocolate, guava jelly, and some crystal flasks, to the General's lady.

By the beginning of June there was ominous activity among the British on the Hudson, and the wives were advised to pack. As the army began its march to defend the Highlands, Martha once more took the road which ran through Philadelphia to Mount Vernon. Awaiting her at the end of the journey was Nelly's third daughter, named for her mother, the first Custis baby to be born in the new home at Abingdon. "Mrs. Washington, according to custom, marched home when the campaign was about to open," Washington wrote to an old friend in Virginia.

Kitty Greene took the children back to Rhode Island, having confided to Martha in tears that another baby was due in time to spoil her return to Headquarters next Christmas—unless, she added defiantly, she brought it along and had it there. Martha shook her head, but sympathized, and warned that they might not be so comfortably situated next winter. Lucy Knox lingered on in the Pluckemin house, where in midsummer baby Julia died of a teething complaint, and was buried in the Dutch churchyard. When she finally set out for Boston, Lucy had hopes that Julia would be replaced, perhaps with the much desired boy, in the spring.

Washington spent most of the summer near the Hudson, often at West Point, watching the British at New York, waiting for news from the South, hoping the French would hurry their reinforcements and supplies, once Lafayette had had time to present his case at Paris. There was almost no hard money, and rations were dull and scant. Time dragged, both at Headquarters minus its women and lacking Lafayette's high spirits, and at Mount Vernon where the continued absence of its master robbed all accomplishment of zest.

When the news did come from Savannah, in November, it was about as bad as possible. A joint attack by D'Estaing and Lincoln had failed. D'Estaing had returned to his ship with a wound, and sailed away again to his West Indies base. Gallant, picturesque Pulaski was killed in the action.

John Laurens, having rushed down to join the fight for the South on a sort of leave from Headquarters, rode all the way back to plead for reinforcements for Lincoln, who had fallen back to Charleston, and to urge Washington to come down himself and turn the British out. It wasn't feasible. Washington sent his cousin William with the remnants of Baylor's cavalry, and detached two Virginia regiments, which were all he could spare.

As the autumn of '79 drew near, it was evident that the British had wasted the campaigning weather around New York, nobody had won the

war, and Washington was still in the field, unbeaten. He had refused to
take the bait of little nuisance raids in Connecticut and Jersey, and thus
lay himself open to the consequences of an unequal show of force. Clinton, on the other hand, had not himself been strengthened for any decisive move. In the American army clothes and shoes and blankets were
worn out or nonexistent as usual, and the Quartermaster Department
was still hopelessly snarled in Congressional red tape in spite of Greene's
energetic effort, so that he even threatened to resign. Ammunition was
so short that they had given up firing the morning and evening gun. The
desperate list of necessities drawn up at Headquarters ran from traveling
forges to sealing wax, from horseshoes to ink powder.

When Martha at Mount Vernon began her preparations for the annual
journey to join the Family, it was still not decided where the Commander
in Chief would spend the winter. In order that she might travel part of
the way before the roads got bad, Washington requested Deputy Quartermaster Mitchell and his wife at Philadelphia to find lodgings for her there
until she could be sent for. He knew that she preferred living in hired
rooms to being someone's guest, and he discouraged with implacable
courtesy several well-meant invitations, so that when she arrived at Philadelphia in a snowstorm she was conducted by the Mitchells to the Pem-
berton house, where they had rented for her use a handsome front parlor,
a bedchamber, her own kitchen, and several rooms for servants. Here she
was caught by another heavy snow, and although Washington was now
established for a second winter at Morristown, she could not get to him
in time for Christmas.

Thanks to his foresight and to the Mitchells' thoughtful provision, she
was able to entertain her friends when she wanted company, for she
found everything laid in for her use—wood, candles, even tea and sugar.
But it was an odd, between-worlds experience at Christmas time, away
from everyone she belonged to, however hard the sympathetic Philadelphians tried to make her feel at home.

They were not going to be so lucky as to have another mild winter,
and she arrived at Morristown at the end of the year in a blizzard which
would have done credit to Valley Forge. Moreover, George had just received the discouraging report that Clinton had sailed from New York
with a large force—presumably to operate northward from captive Savannah against Lincoln at Charleston.

Washington had left his former Morristown lodgings at the tavern to
his officers, and moved into a large white mansion at the edge of town

owned by the widow of Jacob Ford, who had died on duty with the militia in '77. Mrs. Ford offered the house to him, and would accept no payment for its use. She had five children, the eldest boy barely of an age to carry a musket in the militia. Except for the dining room and a smaller chamber behind it on the right of the entrance and next to the kitchen, which she retained for her own use, Washington's Family had the run of the house. This gave him a handsome parlor and a small office behind the stairs, which were cunningly constructed so as not to intrude on the wide entrance hall—a reception room in itself, with an outer door at either end. Upstairs, four large bedrooms were at his disposal, and quarters for servants over the kitchen. It was much the best house they had had since Cambridge, but with a larger staff he was still obliged to build additional space. Log rooms were constructed at either end for office work and dining.

Again Martha was shocked by how thin and worn everyone looked to her unaccustomed eyes, and again she watched anxiously for the gradual relaxation of strain which it seemed to her always came about after they settled into the winter routine—and wondered again if it was only that she got used to the way they looked when she had been with them awhile.

The food situation was just as bad as ever; paper money would not buy its weight of anything, and they had reached the disagreeable necessity of impressment for supplies. Just as she had arrived at Valley Forge at the time of greatest distress, so at Morristown a desperate situation existed in January, 1780, with violent snowstorms blocking the transport of what food and forage could be obtained.

Lucy Knox was detained at home by the prospect of a child in the spring, but Kitty Greene had made a reckless journey to reach the camp in time for the birth of her fourth, leaving the others behind again in the care of relatives. It was a foolhardy thing for her to have done, but Kitty was never a prudent creature. Little Nat was born at Morristown during a blizzard at the end of January, and the whole army partook of his father's pride when the ordeal was safely over. Pathetic homemade gifts, lovingly contrived by the numb fingers of shivering men who were faint with hunger were brought by the dozens to the Greenes' door for the baby. Kitty cried over them, and cried again because there was nothing to give in return but gratitude and compassion.

The Ford house stood isolated and at a distance from the main camp, which lay on the other side of the town, and the British outposts were uncomfortably near, so Washington's Lifeguard occupied fifty log huts in the meadow just across the road. A system of beacons and signal guns was arranged which at the first boom brought the Lifeguard inside to barricade the doors and take posts at the open windows with their muskets until the regular brigades could form on their parades and march up the road to their alarm posts. When the signal went at night, as it usually did, the bedrooms were not exempt, and Martha and Mrs. Ford more than once held as it were front line positions behind the curtains of their respective beds with the covers pulled high, as much against the icy blasts from outside as for modesty's sake. At such times the Commander in Chief always made the rounds, candle in hand, to reassure the ladies.

Colonel Moylan had married one of the Van Horne sisters at Middlebrook, and now everyone was watching with undisguised interest and astonishment the spectacle of Hamilton falling in love. Betsy Schuyler was not the prettiest girl in the world, though Hamilton had good looks enough for two. But her father had the finest house in Albany, and her disposition was soft and tactful and affectionate. "Hamilton is a gone man," his friend Tilghman wrote with amusement, for their self-sufficient Hammy had hitherto been remarkably elusive, and was so ambitious that it was often quite plain that the position of secretary-aide to General Washington was something less than he felt himself capable of.

General Schuyler had retired from the army in poor health to become a member of the Congress, and he brought his family with him to Philadelphia. His sister was the wife of Dr. Cochran, Surgeon General to the army, who had a house at the Morristown camp, and Betsy came to make her aunt a visit. In spite of the snow which went into four-foot drifts, and the murderous cold, the young people of the neighborhood, which was full of Hamilton's old friends, contrived considerable gaiety —sleigh-rides between the country homes of the Stirlings, Boudinots, and Livingstons; subscription dances in the commissary storehouse (which was never overcrowded with supplies); and musical evenings in the parlor at Headquarters and the lodgings of the officers. When Betsy's parents came down from Philadelphia it could be seen that there would be no objection to Colonel Hamilton as a son-in-law, even after an interview between him and General Schuyler in which he manfully revealed his illegitimate birth in the Islands and his lack of personal funds or prospects beyond the army service which now engaged him.

The winter got worse as it went on, but Martha refused to fall back on invitations from Philadelphia to take a few weeks' respite there as someone's honored guest. George could not leave his men, and she would not leave George. Meanwhile the distasteful business of Arnold's court-martial, on charges arising out of his unwise administration of Philadelphia after the British left it, finally ended in a half-acquittal with a recommendation for a public reprimand in General Orders by the Commander in Chief, which Washington managed as tactfully as possible, aware nevertheless that it left Arnold bitterly resentful and without a command. He had married frivolous Peggy Shippen the year before, defiant of his debts and his unpopularity, and a child was due in the spring.

When the snow at Morristown finally began to melt, there was bottomless mud, which hampered the feeble horses hitched to loaded wagons just as cruelly. Forage was always a pitiful problem, as farmers refused to go on boarding horses indefinitely without being paid, nor to sell forage on credit so they could be fed at the camp—yet Congress itself had neither specie nor credit, and paper money in ratio to sterling was sixty to one. The army lived precariously on what the commissaries could rake in from day to day.

May brought a letter from Lafayette, who had arrived at Boston from France in an express frigate by the King's favor, and was on his way back to Headquarters. They had begun to wonder if he might not forsake them entirely, and Martha was thankful that this time George's trust and affection were being justified, and the lad they all loved like a son and a brother would soon enliven the camp again with his gay presence. George brought the letter to her, almost weeping with delight. "Here I am, my dear General," it began characteristically, without the formality of an address, "and in the midst of the joy I feel in finding myself again one of your loving soldiers, I take but the time to tell you . . . that I have affairs of the utmost importance, which I should at first communicate to you alone. . . ."

Hope, which by his own admission had almost deserted Washington, rose again to meet Lafayette, who had been away nearly fifteen months. He had not failed them. And he brought good news, or he would not have written like that.

When the Marquis arrived at Morristown he was in the grip of a bad cold, which allowed Martha to confine him to the guest room across the hall and to make a motherly fuss before he was pronounced well enough to proceed to Philadelphia and report to Congress that six ships of the Line and six thousand trained French troops under General Rochambeau might be expected to land at Rhode Island early in June. In the midst of their rejoicing at Headquarters, the specter rose in Washington's mind: how to subsist six thousand guest soldiers, no doubt accustomed to the best, when his own men and horses were starving? Lafayette undertook that too, and rode off to Philadelphia with the greatest confidence to confer with the French Minister there, and to tackle Congress and the Commissary Department single-handed. He left behind him at Headquarters a certain flatness and reminiscent smiles. His new son, who had been born while he was still in France, had been christened George Washington Lafayette.

But even the distressing facts which Washington was compelled to exchange for Lafayette's encouraging achievements abroad, were easier to bear now that he was back. Word had come up overland, six weeks in transit, that General Lincoln was besieged in Charleston, and the French could not arrive in time to remedy that. DeKalb was dispatched southward with some Maryland and Delaware troops, accompanied by Lee's Legion. They were too late. On the 31st of May, just as a near-mutiny in the Connecticut Line, where the men had been ten days without meat, had been effectively dealt with by the regimental officers—themselves on a self-imposed "felon's diet" of bread and water—a messenger arrived at Headquarters with a copy of a New York *Gazette* which carried a report that Lincoln's Charleston garrison had surrendered with all its arms and equipment to Clinton and Cornwallis.

At first the stricken Family maintained that such a thing was not possible, it was a damned Tory lie. But Martha saw them watching the impassive face of the Commander in Chief like frightened children waiting for a clue from the grownups. George was magnificent. He never, so the Family told each other repeatedly in the days that followed, turned a hair. In fact, it was almost as though he took a grim satisfaction in the completeness of the Carolina disaster. Perhaps, he said, nothing less would have roused the country from its fatal dream of peace by some miracle of the French alliance. If so shattering a blow only shocked Congress out of its chronic state of wrangling muddle, he considered that it might yet prove to be a blessing. As for Lincoln—they would soon get him back by exchange, and some of his officers with him.

But later that night, in the sanctuary of the bedroom, he sat for a long time silent, his head in his hands. And when she ventured to go and lay her arms around his bent shoulders he leaned against her gratefully, and she held him, wordless but strong, for this was her own war, against the loneliness of his private courage and despair.

Congress appointed Gates, of all people, to the Southern command in place of Lincoln, who would be released on parole until exchanged. They were so well aware, at Philadelphia, that Gates would never have been the choice of the Commander in Chief for so important a post, that they did not even consult Washington before notifying Gates, but he made no protest then or later, and the further Gates was from Head-quarters, the easier life there would be. Gates set out at once from his Virginia estate where he had spent a comfortable winter on leave from his Hudson River command, with orders to overtake (and outrank) De-Kalb and Harry Lee, who were already well on the way to the Carolinas.

Almost immediately there was a stir at New York. British transports were returning from Charleston with a force of veterans under Clinton, who had left Cornwallis in Carolina to hold the South and would now presumably himself attack the fortifications at West Point, or make another move on Philadelphia. Skirmishing broke out along the Jersey shore, and young Jacob Ford was brought home with a wound, which fortunately would not kill him. Martha's sympathy overflowed to the kind, generous woman who had given them her house for the winter, and she took part in the nursing and coddling which encouraged the lad to recover. Then the army was under orders from the Commander in Chief to make ready to march on short notice, and the wives began to pack.

The end of June brought Martha home to Mount Vernon for another anxious summer of waiting. If the Carolinas were overrun, Virginia would be next, as Cornwallis rolled north to meet Clinton marching south. "When yours and my dear Fanny's letters came to my hands I was in expectation of leaving camp every week," she wrote to her brother-in-law Burwell Bassett from Mount Vernon in July. "I left the General about the middle of June. The last I heard from him he was going up to the North River. I got home on Friday, and find myself so much fatigued with my ride that I shall not be able to come down to see you this summer and I must request you to bring Fanny up, as soon as you can. I suffered so much last winter by going late that I have determined to go early in the fall before the frost sets in. If Fanny does not come soon she will have but a short time to stay with me. We were sorry that we did not see you at camp. There was not much pleasure there, the distress of the army and other difficulties, though I did not know the cause. The pore General was so unhappy that it distressed me exceedingly. I shall hope to see you soon after the Assembly rises, with Fanny.

Please to give my love to the boys, who I should be very glad to see with you. . . ."

Even to the man who had been her sister Nancy's husband, she could be discreetly vague about the difficulties at Headquarters, though everyone suspected that she knew a great deal more than she admitted. It was her feminine privilege not to understand, to profess bewilderment at army affairs which were beyond the province of wives. Her loyalty and infinite prudence schooled her never to repeat or to speculate on what she overheard or apprehended while in the household of the Commander in Chief, and interested friends found it useless to quiz her on her return to Virginia. She always said she did not know, that nobody told her anything. Aware that she had George's utmost confidence, and must know better than anyone in the world what his thoughts were, whether he told her or not, her baffled visitors could only admire her willingness to appear stupid rather than betray his secrets.

Reverberations of events from both directions rocked Mount Vernon during the black months which ensued, during the summer of 1780. The French did arrive, on the 14th of July, at Newport—disciplined, spectacular troops in immaculate white uniforms like toy soldiers out of a box, who were reported not even to touch the fruit which grew on the trees in the grounds of their encampments. The French were able to buy their own provisions with hard money, which ironically shortened the supply for the ill-fed, penniless army they had come to assist.

In August came the shattering report of Gates's defeat by Cornwallis at Camden in South Carolina—defeat which became a rout in which he personally led the way on a fleet horse in a headlong flight of a hundred and eighty miles to Hillsborough. Mount Vernon heard about it before the express reached Washington in New Jersey, and a gasp went through the River plantations. This was worse than Dunmore. With Charleston occupied by the British, Gates had lost another whole army which had been sent to hold the door to Virginia, and what was to stop Cornwallis now?

Martha's anguished sympathy for George, outweighing as always her own anxieties, followed the awful tidings to the Jersey Headquarters. Not even his patient optimism in the face of repeated disappointments could find an arid moral advantage in this latest disaster to American hopes. What would George do now, she wondered helplessly. Whom could he send, and where would he find a third army? Would he come himself now, to defend the South? In spite of herself, there was a guilty lift of the heart. If he came South the route would surely bring him through Mount Vernon. If only for a day—a few hours—he would be at home again.

But instead he rode in the opposite direction to confer with the French general Rochambeau, who rode down from Newport to meet him halfway at Hartford. He was at a dreadful disadvantage now, because of Gates. The French would think very little of his soldiers after Camden. His soldiers did well enough if they were properly led, but who would tell Rochambeau that, Martha wondered. Lafayette, who went to Hartford with him, would probably speak up, even out of turn. Nothing intimidated the Marquis.

On the way back to his Headquarters from what was a rather fruitless interview (for the French were reluctant to move at all before their second division arrived from overseas) Washington encountered the ultimate treachery at West Point. He had given Benedict Arnold the inactive command there, to recover from his Saratoga wound and live down his Philadelphia record, only to be repaid by Arnold's fantastic design to surrender to the British the West Point fortifications, and possibly even the person of the Commander in Chief as well. The conspiracy had been discovered only just in time, and by what a narrow margin Martha dared not contemplate, for George's capture and trial for treason was her most persistent nightmare. The possibility of his being taken prisoner was perpetual, but surely, as he had so often observed before now, Providence had once more taken a hand to preserve him. Arnold got away and joined the British army. Arnold was the traitor, but there was only young Major André, his unfortunate British go-between, to hang.

Perhaps because of the fright they had all got about West Point, Washington chose to cover that vital spot with his own army during the coming winter. Now that the very worst had happened in the South, a somewhat shaken and chastened Congress left the next nomination for that command to Washington, and without hesitation he named General Greene for the almost impossible task of gathering up the remnants of Gates's beaten army, which had straggled after him to Hillsborough, and with the help of Steuben and Harry Lee—DeKalb was killed leading his troops at Camden—to make another attempt to entertain Cornwallis in the Carolinas. The decision was Martha's private disappointment. Instead of enjoying even a brief reunion at home, she must set out again for another Northern winter within sound of the drums.

CHAPTER SEVEN

The Turning Tide

1780–1783

SHE ARRIVED AT NEW WINDSOR HEADQUARTERS on the Hudson before Christmas, to find the Family inhabiting a small stone-built house overlooking the River. It was a superb setting, facing the wooded snow-clad hills of the eastern shore, but the house was modest and inconvenient, and they all spoke wistfully of Morristown and Mrs. Ford's hospitality. By the usual standards, George was almost alone, as the steadfast Tilghman was the only regular aide left on duty at the end of the year.

Hamilton was at Albany getting married to Betsy Schuyler, and Colonel MacHenry had gone along to see the wedding. The death of Colonel Harrison's father had called him home to Virginia to untangle his family affairs, and Colonel Meade, whose wife had died during the first year of the war, was also on leave, and courting, so the story went, the widow of William Randolph of Chatsworth. Lafayette and John Laurens were at Philadelphia, trying to improve the situation with regard to the belated French supplies and reinforcements. Since Greene was in the South, Kitty had not come to camp. Washington forwarded their letters by the Head-quarters riders, and usually added a few lines of his own. "Mrs. Washington, who has just arrived at these my quarters joins me in most cordial wishes for your every felicity," he wrote to Kitty in December, "and regrets the want of your company. Remember me to my namesake. Nat, I suppose, can handle a musket. With every sentiment, etc. . . . ." It was

the kind of little jest which often delighted his more intimate friends—
Nat was the Morristown baby, born the previous January.

Lucy Knox was installed at a comfortable stone house between Headquarters and Newburgh, with little Lucy and six-months-old Henry, Jr.
It was much handsomer than the Washington Headquarters, but stood
too isolated inland to be considered safe for the Commander in Chief,
who needed easy access to the river landing. Again the choice of Martha's
dwelling place had been subject to strategic necessities.

Nevertheless they had the best Christmas in years, including three real
turkeys for dinner, at which there were, for once, both beef and mutton
as well, plenty of pudding, apples, nuts, cider and, during the evening
while the band played, spiced wine.

It was obvious to Martha that despite his touching pleasure in her
company, and his willing response to the holiday cheer, George's spirits
were low. The meeting with Rochambeau at Hartford had established
between two great gentlemen a remarkable understanding of each other's
desires and difficulties, but was otherwise unproductive. Martha wanted
to know more about the French, and he told her how Rochambeau had
been present as a young cornet at the siege of Maestricht before he himself had ridden out with Braddock. She could see that his almost boyish
admiration for any veteran of the European campaigns had been freely
bestowed on the French general, although Rochambeau had still to live
down D'Estaing's double failure, while Washington on his part had to
make up for Gates at Camden. With Lafayette and Hamilton to interpret,
while Rochambeau had a little English at his command, the two generals
had parted friends, in spite of Washington's disappointment at the inadequate size of the French force—not half what had been promised—
and Rochambeau's equal dismay at the condition of the American army
which he was required to support.

When she asked what Rochambeau himself was like, George hesitated
—not like Lafayette, of course, no one was—he would be called a handsome man, certainly, and was superbly uniformed. He was as much
diplomat as soldier, with the manners of a courtier. To his troops he was
severe, a martinet—American soldiers would never stand for it. He suffered
bouts of rheumatism, and sudden fits of temper called *bourrasques,*
which blew over. He found himself in an irksome position, subordinated
by his French orders to an unknown American Commander in Chief,
and rank for rank his soldiers were to be considered junior to the
Continentals. His son was the Adjutant-General, and was being sent

back to France with memorized dispatches for the King—a fine young man, wearing the splendid white and green kit of the Saintonge regiment. There was an aide called de Chastellux, who spoke English and was exceedingly popular everywhere—he was keeping a journal of his experiences in America and intended to publish it as a book. They had invited de Chastellux to come to New Windsor as a guest, so no doubt she would soon meet him herself. He was not, of course, Lafayette—who was?—but he was an Academician, and had attended all the Paris *salons*. He wanted to travel in America, see all the battlefields and the fine houses—he wanted to see Mount Vernon. And there was Lafayette's brother-in-law, de Noailles, who was said to be in love with Marie Antoinette—in this he was not alone, for a handsome Swede named Fersen, also on Rochambeau's staff, had been sent out of France on account of his known attachment to the Queen—

George paused inquiringly, for she was watching him with an idle needle and an expression of surprise—she had thought he went to Hartford to talk about the war. The aides, he explained, always chattered, and knew everything. The war was dull, he had nothing new to tell her about that.

The French went on sitting at Newport awaiting their second division and word from their fleet, without which they were disinclined to commit themselves to a campaign. The promised reorganization of the American army by Congress made no visible progress—Pickering was Quartermaster since Greene went South—and the Continentals were facing another hand-to-mouth winter of near starvation and frostbite. When at the turn of the year a part of the Pennsylvania Line stationed near Morristown under General Wayne mutinied, Martha felt sure that now at last things had come to the long-dreaded breaking point. Wayne acted with promptness and severity to put down the disorder, but before January was out the same thing happened at Pompton among the Jersey troops, and there had to be a hanging.

It was no worse than George had been expecting and predicting to Congress and the state Governors ever since the winter of '76, but now that it had actually happened he took it very hard. He dared not leave his own men in order to enforce discipline elsewhere. He could only take up his pen again to entreat Congress and the Governors to find some means of paying and feeding the exhausted, grumbling troops who had already endured more of privation than could be expected of human nature. It was a grim and alarming situation.

Meanwhile Headquarters was enlivened by the return of Hamilton and his bride, good-natured, helpful Betsy, who was soon almost like a daughter to Martha, and whose smiling, unruffled presence was very good for the stretched nerves and stale fatigue which the war had imposed on the men who were trying to run it. Martha, with whom Hamilton had never been a favorite, began to think Betsy might make something of him as a human being after all—his own ambition would take care of his career—and there was no doubt that he was very much in love with his wife. At the same time he was undergoing a good deal of personal frustration in other directions.

His friend John Laurens had been dispatched from Philadelphia on an important secret mission to France, to negotiate a loan and the quick delivery of supplies and reinforcements. And his friend Lafayette had been given the detachment which was being sent South from the main army against a small British force led by Benedict Arnold, who had undertaken to sever Greene's northern communications and destroy his stores and bases in Virginia. Twice over, Hamilton had just seen appointments he believed were better suited to his own talents than scribbling at a desk all day as a mere secretary to the Commander in Chief, go to men who he was sure were no more capable than himself, much as he admired them both. His temper was touchy and his pride was raw.

Martha watched Betsy's wifely tact and tolerance with compassion and respect, while it occurred to both women to wonder if Hamilton's recently acquired domestic status had anything to do with his being left at his routine post while men without new wives tacked on got the adventures. It was absurd to suppose that either Congress or the Commander in Chief would deprive the Cause of a man's best services simply because he was a bridegroom. But it was a coincidence. It put a chill on Betsy's happiness, and it roused sympathy for her in Martha, who could see with no trouble at all what Betsy was thinking.

She had anticipated that Betsy's married life would never be an easy one, but it seemed a pity that the rub should start so soon. It would be an irony, she thought behind her usual discreet silence, if young Colonel Hamilton had been too clever for his own good. He had made a brilliant marriage into a distinguished and wealthy family, and he had thoroughly charmed his in-laws. He had moreover acquired a nearly perfect wife, easy to love, uncritical, and with all the social graces. Having thus made sure of a snug future when the war was won, he now saw the thing he wanted even more, which was a chance to cut a dash and make history,

riding right out from under him with Lafayette. Give him credit, he
labored hard and tirelessly on the preparations for Lafayette's expedition to the South, and there was no flaw in his daily attitude toward his
fortunate friend. But it must go hard with him to stay behind twice
over, thought Martha, able to be a little sorry for him.

Simultaneously, new tension was being generated between Headquarters and the French at Newport, whose fleet was needed quickly to
deal with Arnold in the Virginia waters. George intended another personal interview with Rochambeau, but his plans to go to Rhode Island
had given way before the emergency of the Jersey mutiny. Martha had
never, since the war began, seen him so distracted and discouraged. It
was the sixth winter since Cambridge, and the years had taken toll of
him until she doubted how much more he could endure. Lafayette, who
would have given his right arm in defense of his beloved chief, was the
innocent cause of additional strain on Washington's beleaguered composure.

It was a small house, with the staircase running up from a central
hall between Martha's parlor and the office, so that she was seldom unaware of the comings and goings of the Staff. She was sitting with Betsy
over their endless mending and knitting one afternoon in February when
they heard with astonishment a sudden exchange of angry words in the
hall, raised voices, and the bang of the outer door. Martha, being long
acquainted with George's rare, white-faced rages, which were conquered
almost as soon as they flared, sat quietly where she was, in the parlor—
even her knitting-needles motionless. Betsy half rose from her chair, her
eyes round and scared, but Martha shook her head. They waited, making
conversation, pretending it hadn't happened, and no one came to en-
lighten them, until Betsy could no longer bear the silence beyond the
door and went to corner Tilghman on his lawful occasions and beg an
explanation.

Poor Tilghman was by then perspiring freely, having been in the
middle of it. It appeared that the Commander in Chief had asked Hamilton to do a simple errand and Hamilton had delayed on the staircase in
a casual encounter with Lafayette longer than the General's patience
allowed. He had spoken sharply to Hamilton about the wait. Hamilton
had replied furiously with an impulsive resignation from a position where
he could be tyrannized over. Washington had promptly accepted the
threat, and Hamilton flung out of the house.

At this point in Tilghman's narrative Betsy burst into tears, but Tilghman assured her that the General had at once cooled off and sent him to express regrets to Hamilton and invite a reconciliation. Lafayette had gone out before the lid blew off, but he had returned and was with the General now. So far, Hamilton was holding to his resolution to quit Headquarters, but had agreed to continue in his almost essential duties until after the impending conference with Rochambeau at Newport. Tilghman was convinced that by then it would all have simmered down. Everybody was tired, remarked the even-tempered Marylander, in cheerful understatement. It would never have happened if things were going better.

But Martha, witness to George's chagrin in their room that night, had all she could do not to wring her hands. Hamilton now. She had been afraid of it, with Hamilton. Again, again, they failed to measure up—blind and intolerant and unimaginative, they thought only of their own grievances, and took no account of the burden he carried, the pressure on his nerves, his unrelenting fatigue and endeavor. Not Tilghman, of course, his devotion to the General was as selfless as George's to the Cause; not Lafayette, who after an affectionate farewell was soon off southward "in pursuit of glory," as George put it with his rueful smile. Lafayette's final marching orders had been written out in the beautiful penmanship of a now self-possessed Hamilton, still discharging his despised secretarial chores with all his accustomed efficiency, and preserving a punctilious politeness at all times. Martha observed him without illusion. He would not give in, as they all thought he would. He was hard and calculating and obstinate, behind that almost girlish complexion and those candid-seeming violet eyes. It was plain now that he had always been too good, in his own estimation, to be at General Washington's beck and call. The episode had underlined his fundamental lack of personal affection for the Commander in Chief, of the kind which enabled men like Tilghman, Harrison, Meade or MacHenry to overlook George's occasional exacting moods, out of the love they bore him. Hamilton had no love for anyone, really, but Alexander Hamilton. Poor Betsy—Martha thought, with a knowing sigh—would find out, to her sorrow, that he did not change.

The meeting between Washington and Rochambeau at Newport, which finally took place in March, was cordial but in the end accomplished little. The second French division had not yet sailed, being blockaded by the British in home waters. The French Navy failed to cooperate. And although the Commander in Chief captivated all Newport with his tall uniformed dignity at the balls and receptions in his honor, he returned to New Windsor weary and unhappy.

In the South General Morgan had won a small victory at a place called the Cowpens, where Colonel William Washington had distinguished himself, but Greene was on the run from Cornwallis. Morgan's health had broken down to such an extent that he was leaving Greene's command to go home—another good man worn out and thrown away. Suppose the Commander in Chief some morning said, I am tired, I'm going home. Suppose Greene said, This is no good, send someone else to do it for me. When an officer quit, it was called resigning. In the ranks it was desertion, and you flogged them. But how long could anyone hold out, like this? "We are at the end of our tether," Washington wrote to John Laurens, who had arrived at Paris. Without more aid from the French—much more, and promptly—and without better recruiting measures in the States, they might as well all go home. Even then, he must be the last to leave.

Martha accompanied Betsy on a visit to Albany during George's absence in Rhode Island. Mrs. Schuyler had recently been disappointed of a son, whom she had promised to name for the Commander in Chief, but he wrote her that he most cheerfully accepted sponsorship of the daughter who had arrived instead. His namesakes were already numerous.

Martha regretted that he had not seen Kitty Greene while he was in Rhode Island, for it was necessary to dissuade her at once from attempting to join her husband in Carolina. General Greene would apparently be skirmishing all winter. His headquarters consisted of a tent which was pitched at night and struck in the morning. Even without the children, Kitty's presence there was impossible. Because her youngest was sick she was prevented from coming into Newport for the festivities of Washington's visit, and he had hastened back to New Windsor without detouring to pay a call on her at home. Instead, he had written her that she was not to go to Carolina. It would have been kinder, Martha thought, if he could have explained in person, but that was war.

In April Hamilton ended his four-year tenure as aide to General Washington, and with Betsy in tears beside him set out for his father-in-law's house at Albany, where he proposed to establish a law practice. Tilghman, who dated back to the New York summer of '76, was now the senior aide, since Harrison's health had suffered so severely during his long service that after only a brief return from leave, he unwillingly departed again to become chief justice in his old Maryland neighborhood.

Martha was relieved to see David Humphreys back at Headquarters after a visit to his parents in Connecticut. He was a large, jocund man, son of a clergyman and a graduate of Yale, who wrote poetry in his spare time. He had been attached to old Putnam's staff, and during the Valley Forge winter was stationed at West Point, where the snow was almost as deep as in Pennsylvania. After Putnam's stroke, Humphreys came to Greene at Morristown in '79, and when John Laurens first went South Humphreys took his place as aide to Washington, and won the quick approval of the General's wife.

Except for these two, the old Headquarters Family was scattered, and the once coveted post was becoming stale and threadbare. Colonel Meade had married the widow Randolph and then gone to join Steuben's corps in Virginia. MacHenry went with Lafayette to try and run Arnold to earth. Gibbs of the Lifeguard was still available for odd jobs of copying orders and riding errands. George Augustine Washington, son of George's brother Charles, had joined the New Windsor Family as secretary-aide. He was a pleasant, willing soul, and everyone was very fond of him, and went to a great deal of trouble to help him nurse his perpetual colds. Washington had for him a special tenderness, believing that he saw in the boy a resemblance to the beloved half-brother Lawrence, who died in '52. To fill in for Harrison, who would have been missed if he had been replaced by the Angel Gabriel, they had Jonathan Trumbull, son of Washington's good friend the Governor of Connecticut, and brother to the painter, who was now in France. He was full of the Trumbull charm, tidy with his paper work, never in a hurry. There was no doubt that life was easier at Headquarters without Hamilton's drive and efficiency. Things got done somehow, and nobody went round raising a dust. But Martha missed Betsy.

The war had become a matter of mere endurance now, and even among the officers of the Line there had been a plague of resignations. Sullivan had followed Schuyler into Congress, for reasons of health. Theodorick Bland, James Monroe, and Aaron Burr, all young men, simply retired from the army to pursue their private careers, and Varnum, one of the mainstays at Valley Forge, had resumed his Rhode Island law practice with a little militia duty on the side. Even in George's own family defection had occurred, when his aide and nephew George Lewis married and set up housekeeping near Fredericksburg and was seen no more at Headquarters. Palfrey, having asked for leave of absence, was appointed consul general to France—and the ship on which he sailed was never heard of again. Mifflin and Reed were legislating for Pennsylvania. Putnam was permanently disabled; Charles Lee and Arnold were good riddance.

The Washingtons' anxiety for their James River friends in Arnold's path was acute. He had come ashore at the Byrd plantation called Westover, but had done little damage there, perhaps because the widowed Mrs. Byrd was a distant connection of his wife's. After a quick raid on Richmond he retired into Portsmouth, and Jefferson, who was Governor of Virginia now, reported that he kept close to quarters. Lafayette wrote from Williamsburg, having gone there by sea from Head of Elk to reconnoiter, that so far Arnold had accomplished nothing very alarming, but that British reinforcements were on the way to him.

George fell into a bitterly homesick mood, longing for the peace and comfort of Mount Vernon. Nelly Custis, at her fourth try, had had a son in January. He had been christened George Washington Parke Custis, and was to be known for years as "little Washington." It seemed as though they had not heard from Lund so often of late, and a British fleet was known to be operating in the Chesapeake. George's nostalgia took form in a letter to Lund one late evening, while Martha sat knitting by the same candles—she was making a queue-bag for General Knox. How many lambs were there this spring, George wanted to know from Lund. How many colts to come; was there any paint and oil to be had thereabouts; was Lund going about the repairs of the pavement to the piazza; had he made good the decayed trees at the end of the house; had he reclaimed any more land for a meadow? "An account of these things would be satisfactory to me, and infinitely amusing in the recital, as I have these kind of improvements very much at heart," he suggested wistfully. There was a bay horse Martha had taken a fancy to while she was at home, she reminded him—brother to one she had to her carriage now which had gone lame. . . . For a while, bending over his paper in the candlelight, filling page after page with his firm, beautiful script which never scribbled, Washington forgot the war.

When next they heard from Lund it was to learn that a British ship had come up the Potomac and paid a visit to Mount Vernon, and that Lund as Washington's steward had actually received the enemy civilly and tendered refreshments. Resistance would have been futile, of course, and any armed demonstration would have been worse than that and would doubtless have resulted in the total destruction of the property. As it was, the British had left without firing the buildings or doing any permanent damage, except that they carried off with them, presumably as servants, a number of the Negroes. George and Martha at New Windsor read the list of these with grief and anger—Gunner the bricklayer, Watty the weaver, Thomas and Peter, just lads in their teens, three young maids, three old men. What would become of them in British hands?

Washington wrote severely to Lund: "It would have been a less painful circumstance to me to have heard that in consequence of your non-compliance with the request they had burnt my house and laid the plantation in ruins. You ought to have considered yourself as my representative and should have reflected on the bad example of communicating with the enemy and making a voluntary offer of refreshment to them to prevent a conflagration. . . . It was not in your power, I acknowledge, to prevent them from sending a flag on shore, and you did right to meet it. . . . But to . . . commune with a parcel of plundering scoundrels and request a favor by asking the surrender of my Negroes was exceedingly ill-judged and 'tis feared will be unhappy in its consequences. . . ." What rankled most was that the enemy had drunk his wine, and at Lund's invitation.

In the middle of May Rochambeau's son returned from France with dispatches, and another conference—their third—was fixed to take place at Wethersfield on the 21st. It was imperative that some plan of campaign should be determined on for the summer. Tilghman, Humphreys, Trumbull, and General Knox went to Connecticut with him, leaving George Augustine Washington and Gibbs of the Lifeguard responsible for Martha at Headquarters.

She had no warning of the illness which descended upon her almost as soon as George was out of sight. Perhaps she was just tired, like the rest of them. Perhaps the food was just not adequate. In any case, before he returned she was prostrated with a bilious attack which went on into a kind of jaundice, and left her weak and depressed for the rest of the summer. Her devoted colored maid Oney never left her side, and she was not really in any danger, but it was a devastating experience, and she wished for the companionship of gentle Betsy Hamilton. Everyone did his best to cheer her, and Lucy Knox was kindness itself, in spite of her rather overwhelming personality, making frequent visits to bring gruel and sweets and fruit, accompanied by her lively, affectionate children. The Lifeguard foraged for tender fowls and fresh vegetables. They all seemed to think of food, and food was the last thing she seemed to want now. She found herself dreaming of Mount Vernon, in her longing to go there—but not without George, and besides he would worry about her being there in case of another British visitation. Lund had been quite wrong, of course, to pander to the British, but secretly she was grateful to him for saving the house, if such action had been necessary to save it, in spite of George.

The alternative to Mount Vernon would be Philadelphia, which was hot and full of flies in the summer, and required tedious social duties which Martha felt less than ever able to stand up to. Tears ran down into the pillow as she lay in bed obediently trying to gather strength so as not to alarm George on his return—tears of sheer weariness and inward rebellion. It seemed as though the war would go on forever—their lives were wasting—they were turning fifty—and still the end of the war was not in sight. Then she would dry her eyes on the sheet and remind herself how much worse it was for George, who had not been home to Mount Vernon since the summer of '75, and how it would upset him if she gave in now. The day he arrived back from Wethersfield she rose from bed and dressed, shaky and queasy, and took her place at the dinner table, which of course reassured him. Men were easily fooled.

The usual spring upheaval was beginning again all around her. They had reached a decision at Wethersfield to organize a joint movement against the British in New York in the expectation that a French fleet under Admiral DeGrasse would assist, though there was considerable pressure from George's old colleagues to induce him to come South for the summer campaign. Already Rochambeau's army was on the march toward the Hudson, where the Americans waited. By threatening New York they hoped to prevent General Clinton from sending reinforcements to Cornwallis in Virginia, and in this they were successful—Clinton even drew on Cornwallis for men, which in the end proved fatal.

So the weary campaigning got under way again. Martha set out southward late in June, still feeling a great lassitude and with a humiliating tendency to tears. She was to go no further than Philadelphia for a while, where the Morrises, the Blands, the Powells, and the Biddles, among other old friends, would doubtless kill her with kindness.

Throughout July the two armies lay outside New York waiting for news of DeGrasse and for American recruits, hoping to outnumber Clinton sufficiently to risk an assault. Cornwallis had taken possession of Williamsburg, having forced the Virginia Assembly to move from there to Richmond and on again to Charlottesville, and even then a cavalry raid almost caught Governor Jefferson, who would almost certainly have been hanged.

A British army at Williamsburg. Martha in Philadelphia, where all the news was promptly known, found it hard to imagine. And what about her mother at Chestnut Grove in New Kent County, and her brother Bartholomew and his family nearby, and the Bassett household at Eltham where Nancy's daughter Fanny lived with her father and two brothers? Lafayette was thereabouts, of course, to harry Cornwallis and keep him from having things all his own way. But Lafayette confessed himself not even strong enough to get beaten, and could only dodge about, an impudent mouse to Cornwallis's clumsy cat, until he risked a skirmish at Green Spring near Jamestown which could have meant disaster. It was Cornwallis who withdrew that day, and marched for Portsmouth, and thence to Yorktown, which made so little sense to George that he was convinced there must be something very sinister behind it. In Philadelphia, where the chimney-corner strategists were, it was plain that at Yorktown Cornwallis had got himself into a trap, which only needed to be sprung. Even so, Washington and Rochambeau with their combined armies were four hundred and fifty miles from Yorktown, watching for DeGrasse to appear off Sandy Hook.

Martha had got away from Philadelphia and reached Mount Vernon and the delicious comfort of her own bed before she heard of the abrupt change of plans on the Hudson. On an overnight decision, George was coming South after Cornwallis, instead of tackling Clinton at New York. She did not understand why, she did not at all care what the reason was; something about DeGrasse arriving in the Chesapeake instead of where he was expected; something about John Laurens having returned with a whole trunkful of French money; it did not matter why, it was enough that the war was suddenly headed for Virginia, and that George would be able at least to cross his own threshold again on the way to Yorktown.

A frenzy of preparation began at Mount Vernon. Completely restored to health by the prospect, Martha drove her willing helpers without mercy. Everything which easygoing Lund had overlooked, or forgotten, or put off, must instantly be attended to. It was not just that the master's raking blue eye would miss nothing in his first inspection. He was bringing guests with him—French guests, who must not only be entertained but impressed, besides his loyal Family to whom Mount Vernon was already a legend. The ovens and the spits and the great kettles in the kitchen were busy all day long. Delicacies which had not been concocted since the war began, and all his favorite dishes to which he had been so long a stranger, must be prepared in quantity—there was no telling how many would arrive in his suite. No matter if the rest of them ate leavings for weeks, his table must do him proud while he was there. Jack and Nelly would drive over from Abingdon with the children—he had never seen a single one of Jack's babies, and little Washington was now old enough to laugh and grasp at a finger. George had never seen the still unfinished banquet room, or the library, or the new bedroom above it, which could be reached by their little private stair. . . . More than once they saw her turn aside and wipe her cheeks with her fingers—she wept for sheer joy.

When he came, it was not at all as she had pictured it, supposing that an aide would gallop up to the door well ahead of him to give her some notice of his progress and the number of guests he brought with him— to be followed in due course by the bright cavalcade of his mounted suite, after everybody from the stableboys to the butler had been posted at his appointed place and task, herself and the Lunds waiting on the doorstep of the west front as he came up the drive, and a little ceremony of welcome and introductions all round, with a collation laid out and the beds aired and ready.

The sound of horses' hoofs in the drive long after everyone had gone to bed on the night of September 9th she took to be Humphreys or Tilghman with the message. She hurried into a dressing gown and went to the top of the stairs with her candle. It was Humphreys, yes, but only because he had managed to keep up with George, who had ridden the sixty miles from Baltimore in one day to snatch a few precious hours in his home before the rest of the company arrived. They were already in the lower hall, and Billy his body-servant was calling for lights and boys to tend the horses, so that amid a confusion of running feet and incredulous exclamations and high Negro laughter she called George's name from the landing, and he turned and took the stairs like a boy to her side.

Humphreys waited at the bottom step, making his bow with an affectionate grin, relieving her of the candlestick as she gave him her hand. Of course they were hungry, of course they wanted food and wine as badly as they wanted beds. Half-dressed, twittering colored servants, pausing in mid-course to peep at the master, soon had the family dining room alight and the table laid, and the kitchen was in a bustle. Humphreys complained good-naturedly of being lame and sore from the pace the General had set, and collapsed into a chair with his booted legs outstretched, but George moved easily about with a candelabra in his hand, inspecting the new dining-room mantelpiece, which had been installed since his departure for the Philadelphia Congress all those years ago, looking into the library beyond, which still awaited its shelves, and peering up the little stairway to the bedroom above it.

Then Lund appeared, summoned by an incoherent pickaninny, and stayed to drink a glass of wine with them, while the travelers consumed cold chicken and fresh bread and cake. Before George would go up to rest, he and Lund must carry off a candelabra for a quick visit to the new banquet room on the north side, inadequately furnished and lacking its chimney piece, but with a long table set up down the middle and a collection of chairs assembled to seat the expected visitors at the feast.

From Humphreys, meanwhile, Martha gathered the latest news of the war. General Lincoln had been paroled and exchanged after his Charleston surrender the previous May. Temperate, benign, and dedicated to his vigorous belief in ultimate victory, still walking lame from his wound, he was now at Head of Elk, loading the troops into what boats were available there. The rest of the army and its baggage were marching for Baltimore, where more boats were waiting, though the wagons must make the whole journey overland along with some of the guns. DeGrasse with his ships was believed to be in the Chesapeake; Lafayette was apparently planted at Williamsburg. Cornwallis was cut off from reinforcements by land or sea, and could never fight his way out through the combined armies. The Yorktown trap was ready to be sprung.

Martha listened to the cheerful aide, wondering if George was as sure, and prayed that he might be spared another disappointment. At last they saw Humphreys installed in state in the ground-floor bedroom, which he would be turned out of when the French came, and the Washingtons climbed the stairs hand in hand to the new chamber where for six years Martha had slept alone. There George sat down, sighing with relief, in his own chair by the hearth, surrendering to Billy's expert pull the shining, spurred riding boots, and rose again, tall as ever, to hand over the sword belt and the heavy blue coat with its gold epaulettes. The door closed on the colored man's soft good-night, as he retired with the garments that would return in the morning brushed and polished to perfection.

She had stood watching the familiar nightly ritual, and when they were alone she ventured to ask how long he could stay at Mount Vernon. Not long—for Rochambeau would catch up with him tomorrow. There were a thousand things to see to while he was here—the Fairfax militia must be had out to work on the roads before the wagons came; fresh horses must be found for the French; there was always the need for provisions and forage; they were not yet actually in touch with DeGrasse. But how long, she persisted, standing before him, small and determined, in her dressing gown and cap, grasping her happiness firmly against his preoccupation, and he took both her hands. Poor Patsy—she would have tomorrow, and the next day—beyond that he could not say. The Staff were grumbling, they all wanted rest. They had not had his reasons for pressing on to Mount Vernon. Martha drew a long breath. She had been dreading he would ride away toward Yorktown in the morning.

George's military Family arrived in time for dinner the following afternoon, and before evening Rochambeau and his Staff also, to be installed in the best bedrooms, while the American aides were quartered in the rooms on the third floor. There was no shortage of food and delicacies at Mount Vernon, where the late garden stuff was still in its prime, and the guests were visibly impressed with their entertainment. When Chastellux rode in with his suite on the 11th, the hospitality of the house expanded to accommodate them all as well.

Then the Custises came, with a carriage full of pretty children to display to George, and their mother and Martha watched helplessly while Jack developed a belated martial zeal, so that nothing would do but he must go along to Yorktown to see Cornwallis treed. There was no time to get a uniform, but he had a dark blue coat, and Martha rummaged out a broad green ribbon which, worn aslant a white waistcoat, would mark him as one of the Commander in Chief's aides. He sent for his own favorite horse, and another for his colored body-servant in the Custis livery, who led a third. A gentleman volunteer with the best of them, Jack Custis rode away beside Tilghman, Humphreys, and the others, when the journey to Yorktown was resumed on the 12th. Nelly managed not to cry till they reached the further end of the west drive and turned for a last wave before passing out of sight.

Then the waiting began at Mount Vernon. They were joined before long by stout Lucy Knox, pregnant again, who had been invited to share the suspenseful days with his Excellency's wife, though it was a little farther behind the drums than she was usually to be found. Martha, who always thought Mrs. Knox a trifle pervasive, stifled a secret wish that it had been Kitty Greene instead—but General Greene was still in South Carolina and was going to miss the fun at Yorktown.

Cut off, left behind, perishing daily for news, the female household at Mount Vernon existed in hope and prayer and patience. Early in October they heard of Greene's successful engagement at Eutaw Springs, while Washington's army was still making its cautious preparations to invest Yorktown, and the British there contented themselves with throwing artillery fire at the American camp, which took no notice. Within a few days, they knew that the siege had begun.

Often rumor outsped the letters they received from their men. There were false alarms, good news, and bad. Martha held on grimly, waiting for George's brief, cautious letters, refusing to be premature either in despair or rejoicing. Lucy Knox had letters too, and Jack's came to Nelly, supplementing George's own. The first notable casualty was the beloved Colonel Scammell, who was famous in the Family for being able to make the grave Commander in Chief laugh out loud. He had been wounded on an early reconnaissance and taken prisoner into Yorktown, then paroled and carried under a flag to Williamsburg. The American doctors there labored to save him, but the wound proved mortal, and the army grieved.

Anxiety stretched tighter at Mount Vernon. Nelly, who had never set eyes on Scammell, wept because it might have been Jack instead. Martha and Lucy, who had loved him dearly for his heartening presence during many a dreary month at Headquarters in the past, shared the army's sense of personal loss. Who next, they wondered privately, each keeping a brave front for the other. So near the end—it *could* be the end—each death now seemed worse than waste. Anyone could still fall. Martha shut herself into the bedroom and went to her knees. No one told them that Washington himself was one day spattered with dirt from an incoming cannon-ball which sent some of his more prudent companions dodging for cover and beseeching him not to expose himself needlessly at this crucial time.

It went so slowly, at Yorktown as well as at Mount Vernon. They had to wait for the heavy guns to arrive; they had to wait for the French fleet to maneuver; they had to manufacture fascines and gabions. Once Washington wrote of a heavy rain which interrupted the British cannonade. He was too economical of ammunition to return the fire until he was ready.

Then Harry Knox wrote Lucy that his howitzers and 24-pounders were in position on the right, and he had invented an elegant carriage for the mortars. Martha thought of her Williamsburg friends, who were not used to gunfire as she was, and wondered about the Nelsons' houses inside the British lines at Yorktown. Thomas Nelson, Jr., was the Governor of Virginia now, succeeding Thomas Jefferson, but he stayed with the army.

If George fired into Yorktown as he had pelted Boston, he might demolish that nice brick house of Tom Nelson's, and the other one which belonged to his uncle, the Old Secretary. She had not thought enough about the Boston houses, she realized, just because they were not inhabited by friends of hers. Later, she would hear how Governor Nelson himself enthusiastically directed the gunners' aim at his house because he knew that it sheltered Cornwallis and his Staff.

George wrote of Cornwallis's "passive" conduct, which perplexed them all. "He either has not the means of defense, or he intends to reserve his strength until we approach very near him," he surmised. There were more casualties, of course, as the American engineers proceeded doggedly with the placing of their batteries and the digging of their parallels—but nameless ones, to the women at Mount Vernon. When Nelly read out Jack's envious account of a brilliant sortie in which Lafayette, John Laurens, and Hamilton all participated without collecting a scratch amongst the three of them, Lucy's comment was outspoken—Hamilton, showing off as usual, she remarked. Having inveigled the Commander in Chief into giving him a place in the Line, after that disgraceful performance at New Windsor—and if she might be permitted to say so, His Excellency was too lenient by far—Hamilton had succeeded in joining the heroes at the kill. It took courage, Martha reminded her fairly, to keep up with Lafayette and Laurens. Oh, Hammy had courage, Lucy conceded. In fact, Hammy was made of solid brass.

But Jack Custis was frail flesh and blood, not inured to the rough and tumble of a campaign, wet autumn weather, chancy food, broken rest, and high nervous tension. He caught a cold, he had a colic and couldn't eat, it was nearly over now, and he meant to see the end of it —which he did, from a carriage beside the road because he was too weak to sit a horse among the aides while the British army laid down its arms. The letter in which George told them how Cornwallis, ill of sheer chagrin, had sent out his sword by a deputy in token of surrender, ended with a paragraph which sought to reassure them while at the same time conveying the news that he had sent Jack to Burwell Bassett at Eltham for home nursing—and he thought Martha should accompany Nelly there at once.

Fright for Jacky robbed them of the victory, as they set off in Martha's chariot with a hastily packed trunk, leaving the three youngest children with Mrs. Knox at Mount Vernon. They found Jack prostrate in bed at Eltham in the care of their old friend and neighbor, Dr. Craik, who after serving with George at Fort Loudoun a quarter of a century ago was now Chief Physician to the Continental Army. Martha had seen camp fever before, and she did not have to be told that Jack was very ill. Determined not to interrupt the colossal amount of business at the Williamsburg Headquarters which followed the formal capitulation of the British army at Yorktown, she held out against Nelly's panic for several days, and then sent an express with a letter entreating George's presence. Even now, he was able to find time for concern for his stepson, and he rode out at once, near midnight on November 5th, attended only by Colonel Humphreys and Billy, and arrived at Eltham a mere matter of hours before Jack died.

Anticipating the collapse of both Jack's wife and his mother, Washington was witness to the small miracle of Martha bearing up for Nelly's sake. After the first flood of tears, which was conquered in the privacy of their room, she rallied resolutely to support Nelly through the funeral, while Jack was buried in the garden at Eltham. A few days later, having sent the Family on ahead, Washington rode beside the coach which carried the two women and little Eliza back to Mount Vernon.

Gradually it dawned on Martha that the war was not over, just because Cornwallis had surrendered, though the back of it might prove to be broken as time went on. So long as the British still held Charleston and New York, nobody in the American army could quit and go home, and another winter at Headquarters was impending. Without an audible sigh she prepared to accompany George to Philadelphia, and thence to whatever borrowed house and limited convenience would be their lot as 1782 came in.

Washington had sent reinforcements from Yorktown to Greene in South Carolina, and Rochambeau with his troops would remain at Williamsburg for the winter. The rest of the army was bound for the Hudson again, under General Lincoln, to prepare for a new campaign. They could not throw the British out of New York without the cooperation of the French fleet, George explained, and DeGrasse would not return to American waters till the following summer. George was sorry for her, and tried to tell her that she needn't come, that she had best stay with Nelly for a while. She saw that he expected her to be broken by the loss of Jack, and that he was prepared to do without his wife while Jack's mother mourned—which only strengthened her resolution that his greatest victory in six long years should not be sacrificed to her grief. It did not seem to occur to him either that now more than ever he was the rock, the reason, and the magnetic pole of her life. Perhaps she had let it go too long, when the children were small. Perhaps now he would never be sure that without him her days were savorless and empty. It was a little late for speeches. She could only follow him faithfully, cheerfully, willingly, where his unrelenting destiny required.

As there was still no telling when they would be free to return to Mount Vernon to live, they agreed in consultation with Nelly that Jack's uncle Bartholomew Dandridge should be requested to undertake the guardianship of her four small children. Nelly was now approximately the same age that Martha had been when Daniel Custis died, and it was not improbable that she would marry again. During the busy week which George allowed himself at Mount Vernon, he discovered that Jack's affairs had been shamefully mishandled by a dishonest manager, and that in his own case Lund's accounts for Mount Vernon were in great confusion. Without time to act for himself, he put Jack's estate into George Mason's hands for legal unraveling, and wrote to Bartholomew urging him to accept the responsibility for the children. Congratulations on the Yorktown victory mingled with condolences for Martha's loss, and Washington's conscientious acknowledgment of both kept him at his desk for precious hours which might well have been spent elsewhere on the plantation.

When he left Mount Vernon on November 20th Martha was beside him in the coach, composed and uncomplaining. He doubted if they would get past Philadelphia before Christmas, for Congress must be made to realize that the only assurance for peace was the ability to continue the war. All the old arguments and demands for men, clothing, provisions, and shelter must be rehearsed again, in an atmosphere of groundless optimism; groundless because there were still two British armies in possession of American cities, and the Commander in Chief had not the wherewithal to dislodge either one of them. Unless adequate provision was made at once for the next campaign, the Yorktown triumph might still go for nothing. Martha, who had innocently committed the same error of optimism, felt rather sorry for Congress.

Benjamin Chew's new house in South Third Street had been prepared for their use, and it was evident that they were expected to spend Christmas in Philadelphia. Their journey there had turned into a royal progress, and whenever General Washington appeared in the streets or at church a crowd gathered to admire him. He found it embarrassing, but his wife delighted to see him honored, and added her friendly smile to his rather stately bows.

In the face of a thinly attended and uncooperative Congress Washington battled doggedly to prepare for the worst. General Lincoln was elected Secretary for War; Knox and Robert Morris were given the vexatious job of arranging for the exchange of prisoners. Lafayette went home to France, promising to return soon, promising meanwhile to speed the peace negotiations at Paris. It was like parting with another son.

In the middle of December Kitty Greene arrived in Philadelphia on her way to join her husband in South Carolina. George Washington Greene, born while the army was at Cambridge in 1775, was to be left for education with a clergyman's family at Princeton. It was good to see Kitty again, and they were sorry to see her off, dauntless as ever, on the long journey southward.

The Washingtons ate Christmas dinner with the Robert Morrises and were entertained affectionately everywhere. There was not the febrile gaiety of the season which had followed the reoccupation of the city under Arnold's administration, and there was now true cause for a certain amount of self-congratulation and relief. But at the heart of it there was still the war, quiescent, coiled, enigmatic.

In March of 1782 they started for Newburgh on the Hudson, a few miles from New Windsor where last year's Headquarters had been. In another little gray stone house overlooking the magnificent River panorama they sat down to wait. A few of the faithful still composed the Family—Humphreys, Walker, and Trumbull would remain throughout the year. George Augustine, Charles Washington's son, who had served as an aide to Lafayette at Yorktown and then rejoined his uncle's Staff, was sent home to Berkeley County in the spring to recuperate from a chest complaint which was feared to be tuberculous. Tilghman too, after an epic ride to carry the news of the Yorktown victory to the Congress at Philadelphia, had fallen ill of fever and fatigue and had gone home to Maryland on leave. He spent his furlough there courting his cousin Anna Maria, and returned to Headquarters during the summer to confirm rumors of his intention to marry. When he left them again for his wedding his health was still low, and they all felt it was doubtful if he would ever take up his military duties again. And at Newburgh the news reached them of the death of George's brother Samuel at Harewood in the Shenandoah Valley, leaving children of all ages by his several marriages. His sister Betty's husband, having broken his always delicate constitution and expended his fortune in the service of American independence, supplying arms from his foundries and equipment from his personal funds, was also dead at Fredericksburg.

Hopes and rumors of peace fluctuated with the passing weeks, now up, now down. The British never knew when they were beaten. The Americans, who came of the same stock, had long suffered from the same disability. Patiently, Martha watched the summer of '82 coming in, and nothing settled—nothing at all. Clinton at New York was replaced by Carleton from Canada, a reasonable man, disposed to negotiate, but without the authority to do so alone.

In July, protesting that there were still no signs of any more fighting, Martha departed for Mount Vernon, where many small domestic problems awaited her. And at the end of the following November, with another whole year gone, Washington gave up the secret hope of wintering at home and sent for her, and they prepared philosophically to sit out one more army Christmas at Newburgh. Rochambeau had decided to remove his troops to the West Indies, and many of the French officers came all the way to Headquarters to say good-by to the Washingtons and the Staff. It was a gloomy Christmas they all left behind them at the camp on the Hudson.

Early in January, '83, Washington was writing with his characteristic private irony: "The army are as usual without pay; and a great part of the soldiers without shirts; and though the patience of them is equally threadbare, the States seem perfectly indifferent to their cries. In a word, if one was to hazard for them an opinion on this subject, it would be that the army had contracted such a habit of living without money that it would be impolitic and injurious to introduce other customs in it!"

When General Stirling died on duty at Albany he was much mourned and Martha wept in sympathy for his wife and daughters. Young Laurens had been killed in a trifling skirmish in South Carolina—a tragic, futile loss. The record, among the officers who had been her friends, of failing health and early death was a depressing one, for a time when the guns had fallen nearly silent. A letter from John Augustine Washington revealed that their brother Samuel had died deeply in debt, and that their mother at Fredericksburg was complaining that she could not pay her taxes. On both these scores George experienced a helpless exasperation. Samuel had always been a family problem, and his mother was amply provided for, both by his own arrangements and the near proximity of his sister Betty Lewis. It was clear that his own personal and business affairs would take a great deal of untangling if ever he was free of the war, and they weighed increasingly on his mind.

Charleston was at last evacuated, and only New York remained in

British possession. It was infuriating to know that the war was actually over, and that it was won, and still the peace was not signed. Most people blamed the King for the delay. At the end of March there was a ray of light—a treaty for the suspension of hostilities (when not a gun had been fired on either side for weeks) was completed at Paris.

But still nothing happened at New York, and nobody could go home.

As that endless spring of 1783 stretched into summer, Washington wrote to Lafayette in France: "We remain here in a listless state, awaiting the arrival of a definitive treaty, the uncertainty of which, adding to the great expense of subsisting the army, have induced Congress to furlough (which in the present case is but another name for discharging) all the soldiers who stood enlisted for the war . . ." as apart from those who had enlisted for a specified time, such as three years, and should remain on that basis. He had repeatedly stressed to Congress the advisability of putting money, however small a token payment, into the hands of the soldiers as they set out for home. The condition of the Treasury was such, however, that only a printed voucher entitling them to collect pay from their home States was issued.

The whole proceeding of ending the war turned into such an anticlimax, as the final negotiations in Paris dragged on, that the officers at Newburgh abandoned their intention of giving themselves a farewell dinner, while the regiments were allowed to disintegrate and melt away down the road without ceremony of any kind—no bands, no flags, no parade, no special issue of rum because there wasn't any—just a general, bewildered flatness and petering out. The men were granted their muskets as a farewell gift, and the familiar hard weight on their shoulder was often the only companion and the only possession of the homeward bound.

At Headquarters they began in a desultory way to pack, and Washington ordered some stout trunks made in which to transport his private papers to Mount Vernon. Also, he began to think of purchases for the house itself, in a return to the plans he had entertained as far back as '75. A tidy sum was owing him, when he presented the accounts for his expenses to Congress, as he was prepared to do when the time came that he could resign his commission and return to Virginia as a plain citizen and farmer again. Hospitality would be required, as the neighborhood welcomed him home, and his establishment required silver plate, china, and glass to dress the new banquet hall and ballroom. Moreover, he would have time to read again, and he ordered books for the library, even a French-English dictionary.

At the end of June there was another mutiny in Pennsylvania among troops who accepted the penniless discharge less philosophically than those under the General's own eye, and the discontented men carried their arms into Philadelphia to lay their demands and grievances before Congress—which promptly decamped to Princeton, and sent to Washington for some of his troops to control those in Philadelphia. He dispatched the same officer who had done the same job before in Jersey, and by the 4th of July order was restored. Congress remained in Princeton, at some inconvenience to themselves, but taking no chances.

One of the first evidences of the gradual return to normal was the arrival during July of a letter from George William Fairfax in England, with congratulations on the successful end to the war. None of the letters he had written during the hostilities had come through, and one which was intercepted had very nearly brought him serious consequences, and he was convinced that some of his English relations would have gladly seen him hanged to get his lands. An influential friend at Court had intervened on his behalf, and now, wrote George William, suddenly he was made as much of for being an American as he had lately been despised, and was pestered by intending travelers for introductions to the successful American Commander in Chief.

It was necessary in George's reply to break it to the Fairfaxes that their house Belvoir had suffered damage from a fire during the occupancy of the clergyman to whom it was rented, and was no longer habitable; "but mine (which is enlarged since you saw it) is most sincerely and heartily at your service, till you can rebuild it," he added with some pride and with Martha's entire approval. Twenty-three years, since Sally Fairfax had offered the Pamunkey bride the hospitality of Belvoir. Now the Fairfax fortunes had declined, and Mount Vernon could provide asylum and a generous welcome to old neighbors.

To relieve the general tedium at Newburgh Washington set out on a tour of the northern posts, as far as Ticonderoga. Humphreys and Walker went with him, and Trumbull remained with Martha, to attend to correspondence and emergencies at Headquarters—"like a gallant knight of ancient time, for the protection of the castle and defense of the virtue and innocence of the ladies," he wrote gaily to his friend Colonel William Stephens Smith, one of the Yorktown aides who was now acting on the commission for prisoners of war.

As at New Windsor two years before, Martha was stricken in George's absence with a prostrating fever and colic—as though once the daily neces-

sity for presenting a serene front was removed her resolution failed, and
all the ills she had held at bay took charge. Attended by her maid Oney,
and visited faithfully by Lucy Knox, who urged her to accept the hospitality of the much larger house which the Knoxes again occupied, some
distance from the River, Martha continued to lie in the small back bedroom which opened off the dining-reception room on the ground floor
—there were no upstairs chambers at Newburgh—enjoying the scent of
her herb garden baking in the hot sun outside her window. It would not
do for George to return and find her fled to the luxury of Mrs. Knox's
spacious rooms in the forest shade.

She was anything but recovered when he did come back, and what
was worse, a summons to Princeton from Congress awaited him. Its purpose was vague, and he felt justified in replying that he could not leave
Newburgh until the state of her health permitted her to accompany him.
They had intended that she should travel straight from there to Mount
Vernon to await his release, which they told each other must come now
some time within reason, but Congress informed him that a furnished
residence called Rocky Hill near Princeton had been engaged for them
to live in, and apparently expected them to make an indefinite sojourn
in the vicinity until the peace negotiations were concluded at Paris.

They would have found it much more convenient to send everything
from Newburgh to Mount Vernon in one move, and they had been packing to that end. On the other hand, the stay at Princeton would break
the journey for Martha, and provide a welcome reunion with her former
Jersey neighbors. She was able to start by the middle of August, and
they made another progress together through an affectionate countryside
to the widow Berrien's handsome mansion outside Princeton.

Rocky Hill was as different from the little stone dwelling above the
Hudson as they could have wished, short of Mount Vernon itself. A long
white house with a second floor verandah and high cool rooms, it might
have been designed to comfort Martha's convalescence, and except for
a relapse soon after the journey, and a simultaneous illness on the part
of both Humphreys and Walker, the Headquarters Family embarked on
a delightful social season which compensated for the infuriating inertia
at Paris.

It was sometimes sobering to contemplate the changes the passing
years had brought to Princeton, since the winter of '77 when the Commander in Chief of the American forces had first turned back the British army there. His comrades of that day were many of them far to seek.

Stirling, Mercer, and Charles Lee were dead, and Baylor was an invalid from his Tappan wound; Knox had been left on sentry-go at West Point, and Greene was still mopping up in South Carolina; Harrison as a chief justice in Maryland and Tilghman with a business established in Baltimore were both family men, and another of their friends from the Morristown winters, Elias Boudinot, was President of the Congress, where Colonel MacHenry, having served on Lafayette's staff through Yorktown, was now a member, as was the perennial Mifflin; Hamilton had already served and departed from a brief tenure as member for New York, returning to his law practice there.

The pretty college town which had echoed to gunfire that bleak January morning in what seemed like the dawn of time was now at midsummer, full of visitors, gay with balls and dinner parties and the bright gowns of women, while the Congress relaxed in spite of present complications in the sure promise of a hard-won peace. Old friends met again with reminiscent laughter, and reunited families began to lay plans for a not too distant future. Undeniably, there were, of course, stretches of boredom for all of them, when they wanted only to be done with it and go home. The news of the Treaty's arrival at New York was finally announced at the end of October, two years after the surrender at Yorktown, but the long delay had almost robbed them of any new elation.

Everyone remarked that General Washington looked well and had even put on a little weight, and was in noticeably good spirits. But his family affairs at Mount Vernon had begun to press, especially since a letter from Lund, which related, apparently with disapproval, that young Mrs. Custis was showing a great deal of interest in their neighbor David Stuart, whom she had known all her life. Lund—or possibly Mrs. Lund —seemed to feel that it was a little soon, but Nelly was now two years a widow. George and Martha, though they had had no previous intimations regarding Dr. Stuart, who was a responsible widower with grown children, were not altogether surprised. To Lund's possible expectation that the Washingtons would want to take steps, George replied with one of his tactful, sagacious letters which always left Martha smiling and impressed all over again by his profound knowledge of the female heart —especially as this time she could not but reflect that she had once found herself in Nelly's shoes: "For my part," he wrote to Lund, "I never did, nor do I believe I ever shall, give advice to a woman who is setting out on a matrimonial voyage; first because I never could advise one to marry without her own consent, and secondly because I know it is to no purpose to advise her to refrain when she has obtained it. A woman very rarely asks an opinion or requires advice on such an occasion until her resolution is fixed; and then it is with the hope and expectation of obtaining a sanction, not that she means to be governed by your disapprobation, that she applies. . . ."

At Princeton the remaining question was when the British would find it convenient to evacuate New York, their last post on the American continent, and they seemed to be in no great hurry. It would be necessary for the Commander in Chief to return to the Hudson River Headquarters in order to make a formal entry into the city on the heels of Carleton's departure. Time was running fast, and the Washingtons had promised themselves (and Nelly's children) that they would spend Christmas at Mount Vernon. This was still possible, but it began to look like a near thing. Early in November, Washington saw Martha off homeward in the chariot, riding with her as far as Trenton, with a couple of aides in attendance and a led saddle horse for his return journey. He paused at the ferry house, where the current still flowed strong and gray and cold, and turned a long glance backward in his memory to a night when the Delaware was dark with open boats full of silent, shivering men, and frantic horses were being swum through floating chunks of ice toward the Jersey shore.

Looking after him through the chariot window as he rode away with his little suite, toward his duty at Princeton, West Point, and New York, Martha comforted herself with the knowledge that he ran no hazard now, and their next meeting would be at Mount Vernon, and he would have come home to stay. Never again would it be required of her to drive northward along this road to a winter within sound of the drums. The war was over. The war was won. Alone in the chariot except for the silent, sympathetic Oney, the General's wife wept a little, because she was so happy.

They had only a month to make ready for his first Christmas at Mount Vernon in eight years. Besides the long list of commissions he had given her to take up with Lund, who had been much preoccupied with building a new house of his own to be called Hayfield, on land adjacent to the Home House on the west, she had a list of her own—a woman's list, of things which did not occur to him. Nelly came to stay, and brought the children, and was a great help. Martha asked no questions about Dr. Stuart. She didn't have to. It was plain enough how things were going in that quarter.

There was nothing to dread and everything to look for now, in the brief messages which came from the North. She measured his progress against the days left in the calendar. He could never manage it now, they said, despairing. But he had promised to try. Somehow, in spite of the British, in spite of Congress and the weather, in spite of time itself, he would be home for Christmas. His luggage came first, in a train of wagons shepherded by an officer of the Lifeguard, with explicit orders for its disposal and that of the teams and wagons and men who accompanied it. She felt it was a good sign.

On November 25th he was in New York, enduring an endless succession of dinners and speeches, congratulations, and fireworks. He was also doing some shopping for Mount Vernon. On December 8th he had reached Philadelphia again, and more of the same, though Congress was still absent, having removed from Princeton to more comfortable quarters at Annapolis. Hard riding brought him to Baltimore on the 17th—where the citizens had prepared a ball in his honor. He arrived at Annapolis on the 20th, and Congress held him there for three more days before he was permitted to tender his formal resignation with appropriate ceremonies. Humphreys and Walker were to accompany him home, and they had stationed Billy outside the State House with the horses, so that they could go straight from the last Congressional handshake to the saddle. Toward mid-afternoon on Christmas Eve, they rode up to the west door at Mount Vernon.

This time it was the way Martha had pictured it again and again in the course of keeping up her courage during the war—the day that he would come home to stay, not disabled, not broken in health, not obliged to sacrifice the rest of his life for the good of his country. Now the nightmare was over, and the dream had come true. Nelly's children ran to meet him—and Martha knew a strange, echoing moment which recalled a time twenty years before when Jacky himself and his sister Patsy had welcomed back their beloved Pappa from Williamsburg in exactly the same way. Now it was Jacky's son and daughter. Grandchildren at Mount Vernon, already? The war had robbed them of eight years. Lund's family hastened up from his new house to join in the welcome, and the servants gathered along the drive to touch the General's horse as it was led away, and then lingered to watch the door till he reappeared to smile and wave to them again.

Inside the house, there was the pleasant bustle of settling the aides into the rooms which had been ready for them for days, while the saddlebags were carried upstairs in Billy's charge. Dinner was set back to give the travelers time to wash and refresh themselves, and the candles were lighted in the family dining room as the short winter day drew in. Preparations for this meal had been made and remade many times, and every servant knew his place and his part, but still there was a happy scurry behind the scenes and a giggling in the pantry, from almost unbearable excitement and joy. The war was over. The master had come home. The war was won.

Martha sat next to him at the table, with Humphreys at the other end to do the carving. The children were flushed and talkative with the privilege of sharing the meal, and Nelly, in love again, had never looked prettier. Just by putting out her hand Martha could touch his sleeve—she did so, for the pleasure of proving that he was actually there, and he turned to her quickly, with that softening and lightening of his face which was her own particular possession. She found that she had nothing to say—but he understood, and his fingers closed hard over hers and held them, out of sight behind the table, while he asked the blessing.

When she raised her head she saw everything through a blur, and the candles dazzled. This was her moment. For this she had encountered the guns at Cambridge, the stench and hunger at Valley Forge, the pitiless cold at Morristown, the small, dull rooms on the Hudson, the everlasting drums and the endless waiting. For this she had watched him growing old before her eyes, graying, taking to spectacles, the lines etching deeper into his face, as the long struggle took toll of him, while he stood like a rock and endured it. And now he had won.

Pride of him, love for him, thankfulness to God, stood in her eyes and blinded her, as Humphreys rose in his place to wield the carving tools with his accustomed skill, and the wine glasses were filled. They had survived, and Mount Vernon had survived, and here they were together again, beginning again, even with small children in the house again—but with the war behind them, instead of looming on the horizon. His duty was done, his obligations discharged; they could ask nothing more of him now in the Congress, he had given them eight whole years. What was left of time, at their age, belonged to her and to Mount Vernon and to Jacky's babies. Still unable to see, still clinging to his hand behind the table, she felt him get to his feet and raise his glass in his only, his invariable toast—"All our friends!" he said, and then, with his best bow, he turned and drank to her.

CHAPTER EIGHT

False Dawn

1784–1789

EACH TIME THE SUMMER CAMPAIGN had driven her back to Mount Vernon during the war, she had noticed first of all the silence—no drums beating reveille before daybreak, no express riders pounding in at midnight, no rasp of command and slog of marching feet, no clattering aides, no spurs on the stairs. Now they experienced together with mutual delight the winter-locked tranquility on the Potomac.

They were housebound by snow and cold all through January, and visitors could not get to them, after Walker and Humphreys had ridden away—each aide with a present from the General of one hundred dollars as pocket money. To no one's surprise, Jacky's widow married Dr. Stuart, and they settled in at Abingdon which for five years had been home to Nelly and which she preferred to Hope Park where Stuart had raised his first family. The two elder Custis children, Eliza and Patty, remained with their mother, and Martha was given the upbringing of little Washington and little Nelly, so that the places of her own lost Patsy and Jack were filled by the second generation. Next summer they would all come to visit at Mount Vernon, and it would be like the old days again, with George riding his rounds of the farms and watching things grow, and neighbors driving in at dinner time—always someone driving in; laughter and security and reunion and plenty to eat; nothing to fear, nothing to regret. They had seen it through, and it was done, and they were at home again, and he had not been sacrificed. The years stretched ahead of her, sunlit and free—downhill all the way, now, in peace, together.

The Lunds were living at their own house, Hayfield, nearby, with a child coming in August, after one stillborn a year ago. The reckoning with Lund had been an embarrassment, for he disliked traveling and had left the western lands untended, had not even collected some of the rents or outstanding debts, and his accounts were as always in a sorry mess. Perhaps to make up for these shortcomings, he had drawn no pay as steward since '78—so the estate owed him five years arrears, which constituted simply another debt, as George would not accept the recompense. It was necessary for George to spend tedious hours at his desk in the new library, in a noise of carpentry as the bookshelves went up, endeavoring to sort out his own dues, many of them long past payment, and the often unsuspected claims of his creditors.

His army papers and letterbooks for the whole war period had come home in trunks full of bundles, after countless moves from one headquarters to another during the years between Cambridge and Newburgh. It would take a good secretary months to bring order out of that particular chaos, and no such person was now available. He needed a secretary just for his private correspondence, for everybody wrote to him about everything under the sun, from missing soldiers to the future of the Confederation. Many of his former officers, reluctant to lose touch with him, engaged him in letter-writing from their respective postwar locations. Some of them, like Humphreys, William Stephens Smith, and Steuben, were without employment and facing financial distress. Some of the others, like Knox and Hamilton, having gone into politics themselves tried to involve him again in public affairs. And some, like Lafayette and Tilghman and Trumbull, just wanted to hear from him because they could not bear to get along without him. He enjoyed his mail, even though it became a burden, and the letters from his recent comrades were read aloud in the evenings, and their affectionate messages to Martha were received with pleasure and acknowledged in full.

Not one of his punctilious replies was ever scribbled in haste or scamped of the courteous flourishes which good manners required. "At length, my dear Marquis, I am become a private citizen on the banks of the Potomac and under the shadow of my own vine and fig-tree, free from the bustle of a camp and the busy scenes of public life," he wrote to Lafayette in February. ". . . . I am not only retiring from all public employments, but I am retiring within myself; and shall be able to view the solitary walk, and tread the paths of private life with heartfelt satisfaction. Envious of none, I am determined to be pleased with all; and this my dear friend, being the order for my march, I will move gently down the stream of life until I sleep with my fathers. . . ."

Martha listened and nodded with her sympathetic smile, and noted that he then passed on quite briskly to a description of the evacuation ceremonies at New York, and an urgent invitation to Madame Lafayette to join her husband in a visit to the domestic scenes of Virginia.

Gradually the familiar plantation routine absorbed him, as though he had never been away—several hours at his desk before breakfast, a ride when the weather permitted till dinner time, a change of dress, with powder, an unhurried meal, often with guests who finally braved the cold, more writing till dark, a family supper, and in the evening a game of whist or a book read aloud in the parlor. He had brought back with him from Princeton Goldsmith's *Natural History,* Voltaire's *Letters,* Wildman on *Trees*—all these Martha heard contentedly, busy as usual with her needle, after remarking that Locke's *Human Understanding,* to which Tom Jefferson was said to owe so much, made her sleepy.

Pressed as he often was, behind hand as he was in all the estate work, they nevertheless enjoyed what seemed to them a magnificent leisure. Mount Vernon's affairs might be tangled and exigent, but they weighed less than the Cause. The claims of anxious relatives and impatient creditors might be worrisome, but it was not like watching his men and horses starve. And often as they sat together in the warm candlelight with a generous fire burning on the hearth, surrounded once more by their own belongings and comforts, they would recall those other rooms at Valley Forge and Newburgh, where they had cherished what then appeared an almost hopeless dream of spending another such evening as this one. The sense of achievement, of deliverance, more than once brought a mist to Martha's eyes, seeing him bent above his tireless quill, preoccupied, intent, but in his bones aware of her sitting near him, as she was in hers that he was within reach of her hand. He wore his spectacles for reading and writing, and was having trouble to get false teeth that were comfortable. She too used spectacles for her fine sewing, and they had little need for powder in their hair. But he was up to his normal weight again, and his face, in spite of the frown the relentless columns of figures brought, was smoothing out.

There was still plenty to bear down on him. He would have to sell or lease western lands to finance Mount Vernon until he got it running properly again as only he knew how to do. The demands on him for money were appalling, and he had never had enough ready cash. His widowed sister Betty was living in the beautiful house Fielding Lewis built for her at Fredericksburg, but she had very little money to keep it up, and there were three sons under twenty. His mother, more unreasonable each year, mismanaged her small farm and complained of her overseer and of poverty. Sam's orphaned family at Harewood in Berkeley County, three unruly boys and an infant daughter, were in the dubious care of his eldest son Thornton by his second wife. John Augustine's Bushrod was studying law at Philadelphia and overspending his allowance, and his younger brother Corbin was without prospects of any kind. Charles' George Augustine, the General's favorite nephew and late aide, was trying to recover his health in the sea air of Rhode Island, but was marked, they feared, for Lawrence's fatal disease.

On Martha's side, the Bassetts and the Dandridges were comparatively solvent and self-sufficient, and Fanny Bassett, now a charming seventeen, came to Mount Vernon for a visit, which was almost like having her mother back again.

In April, they had a letter from Lafayette, setting the date for his promised return to America, and presenting his family's affectionate compliments to Mrs. Washington: "Tell her that I hope soon to thank her for a dish of tea at Mount Vernon," he wrote. "Yes, my dear General, before the month of June is over, you will see a vessel coming up the Potomac and out of that vessel will your friend jump. . . ."

But it was August, and the ship took him to Philadelphia. "There is no rest for me till I go to Mount Vernon," he assured them from there, and on the 17th he came, tall and magically invigorating as ever, still the dandy even without a uniform, boiling over with excitement and affection. He seized and kissed the delighted General on both cheeks, he caught and kissed both Martha's outstretched hands, he tossed and kissed the children, he drank healths, he made toasts and little speeches, he praised the food, the new rooms, the landscaping plans—he blew through the house like a happy hurricane, and they all felt transported by his unaffected joy.

He brought with him nostalgic letters to George from Rochambeau and Chastellux. He wanted to hear all the news about his wartime comrades in America, and sat down with his hosts the first evening over a bowl of iced punch to call the roll. The Washingtons were concerned about the situation of Baron Steuben, for whose caustic military caution

Lafayette had once had a youthful intolerance, but the dynamic drill-master was now just a lonely, stout-hearted old man, without resources in a country not his own, quite unfit to earn his living if there was no army to work at. He had served steadily from Valley Forge to Newburgh, and had not received a fraction of the pay which Congress had promised him as Inspector General. Unattached to a family of his own either in Europe or America, he had for a while kept up a lively bachelor establish-ment in New York with a few of his younger officers like Walker and William Stephens Smith, who one by one had gone their own somewhat precarious ways. He was at present living almost alone in his shabby, run-down house outside the city, unable to afford better lodgings, unwill-ing to accept hospitality from old friends which he could not repay in kind, asking only for enough of what money was due him to pay his debts and his way back to Europe. The State of New Jersey had offered him the confiscated property of the Tory Zabriskie in Bergen County, which had once served briefly as Headquarters during the war, and he had refused it for the owner's sake, thus leaving himself homeless. Generous, hospitable, and proud, the Baron had always kept himself poor by lending and giving what little money he came by, and at York-town had sold his last few personal valuables to finance a dinner to the French officers in return for entertainment accepted from them. Congress was now treating him like any shiftless foreign vagrant, which was dis-graceful and would not look well abroad.

Washington felt keenly that something should be done about Steuben without delay, but he had already found that Congress took even less notice of the master of Mount Vernon than they had of the Commander in Chief. He had recommended his aide Colonel Humphreys for the post of Foreign Secretary, and they had promptly appointed John Jay instead. Humphreys was glad to take a job as secretary to Thomas Jeffer-son on the commerce commission which had sailed for France in July. Tilghman, Moylan, Varnum, Bland, Fitzgerald, and MacHenry—all safe, Lafayette was glad to learn, in business and politics for themselves, and all raising families, except MacHenry who was in the Maryland Senate now and he would doubtless go soon. Baylor had died at Barbados at thirty-two, of that Tappan bayonet. Harry Lee had a wife and son at Stratford, and was in the Virginia Legislature. Hamilton was practicing law in New York. General Greene had been presented with a plantation home on the Savannah River, in recognition of his part in the Southern campaign, and was planning to spend his winters there raising rice and cotton—it was sixteen days by water from Rhode Island, but he and his family seemed to think nothing of that. General Wayne, who had served with Greene till the end of the war and had been given the honor of leading the army into Charleston on the day the city was evacuated by the British, had also been voted an estate in Georgia only a few miles from Greene's, and talked of settling there—without his wife, who was now permanently estranged. Knox had succeeded Lincoln as Secretary of War, and his family grew yearly. Lincoln, in retirement on his Massachusetts farm at Hingham in happy domesticity, was nevertheless very embarrassed financially. Colonel Harrison at Port Tobacco was a near neighbor to Mount Vernon, and they would ask him in for dinner and a talk about old times. Meade was living out in the Valley with his second wife and a little family; Walker was secretary to Governor Clinton of New York, and had married the pretty Quakeress he had loved for years. George Augustine Washington—the shadow fell. He had gone to the West Indies last spring—on a hundred guineas provided by his uncle— and had recently written from Bermuda to say that he was still so little improved in health that he thought of trying Charleston next, where his cousin William Washington lived with a South Carolina wife.

When the tale was all told, and everyone accounted for, Lafayette looked round rather solemnly in the firelight at Mount Vernon and pointed out, unnecessarily, that they in that room were among the fortunate ones.

While the Marquis made his tour of the country, as far north as Albany and Boston and then by sea to Williamsburg, to renew old friendships, George set out with Dr. Craik and his son William, and Bushrod Washington, for an inspection of his western lands. Martha thought they were like four schoolboys together, assembling their traveling kit, choosing horses and servants, hunting out old maps and surveying tools. It was a holiday—George's first in many years. He chose to spend it the way he had loved best and longest—in the saddle. He would collect his rents, straighten boundaries, investigate trespassers, lay out a program of improvement on his frontier property—and except that on the way he must go to see his brother Charles at his place called Happy Retreat near Samuel's Harewood, and learn the worst about the dismal affairs of the Shenandoah Washingtons, he would thoroughly enjoy himself. The winter had kept him too much confined at Mount Vernon. He was used to exercise and hardship and activity, during all those years as Commander in Chief. The change was too sudden.

After a candlelight breakfast, Martha watched the cavalcade out of sight down the westward avenue in the dawn—two Craiks, two Washingtons, and three mounted servants leading extra horses which carried baggage. Then with a private sigh of relief, she gave her orders for the day and climbed the stairs and went to bed, defiantly, in the morning, and closed her eyes. The time had come, as it had in the little house on the Hudson, when she had to let go. She was roused in mid-afternoon by Mrs. Lund, in a state of anxiety. The maid Oney said she was not to be disturbed, it was true, but did she realize that she had not had any dinner?

Lying back comfortably against her pillows, Martha murmured something about being tired, but accepted with resignation the tempting tray Oney brought to the bedside, and then drifted off to sleep again. Mrs. Lund was frightened, for it was not like her, and Dr. Craik was now out of reach. When Martha woke again she begged them not to fuss, because she only wanted a rest. She only wanted for a few days not to have to hold up for George, she might have said—just to be tired, all by herself. Oney hovered, and the children came in to stare, and neighbors whispered in the rooms below. She did not care. He would not know until he got back, and by then she would be all right again.

She might have been, but once released from daily supervision everything at Mount Vernon began to fall apart. Sickness spread in the quarters, and both the children were afflicted with diarrhea, from which fat, jolly baby Washington bounced back before long, but it left little Nelly puny and reduced. George came home sooner than they had expected him, his travels curtailed by Indian unrest on the Ohio frontier which he was urged to avoid—and caught the household in confusion, and discovered that she had been ill along with the children. So she gave up trying to conceal it from him, and listened patiently to Dr. Craik, who was inclined to run on about the nervous strain of the war years, and her time of life—which it didn't take a doctor to know.

The family conference with Charles had produced no solution to the Washington problems in the Shenandoah Valley. Thornton had married well, and wanted to leave Harewood, which could not run itself. His half-brothers were eleven, ten, and eight, and there was a baby girl by Sam's wife, who had not long survived their father. The boys could be put to school, if someone would foot the bills, but little Harriot could not be left forever on the hands of Thornton's wife, starting a family of her own, and colored nurses. Already the child, about Nelly's age, was

spoiled and unmanageable. Must they have her at Mount Vernon, along
with Jacky's two, who knew how to behave themselves? Well, perhaps
not yet. The boys first. There was a boarding school at Georgetown that
would do for the two youngest ones.

In November George went down to Richmond to meet Lafayette, who
was returning overland from Williamsburg on his way back to the
Potomac for a second brief visit before he sailed for France. He brought
news of their friends in the North, where he had for the first time set
foot in New York City, and received a splendid reception at the Battery.
Mrs. Knox was going to have another, he reported, and Aaron Burr's
wife, who had been that charming widow Mrs. Prevost, whose hospitality
the General would recall at Paramus in '78, had given him a daughter
called Theodosia. But Lafayette was now thoughtful, and he asked questions to which they did not know the answers at Mount Vernon. George
listened, and queried in his turn, and then he too looked grave, and they
invited Harry Lee to come over from Stratford to dinner, and brought
Colonel Fitzgerald down from Alexandria, where he ran a prosperous
shipping agency. They all sat a long time over the wine when the cloth
had been drawn, and their voices dropped, and nobody made any jokes
—and that was like old times too, but not what Martha liked to recall.

They had won the war, she thought with an impatient jab of her
needle, and the British had gone, so what was there to worry about
now? They had settled it, hadn't they, at Yorktown, and two years later
at Paris where the Peace Treaty was finally signed. Who was it now,
making the trouble, besides the Indians? Gradually, as she listened in
silence, it began to appear that the thing they had been fighting for
wouldn't work. But that would make them a laughingstock all over
Europe.

They were quoting Locke again, and Lafayette advised them to read
Montesquieu. And then George said—she could usually make something
of it when he spoke—he said it was as clear as A B C to him that unless
the states could be persuaded to control their jealousies of each other,
and renounce the idea that each one of them must be all-powerful within
itself, they had beaten Great Britain to very little purpose, and would
be conquered again by their own prejudices, while England howled with
laughter, and no one could blame her for that. So long as the Congress
had not sufficient power to enforce its will, said George, there would be
squabbling and controversy. Even during the war, when the colonies were
united by a common peril, there had been an almost fatal rivalry between

them, and between the North and the South. Without the war, each separate breach would widen. Harry Lee remarked that there was talk in Congress of revising the Articles of Confederation, and designing a new Constitution, with a more centralized authority.

Unnoticed by any of them, Martha swept the table with a glance of exasperated surprise. A Constitution? Then what about that document of July, '76, which had set all the bells of Philadelphia ringing and was celebrated with bonfires and fireworks till the storm drove people indoors? But she asked no questions. Usually if she waited long enough she began to understand.

The time for Lafayette's sailing drew near, and he made the Mount Vernon rounds with George for the last time—to see how the new greenhouse was progressing, and the planting along the serpentine walk to the west of the mansion; to pay the daily visit to the horse Nelson, now retired to pasture and a green old age, because he had had the honor to carry the Commander in Chief on that glorious day at Yorktown— he always came frisking to the fence like a youngster again to feel the master's hand. George accompanied Lafayette in the carriage as far as Baltimore, and came home depressed and quiet, convinced that he would never see the boy again.

Then Fanny Bassett arrived from her father's house at Eltham for a Christmas visit, and having this favorite niece of Martha's in the house always brightened things up. It proved to be a mild winter, and Fanny was much in demand in the Alexandria neighborhood for balls and weddings, often attended by young Dr. Craik, who conveniently had sisters Fanny's age. Betty Lewis' sons, the Fredericksburg nephews, came and went, along with the countless Carters, the Fitzhughs, a Calvert, a Lee or two, and Bushrod Washington, back from Philadelphia to start a law practice at Alexandria—the house sometimes rang with young people.

As the days grew shorter, George was still spending hours at his desk in the new library conducting his own correspondence, and his diary had resumed its tranquil chronicle:

April 13. Received from Colonel Henry Lee of Westmoreland, 12 Horse Chestnut trees (small) and an equal number of cuttings of the Tree Box . . .

April 27. Rid to Muddy Hole [farm]. Upon my return found General and Mrs. Moylan here . . .

May 9. The blossom of the crabtree is unfolding, and shedding its fragrant perfume. That of the black Haw has been out some days and is an ornamental flower, being in large clusters . . .

May 14. My nephew George Augustine Washington arrived here from Charleson after [having] been to Bermuda and the West Indies in pursuit of health, which he has but imperfectly recovered . . .

May 18. The locust blossom is beginning to display . . .

May 20. A Mr. Noah Webster came here in the afternoon and stayed all night . . .

May 25. Had peas for the [first] time in the season at dinner . . .

It was always Martha who insisted that the children should be quiet while Grandpappa was thinking, and that he should not be interrupted —until sometimes Grandpappa grew lonely among his tiptoeing household and showed a smiling face around the door, which was the signal for juvenile rejoicing. In the evenings after supper when the young people had been sent off to bed he often worked as late as nine o'clock, and then he liked Martha to sit in the same room with her needlework and send her compliments in the letters he was writing, and provide the bits of family news and neighborhood doings with which he salted the final paragraphs for old friends. To Lafayette: "The little sprig at Annapolis, to whose nod so many lofty trees of the forest had bowed, has yielded the scepter . . . and last Thursday placed it at the feet of Mr. M—, who perhaps may wield it with as much despotism as she did." To George William Fairfax, who seemed not to have received several letters of earlier dates: "to beg that you would consider Mount Vernon your home until you can build with convenience, in which Mrs. Washington joins very sincerely. I never look toward Belvoir without this uppermost in my mind. But alas! Belvoir is no more! I took a ride there yesterday to view the ruins, and ruins indeed they are . . ."

The spring of '85 brought a double blow to Martha in the death of both her mother and her only surviving brother, Bartholomew, who at forty-eight left a widow, a son named for him, two younger boys, and another Patty. Grief robbed her of the ability to conceal her persistent lack of good health, which began to cause George real concern.

Moreover, with all those other likely boys to choose from, and with everything there was to be feared from his recurrent illnesses, Fanny confessed that she had been in love with George Augustine for a long time—she had turned eighteen—and had promised him that she would never marry anyone else.

George sat down to write to her father, one of his tactful masterpieces of non-interference. Martha's mind went back to Nelly Calvert and poor Jack, but this time, except for George Augustine's weak chest, it seemed an ideal match—her beloved niece and George's favorite nephew, childhood sweethearts, probably willing to make their home at Mount Vernon, or build a place nearby. George could give them some land, he had plenty of that. Her interest in things began to revive.

Her brother-in-law Burwell Bassett came up from New Kent to discuss it, bringing Fanny's two brothers, and Charles Washington arrived from the Valley. All the Bassetts and George Augustine went on to Abingdon with Fanny to celebrate the engagement there too, taking with them little Nelly and even baby Washington for a visit with the other Custis children. The next day Charles returned home, so that on the 30th of June George was able to set down in his diary with some satisfaction one of the rare personal items which occurred there: "Rid to my hayfield at the meadow, from there to my Dogue Run and Muddy Hole plantations, and dined with only Mrs. Washington, which I believe is the first instance of it since my retirement from public life."

The house was soon full again, with the Stuarts and all the children from Abingdon for a return visit. On the advice of Dr. Stuart, George Augustine had agreed to a few weeks' complete rest at the Springs before the wedding, and the Bassett boys were to accompany him. In another family conference it was decided that he and Fanny would live at Mount Vernon, at least until there were children, and he would resume something of his old Headquarters duties as copyist and assistant to his uncle, who was still hoping to hire a man to act as tutor to Nelly and little Washington, and take charge of the accounts and correspondence of the estate. Washington weddings were in the air, as John Augustine's son Bushrod was to marry Julia Blackburn in October.

Jefferson wrote from Paris that a M. Houdon had been chosen by himself and Dr. Franklin to come to America to execute a statue of Washington which the Virginia Assembly had directed made for the sake of posterity. There was not time, Jefferson explained, to ask his permission and await his answer. M. Houdon had just finished a work of the King of France, and his bust of Voltaire was said to be the finest thing of its kind in the world. He would bring with him a trained workman or two, who would not of course expect to consort with the family, and he would need an interpreter, which could doubtless be found in Alexandria.

Washington could only groan. He had already suffered much from painters, in the interest of posterity.

M. Houdon crossed the Atlantic in the same ship with Dr. Franklin, who had recently turned over his ministerial duties in France to Jefferson, and was coming home to Philadelphia at seventy-nine, after almost nine years at Paris. Washington sent a courteous welcome and invitation to Houdon's party, and they arrived unannounced at the Mount Vernon river-landing at midnight on a Sunday, having been delayed by an accident on the voyage down the Potomac from Alexandria. The household had gone to bed, and the strangers set all the dogs to barking, while hastily clad servants ran here and there with luggage and lights, the kitchen was summoned to action, bottles of wine were opened, beds were prepared, and hospitality provided for the sculptor, his three young men assistants, and a Mr. Perin of Alexandria who had come along because he could speak both French and English.

The whole thing was inopportune. The boys were back from the Springs before their time, preparations for Fanny's wedding were afoot, many family guests were expected—and yet George was required to submit to the tedious indignities of a life-mask and a welter of plaster of Paris. He nevertheless found the process novel and of interest—even though he must also permit himself to be followed about and surveyed in all attitudes and moods. Houdon was a pleasant fellow, and brought letters from Lafayette and Jefferson and Humphreys in Paris. He and his minions were still at Mount Vernon when on October 15th George wrote in his diary: "After the candles were lighted, George Augustine Washington and Frances Basset were married by Mr. Grayson . . ."

It was a happy Christmas on the Potomac, and everyone attended the races at Alexandria. Martha was in better health than for nearly a year, and Washington felt really well, all the time, and was in the best of spirits, especially after the hunting began.

In November Lund proposed that someone else, possibly George Augustine, should take over his duties at Mount Vernon and allow him to retire to the management of his own place nearby. George Augustine was willing to try, and it was agreed that a house should be built for him and Fanny on land adjacent to the Home House. There remained the problem of a tutor-secretary, which was solved early in the year by the recommendation of a young man named Tobias Lear of New Hampshire, who was chosen by General Lincoln from among his son's associ-

ates at Harvard, and was hired without an interview. The schooling of
Sam's two youngest boys, George Steptoe and Lawrence Augustine
Washington, was proving very expensive, and they were an irresponsible
pair at best. Washington removed them from Georgetown to an academy
at Alexandria, hoping to keep a tighter rein, and finally brought their
half-sister Harriot to Mount Vernon, where her willful ways and lack
of discipline created discord and tears in the once peaceful nursery department.

Young Mr. Lear, Harvard, '83, was good-natured and companionable,
and before long became an indispensable member of the family. During
the summer of '86 Colonel Humphreys returned to Mount Vernon after
two years abroad. They received him with joy and entreated him to stay,
and listened spellbound to his stories of his European adventures and
acquaintances. He had been introduced to Paris society as a colleague of
Jefferson and under the wing of Dr. Franklin, to say nothing of the cordial
wartime friendship renewed with Lafayette. His good looks, bachelorhood, and somewhat bluff American ways made him popular in French
circles, if only as a novelty. John Adams, already overseas on government
business, was added to Jefferson's commerce commission, and had sent
to Massachusetts for his wife and family, who were with him at Paris. In
Humphreys' expert opinion, young Abigail Adams, just turning twenty,
compared very well with the European girls.

Later on, after Adams had been appointed the first American Minister
to Great Britain, Humphreys had encountered them again during a visit
he made with Jefferson to London. Colonel William Stephens Smith,
whom Martha recalled as one of the more spectacular members of the
Headquarters Family at the end of the war, was acting as Adams' secretary. Extravagant, enterprising, and always a little more than life-size,
Smith was by no means sobered by the opportunities of diplomatic
service, and everyone prophesied that he would marry Abby Adams, if
she looked no higher. The manners of the British Court toward Americans were distinctly cool—the King was not a good loser. Humphreys
had gone many times to the theater in Paris and London, and pronounced
Mrs. Siddons the most superb actress he had ever seen.

But while he was at home in Connecticut for a visit to his parents
before coming South, he had received a rude shock at the state of American affairs. It was the same story other guests had brought to Mount
Vernon—legislative dissension, empty treasuries, worthless paper money,
criticism of a government which was powerless to redress the complaints
it suffered from.

Only a few days after Humphreys' arrival at Mount Vernon they were saddened by the news of the death from sunstroke of General Greene at his Savannah River plantation, which raised the delicate question of how Kitty and her children could manage without him—the eldest, born at Cambridge, was only eleven years old. George wrote to her with a prompt offer to assist with the expenses of the boy's education—it was by no means the first or last offer of its kind among his many needy acquaintances—but Kitty gratefully refused and brought the children to the household of relatives in New York. Tilghman also had died very suddenly at forty-two, from the lingering effects of his continuous wartime service at Washington's side. Each time they lost one of the Headquarters Family, all so much younger than George, Martha would flinch and turn an anxious glance on him for reassurance. He was well. He was safe. He was strong. He had years to go. It had caught the boys too young, perhaps, and they had not had his frontier training. He stood the war better because he was already inured to hardship from his strenuous youth.

Humphreys had brought with him from France the newly published volume of Chastellux's Journal of his travels in America, and he read it aloud to them, translating as he went—he would have liked the job of preparing the English edition, if it had not already been announced in London. The Washingtons listened with reminiscent laughter and some shaking of heads, reliving the old perilous days in Jersey and the boredom on the Hudson. This led to a renewed discussion of Humphreys' pet hope that Washington would write his own memoirs, drawing on the mass of private and official papers which reposed in his trunks. Washington always said no, but offered all the material to Humphreys if he would stay at Mount Vernon indefinitely and write a history of the war, as well as his projected Life of General Putnam, under whom he had served devotedly until Putnam's retirement in '79.

The happy prospect was soon canceled by Humphreys' election to the Connecticut Assembly, which forced him to leave Mount Vernon after only a month's stay, promising to return and complete both literary tasks as a member of the household again. No one was more uneasily aware of the need of good men in the legislative department than Washington, who could only encourage his former aide to take his place in the troubled New England scene, and hoped for a full report from him on the unrest in the North. Harry Lee at the same time left the Virginia Assembly for the Congress, now established at New York, while Madison and Monroe assumed leadership at Richmond, under Edmund Randolph as the newly elected governor.

Madison and Monroe. Martha had not made up her mind about either one of them. Monroe was a Westmoreland County man, nephew of Judge Jones at Fredericksburg. He had left Williamsburg College to join the army at the beginning of the war, but was one of those who resigned midway, returning to Virginia to study law. That could only count as a mark against him, though he went out again when Arnold came up the James. From the Virginia Assembly he had progressed to the Congress as a protégé of Jefferson's, and while in New York had somehow managed to marry Elizabeth Kortwright, whom everybody had expected to do better than an unprepossessing Virginia delegate with no particular prospects. They had now settled in a Jones house at Fredericksburg, with a comfortable law practice.

Madison had wit and quiet charm, and a Princeton polish, but no army record whatever, and was also one of Jefferson's friends. He had gone to Congress in the latter part of the war—Martha remembered him from the Philadelphia winter of '81—and then went into the Virginia Legislature and a law practice at Richmond. The two men seemed oddly congenial associates, and secretly Martha bracketed them in a common suspicion—they were up to something about George. They kept writing to him, and she could see that their letters disturbed him. When they arrived at Mount Vernon together on their way home from the Congress in October, she felt a growing uneasiness.

There had been a meeting of commissioners at Annapolis, too sparsely attended, which nevertheless set the following May for a general convention at Philadelphia to consider the alarming spirit of disunion among the United States, and to devise a remedy—thirteen years to the very month, since that First Congress in '74. There was no longer any doubt about what was afoot with regard to George. His name would head the list of Virginia delegates to Philadelphia—again.

He would not consent to it, he told them, first because of his own inclination for private life, and secondly because he had announced his retirement so firmly and repeatedly. Madison was the man to act for Virginia now, George said. Madison was young, a brilliant debater, schooled in law and Congressional procedure. Madison must take charge. They went away, unconvinced.

It was David Humphreys up in Connecticut who brought the house down over Martha's head, just in time to spoil Christmas. A man named

Shays had raised a rebellion in Massachusetts and led an armed rabble
toward the arsenal at Springfield. Both Lincoln and Knox had taken a
hand in its prompt dispersement, but this looked like civil war. George
was appalled and bewildered at the speed with which his brave new nation was crumbling into anarchy. He read out Humphreys' letter to Martha and George Augustine and Fanny, in incredulous tones: "Congress,
I am told, are seriously alarmed and hardly know which way to turn or
what to expect," Humphreys had written. "Indeed, my dear General,
nothing but a good Providence can extricate us from our present difficulties and prevent some terrible catastrophe. In case of civil discord, I
have already told you it was seriously my opinion that you could not
remain neuter—and that you would be obliged, in self-defense, to take
part on one side or the other, or withdraw from the Continent. Your
friends are of the same opinion . . ."

Withdraw—where? There was speechless consternation in the quiet
parlor at Mount Vernon. But because of David Humphreys' shocking
outspokenness, Martha was better prepared for the letter from Governor
Randolph which arrived a few days later: "I freely, then, entreat you
to accept the unanimous appointment of the General Assembly to the
Convention at Philadelphia," it read. "For the gloomy prospect still ad-
mits one ray of hope; that those who began, carried on, and consum-
mated the Revolution, can yet rescue America from the impending
ruin. . . ."

But for the children, that Christmas of '86 would have been ruined
indeed, disappointed of Humphreys' jovial company, and overhung with
anxiety about the Massachusetts trouble and the uncertainties confronting the proposed Convention at Philadelphia. George would attend it, of
course, however much he might temporize and postpone his decision.
Martha was already resigned to that, if he was not. She knew very well
he had not spent eight years trying to save his country from its own
ineptitudes only to let it sink now, if any effort on his part could once
more hold it up. He would go to Philadelphia. And after that—she could
not imagine what they would demand of him after that.

The year 1787 began badly, with the death of John Augustine, always
George's most dearly loved brother. Bushrod being grown and a lawyer,
his father's estate was in good hands, and for once George had no inconvenient obligations. The perpetual complaints of his mother at Fredericksburg seemed to indicate some wish on her part to come to Mount
Vernon for her declining years, and at this George really balked. He

wrote her another of his painstaking letters, advising again how to reduce her responsibilities and expenses, and regretting once more that he
could not undertake personally to direct her overseer and keep her accounts.

Both he and Martha came close to panic at the idea of trying to assimilate the strong-willed, unobliging old lady into their own overflow-
ing household, and he had a guilty dread that it might be apparent in
his letter, where he strove with his usual good manners to explain away
what he felt to be a lack of hospitality: "My house is at your service,
and I would press you most sincerely to accept it, but I am sure, and
candor requires me to say, that it will never answer your purpose in any
shape whatever," he wrote after anxious consultation with his wife and
his conscience. "For in truth it may be compared to a well-resorted tavern, as scarcely any strangers who are going from north to south or from
south to north do not spend a day in it. This would, were you to be an
inhabitant of it, oblige you to do one of three things: first to be always
dressing to appear in company; second to come into [the room] in dis-
habille; or third, to be as it were a prisoner in your own chamber. The
first you'd not like; . . . the second, I should not like . . . and the third,
more than probably, would not be pleasing to either of us. Nor indeed
could you be retired in any room in my house; for what with the sitting
up of company, and the noise and bustle of servants, and many other
things, you would not be able to enjoy that calmness and serenity of mind
which in my opinion you ought now to prefer to every other consideration in life. . . . But by the mode I have pointed out, you may reduce
your income to a certainty, to be eased of all trouble, and if you are so
disposed, may be perfectly happy; for happiness depends more upon the
internal frame of a person's own mind than on the externals in the world.
Of the last if you will pursue the plan here recommended I am sure you
can want nothing that is essential. The other depends wholly upon yourself, for the riches of the Indies cannot purchase it. . . ."

When he had sent the letter off to Fredericksburg with that lingering
self-doubt and self-reproach which his mother could always rouse in him,
Martha dared to draw a long breath, and sent up a fervent prayer that
he had settled it this time.

Pressed on all sides to commit what seemed to him at least an in-
consistency, by attending the Convention at Philadelphia in May, he admitted to Martha a fear that from there he might be swept again into
the sort of public duty which they had so recently escaped. He was fifty-

five. He had just begun to enjoy himself in his own way. The renewed demand of his country for his time and attention, caused largely by the recent upheavals in New England, was as exasperating to him as the whine of a teething child. He wanted to live his own life for a while. Lund's retirement, although he was still in the neighborhood, had left many extra duties about the estate which it was unfair to expect George Augustine to carry alone, even for the few weeks the Convention would require. May was a bad time to go, at the start of the growing season. George had been visited by a rheumatism so severe as to put his arm in a sling for several days. His letter to Governor Randolph, finally yielding to the wishes of his friends, was as little gracious, as nearly disgruntled, as any he ever penned. Once committed, he shouldered the new burden with his usual serenity, and reproached no one for forcing his decision.

The Robert Morrises had cordially invited the Washingtons to be their guests again, during the Convention, but Martha's niece Fanny's first child was born at Mount Vernon in April, and she was slow to recover her strength, while George's niece Harriot remained a small disturbance in the house, and the Custis children would be unhappy without their grandmother. Martha was willing that he should go to Philadelphia without her, but she wanted it understood that if the thing dragged on too long, or if he was ever unwell or needed her, he had only to send. Philadelphia, she reminded him with a backward glance at Cambridge and Newburgh, was not far.

A few days before he was to set out, an express from Fredericksburg brought word of the illness to extremity of both his mother and his sister Betty, and he was compelled to change his plans in order to ride in the opposite direction. He found his mother out of danger, and Betty merely exhausted with nursing. They promptly improved at sight of him, and he returned home the following day. As usual with him, under the stimulus of emergency his own health rallied.

He rode the rounds once more with George Augustine, to go over the work to be done and the possible difficulties arising in his absence, aware as he did so of a dreamlike sensation of having done the same thing before in another life—only then it was Lund he left in charge, and at Philadelphia in '75 he had somehow become Commander in Chief. This time—but they didn't need a general now, and surely he was no good to them in Congress, he couldn't make a speech.

In spite of his reluctance to leave home, the prospect of meeting again as fellow delegates some of the men who had once been his daily companions in the field, and whom he had hardly thought to see again, raised his spirits as he started North, charged with messages and small tokens from Martha to her Philadelphia friends. And although the proceedings of the Convention were at once voted secret, and no member set down in his letters home anything of the deliberations in the chamber or his own conclusions, Martha at Mount Vernon awaited eagerly the social news from that once familiar scene.

The warmth of Washington's reception was surprising, even to her. An escort of old friends and comrades rode out to meet him and all the bells in Philadelphia were rung as he entered the city. After nearly four years in seclusion he was still the most popular man in America, unforgotten and genuinely loved. There was still a conviction in the streets that he had saved them before and could do it again. There was still magic in his tall, unassertive presence, even without an army at his back. Washington was there. Now the right thing would be done.

At Mount Vernon they received that impression more from the newspapers than from his letters, which were on the old familiar homesick note. He sent some pecan nuts for planting; he hoped the stray doe from his tame herd was not lost; would they please forward the last volume of his diary, which he had left by mistake on his writing-table; and had the seeds of the honey locust come up?

He had been made, contrary to his wish and by unanimous vote, President of the Convention. How did that sit, Martha wondered in wifely satisfaction, with the slippery Thomas Mifflin, who was now Speaker of the Pennsylvania Assembly?

Notwithstanding his usual preference for independent lodgings, George was persuaded to stay with the Morrises after all, and everyone regretted Martha's absence and sent her the fondest regards in the letters he filled with the kind of personal details he knew she would best appreciate. He wrote that he had attended the wedding of Colonel John Eager Howard—hero of the battle at the Cowpens in Carolina in '81, and now one of Baltimore's wealthy and respected landowners—to Peggy Chew, around whose home at Germantown the fighting had surged in '77. He confessed that he was sorry to find that George Mason, a reluctant member of the Virginia delegation and now on his first visit to the city, was bored and impatient with the Philadelphia entertainment, coming to it belatedly as a stranger. Of the old Headquarters Family, Hamilton was there from New York, MacHenry from Maryland, and Varnum of Rhode Island, besides the Virginians, Edmund Randolph, Harry Lee, and Mason. There were many delegates who were unknown to him, and very few members were left from the original Congress of '74 besides himself, William Livingston, and Rutledge of Carolina. He had gone to pay his respects to the aged Dr. Franklin who, although one of Pennsylvania's delegates, was seldom able to attend the sessions any more. They were having the same hot summer weather she would recall from '76, when she was inconvenienced by the inoculation. During a brief adjournment for work by a committee on the new Constitution, he had ridden up to Valley Forge and looked round the whole camp—that took you back.

In June he wrote asking for some books to be sent to him, and more clothes, "as I see no end to my stay here." He wanted his blue coat with the crimson collar, and the one without lapels and lined with white silk, and his new umbrella which they would find in his study. What progress on the greenhouse? Send measurements for Venetian blinds for the dining-room.

To everyone's dismay at Mount Vernon, George Augustine's conscientious exertions on the estate business brought on symptoms of his old weakness—he got wet in a shower, caught a cold which settled on his chest, and could not get rid of a cough. George wrote at once to say that he was not to attempt more than his strength would bear, and Fanny was frightened, and they put George Augustine to bed while the dependable Mr. Lear took over as best he could from day to day.

The new Constitution was signed by the delegates at Philadelphia in mid-September, and Washington reached home on the 22d, bringing gifts for the children and remembrances for Martha from their friends—besides a recurrent thoughtful silence. She watched him wisely as he moved about the house and surveyed the improvements to the grounds. His face was calm, but somehow secretive and masked, as it used to be before a new campaign began.

He told her about signing the Constitution himself first of all, as President and Virginia delegate. Mason and Edmund Randolph were two of only three who withheld their signatures altogether, because they did not believe that as it stood the document embodied the necessary solution. George was willing to concede that it was far from perfection, but it was the best that could be arrived at so far, and in his view was the only present alternative to anarchy, and furthermore, could be amended as time went on. It was largely the work of Madison, Gouverneur Morris,

Rufus King, and Randolph himself. It provided for a Senate and a House of Representatives, a Court of last resort, and a Chief Executive to be chosen by electors from each state. It had now to be ratified by nine of the thirteen state Assemblies, which would entail months of debate in each. He was disappointed in his old friend George Mason, and more than ever impressed with Madison. Besides Mason, Patrick Henry (who had refused to attend the Convention) Richard Henry Lee, and Benjamin Harrison all had objections—the old guard. Well, then, George could only leave them behind and go forward with the young men, Madison, Hamilton, Harry Lee, and King. Randolph, they thought, would come round.

He found his crops injured by the severest drought in memory, but even his being at home all summer could not have prevented that. He was much concerned about George Augustine's health, although it had taken a turn for the better again and allowed the boy to be up and around. Bushrod's brother Corbin had recently married a Chantilly Lee, and there was a baby boy, though Bushrod was still childless. It was time to choose an heir for Mount Vernon, and Washington began to take careful notice of the second and third generation of nephews.

A letter from Colonel Humphreys in Connecticut announced the death of both his parents within a few weeks of each other, and his desire to return to Mount Vernon for the winter, bringing the unfinished manuscript of his Life of Putnam. George handed the letter to Martha to read, because it contained a sentence which confirmed the unspoken apprehension which she had refused to recognize and he had refrained from putting into words. "What will tend, perhaps more than anything, to the adoption of the new system," Humphreys had written of the Constitution debates which raged in the state legislatures, "will be an universal opinion of your being elected President of the United States, and an expectation that you will accept it for a while." She sat silent a long time with the letter in her lap. Protest would be useless, she knew. He had no more desire to be President than he had had to be Commander in Chief, she knew that too, but if they called him, he would go.

And she, of course, would go with him. Philadelphia, again? They would have a house of their own there, she supposed, and she could take the children along, and Mr. Lear would continue as secretary. But who would look after Mount Vernon if George Augustine was constantly ill? How long would they have to be away this time? As usual, she did not ask the questions. Not for a while. He said there would be a long wrangle first in most of the states over the ratification.

Meanwhile Colonel Humphreys would be back in time for Christmas, and he was always a robust and cheerful addition to the household. He arrived providentially a few days after the news of George William Fairfax's death in England, which left Sally alone and in poor health at Bath. Humphreys' presence was a blessing at such a time, when memories crowded in—the most useful and companionable guest Martha could have wished for, always ready to ride the rounds of the farms or go hunting with George, play games or read aloud in the evenings, or enter into the amusements of Nelly's young friends. Hearty and genial himself, he brought out the latent wag in Washington too, and was fond of recounting their small adventures together—his favorite being the time he had challenged the chief on their morning ride to jump a hedge they had come upon. Washington agreed, and invited Humphreys to go first, well aware that the landing was in a muddy bog on the far side. While Humphreys, having cleared the hedge like a breeze, was dismounted, mired to the knees and attempting to extricate his indignant horse, Washington rode up to the take-off to watch the struggle, and dissolved his guest into helpless laughter by remarking blandly, "Ah, Colonel, you see, you are too deep for me."

Because of Humphreys, Christmas passed quite gaily, and before January was out he was lending a hand with the correspondence, which was now full of letters about the necessity for George to accept the Presidency. All summer the roll-call of the states went on as one by one they fell into line. By the end of June, '88, eleven had ratified, and it was plain that there was no second choice for President—it was Washington all the way, with John Adams, who had come home to a seat in the Congress, running ahead of Hancock, now Governor of Massachusetts, for Vice President. Martha wondered about Abigail Adams. She had followed her husband across the Atlantic to France and England. Would she mind moving to Philadelphia, or did she enjoy public life, as Dolly Hancock did? Why couldn't the Presidency have happened to the husband of Mrs. Hancock, who would have been an ornament to the formalities which it would entail? But Martha knew why. John Hancock was not George Washington, never had been and never would be.

It was not as simple as that in George's mind, when they finally sat down to face it together. Once more the agonizing choice was before him, and however he turned and twisted and stood back from it, it was really no choice at all. He tried to explain it to her, thinking aloud as he always could do in her receptive silence. If he refused to serve, and the new plan of government was abandoned for lack of a leader who believed in it, the whole idea of independence—liberty—was bankrupt, and the states would split up into small, hostile communities, perhaps into bitter North and South factions which might even go to war with each other and with the western frontier. And yet how, for all the urging of his friends, could he either accept or decline until he was officially notified by the electors that he had been chosen? And what would become of his reputation, now regarded as a sort of talisman, if under this new responsibility he should make some irretrievable blunder? After all, he reminded her, he had led men into battle before he went to Cambridge; but the duties of a Chief Executive were a closed book to him. It was not the same as 1775. Then they wanted a soldier, and he was a soldier. Now they wanted something of him that was not in his line.

Worst of all—and this would set him pacing the floor—he had not had time to get Mount Vernon back on its feet financially. If he left it now, he would have to borrow money—a large sum of money—for his immediate expenses.

There would have to be new clothes for both of them, and for the children, on a much grander scale than was required at Mount Vernon; new liveries for the servants; possibly a new carriage; he must maintain a certain amount of state and ceremony, not because he was President, but because the President happened to be Washington. It was no longer just the dignity of the army which was placed in his hands; as the Chief Executive he would represent the country itself. He was resolved once again to refuse to accept a salary, and only take reimbursement for what he laid out during his term of office. And for that he must borrow at interest. It was humiliating.

They were glad of Humphreys' continued presence at Mount Vernon that winter. He had settled with great good will into something like his old duties as secretary-aide, working on his memoir of General Putnam in his spare time. He passed a second Christmas in the house, and was always an enlivening influence, as their precious interval ran out.

When the electors met at New York in March the family at Mount Vernon had stopped saying "if" and had begun to lay plans for an indefinite absence from home. There were many complications, some of them quite ludicrous, such as the episode of Sam's two youngest boys, always in a scrape, when one of them tried to rescue the other from a caning by their schoolmaster, actually jumping on the old gentleman's back and pummeling him until pulled off. Charles—not to put too fine a point on it—had taken to drink, and as Sam's executor was allowing the property at Harewood, as well as his own at nearby Happy Retreat, to run down. Bushrod, as the family lawyer, was dispatched to look into that. Harriot was to remain at Mount Vernon in Fanny's care, and the two youngest Custis children would go with their grandmother as part of the Presidential establishment.

It now appeared that the first seat of the new government would be at New York instead of at Philadelphia, and the Washingtons were expected to occupy the house in Cherry Street which had been the residence of the President of the late Congress, newly furnished and redecorated for their use. George sent Mr. Lear and Billy the body-servant ahead to make the final dispositions there, and find a cook and some other local servants, retaining Humphreys to accompany him when the summons came. Rather than send one of these two indispensables back to escort Martha and the children, with their maids and nurse, from Virginia to New York, George engaged one of the Fredericksburg nephews, Betty's son Robert, to act as junior secretary to Lear and in particular to make Martha and the children his personal charge. At the end of March George paid a last visit of duty and respect to his mother, aware that he would probably not see her again.

Martha was fully prepared for the result of the election, even resigned to it, long before that April day when Secretary Thomson came to Mount Vernon with the official message from Congress. The votes had been counted. There would not be one against George, she knew. It was a kind of destiny, as he had written from Philadelphia in '75. She was just starting down the stairs for dinner when she heard the sounds of the Secretary's arrival in the lower hall—no different from those of any other guest seeking a night's lodging or a meal, and yet she paused instinctively, gripping the stair rail, while they went into the dining room and shut the door. Someone ought to put dinner back half an hour. Humphreys would see to it, perhaps. She turned, and made her way on tiptoe back to the bedroom and shut that door too, and when she sank into the chair by the fire she was trembling.

It was not a sudden thing. It had been drawing nearer for months. But now that it was here, it found her shaky and breathless. She reached for her knitting, and at first she could not seem to guide the needles.

When George came to the bedroom door a little while later to announce their guest, the face she lifted to him was composed and questioning. As always in a crisis, he seemed an inch taller than ever before —calm, unhurried, sure of his way—it was no wonder, she thought with a mixture of pride and ruefulness, that they could not do without him. As always, her spirit lifted to his. She put the needles safe, with fingers that were cold and steady—laid the knitting aside, and rose, brushing the folds of her skirt into place as she crossed the room to join him. Just inside the door he paused and took her into his arms, and she clung to him, wordless and dry-eyed. Then they descended the stairs together to the dinner table.

Two days later, accompanied by Secretary Thomson and Colonel Humphreys, with young Christopher to act as valet in Billy's absence, George set out for New York in the chariot and four. When the sound of the wheels had died away, Martha turned back from the west door and groped for the familiar curve of the banister in sudden blindness. She climbed slowly, holding to the rail like an old woman, to the refuge of the bedroom they had shared since his return six years ago. The bed with its four slender posts supporting a white canopy invited collapse on its broad bosom, but she swerved from it to the chair beside the hearth and sat down carefully, as though any jar might shatter the frail composure she still preserved. Tears, she believed, were for younger women who had not endured the hard schooling she had known.

How many times, she wondered, had she seen him go from her since that day in '58 on the Pamunkey when she had first experienced the flatness he left behind him, the extinguishment which took place within her when she had said good-by to him. This time there would be no danger ahead of him, as there had been before. That is, the war was over. And yet, even in the darkest days of the fighting there had been no desolation to compare with what she was feeling now. Her face twisted, and she hid it in her empty hands, and felt hot tears run down her fingers. The door was shut, and no one would dare to open it. She gave herself up to the luxury of heartbreak, alone and private in their room, which he had left to do his solemn duty once more as he saw it—as she saw it too, while he was there to convince her. Thirty years since that day on the Pamunkey, and it got no easier to see him go.

It was all beginning again, when she had thought it was finished, for him, and she knew that the honor and the glory and the circumstance were nothing to him either, compared to the plantation life they both loved, in the midst of their family and friends. Their good years were slipping away, the time they had meant to enjoy together here in tranquility, watching Jacky's children grow up.

Four more years were required of him now, by this new task. But in four years, when they would be free to come back home, they would be really old. All the best of it would be gone—stolen, or given, it didn't matter which way you looked at it; demanded of them, anyway, by this compelling idea called America, which was to him like the child he had never had. America was his nursling, and America was having growing pains and nightmares, and he had been called again to its rescue. She had no doubt that he coud save it again. She had no choice but to stand at his side, smiling and serene, while he did so.

CHAPTER NINE

Lady Washington

1789–1797

SHE MISSED THE INAUGURAL CEREMONY, but it did not occur to her to mind that, just as it had not yet occurred to her that the President's lady would be a much more conspicuous and important person than the wife of the Commander in Chief. She was accustomed to what she thought of only as reflected glory during her journeys to and from Headquarters during the war. But when she arrived at the Cherry Street house late in May, it had been demonstrated to her all along the road that his popularity, and hers, had reached a new level, far above anything she had experienced before. Without Bob Lewis, smiling and competent, at her side, and the children's unself-conscious pleasure at the parade which her progress northward became, she would have felt quite overwhelmed.

Once more she settled down in a house not her own to make a home for George, and this time for the children as well. Lear and Colonel Humphreys had already organized a smoothly running household, with Sam Fraunces as steward to do the marketing and to serve the meals. He had left his famous tavern on Pearl Street in his wife's capable hands, and moved in on the President to produce a series of imaginative dinners which taxed even the hearty appetites of the young secretaries, and brought several remonstrances from Washington on the grounds of extravagance.

There were fourteen white servants; a coachman, two footmen, a porter, a houseman, all dressed in the splendid scarlet and white Washington livery, with cocked hats, white gloves, and polished shoes; a cook, two kitchenmaids, two housemaids, two washers, the steward, and a French valet skilled in hairdressing. Billy, the colored body-servant who had never left Washington's side throughout the war, was getting old now, and had injured both knees in a fall, and found consolation in the bottle, but Washington indulged him, and Christopher was there to do most of his work. Martha's two personal maids, Oney and Molly, and the postilions and grooms, made a total of seven slaves from Mount Vernon. Most of the servants hired in New York came in by the day, but the house was overcrowded from the start.

It stood at the junction of Cherry and Queen Streets, five windows wide and three stories high, with a raised stoop and steps up either side. Its east windows looked toward Long Island, its garden sloped to the river. It was too far uptown from Wall Street to be fashionable, and not far enough to have the pleasant country surroundings which the Adamses enjoyed at Mortier's, now known as Richmond Hill. It had a handsome carved staircase, and the walls of the hall were wainscoted. Mrs. Osgood, the wife of the owner, and General Stirling's daughter Kitty Duer, whose husband was in the Treasury, had been given charge of the interior, and had furnished it with handsome mahogany, a quantity of plate and china, new wallpaper, and Wilton carpets.

On the ground floor were the large dining room for entertaining, and the small breakfast room, which was also used as a sitting room by the secretaries, and sometimes as a schoolroom by the children. The window seats were deep and comfortable, the fireplaces were tiled in blue and white. The second floor consisted of a drawing room, with a partition removed to enlarge it, and the family bedrooms. On the third floor the secretaries slept two or three to a room, and the maids and footmen overflowed into the attic. There were sixteen horses in the stables—six cream-colored ones with white manes and tails, to draw the coach; two white chargers, always the General's favorites; and the rest were bays, for the open carriage and for saddles.

Washington rode out daily in the fine summer weather, attended only by a groom and one of the secretaries, to make informal calls on the members of Congress who were old friends—William Livingston, Colonel MacHenry, the Robert Morrises, Madison, Rutledge, and two Pinckneys; the Vice President, John Adams, whose wife was expected to join him in June; Hamilton, now Secretary of the Treasury, and his amiable

Betsy; and the Knoxes, installed at Number Four Broadway, across the street from where they had been so luxurious in the tense summer of '76.

Hamilton's staunch support of the new Constitution, and his expressed conviction that no other President but Washington was possible, had re-established the friendship damaged by the scene at New Windsor eight years before, and Washington was never a man to cherish a misunderstanding, but it was noticeable nevertheless that among the younger men Madison was the one he most relied on. Knox, as large as ever, was still Secretary of War, and his uninterrupted correspondence with Washington since the parting at New York in '83 had kept them on the old intimate footing. Lucy had named her latest, born the previous November, George Washington Knox; a fine, black-haired, black-eyed boy, to console them for the death of baby Caroline during the Convention year. As the summer of '89 went on there was no doubt that the Knox family would increase again roundabout January. Edmund Randolph had been named Attorney General for the United States at a salary insufficient for the needs of his growing family. John Jay preferred an appointment as Chief Justice to his former post of Foreign Secretary, and they were trying to get Jefferson back from Paris to replace him in the State Department.

Colonel Humphreys, because of his experience abroad, had been made a sort of chamberlain or master of ceremonies, and was flooded with unsolicited opinions about the etiquette and protocol of the new government. One would have thought the most vexatious of all the questions confronting them was how to address their Chief Executive, who had even been referred to unofficially as *His Highness,* which was promptly condemned as excessive and in bad taste, to say nothing of setting a dangerous precedent. *Excellency* put him on a level with the Ministers, which was not high enough—besides, he had already been called *Excellency* for years, during the war. A solemn committee finally rendered a decision for the title of *the President,* no more, no less.

Martha adopted it tolerantly. To little Jack and Patsy at Mount Vernon he had once been Pappa. Then for eight years, she had spoken of him as the General. Now, in a letter to Fanny, she wrote for the first time *the President,* and in the next paragraph forgot: "I set out [from Philadelphia] on Monday with Mrs. Morris and her two daughters, and was met on Wednesday morning by the President, Mr. Morris, and Colonel Humphreys at Elizabeth Point with the fine barge you have seen so much said of in the papers, with the same oarsmen that carried the President to New York," she told Fanny with satisfaction. "Dear little

Washington seemed to be lost in a maze at the great parade that was made for us all the way we came. The Governor of the State [Clinton] met me as soon as we landed, and led me up to the house. The papers will tell you how I was complimented on my landing.

"I thank God the President is very well, and the gentlemen with him are all very well. The house he is in is a very good one, and is handsomely furnished all new for the General. I have been so much engaged since I came here that I have never opened your box or directions, but shall soon have time as most of the visits are at an end. I have not had one half hour to myself since the day of my arrival. . . . My hair is set and dressed every day, and I have put on the white muslin habits for the summer. You would, I fear, think me a good deal in the fashion if you could but see me. My dear Fanny, send me by some safe conveyance my black lace apron and handkerchief, they are in one of my drawers in my chamber—and some thread lace or joining net, it is in one of the baskets on the shelf in my closet. They were fine net handkerchiefs which I intended to make cap borders of. . . ."

One of Humphreys' first problems was the mob of visitors which invaded the President's house, from old soldiers who simply dropped by for a sight of him again, to the needy applicants who considered that they had some sort of claim for a government post and salary. Obviously if he made himself available to all of them, he would get nothing else done. The question was where to draw the line, and whose feelings would be hurt. Hamilton advised one levee a week and several formal entertainments on special days and anniversaries, and an occasional family dinner to friends in Congress. A howl at once went up that such a course was not sufficiently democratic. Washington listened patiently, and then arranged his own life, on a middle course—a weekly levee on Tuesday afternoons; a weekly dinner on Thursdays; an evening reception by Martha, which he would attend as a guest himself, on Fridays; small dinner parties composed of government officials and noted strangers; a little time to himself for intimate friends; and *nobody* on Sundays.

A further embarrassment was the mail, which was full of more applications for salaried positions from old associates who should presumably have had a competence at home, yet found themselves in want of additional income—like Lincoln and Moultrie and Sullivan; or those who had sons or relatives to place in the world; as well as the usual ambitious strangers and the inevitable cranks. It was soon obvious that the secretarial staff would have to be enlarged, and when Dr. Stuart wrote that General

Nelson had died at Yorktown, leaving his widow and a large family almost destitute, Washington offered to take his eldest son Thomas into the New York household as assistant to Lear, with board, lodging, and washing, three hundred dollars a year, and horses kept at his own expense—which was gratefully accepted.

The second day after Martha's arrival was a Friday, and she was pitched at once into her weekly drawing room, for which Humphreys had made the arrangements and sent out the invitations. Seated with the utmost composure on a sofa, while George circulated informally, and the secretaries escorted the ladies to and from their carriages, and Humphreys standing at her side made the necessary introductions, she had a smiling welcome for each guest, and a warm greeting for those who were already known to her—General Stirling's widow and her married daughters, Mrs. Watts and Mrs. Duer; several Livingston ladies; Betsy Hamilton; Governor Clinton's wife; and Lucy Knox. Fraunces had provided a handsome array of cakes and candy, with tea, coffee, and lemonade, and the evening ended in a general glow of good will at 9 P.M., a pronounced success.

Her first public appearance was made at the theater, in the President's box, with the Robert Morrises, the Knoxes, and General Steuben as guests, besides the young gentlemen of the household. The play was *The Clandestine Marriage,* acted by Hallam, Wignell, and the lovely Maria Storer, and George thought it not as entertaining as *The School for Scandal,* which he had seen for the first time the previous week. A few days later the good-natured Mr. Lear took the children to see Sheridan's comic opera called *The Duenna,* which was followed by a Robinson Crusoe Pantomime and an Allegorical Finale.

With Martha's arrival the social pattern of the President's duties was established. The formal dinners began at 4 P.M., and there was no waiting for unpunctual guests. If no clergyman was present, Washington himself said grace. In a mixed company, the President and his lady sat across from each other, halfway down the long table, with a secretary at the head and the foot, to aid the serving and the conversation, which often suffered from dullness if the guests were strangers to each other or allowed themselves to be awed by the presence of their always untalkative host. Fraunces, in a dazzling white apron, white silk shirt and stockings, velvet breeches, and powder in his hair, presided in the dining room and placed the dishes on the table, uncovered, while the carving and helping were mostly done by the secretaries. When the ladies retired to the drawing room it was Washington's habit to follow them after fifteen minutes for coffee, leaving one of the secretaries to entertain the gentlemen who wished to linger over the wine. If there were no other ladies present, Martha sat at the head of the table, with a secretary at the foot, and the President half way between. For the family meals they reverted to the side-by-side chairs at the head of the table, with a carver at the foot.

Lear, Humphreys, Bob Lewis, and young Nelson made an amicable division of duties among themselves. They were all bachelors in their twenties, and all charming, well-mannered, and considerate. It fell to Lewis as Martha's particular property to receive and announce her callers, supervise the refreshments, retrieve gloves and scarves and fans, and attend her in the carriage on shopping trips or excursions with the children.

These four were joined before long by Colonel Jackson, one of General Lincoln's old reliables, who had served him as aide and been taken prisoner with him at the Charleston surrender in 1780; he had also accompanied John Laurens to France in '81, and since then had acted as assistant secretary of war and as secretary to the 1787 Convention, when Washington took note of his discretion, ability, and good looks. Jackson became the devoted bodyguard of the President, always at his side, walking, riding, or driving in a carriage, always correct, cheerful, and good company.

A tutor was engaged for little Washington, as Lear's secretarial duties made increasing demands on his time, though he remained in charge of the children's outings to the theater and the museum and the waxworks. Mr. Reinagle came in to teach Nelly the pianoforte, and she was required to practice daily, which often reduced her to tears. "She is a little wild creature, and spends her time at the window looking at carriages, etc., passing by, which is new to her and very common for children to do," Martha wrote to Fanny. Nelly was ten, and was not so much indulged and humored as poor Patsy had been in her affliction. In the autumn she was to go to Mrs. Graham's school in Maiden Lane as a day pupil, and learn such extra accomplishments as drawing, japanning, filigree, and French, and make the acquaintance of other children her age, which there had been less opportunity for her to do at Mount Vernon.

Before things had had time really to settle into a routine, George was taken with a fever, and there was a sore place on his left thigh where his sword hung, which rapidly developed into an abscess, causing him great pain and inconvenience. Dr. Bard, the town's most fashionable physician,

was called in, along with his son, who was a surgeon, and a deep incision
was made. For several days the President's life was almost despaired of.
His bedroom windows stood open in the summer heat, and Martha was
driven to distraction by the normal street noises of the city, which repeatedly roused him from his light woodsman's sleep just as he had
escaped from pain into a doze. Straw was laid down outside the house,
a rope was stretched across the roadway, and a footman stationed to still
the hawking-cries of the watercarts, milkmen, chimney sweeps—everything was cried in the streets, from firewood to clams, and after the
quiet years on the Potomac the din of New York seemed deafening.

A stream of anxious callers stopped by to inquire, and leave messages
of sympathy. Members of Congress, old and new, singly, in pairs, or
with their wives, came in carriages, bringing flowers, fresh strawberries
and other sickroom delicacies and concoctions, and their best wishes. The
whole city was suddenly hushed and waiting, until at last the word
was given out that a satisfactory drainage had been established and he was
out of danger.

Martha was then persuaded to leave his bedside for some rest. Almost
the first person she received when the worst anxiety had passed was
Abigail Adams, wife of the Vice President, newly arrived from Massachusetts and accompanied by her daughter, young Abby, now married
to the expansive Colonel Smith, and mother of two babies.

With her husband in the Philadelphia Congress instead of in the army,
Mrs. Adams had not shared the Headquarters life which formed a lasting
bond between Martha and women like Lucy Knox and the Stirlings, but
they had a mutual friend in Mercy Warren, who had frequently made
the journey from Plymouth through Cambridge to Watertown, where her
husband attended the Massachusetts Assembly in '76. Mercy and Abigail
were fluent letter writers, which Martha was not, and they had kept
each other informed, even during the years Abigail had spent abroad with
John while he was a commissioner for the United States in France and
the Netherlands, and then Minister to Great Britain. Abigail at Braintree
had received Mercy's impressions of the Commander in Chief's wife at
Cambridge long ago, and she was now able to write from New York to
her sister in Massachusetts that Mrs. Washington had received her with
the greatest ease and politeness. "She is plain in her dress, but that plain-
ness is the best of every art," her letter ran on. "She is in mourning.
Her hair is white, her teeth are beautiful, her person is rather short than
otherwise, hardly so large as my ladyship, and if I was to speak sincerely,

I think she is a much better figure. Her manners are modest and un-assuming, dignified and feminine, not the tincture of hauteur about her. *His Majesty* was ill and confined to his room. I had not the pleasure of a presentation to him, but the satisfaction of hearing that he regretted it equally with myself. Colonel Humphreys, who had paid his compliments to me in the morning and breakfasted with me, attended Mrs. Washington, and Mr. Lear, the President's secretary, was the introductor. Thus you have an account of my first appearance. . . ."

Colonel Humphreys was an old friend of the Adams family from their European days, and was capable of furthering an early meeting between the two ladies for Martha's sake, well aware from his knowledge of both that they would take to each other. They had much in common, to begin with. Abigail at Braintree had heard the guns at Bunker Hill before Martha came to live with the daily cannonade at Cambridge. Both were the staunchest of wives, and had already endured much out of devotion to their husbands' service to the country. Both had once congratulated themselves that the public duty was done, and that their remaining years could be spent at home in the uninterrupted family life they preferred. Both had been snatched back into the breach when the infant nation faltered and everything won at such cost seemed in danger.

It was amusing to them that Abigail was now living in the house where Martha had spent those anxious weeks before the fighting began on Long Island in the summer of '76—a beautiful location above the Hudson with a superb view of the Jersey shore, an upstairs gallery, a piazza, and a garden with graveled walks and shade trees. Compared to Abigail's Rich-mond Hill, the Cherry Street house was small and stuffy, no place for an invalid in July weather. After her second visit there she wrote again to her sister that the President had sent for her to his chamber: "He was lying on a settee, and half raised himself up, congratulated me on my arrival in New York, and asked me how I could relish the simple manners of America after having been accustomed to those of Europe. . . . The President has had a bed put into his carriage, and rides out in that way, with six horses in his carriage and four attendants. Mrs. Washington accompanies him. I requested him to make Richmond Hill his resting place, and the next day he did so, but he found walking upstairs so diffi-cult that he has done it but once. . . . Mrs. Washington is one of those characters who create love and esteem. A most becoming pleasantness sits upon her countenance and an unaffected deportment which renders her the object of veneration and respect. . . . I found myself much more deeply impressed than I ever did before their Majesties of Britain. . . ."

As soon as he was able to take carriage exercise, with Martha at his side, Washington began to make one of his miraculous recoveries, for he always suffered most from confinement. They were surprised to notice during their drives how much evidence remained of the disastrous fires which had swept the city during the British occupation. They took pleasure in the churches and tidy fenced churchyards, and the fine dwellings in many-styled houses, Dutch, French, and English, all mixed together; they admired the handsome stores and taverns, and the shade trees in the streets. Without the cosy red-brick symmetry of Philadelphia, it was a hodgepodge, cluttered, naïve sort of place, but it had a certain charm.

By August Washington was holding his levees and dinner parties again. During one of these, interrupting General Steuben's flow of funny stories, the letter was brought in to him which announced his mother's death at Fredericksburg. It was not unexpected, and her long illness had exhausted Betty with nursing and worry. Entertaining in Cherry Street was suspended for a week, and mourning cockades, sword knots, and sleeve bands were ordered for the members of the household, including the servants, but the children were soon allowed to go to see the waxworks. On Dr. Craik's advice from Alexandria to take more exercise, Washington resumed his morning walks, accompanied by Lear and Jackson, who walked abreast and two paces to the rear, in a smart little procession of three, dispensing bows and greetings as they went. He also took up his diary again, to record the company at the official functions and his private calls and conferences.

When Congress adjourned in the autumn he made a tour of New England, traveling in the open carriage drawn by four bays, with a liveried coachman and postilions. Lear and Jackson rode horseback on either side, and there followed a baggage wagon with a driver, a mounted valet, and a colored groom leading a white charger—six servants altogether. The population cheered itself hoarse along the way, and plainly their confidence in the President was as great as it had been in the Commander in Chief.

Martha remained in Cherry Street, getting Nelly settled in Mrs. Graham's school, while a Mr. Wright undertook his duties as tutor to little Washington. She was homesick, and often rather bored, and she missed the familiar domestic interests at Mount Vernon and the companionship of Fanny and George Augustine, whose second child, Maria, had arrived in time to console them for the death of their first. Martha's New York associations were of necessity somewhat formal. Only a few of the Congressmen's wives had come to share the crowded lodgings and boarding-house food which was all the city provided, at enormous expense, and she was without the comforting backlog of old acquaintance which would have been available in Philadelphia. "I have by Mrs. Sims sent for a watch . . . I hope such a one as will please you," she wrote to Fanny in October. "It is of the newest fashion, if that has any influence on your taste. The chain is of Mr. Lear's choosing, and such as Mrs. Adams the Vice President's lady and those in the polite circles wears and will last as long as the fashion—and by that time you can get another of the fashionable kind. I send to dear Maria a piece of chintz to make her a frock. The piece of muslin I hope is long enough for an apron for you, and in exchange for it I beg you will give me the worked apron you have like my gown that I made just before I left home of worked muslin, as I wish to make a petticoat of the two aprons, for my gown. . . . I live a very dull life here and know nothing that passes in the town. I never go to any public place. Indeed, I think I am more like a state prisoner than anything else, there is certain bounds set for me which I must not depart from—and as I cannot do as I like, I am obstinate and stay at home a great deal.

"The President set out this day week on a tour to the eastward, Mr. Lear and Mr. Jackson attended him. My dear children has very bad colds, but thank God they are getting better. My love and good wishes attend you and all with you. Remember me to Mr. and Mrs. Lund W. How is the poor child? Kiss Maria, I send her two little handkerchiefs to wipe her nose. . . ."

Abigail Adams was always a welcome visitor in Cherry Street, with her shrewd, sophisticated opinions of the mighty, both in America and abroad, and her breezy attitude towards the restrictions and etiquette which hedged the President's lady. There were still two schools of thought about how the President should conduct his new Republican court, and whichever way he stepped there was criticism. It had been given out that the Washingtons would not accept private invitations, and so they never received any—but this did not mean that calls should not be returned punctually on the third day, and left room for informal visits during a carriage drive, which leeway Martha often took advantage of. The friendship between the wives of the President and the Vice President was doing much to smooth John Adams' habitual prickles of jealousy and self-importance. Although he had been the first to elevate George Washington to leadership, back in '75, the heights to which the Virginia colonel had since then attained through no ambition of his own often irked the sensitive ego of the little man from Braintree, who owed more than he would ever know to his wife's unfailing tact and loving tolerance of his difficult ways.

The October letter to Fanny was the low-water mark of Martha's first year of Presidential state. George returned from the New England tour restored in health and spirits. He had had a rattling good time, and could not but reflect with satisfaction on his last view of the same scenes in the summer which saw him hurrying southward to meet the British at New York at the uncertain beginning of the long war. That much, at least, was behind him. He came back fresh to the problems which awaited him now, with a renewed faith in his star. The shadow cast by his mother's death had faded, and his illness could be forgotten. Reestablished in the house which held Martha and the children, and was therefore a home, he was suddenly more at his ease, less conscious that every move he made created a precedent for presidents, more confident that he could somehow carry this new load without committing any disastrous—some of Lafayette's words had entered his vocabulary forever—*faux pas*.

Martha as always responded to his mood. They began to go out more —to the Assembly balls, and to see the museum curiosities, and to attend the theater in John Street where the director had composed a special tune called "The President's March," which was always played when they entered their box. Their social circle widened and warmed—the Schuylers, the Hamiltons, the Jays, the Knoxes, the John Adamses, the Rufus Kings, the Varicks, the Clintons, the Duers—it was really not so bad. They gave children's parties on Saturday afternoons, sending the Presidential carriage for the young guests, serving Fraunces' wonderful cakes and ice cream. They converted part of the attic into a playroom, where the children could perform amateur theatricals and concerts. Nelly's new school friends brought music and laughter and dancing feet into the house.

Kitty Greene was in New York that winter, and talked of selling the plantation on the Savannah for money to live on and educate the children. She was still a bright, beguiling creature, with pretty clothes and the ability to evoke laughing memories of the grim old days in Jersey and Pennsylvania. She enjoyed dining with the Washingtons and attending the theater in the President's box, as did General Steuben, who still awaited on borrowed funds a decent settlement from Congress for his back pay, and was meanwhile much in demand by all the fashionable hostesses for his courtly manners and his stories, which were always suitable to his company.

Martha was busy with Christmas shopping for the children, and the plans for a joint New Year's Day reception, which fell on a Friday anyway. George gave her a set of the fashionable seed-pearl pins and earrings which cost £16, and paid £42.16 for fur cloaks for each of them. Best of all, in spite of the bitter controversy raging in Congress over the permanent locality for the Government, which apparently might wind up in any one of half a dozen cities, they took a bigger house.

The French Minister was returning home at the end of the year, which left available his mansion known as Macomb's, on Broadway below Trinity Church, considered the finest house in the city. It had four stories and an attic, and its spacious, high-ceilinged rooms were suitable for entertaining on a Presidential scale. From the large front hall a splendid staircase rose to the top story, and glass doors opened from the rear of the main drawing room on to a balcony overlooking the Hudson. The dining room would seat up to twenty guests, whereas fourteen was the limit in Cherry Street. Its rent was $1,000 a year, which would be paid out of the $25,000 a year agreed on as the "compensation" for the President's expenses during his term of office.

Preparations for the move amused George all through February, as his exile from Mount Vernon deprived him of games of that kind which he always relished, and he chose to make the shift from one house to the other on his fifty-eighth birthday, before the alterations at Macomb's had been completed.

The spring of 1790 brought other changes to their household, with the marriage of Tobias Lear to his childhood sweetheart in New Hampshire. The attachment had been taken note of by Washington during the New England tour, when he was entertained at the home of the bride's parents, at what amounted to an engagement party. He had at once recognized in Polly Long an ideal substitute for Fanny as a companion to Martha, who was accustomed to having at least one young person about the house besides little Nelly, who was only eleven. Bob Lewis took over the bookkeeping for the Presidential establishment, and in April Lear was given several weeks leave for his wedding, after which he was to bring Polly back with him to live at the Macomb house.

Dr. Franklin died that spring at eighty-four, and Robert Hanson Harrison at forty-five—another of the Headquarters Family whose health had given way, even in the mild climate and leisurely life of his native Maryland, from where he and his family had paid frequent visits to Mount Vernon after the war.

Thomas Jefferson arrived in New York in March, belatedly and roundabout from Paris via Monticello, where he had delayed to see his daughter

Martha married to a Randolph. He took a house in Maiden Lane, and after a private conference with Washington embarked at last on his duties as Secretary of State. The family of Vice President Adams at Richmond Hill was prostrated with various ailments, and when George set out on a brief tour of Long Island an influenza epidemic had gripped the city, striking down Madison and many others in the Congress. Washington returned home with a cold, which started a fever, and by the middle of May he was again in danger of his life.

Lear was still away on his honeymoon, but Jackson, Nelson, Humphreys, and Lewis united to hearten Martha, who again took up her vigil at the bedside. Outwardly composed, she sat listening with terror and prayer to the labored breathing, only eleven months since she had faced the same stark prospect because of the abscess. Eight years of service in the field had not killed him, British shot and shell had not found him, but daily confinement in a New York house, surrounded by dissension in Congress, spiteful criticism of his honest effort and beliefs, and the complex wear and tear of personalities and politics, had twice within this one year brought him lower than he had ever been during the war. Behind her quiet voice, her cool, steady hands, and her smiling courtesy to the shaken men who were trying to save him, her old, well-disciplined temper surged and boiled. If they had let him alone at Mount Vernon this would never have happened. If they had not come running back to him with their quarrels and uncertainties and foolish feuds and hair-splittings, and then, having obligated him to take command again, if they had not gone on squabbling just as badly as ever, he would be out on a horse this minute, riding the rounds of his friendly Presidential calls, if not the Mount Vernon hayfields, as well as he had ever been. They had elected him by a unanimous vote, and once he was secured, nothing he did could please a fault-finding faction who even had remarks to make about the clothes he wore, the food he set before them, and the nature of the bows with which he received them in his drawing room. Such things were flea bites, as he truly said, but the least he was entitled to was the support and loyalty of the men who had laid this burden on him, and if he died now they had killed him, they were to blame, they had robbed him (and her) of the peaceful old age he had earned without trying to be President too.

Anger and rebellion, righteous and unresigned, swelled within her while she sat stoically by his bed, knitting and waiting. Downstairs the straw was laid on the pavement again, and the callers were at the door, tears in their eyes, prayers on their lips—she would not see them. She blamed them all, even Humphreys with the rest, white-faced and sleepless now, now that the harm was done, for devoted as he was, he had been among the first to point out where George's duty lay. But Humphreys, admiring her courage and her faith, never knew.

They even brought a doctor all the way from Philadelphia, who frankly admitted that he had little confidence in his own ability to bring his patient through alive, and the house where the sick man lay seemed suspended in time, counting each breath, listening for one more—one more—until suddenly the sweat came, the heart steadied and pumped, the color came back, and he had passed the crisis. Cautious Dr. McKnight would not promise recovery until several more days had passed, but Martha knew, and cooled off inside. They had weathered it again. He would get well again. At the end of May, still coughing, but quite himself, George was able to ride out with her in the carriage. The first week in June, he went for a three-day fishing trip for sea bass off Sandy Hook with Hamilton, Jefferson, Humphreys, and Jackson, in Hamilton's sloop. Martha, wrung out and thankful, her natural buoyancy reasserting itself, seized the opportunity for a holiday of her own at the Falls of the Passaic in Jersey, with Abigail Adams, who was also in need of escape from family cares, as her companion.

Lear had hurried back to New York with Polly, and the bride stepped gently into the place of the grown daughter Martha always needed and rejoiced in. Polly helped with the entertaining, she played with the children, she accompanied Martha in the carriage to pay calls, or sat companionably sewing or reading aloud. They soon wondered how they had got along without her.

That summer's session of Congress was acrimonious on at least two counts—the location of the new Federal City which was to be built as a permanent seat of the government, and something called assumption of state debts, which Martha did not pretend to understand. By the time they adjourned in August, and the Washingtons were free to make their first visit to Mount Vernon since the inauguration, it had been settled that the capital city was to be planned and erected near Georgetown on the Potomac, and that until it was ready for occupancy Congress would reside at Philadelphia instead of continuing at New York.

Like the annual breakup of Headquarters, the inevitable changes were accepted by Martha with a philosophical sigh. She had got used to New York, and they had enjoyed the comfortable Macomb house on Broadway less than a year, and weeks of that time had been consumed by George's second illness. But the shift to Philadelphia at least would be for her a return to familiar ground, and reunion with wartime friends, while Abigail Adams would be a stranger there, and farther than ever from her Massachusetts home and family. Most serious to Martha was the loss of Colonel Humphreys, who was going abroad as a special agent to Portugal and Spain after being so long a staunch member of the family circle.

Secretary Robert Lewis and Colonel Jackson would accompany them to Mount Vernon, and Secretary Nelson was to go on leave to Yorktown for a visit with his family. The Lears were remaining in New York to oversee the removal of the President's household goods to the new quarters at Philadelphia. As usual the Washingtons' residence had been chosen arbitrarily, without consulting their wishes, and this time it was the Market Street mansion which had served both Howe and Arnold as headquarters, and which after a fire had been bought and rebuilt and occupied by Robert Morris.

The last few days in New York became emotional, and Washington's farewell dinner to the city officials who would not accompany the Congress to Philadelphia affected even Martha, who had no real cause to love most of those they were leaving behind. They had spent seventeen months in the city—there was little likelihood that they would ever return there—and as the wine went round and the toasts multiplied, sentiment flowed freely.

After a ceremonious departure from New York, and a ceremonious arrival in Philadelphia, Martha gave way to fatigue and remained in bed at their lodgings while George revisited the house in which they were to live when Congress reassembled in December. They had both stayed in it as guests of the Morrises in the spring of the inauguration, but without any idea then of adapting it to their own use. She was always content to let George make the household arrangements, because then presumably he would be satisfied with the result. Having surveyed the accommodations in the light of his recent experience in New York, he wrote out detailed instructions for Lear regarding alterations and additions to be made to the house while the family was at Mount Vernon, and as soon as Martha recovered they resumed the homeward journey.

They were both aware, as the carriage turned in at the gate and swept up the drive toward the wide, welcoming west front, that he might never have seen Mount Vernon again. And their own thankfulness was reflected in the broad white smiles of the servants who gathered to see him arrive, and in the relief and joy of the younger Washingtons as they waited for him to alight, strong and serene as usual, at his own front door. With the excited children swirling about them they were borne in to dinner, after which a general inspection tour lasted until dark.

It was a busy but peaceful interlude. In contrast to the Congressional bickering and the disturbing news from abroad as the French Revolution began to simmer, they almost welcomed the familiar Mount Vernon problems—the perpetual lack of ready cash, the two incorrigible Harewood nephews at school in Alexandria, the unruliness of their half-sister Harriot, who was altogether too much for Fanny's gentle discipline, and George Augustine's still precarious health.

The Lears arrived at Philadelphia in October to supervise the readying of the Morris house. Bow windows were to be let in to the south, or back, rooms used for dining and reception; a partition was required to provide Washington with "a small place for a private study and dressing room"; an addition must be built out at the rear to accommodate more of the servants; and the stables must be enlarged. Nothing on earth could be done to make it as convenient as the Macomb house which they had just left, where the office for the secretaries was a room on the ground-floor front. The exasperating arrangement of the Philadelphia residence required the President's business to be transacted in a third-floor room, so that strangers must climb two pair of stairs past the drawing rooms and private chambers to come to the secretaries' room, opposite the Lears' apartment and the staff bedrooms. But it was apparently the best that Philadelphia could offer, and the Morrises had moved into the house just next to it, which was connected by a walled garden. All this trouble, Martha would reflect with secret impatience, all this crowding and conniving and discomfort, when beautiful, spacious Mount Vernon, with its library and adjacent bedroom, stood waiting as they had planned it for the rest of their lives—wasted, while they huddled into still another house which was not their own, enduring makeshift belongings and people traipsing up and down the stairs all day.

Washington's letters to Lear from Mount Vernon that autumn covered everything from the painting and carpentry to the lamps and mirrors in the new house, and indicated which servants were to be retained or let go from the New York establishment. In the effort to find an adequate substitute for the versatile Fraunces, who had resumed the management of his tavern, a married couple named Hyde had been engaged, and the two of them together did not fill his place, especially in the matter of cakes and desserts. One of the Mount Vernon cooks, a character named

Hercules and known affectionately as Uncle Harklas, was to be added to the Philadelphia kitchen staff along with his son Richmond as scullion. Tradesmen must be interviewed and chosen by Lear, and there was also the expensive necessity for a new chariot and liveries. All these chores he cheerfully undertook and executed and reported on, to the entire satisfaction of the President at Mount Vernon. Schools for the Custis children were another concern—possibly schools for the Harewood nephews and for Harriot as well.

The Lears found Philadelphia already full of opportunists awaiting the Congress. Rents and prices were high, and workmen in great demand. The house was still not finished when the Washingtons arrived at the end of November after a tiring journey over wretched roads. The Adamses had taken a place called Bush Hill, outside the town, which had stood unoccupied for several years. Polly Lear, who had already called on Abigail there, found her in some distress, with everyone in the family ill from the damp and the smell of paint. Mrs. Knox's handsome furniture had been damaged in a storm while coming down from New York by boat, and they had lost another child during the summer.

Philadelphia society was prepared to outshine anything New York could do, and Martha's Friday drawing rooms now lasted till after 10 P.M., and were notable for their beautiful women and splendid attire, as the Morrises, Biddles, Powells, Shippens, Willings, Chews, and Binghams, most of them old friends, came to pay their respects. The ubiquitous Thomas Mifflin was now Governor of Pennsylvania.

For the Christmas reception Martha had a new black velvet gown which cost £40. She felt at home in Philadelphia; everyone under her wing was well; Mount Vernon was not so far away; and a very pleasant social routine soon evolved, much livelier than the humdrum New York life she had described to Fanny, but nothing like what it might have been if she had kept up with the Bingham set, who played cards and danced till all hours. The Washingtons attended the Assembly balls, and St. Peter's Church. When the Hallam Company opened their season at the Old Southwark Theater with *The School for Scandal,* which Washington had so enjoyed in New York, he took eleven tickets. The east stage box of the theater, which had housed the amateur theatricals of the British officers during the occupation winter, had been set aside for him, with red draperies and cushioned chairs, and the United States coat of arms on the front. Mr. Wignall in black full dress and powder stood at the entrance, a silver candlestick holding a tall lighted wax candle in each hand, waiting to conduct Washington's party to their places, while the musicians played "The President's March." A soldier was posted at each stage door and four in the gallery, as much for style as to ensure decorum during the performance. Jefferson, who lived and dressed like a lord since his sojourn in France, inconsistent with his emphatic democratic principles, doubtless thought such ceremony monarchical, but to Washington it was suitable to the dignity of the President—any President—of the United States.

Martha always found the Philadelphia shops delightful, especially Mr. Whiteside's new fancy drygoods shop, which had a display of fine mulls and jaconet muslins and chintzes puffed and festooned in the large glass windows after what Abigail Adams said was true Bond Street style. Martha sent a doll to Fanny's Maria, and painting materials to Nelly Stuart's Eliza and Patty, and bought Nelly Custis a spangled dress for dancing school. Little Washington, not yet ten years old, was enrolled in the Academy, and the Harewood nephews were transferred from Alexandria to the Philadelphia College to study law, at considerable outlay by Washington for their books—£8, to start with—and clothing. Harriot was left at Mount Vernon after all, on Fanny's hands.

Young Secretary Nelson while at Yorktown on his holiday decided not to return to the President's household, and his place was filled by another presentable bachelor, Martha's nephew Bartholomew Dandridge II. There were lively debates in Congress that winter over Hamilton's banking plan, and wary hostesses began inviting him and Jefferson on different evenings. But the government was, on the whole, organized and functioning; the Revolution in France seemed to have been effected without violence; and in the spring it looked to Washington like a good time for another tour.

He had a desire to visit every state in the union, and this time he planned to go South as far as Savannah, and see the southern battlefields while testing the state of public opinion below the James. Colonel Jackson was to be his sole attendant, besides the servants. His departure was sufficiently delayed for him to stand godfather to Polly Lear's first child, named Lincoln after the man responsible for his father's happy association with the President.

George left Philadelphia at the end of March for an absence of about three months, in a new light traveling coach, with Jackson riding beside it, followed by the baggage wagon, a mounted footman and valet, and the slave Paris, mounted and leading a white charger—five servants, eleven horses in all. Although they would stop at Mount Vernon on the way down and again on the way back, Martha remained in Philadelphia, partly for the sake of the children's studies. George sent a letter back from Bladensburg to Lear about things he had forgotten to mention before he started: "I wish you would have all the packages moved out of the garden and have it kept in complete order, *at my expense,* and the paved yard also," he wrote. ". . . . The top of one of the urns in the garden was broke by its falling . . . let it be cemented on again. Furnish Mrs. Washington with what money she may want—and from time to time ask her if she does want, for she is not fond of applying. . . ."

Abigail Adams went home to Braintree for the summer, but her absence now created less of a vacuum for Martha than it would have done in the early days at New York. Young Abby's marriage was not turning out well—a baby every year, and not enough money, and a disinclination on the part of Colonel Smith to get a steady job or to economize at home. He had recently taken a sudden whim to return to England on a mysterious business speculation, leaving his wife and children with his family on Long Island. Martha felt secretly that it was a lesson to herself and George, with Nelly growing up. Abby's first love for Royall Tyler, before the European interlude, had been considered by her parents mere girlish folly, and when she was taken abroad she was forbidden to correspond with him. Now he was courting someone else, and had become a successful lawyer and playwright. It must be unnerving, Martha reflected, to find yourself in the position of having interfered with the course of your child's life, and then sit helplessly by while it foundered. Abigail as a rule had stood up well enough for most of her convictions against the rather pompous opinions of her domineering husband, who was affectionately referred to by her in her family correspondence as *Sir,* in genial recognition of his overstated authority. In some long-distance mood of wifely submission she had concurred against her own inclination when John wrote from Paris a peremptory refusal to consider an engagement between Abby and Tyler, let alone a marriage, and perhaps she hoped that Abby might do better abroad. Now it was painfully apparent that she had not. Still, Abigail was more fortunate in her children than Mercy Warren, not one of whose five sons had turned out really well, in a dreary series of disasters and illnesses. Mercy's fortunes went steadily down, as Abigail's rose. The Warrens' opposition to the Constitution had caused some estrangement with their friends, though Martha still exchanged an occasional letter with Mercy, who had dedicated a volume of her poems to the President.

Mr. Lear's mother came down from New Hampshire for a fortnight in June to see baby Lincoln, and a lifelong friendship at once established itself between the two grandmothers, who enjoyed their driving, shopping, and sightseeing together, accompanied by Polly and the Custis children. Little Washington was Jacky all over again, willful, lazy, resistant to education, and so beguiling that rebukes and punishment melted before his sunny impenitence. Nelly at twelve was already a beauty, dusky like her lost Aunt Patsy, and while Martha spoiled the boy, Nelly was George's weakness and stood in no awe of him. Privately he thought Martha made up for her overindulgence of his namesake by overconscientious discipline of poor Nelly, who was made to practice her music, needlework, and drawing for hours each day, besides attending dancing school and a day school for young ladies, with the daughters of her family's friends.

It was a constant pleasure to Washington to observe the charm and affection of Martha's youngsters compared to Sam's incorrigibles— though the nephews had finally settled in at the Philadelphia College with a show of good will and appreciation of the advantages they owed to his generosity in providing for them. They were growing up now, and there was a constant irresponsible demand for extras which would not come out of their pocket money—a dancing master, a music master and a music *stand,* fancy shoe buckles, silk stockings, French lessons, a hair dresser *three times a week.* As for their half-sister Harriot, George returned from Mount Vernon this time more than ever discouraged about making anything of her. He had found George Augustine so deteriorated in health, and Fanny so preoccupied with that anxiety, as well as with another child on the way, that he again proposed putting Harriot into boarding school, and again postponed the expense.

The situation at Mount Vernon was heavy on his mind when he reached Philadelphia in July from the southern tour. It was plain that George Augustine was not able to handle the estate business any longer and, haunted by the memory of Lawrence's appearance and early death, Washington doubted any probability of recovery by George Augustine. To turn the place over to a stranger to manage without being there himself to orient the man was out of the question. During a comforting visit with his sister Betty on the way north, he had discussed with her a temporary shifting of her son Bob Lewis to Mount Vernon, as Bob was already familiar with its routine, while George Augustine made another pilgrimage to the Springs, always recommended by Dr. Craik as a last resort. Lewis, who wanted to get married, was more than willing, and accompanied the Washingtons and the children, along with Secretary Dandridge, when they made a brief family visit at Mount Vernon in September, before Congress reassembled. As a result of a lengthy correspondence a man named Whiting was then engaged to come and learn.

It was a less carefree winter in Philadelphia that year, as the Jefferson-Madison States-Rights faction united against Hamilton's Federalists, whose policy Washington would have favored but for his determined effort to preserve impartiality and peace. There was friction over the plans and construction of the new Federal City on the Potomac, the site of which Washington visited each time he drove that way. Nelly Stuart's husband was on the building commission and kept him informed of the many tempests raised by the mercurial architect L'Enfant. Affairs in France looked ominous again, thanks largely to the King's vacillation and intrigue, and they feared for Lafayette, who had involved himself in the National Guard army and yet dared to oppose the excessive Jacobin hatred of the Royal Family. Other European monarchies were alarmed and a proposed coalition against France raised the threat of a general European war, in which America owed allegiance to what many people began to suspect might be the wrong side. And back of all this, like a dark fog, hung the lowering question of a second four-year term for Washington as President.

Martha was appalled. They had once even naïvely promised themselves that he might find it possible to resign short of the whole first term of office, once he had seen the new Government safely seated, turning over his place to someone else, possibly the Vice President. When that prospect faded she had begun to count the weeks to the spring of '93. Each time he was ill, each time he was even tired, her private calendar gave reassurance. The time was passing. The day of release would come. There was an end. But now—*another term?*

For once she spoke her mind to him, vehemently and at some length, goaded by sheer panic. He heard her without interruption or protest, and when she paused, breathless and aghast, for this was not the way to help him, he only leaned his head on his hand, hiding his eyes. She was instantly on her knees beside his chair, tugging him back to her. She was sorry, she had not meant to say it, she was taken by surprise, the decision was his, of course, and she would abide by it, she would stay if he did, go anywhere that he had to go. He bent to lay his arms around her, and his face against her shoulder. Poor Patsy, was all he said. Poor Patsy.

From then on, the specter waited, ignored, but always there. *1797.*
They would be sixty-five.

She went about her daily life with apparent serenity again, awaiting
the verdict. Fraunces had rejoined the President's household, bringing
with him a competent housekeeper, and promised to remain in service
as long as needed. For little Washington's eleventh birthday party he
turned out a child's miracle of molded ice cream, and a great white cake
in tiers. When the small boy came down with measles shortly after, di-
gestible jellies and broths and cooling drinks became a specialty. And the
Presidential dinners took on a new interest for the guests.

There was no doubt that the children enjoyed Philadelphia, and
would miss their playmates when removed to Mount Vernon. There were
grown-up compensations too, during the summer, such as visits to the
country houses outside the city, and the July 4th fireworks display, and
always the theater. *The Beaux' Stratagem* was presented in June, followed
by dancing on the tightrope by a child performer known as The Little
Devil, who was billed to dance with two eggs under his feet, beat the
drum in several attitudes on the rope, and throw a summerset over a
man on horseback—a diversion so enchanting that Lear took the children,
and even Uncle Harklas and Oney were given tickets to witness its
repetition.

The Washingtons had begun the fascinating annual game of accumulating things to take to Mount Vernon, this time with the obstinate hope
that the coming winter in Philadelphia would be the last they would have
to spend there—a new plough, made according to New England specifications for use in heavy soils; lightning rods as invented by Dr. Franklin;
glass lamps; a carpet; chocolate; pineapples for preserving; replacements
for Martha's favorite blue and white china; six superior shoats from a
model farm on the Germantown road, to improve the breed at Mount
Vernon; Buffon's *Natural History,* abridged in two volumes, Thomson's
Seasons, and *The Vicar of Wakefield,* to read aloud in the long, peaceful
evenings; a comb for Eliza Custis; a little chair for Fanny's Maria; a
guitar for Harriot because she teased for it, though no one ever thought
she could learn to play it; summer clothes for everybody; and a blue cloth
cape with a scarlet lining for the President—he wore it superbly, with one
corner thrown back to show the color.

The children were taken to have their teeth cleaned; the phaeton was
sent to be repaired; the Lears were given leave to go on a visit to New

Hampshire with the baby; while Fraunces remained in the house to do the preserving and pickling and keep an eye on young Lawrence Augustine Washington, who was to live there in one room while the family were away, to save his lodging bill. His elder brother George Steptoe went home to Harewood to learn something about the neglected estate which was his inheritance. They were young men now, out in society, and had discovered girls, and were to enter the Attorney General's law office in the autumn as a start to earn their own living.

At last, in mid-July, the coach rolled away toward Mount Vernon, followed by the usual procession of baggage wagons, mounted servants, and led horses. Martha held tight to present happiness. One more summer was being snatched from eternity, and for a little while again they would be at home. They could pretend, if not hope, that it was forever. She knew for a fact that George had consulted Madison about the composition of a farewell address.

George Augustine had not benefited to any degree from his sojourn at the Springs, and a recent relapse had left him too weak to leave his bed for more than a short while each day. Fanny was weary with nursing and liable to the disease herself, and she broke down and wept in Martha's arms. Maria, the eldest of her three children, now that the first boy had died, was only four, and it was doubtful if their father would survive the winter. The other news of the neighborhood was full of sickness and sorrow. George Mason, long estranged from Washington in the wrangle over the Constitution, had died at Gunston, and Harry Lee, now Governor of Virginia, had lost his wife. There was always the inexorable mailbag, with letters from people who considered themselves George's friends, urging him into the second term—even Knox—even Edmund Randolph. How could he leave Mount Vernon, with only Whiting to run it, a good man, an honest man, but not a Washington. Bob Lewis was living in Fauquier County with his new wife now, and administering the western property, which was as much as he could do. George's own presence was all that made Mount Vernon pay. Surely someone else could be President now.

Whatever they might dispute about in Philadelphia, they all agreed that only Washington could hold the country together, as the rift between the two parties widened. Only Washington was above the party—and in the middle. Hamilton wrote, pleading his side of the case, which he had been able to build up in Washington's protecting shadow. Jefferson wrote, touching on his own desire to retire to Monticello and rusticate

—denied in order to uphold his beliefs against the opposition—and pointing out that while any one else as President would appear to the country as the leader of one party or the other, Washington possessed the confidence of all.

But the newspaper war had shaken Washington's own confidence in his position—a war of invective directed against the policies and convictions of the rival factions, and also, he felt, at the solitary figure who stood behind both parties trying to reconcile their differences, and failing. Madison argued that the very bitterness of the rivalry required the strong, impartial leadership expected only from Washington. Could *Adams* hold Congress together, and inspire confidence in the country? Who then? It was not just a President the uneasy public looked to. It was the man who bore the magic name of Washington. When he passed through the streets of Philadelphia and people pointed him out, the word they taught the children to say was not the President—the word was Washington.

He contemplated the draft of his farewell address, in the old dilemma —how could he say that he would not until he had been asked officially if he would? If he did not refuse to be a candidate again, wouldn't they say he did not know how to quit? And if he put himself to the vote again, and emerged with only a small majority—or none. . . .

Martha watched him sidewise as he sat in the evenings with an idle pen or a forgotten book, but she kept her needle moving. Everyone said how well he looked, and a few weeks at Mount Vernon had made a notable improvement in his health and spirits, as always. But to the misty eyes of the woman who could remember the tall Virginia colonel of the '50s, he was tired and worn and getting old. His shoulders had a little stoop now, his unpowdered hair was quite white, and he did not hear as well as he used to. He was by no means as decrepit as he sometimes pretended to feel. But every now and then a gesture, an unconscious pose, an unpremeditated remark, stabbed her with the realization that his splendid youth was gone. Quite suddenly, it seemed to her—perhaps with those two illnesses in New York—George had turned the corner. To see him leave this place he loved, to see him committed to more years of exile, disappointment and thankless effort, was a thing she did not know how to bear for him. But all she could do was not to argue and plead and give advice. She must accept his decision with the best grace possible, create what sanctuary she could for him at whatever fireside they shared away from home, and never let him know her pity and her terror.

Before they returned to Philadelphia in October they arranged for George Augustine and his family to spend the winter at Fanny's father's house at Eltham, where the weather was milder than on the Potomac. He was to travel down by boat from the Mount Vernon landing. This left Whiting in full charge of the estate, and meant that Harriot had to be sent to Betty Lewis at Fredericksburg, with a request for firmness and a guarantee of her support. "Harriot has sense enough, but no disposition to industry, nor to be careful of her clothes," George wrote to Betty, incorporating his own observations with Martha's. "Your example and admonitions, with proper restraints, may overcome the two last; and to that end I wish you would examine her clothes and direct her in their use, and application of them; for without this, they will be, I am told, dabbed about in every hole and corner, and her best things always in use. Fanny was too easy, too much of her own indolent disposition, and had too little authority to cause either by precept or example any change in this for the better, and Mrs. Washington's absence has been injurious to her in many respects; but she is young, and with good advice may yet make a fine woman. . . ."

Colonel Jackson had asked for leave to travel abroad, so another Lewis nephew accompanied them back to Philadelphia to assist Lear—Howell, Betty's youngest, unmarried and so far untried. Whiting was to send a written report every week by the post which reached Philadelphia on Saturday. Washington would then have his quiet Sunday hours in which to reply.

The news from France was horrifying—the King arrested and imprisoned, Royalists murdered in the streets by the mob. The Washingtons were naturally shocked by the excesses committed by Danton's government, yet a French-Republican party persisted in America, nursing the ancient grudge against monarchy, preferring anything French to anything English, and Jefferson's democratic aphorisms to Hamilton's hard-headed belief in law and order, which was called monarchical and Anglophile.

Washington's November message to Congress did not announce his retirement. No rival for the Presidency appeared, or was even mentioned. His silence was taken for assent, and in February, just before the celebration of his sixty-first birthday, he was again unanimously elected, though John Adams' majority as Vice President was appreciably less.

Fanny's unhappy affairs reached a new crisis in the same month, with the death at Eltham of both her father and her husband within a few days of each other. Her brother, Burwell II, was there to uphold her, but it was plain that Washington would have to come forward as usual, and provide advice and shelter, if not an income, for his favorite nephew's widow and small children. With Martha at his side, he sat down to write Fanny a warm invitation to consider Mount Vernon her home and to call on him for whatever she needed. He added that he would have to travel down as soon as possible in connection with George Augustine's estate, and what appeared to be the suddenly failing health of Whiting, and he would see her then if she cared to make the journey from New Kent at that time.

Abigail Adams' son-in-law, the floating Colonel Smith, returned from abroad that February, with a hair-raising firsthand account of the boiling cauldron Europe had become. In a private interview with his one-time Commander, Smith made many disturbing revelations and predictions. There would be a general war in Europe, he said—France in her present mood was ready to challenge the whole world, and the massacre of the aristocrats had only begun. The popular French Minister to America, de Ternant, who had served as a soldier in the American army under Lincoln at Charleston in 1780 and traveled widely in America after the war, was now to be replaced by one of Danton's men, Citizen Genêt. America's present Minister to France, Gouverneur Morris, was resented in Paris as much for his ingrained aristocracy as for his outspoken opinions of rabble rule. Lafayette? Colonel Smith could only shrug in the French fashion. Lafayette was a prisoner in Austria, having been taken on the border in flight from his own army. He was safer there than in France. As a constitutional monarchist, he would be torn to pieces if he showed himself now in the streets of Paris. And Lafayette's family? Colonel Smith did not know. In confinement, no doubt, perhaps on the way to the guillotine in his place. Martha wrung her hands.

Escorted by young Mr. Dandridge and the Lears, she and the children were present at the simple inaugural ceremony for the second term, which took place in the Senate Chamber with the doors open to the public outside. There was a great deal of entertaining to follow, which was much enjoyed by Nelly and her sisters Eliza and Patty Custis up from Abingdon —all young ladies in their teens now. But the gay, secure Philadelphia celebrations rang a little hollow to many adults against the terror in France, where the King had been sent to the guillotine and the Queen was said to be doomed, and the fate of Lafayette remained uncertain— "crushed by the wheel he had set in motion," Gouverneur Morris wrote, in a letter which told of unbridled murder which had extended to all classes of citizens, and acknowledged his own far from pleasant situation.

At the end of March Washington made the necessary flying trip to Mount Vernon on George Augustine's affairs, and had no sooner got there than the news exploded in Philadelphia that largely as a result of Louis XVI's execution the French Minister had been ordered out of London, and that France had declared war on England, Holland, *and* Spain. Letters rained on Mount Vernon, and Washington, his mission there only half accomplished, hurried back to town, arriving on the 17th of April. He was tired, very concerned, but not flurried or ill.

Martha had remained in Philadelphia, surrounded by her young visitors, who could not have told the difference between a Girondist and a Jacobin, but who perfectly understood the fact of a public scaffold and a falling knife, and shuddered for the Queen. Philadelphia was tense and excitable, and everyone had something to say, while the Cabinet assembled behind the closed door of Washington's office—Jefferson, Hamilton, Randolph, Knox—it was like the old days, with the British in the River. Martha hushed the children and surveyed her own bewilderment and apprehension. This new word—neutrality. A proclamation of neutrality from George would mean that America must keep out of the war in Europe. But why in heaven's name should there be any question of America's getting into it? The treaty of '78 with France, they told her. She gave them a woman's answer of naïve logic—surely that treaty was dead now, along with the King who had signed it, she said, which left them gaping at her. Oddly enough, that proved to be Hamilton's answer too.

Washington had undertaken a second term partly in the hope of reconciling Hamilton and Jefferson in their bitter domestic feud. He now found himself and his infant nation facing a whole world aflame, while instead of uniting against the conflagration overseas the American public took sides practically along party lines, Hamilton's Federalists insisting that America must remain aloof at almost any price, and the Jeffersonians accepting even the murder of the King in their blind enthusiasm for the idea of republicanism. Once again George must act without a precedent, treading unknown ground. There was no guide to neutrality. What about privateering? What about the seizure of American vessels by the belligerent powers? Should Congress be called into special session? What about the reception of French Royalist refugees in America, who had once been his friends? How could he hold on to both Jefferson and Hamilton, who both talked recklessly now of retiring into private life after embroiling him for another four years? The President was not privileged to resign. Martha was sure about one thing, and said so, to his comfort, more than once. Not war. Not again. Let Jefferson go, if he wanted to risk a war for France. And it took a woman to point out that Jefferson had never smelled gunpowder, and that whatever else you might say about him, Hamilton had.

The diplomatic temperature rose with the arrival of the Girondist Citizen Genêt to replace the Chevalier de Ternant as Minister from France. Genêt was a pompous, tactless troublemaker who conceived that he had a mission in America to raise public opinion against the Washington administration and create a general demand for participation in the European war on the side of France. He had at first some success. Republican clubs were formed, and fiery speeches were made about perfidious England and how she should be dealt with. There was one awkward question: with what was America to threaten England? To declare war in support of France was simply to lay a defenseless country open to blockade or even invasion, while peaceful ports like Philadelphia became a refuge and a battleground for rival piracy.

The unanimous vote of confidence which had brought Washington into the second four years of captivity did not protect him now from personal attacks by the newspapers and the Jacobin societies for his stand regarding the French Revolution. He was accused of everything from betraying an old friend to deserting the principles for which the American war had been fought. He made no reply, but pursued his dignified routine in a serenity more impressive than ever. When he appeared in public his reception was less enthusiastic than it had been, but not a muscle of his face betrayed awareness of hostility. He moved through his levees and Martha's drawing-room evenings with his usual smiling courtesy. But his wife knew the inner conflict of doubt and mortification he concealed. They had imposed the responsibility upon him to direct the nation's course, and now they criticized his every move. No man had less of self-importance or vanity, but in spite of himself he had grown accustomed to the pedestal. To find himself now the target for every kind of verbal mudslinging went very hard. Behind what he considered a shameful affront to the Presidential office, which a man named Washington happened at the moment to occupy, the human being's feelings were grievously hurt.

The summer of '93 was a succession of what seemed to be last straws, beginning with the elopement of George Steptoe Washington, aged twenty, the elder of the two Harewood nephews, with fifteen-year-old Lucy Payne, from one of the "gay Quaker" families of Philadelphia. Eluding the President's certain wrath, the youngsters retreated to the bridegroom's Shenandoah plantation, and announced their sober intention of working it and making it pay. No one could deny that was a more commendable goal than attempting to maintain an establishment in Philadelphia on the doubtful earnings of an apprentice lawyer. Next, Washington received word of Whiting's desperate illness at Mount Vernon, and set out in the phaeton with Secretary Dandridge, arriving too late to see the poor man alive. He returned within a fortnight, forced by the pressure of public events to leave the estate without a manager just at harvest time, and dispatched his nephew Howell Lewis to do the best he could there until the whole family could go down for its usual summer visit, when Washington would be able to interview candidates for the permanent position of manager in Whiting's place.

At the end of July Polly Lear began to run a fever and died before the week was out, at twenty-three. She left a little son, and a devoted husband half distraught, while Martha was bereft of a dear companion. Washington stood beside Lear at the funeral, and the light coffin was borne to the grave at Christ Church by three Cabinet Secretaries—Jefferson, Hamilton, and Knox—and three Federal Judges—Wilson, Peter, and Iredell.

Lear had already had in contemplation some kind of independent business career to provide for a family which had outgrown his private secretary's quarters and pay, which was all the President's household could afford. It was a matter of only a few days' work to turn over his accounts and files to Dandridge, and Lear departed with the baby for New Hampshire where his mother would make a home for little Lincoln while Lear went abroad to establish connections for the shipping agency he planned to undertake at Georgetown. The Washingtons saw him go with regret. He had been an industrious and agreeable member of their family for seven years, and with them had experienced the difficult transition from retirement at Mount Vernon to the daily alarums and excursions of life in the Presidential mansion.

It was not long before they realized that Polly was an early victim of a deadly epidemic. Yellow fever had come up in the West Indies cargoes to the evil-smelling streets along the Philadelphia waterfront, and from there was spreading into the city, until the passing bells tolled all day, and the streets were dark with funeral processions. Rival theories of its

cause and treatment drowned out the politics, and when the authorities
began marking infected houses with a plague sign, and put a stop to the
bells and processions, it was too late to prevent a panic. Within a few
days everyone who could leave the city was on the way to refuge, shunned
along the road and unwelcome at their destination. Business came to a
standstill, though at first the government offices remained open and most
of their occupants stayed at their posts. Drastic remedies like purging and
bleeding and cold baths were condemned by a school of do-nothing
physicians, and argument raged until the acidulous Benjamin Rush remarked that the principal mortality would be due to the doctors.

Martha feared for the children, but refused to be bundled off to Mount
Vernon without George, who of course felt no personal alarm. His
fatalistic contempt for precautions against illness was equaled only by his
iron nerve under gunfire. And as long as Citizen Genêt was at large among
the irresponsible Jacobin clubs he had fathered in his self-anointed Joan-
of-Arc role, there was no turning one's back on him. The matter of an
illegal French privateer in Philadelphia harbor finally sealed Genêt's fate
in the Cabinet, and they determined upon an official demand for his
recall.

By September, sobered and scattered by the plague at home and
Robespierre's Reign of Terror in France, Philadelphians seemed to have
had enough Republican hysteria. Once more Washington had ridden out
the storm with granite composure, and at last on the 10th of September
the Presidential cavalcade rolled southward again toward Mount Vernon. Martha watched the familiar landmarks fall behind in secret, smiling
thankfulness. He had not caught the fever. Three more summers to go.

Affairs at Mount Vernon had never been in worse shape. Howell Lewis
had not taken hold, the white overseers had got out of hand, the slaves
had shirked their work, George Augustine's widowed Fanny was still un-
settled and wanting advice, and she had been serving the best Madeira
wine to any casual visitor. It was arranged that she should occupy with
her children Washington's Alexandria house, which required improvements for her convenience entailing some expense.

Then almost out of nowhere, though he was known to the Chews, a
man named Pearce arrived to run Mount Vernon—a sober, knowledgea-
ble fellow of farming experience, a widower with children, who earnestly
desired to be of use to his distinguished employer. Washington soon felt
that his troubles on that score at least were modified. He found it necessary
in November to meet the Cabinet at Germantown, which was considered

safe from the fever, and while there he lived in a rented house with Secretary Dandridge and two servants, until the first snow put an end to the infection, and everyone came back to Philadelphia for Christmas.

Jefferson insisted on resigning at the end of the year, commenting bitterly that he was cured of politics and that the Cabinet was a cockpit. Attorney General Edmund Randolph moved into Jefferson's place as Secretary of State. Handsome, opinionated, oversensitive to criticism, Randolph was not a popular man with his colleagues, but Washington believed in his ability. Hamilton consented to remain at the Treasury a little longer, though his reputation had suffered from sinister rumors about reallocation of funds, and other more private misdemeanors, besides his flagrant daily cockiness which older, wearier men found very hard to bear. Secretary of War Knox, the last and dearest of Washington's army stand-bys, was ailing and looking wistfully toward his own retirement to Lucy's estate in Maine, where they planned to build a wilderness mansion. Martha would miss the ebullient Lucy, linked by so many mutual memories to the stirring Headquarters days during the war, which sometimes seemed by comparison almost good. Lucy ranked second to Abigail Adams in the Presidential social circle—fat, outspoken, interfering, but a true friend. The Philadelphia climate did not seem to agree with Abigail, who was subject to torturing bouts of rheumatism, and she spent more and more time at home in Braintree—they called it Quincy now—while her forsaken *Sir* wrote long, loving, complaining letters full of Philadelphia news.

The first year of the second term had taken more out of Washington than the other four put together, but his health had stood up to it amazingly well, and he had the satisfaction of knowing that his unswerving policy was at last winning appreciation even in what had once been hostile quarters; that the offensive Genêt was to be replaced—at the price of Gouverneur Morris' recall from Paris—by a Jacobin named Fauchet who could hardly be worse; and that Mount Vernon was in better keeping than it had been since he left it in '89.

The respite was brief. By March the British blockade of the French West Indian ports encountered American neutrality. American crews were seized, and Congress became a bedlam of angry demands for the spirit of '76. John Jay was rushed off to London as a special envoy, and Monroe left the Senate to replace Morris as Minister to France. Trouble was brewing too in the West over the whiskey tax, and Washington's precious summer visit to Mount Vernon was foregone in favor of a house at Germantown where they could all live away from the humid heat of Philadelphia and danger of the fever, but near enough for him to keep a daily watch on what threatened to become civil war.

Martha was happily preoccupied with romance in all directions. Jacky's second daughter, Patty, just turning seventeen, had fallen in love with the son of Washington's friend Judge Peter of Georgetown, and was to marry him in the spring. Everyone was pleased with the match, though her elder sister Eliza felt a little left behind and openly wished that she too was as blissfully in love.

Mr. Lear's little business at Georgetown was prospering, and he had found his way to Fanny at Alexandria—both of them had been bereaved in the same year, both were young and well acquainted with each other— why should not two lonely people with a mutual background marry each other and make a home together for their children? Fanny put it to Martha in a troubled letter which reached Germantown just as George was setting out for Carlisle with Governor Harry Lee and Hamilton, to see for himself the mustering of militia to put down the insurrection in the country round Fort Cumberland which had witnessed his first campaign almost fifty years before.

George had taken time to write to Eliza Custis a fatherly warning against too much haste to fall in love and marry just because she was envious of her sister. "Love is a mighty pretty thing," he had written, while Martha marveled again at his ability to sympathize with the impetuous young, "but . . . is too dainty a food to live upon *alone,* and ought not to be considered farther than as a necessary ingredient for the matrimonial happiness which results from a combination of causes; none of which are greater than that the object on whom it is placed should possess good sense, good disposition, and the means of supporting you in the way you have been brought up. . . ."

It seemed to Martha that by George's own rules Mr. Lear qualified for Fanny. In fact, it looked like such a good idea that she was afraid of sounding too anxious, but in George's absence she undertook a letter to Fanny herself lest the prospect suffer from uncertainty. "The President has a very high opinion of, and friendship for Mr. Lear," she set down from memory of what George had paused long enough to deliver himself after Fanny's letter arrived, "and has not the least objection to your forming the connection, but no more than myself would not wish to influence your judgment either way, yours and the children's good being among the first wishes of my heart. . . ."

At Harewood, where George Steptoe Washington and his bride had actually settled down quite seriously to farming and raising a family, there was a September wedding. James Madison, Congressman from Virginia and one of Jefferson's protégés, still a bachelor at forty-three, married beautiful Dolley Todd, the widowed elder sister of Lucy Washington. Her Quaker husband had been a popular Philadelphia lawyer who died of the fever in '93, leaving Dolley with a two-year-old son. She could have married any one of half a dozen men with livelier prospects and more money than Madison, including Aaron Burr, whose wife had recently died after a long illness. But Dolley chose "the great little Madison," so often in poor health, so retiring socially, whose stiffish ways did not conceal from her his quiet humor and capacity for devotion. Martha said Dolley Todd would be the best thing in the world for Mr. Madison, and welcomed her warmly into the Presidential circle, though she had noticed that as Jefferson's influence over Madison grew, George no longer relied on him as he had done in the early days of the first administration, before Jefferson returned from France.

The year 1795 began with the wedding of Patty Custis to young Mr. Peter, which caused a great flurry on the distaff side, for her sister Nelly went down to be bridesmaid, with a new dress and the loan of their grandmother's watch to wear. George was much amused at a letter which came back from Nelly during the festivities at Abingdon and Georgetown. Unlike Eliza, Nelly was in no hurry for love and marriage, and was not impressed with young men as encountered during her first ball, and declared a resolution "never to give herself a moment's uneasiness on account of any of them."

Knox and Hamilton had both followed Jefferson into retirement, and the Cabinet was in chaos, but George sat down, still laughing, to answer Nelly's letter. Martha, who was not handy with her pen and dispensed her own advice in tactful driblets over the needlework and teacups, always admired his sermons to the girls, and his knowledge of the female heart. "Let me touch a little now on your Georgetown ball," he wrote to Nelly, "and happy, thrice happy, for the fair who were assembled on the occasion, that there was a man to spare; for had there been 79 ladies and only 78 gentlemen, there might, in the course of the evening, have been some disorder among the caps; notwithstanding the *apathy* which *one* of the company entertains for the *youth* of the present day. . . . A hint here; men and women feel the same inclination to each other *now* that they always have done, and which they will continue to do until there

is a new order of things, and *you,* as others have done, may find, perhaps,
that the passions of your sex are easier raised than allayed. Do not, therefore, boast too soon or too strongly of your insensibility to, or resistance
of, its powers. In the composition of the human frame there is a good
deal of inflammable matter, however dormant it may lie for a time, and
like an intimate acquaintance of yours, when the torch is put to it *that*
which is *within you* may burst into a blaze; for which reason, and especially too as I have entered upon the chapter of advices, I will read
you a lecture drawn from this text. . . ."

Which he then proceeded to do, at some length, with his happy faculty
of withdrawing his mind from the vexations of his office to the tranquil
contemplation of his domestic responsibilities and the enduring affairs at
Mount Vernon, creating for himself a brief mental refuge from which he
could return, refreshed and with a new perspective, to the Presidential
grind.

Martha was aware during the spring of some anxiety on George's part
regarding the unpopular treaty with England which Mr. Jay had effected
in London, but when the household moved to Mount Vernon in July
she looked forward without any special misgivings to a restorative summer there before the start of the last winter but one that they would have
to spend in Philadelphia. Once more they were winning against time.
George's health was good; Pearce was more satisfactory as a manager
than poor George Augustine had ever been; Tobias Lear and Fanny
planned to marry in August, and George had given them a little farm
called Wellington as a wedding present, which would establish them in
the Potomac neighborhood. Her natural optimism soared in anticipation
of the happy weeks ahead in the peaceful Mount Vernon routine, brightened by family visits bringing children grown almost beyond her recognition after eighteen months away.

Washington led the homeward procession in a double-rigged phaeton
which he drove himself, leaving the coach to his family, with mounted
servants and his led saddle horse bringing up the rear. It was a hot, slow
trip, during which one of his horses fell sick at Elkton and died. Heavy
rains kept him indoors the first few days after their arrival on the Potomac,
but the mailbag always came through eventually, and the first thing
Martha knew, urgent letters from Secretary of War Pickering and Secretary of State Randolph had determined him to return alone to Philadelphia for what he hoped would not exceed a week's stay. Her disappointed
protest that he would miss Fanny's wedding to Mr. Lear was received

with a tired smile. He showed her Pickering's letter, with its mysterious underlined phrase—*"a special reason* which can be communicated to you only in person." She had never liked the man, even back in his quartermastering days, and as a successor to Knox he left much to be desired.

George had no secretary until an express could fetch Dandridge from New Kent where he had gone on a visit to his people. The letters which came back to Martha from George in Philadelphia were guarded and brief, and she had still no clear idea of what had detained him there for more than a month when he returned in mid-September, weary and depressed. He had signed Jay's treaty, and was under fire again from the Republican newspapers. Well, he was getting used to that now. In the parlor after dinner the first evening at home he told her an incredible story of an intercepted letter from Fauchet to his government which seemed to convict Edmund Randolph of passing secret information to the French Minister and soliciting money in return for throwing his weight as Foreign Secretary against the negotiations with the British. George agreed with her that the supposition was impossible—and then reminded her grimly of Benedict Arnold, whom they had once liked and trusted too.

Randolph's circumstances were against him. His wife was an invalid, he was known to be hard-pressed for funds, and of all the Cabinet he had always been most inclined toward the French. He denied everything, of course, in a most embarrassing scene, and he was preparing a written defense. But even if he could prove his innocence, the harm was done and he could not be retained in a confidential post. Granted that Pickering and his friend Wolcott, who had succeeded Hamilton at the Treasury, had gone off half-cocked and had handled it clumsily and in the worst possible taste—the harm was done. Granted that Randolph had been a good and loyal friend to Washington for years—private feelings could not weigh against the necessity for peace with England, which the treaty would secure. The Fauchet letter existed—though George had read it only in a hasty translation made by Pickering with the aid of a French dictionary. The letter existed, and Randolph had been sacrificed to it. Pickering, with apparent reluctance, took over the State Department, and the wartime aide, Colonel MacHenry, was induced to serve in his place as Secretary of War.

A month remained in which George could attempt to catch up at Mount Vernon and arrange the coming winter's plantation work with Pearce, and enjoy the companionship of his neighbors. He made the most of it, in spite of the postbag and the newspapers which followed him everywhere. On their way back to Philadelphia they paused at Mr. Lear's house in Georgetown, to dine with him and Fanny, and went away very satisfied with the obvious contentment of two people who were well suited to each other.

During the autumn the Republican newspapers, in protesting Jay's treaty, overreached themselves in a kind of self-hypnotic fury of abuse of the President, in which his personal finances and even his heroic war record were dragged out and besmirched. The attack was fanned by the publication of Edmund Randolph's *Vindication,* to which Washington made no reply beyond some caustic marginal notes in his private copy. There was nothing to be gained by arguing publicly with a bitter, ruined man, and no new evidence to produce. But it was harder on him than the Arnold affair, for Randolph was an old comrade and a fellow Virginian. The hostile part of the press made a Roman holiday out of the Randolph story. Beyond the hysteria of the wolf pack on the kill, akin to the blood lust engendered in the guillotine mobs, there appeared to be no accounting for the printed invective aimed at the President, whom the whole nation had recently idolized.

But by the first of the year public feeling had turned against the scurrilous editors and swung round to shield Washington, and the celebration of his birthday in '96 was unprecedented. It began with a peal of bells and a cannon salute at dawn, and Martha waking suddenly in the Morris house in Market Street was for a moment back at Cambridge when the guns on Dorchester Heights opened up on Boston. She counted on her fingers, and it came out an even twenty years. She had heard guns since then, heaven knows—including the ones which greeted her arrival at New York in the first year of the Presidency, when she came across the bay in all the pageantry of the reception prepared for the ornate barge which carried her and the ecstatic children from Elizabethtown. Luckily she had had no inkling then of all that would be demanded of him before they let him go. And they would have to let him go soon now. If he kept safe and well through his *next* birthday, the long ordeal would be nearly over.

Chimes rang out intermittently all day, and a flood of well-wishers crowded the Presidential mansion in a continuous stream, consuming cake and punch. In the evening a gala supper was followed by a grand ball where all the ladies wore white. Martha sailed through the day, smiling and proud and cordial—the final year of bondage had begun. All the

Republican newspapers could do about the overwhelming, spontaneous tribute to the President was a sour reference to "America's political Christmas."

Jacky's eldest daughter Eliza Custis had taken them by surprise, announcing that she intended to marry Thomas Law, a wealthy Englishman lately arrived at Georgetown from India, where he had made a fortune under the administration of Lord Cornwallis—who was now the Royal Governor there—and had acquired three Asiatic sons, whose mother was said to have died. They were handsome lads, and very popular in the Federal City where Law had built a mansion and established a business. Eliza was nineteen. Mr. Law admitted to thirty-nine, and was a relative of Lord Ellenborough, Chief Justice in England—the black sheep, no doubt, Martha felt, for she considered the match unsuitable but was powerless to prevent it since Eliza's mother and stepfather gave their consent. Mr. Law was known to be speculating in city lots at the new capital, and what Washington had seen of him there had left an impression of considerable eccentricity. Moreover, he disliked the difference in ages. It was apparently too late to interfere even if they had wanted to, and he wrote a diplomatic letter to both bride and groom, inviting them to stay as guests in his house if they found themselves in Philadelphia as Eliza's sister Patty had done on her honeymoon with young Mr. Peter—which was a very different thing, Martha reminded him. Eliza's wedding took place in March at Dr. Stuart's house at Hope Park, to which he had removed his family from Abingdon to cut down expenses. Nelly Custis was bridesmaid again, but the Washingtons did not attend.

Lear wrote from Georgetown at the end of March with reference to his proposed visit to Philadelphia on business, and mentioned the illness of his wife Fanny and her little daughter Maria, eldest child of George Augustine Washington. George's reply, offering lodging if Lear did not mind sharing the room occupied by little Washington and Secretary Dandridge, where another bed could be set up, and expressing concern for the invalids, crossed another letter from Lear announcing Fanny's death—at twenty-nine, after only eight months of her second marriage.

Martha took it hard. Child of her favorite sister Nancy, Fanny had been for years like a daughter in the household, and her prospects with Lear had been so bright, after the strain of George Augustine's long, tragic illness. Adding her signature to the letter of condolence which George had phrased in his usual stately and fatalistic style on the subject of death, Martha both admired and envied his philosophy of the immutability of

Providence—while her own loving heart rebelled for poor Fanny, robbed of a happiness she surely deserved. Martha was sorry for Mr. Lear too, who was left with Fanny's little Maria, Fayette, and Charles Augustine Washington on his hands, as well as his own son Lincoln by Polly, all of them under ten years of age. Lincoln was still living with his paternal grandmother in New Hampshire, and presumably she would take charge of the other three as well. Fortunately Martha was fond of Lear's mother, and was quite willing that the children should be left in her care if the Bassetts did not object. Both of Fanny's brothers had families of their own. To take her children under George's roof would be impossible. He was already charged with Jacky's Nelly and little Washington, and with Sam's Harriot.

There was a new embarrassment too in the arrival in America of George's French namesake, Lafayette's son, aged fifteen, with his tutor, M. Frestel, apparently confident of sanctuary in Washington's home. But the Commander in Chief was now the President, and hospitality to French emigrés at the present time was a matter of state and a double-edged complication. It was necessary once more for George to stifle his private impulses in the responsibilities of his office, for he realized that whatever he did with regard to young Lafayette, he would be wrong somewhere—accused either of countenancing those who had been de-nounced as enemies of France, or of *not* countenancing the son of a man who was once a hero to Americans. Temporarily the two young French-men were installed as Hamilton's guests in New York. With Madison's absorption into the Jeffersonian circle, George was turning back, from sheer necessity, to the hard-headed, ambitious Hamilton, who had in a way grown up now, and in any case was clever enough to mind his man-ners and remember which side his bread was buttered on, politically.

A letter from Betty Lewis in April provided another surprise; Harriot, of all people, had caught a husband. Harriot was tamed, by a young man named Parks, to such an extent that she was making herself ill with anxiety lest her Uncle George might not approve the match. Betty, who would certainly be glad to see her difficult charge into the safekeeping of a husband, was convinced that Mr. Parks made an adequate living, was sober and respectable, and that Harriot was truly in love. However much relief George himself felt at the prospect, he replied cautiously, and wrote to his nephew and former aide George Lewis requesting him to look into the man's background. Harriot, having no fortune of her own, could not expect much in that direction, he wrote, but she had always lived well, at Mount Vernon and Fredericksburg, and must be protected against making an impulsive connection which would mean a come-down in her social status. She had not been brought up to marry a poor man, and it would have been as well if she had waited another year until the Washington household was again settled at Mount Vernon. But George Lewis was satisfied with what he learned, and Harriot was headstrong; and Betty, no doubt, was tired. The wedding was set for July.

Mrs. Lear came through Philadelphia with little Lincoln, on her way to her son's house at Wellington, where she would remain for a time with all four motherless children. He was fortunate that so charming and sensible a woman was able to devote herself to his family, and Martha looked forward to Mrs. Lear's companionship during the summer at Mount Vernon. Lincoln was a sprightly, healthy child. The problem was Fanny's Maria, spoiled by her mother's easy going ways as Harriot had been, and in need of a firm hand, possibly a boarding school.

Before they left for Mount Vernon in mid-June George had sent off to Hamilton the notes for a Farewell Address which Madison had begun in '92—they were to be incorporated, with Madison's consent, in the Address which was now being prepared for the coming autumn. Martha drew a long breath when she heard about that. It was another step in the right direction. Young Lafayette and his tutor had joined them for the journey and were to spend the summer with them on the Potomac. He seemed a modest, sensible lad, more than a little oppressed by his situation and the uncertainty of his parents' fate. George assumed with him a cheerful, rallying air which was supposed to cover his own anxiety, and found it hard to explain that as the head of the independent United States he was powerless to intercede on behalf of his old friend, except in a so-far ineffectual personal way through the side door of the American Minister in France.

They were forced to leave Philadelphia without a clue as to the whereabouts of Martha's handsome mulatto maid Oney, who had apparently been seduced into flight by one of the French emigrés. The President could not raise a hue and cry for a runaway slave girl, and had to make his inquiries with discretion and without result. It was a real grief to Martha, for she had reared Oney in the house, and from the age of ten the girl had been her devoted personal attendant. Martha was sure that Oney had been decoyed away by an unscrupulous adventurer, who would only ruin and abandon her, and she wanted to make it known that Oney would be taken back into the household and forgiven, in whatever state she returned. But she had vanished, and her chances of happiness in the circumstances were small. It was some time before Martha gave up hoping that Oney would find her way back to a mistress who had never been anything but kind.

At Mount Vernon they found the dependable Pearce ailing in his turn, a martyr to rheumatism, and the despairing search was begun again for someone to learn the management of the estate from him so that he could retire to a small farm nearby and rest his bones. Young Dandridge, whose attendance on his secretarial duties was sometimes erratic, went off for a holiday, and George was thankful to take on one of his many namesakes, a younger son of Dr. Craik at Alexandria, sufficiently grown and educated—partly at his patron's expense—at twenty-two to help with the letter-writing and accounts. Lear was always ready to lend a hand at Mount Vernon, and Martha had a suspicion that when his grief for Fanny had a little subsided he might be willing to rejoin the household in the old way, for George had never had a more helpful and loyal assistant.

In August George made a flying trip back to Philadelphia, to deal with the necessary recall from Paris of Monroe who, as the American Minister, seemed to be doing all the wrong things there, and to name his successor; and also to confer with Hamilton on the Farewell Address, which was finally published in September, closing the door on any possible campaign to persuade him into a third term. On his way North, dining at Alexandria with another of his former aides, Colonel Fitzgerald, he got track of a man named Anderson, as a suitable manager for Mount Vernon. He visited the Custis girls at Georgetown in their new dignity as Mrs. Law and Mrs. Peter, inspected the buildings at the Federal City, and was back at home in time to catch up on his correspondence and dispose the young of the family for the interval which remained before his return to Mount Vernon in the spring, when his second term would be at an end.

Little Washington Custis, now an irresponsible fifteen, was to enter Princeton in somewhat the same forlorn hope that had placed his father at King's College more than twenty years before. Maria was to go to her uncle Burwell Bassett in New Kent until it could be arranged for her to attend the Moravian school for girls at Bethlehem. Harriot was safely off their hands with her new husband, and the Harewood nephews were grown. George Washington Lafayette and M. Frestel would go back to Philadelphia as members of the President's household, and George Washington Craik was added as junior secretary to Dandridge. Faithful Tobias

Lear promised to be at hand in Philadelphia in March to superintend the final packing up for the homecoming.

Martha began to feel a little giddy with anticipation. Philadelphia took on a certain glow as she returned to it for what would be the last time ever. She had been happy there, for it was not in her nature to fret and pine. She had good friends in the city whom she would be sorry to part from, though it need not be forever, as many of them had hitherto found their way sooner or later to Mount Vernon and would doubtless do so again. The Knoxes were already gone to Maine, and Abigail Adams had become half an invalid at home in Massachusetts. The Hamiltons she could do without, though Betsy still had a place in her heart. The Biddles, the Morrises, and Mrs. Powell, widowed by the fever in '93—they would all come to visit on the Potomac, and when the Government moved to the new Federal City, which nearly everyone but George had now begun to call by his name, the members would be nearer than they were at Philadelphia. George would miss going to the theater, and to Mr. Peale's museum, and the circus. But Mount Vernon made its own entertainment, especially with the children getting married and having babies of their own. Philadelphia had not been all bad luck, now that it was almost over.

They arrived there in a pelting autumn rain, and in the middle of the first contested Presidential election campaign. The field had narrowed down to John Adams and Thomas Jefferson, with some mention of Aaron Burr, Thomas Pinckney, and even Pickering. Adams won, by a scant three votes, with Jefferson second, which made him Vice President—an awkward combination to start with.

Martha's receptions were crowded for the holiday season, and everyone seemed intent on dispelling the memory of the unbridled abuse which had been poured out on Washington, to which had been added a recent attack by Thomas Paine, who considered himself aggrieved because the President had not rescued him from the Paris prison where his own Girondist meddling had landed him—Washington could not even rescue Lafayette. For his last Philadelphia birthday the city outdid itself. The cannon were fired, the ships in the harbor were dressed, flags flew everywhere, the militia turned out in uniform, the servants were given liberty, and the schools were closed. There was a ball in the evening, dancing and supper for twelve hundred guests at Oeller's new hotel, and everyone was moved almost to tears at sight of the tall, stately figure in black velvet and powder, bowing to his well-wishers. On the evening of March 3d he gave his own farewell dinner party, and everyone choked up again.

On the 4th, again in black velvet and powder, and wearing a military hat, he walked alone to the Congress Hall as the cannon boomed, and took his place beside John Adams, who was dressed in pearl-colored broadcloth, for the inauguration ceremony. He then accompanied the new President on foot back to his hotel through a crowd which watched and followed them almost in silence, awed and stirred beyond its own comprehension. Abigail Adams had not come down from Braintree for the occasion.

A few more days must pass in paying and receiving private calls and, as Adams had declined to purchase the contents of the Presidential mansion, disposing of some of its furnishings as gifts to their friends and arranging for the rest to be put up for sale. A pair of lamps were set aside for Mrs. Powell, wine coolers for the Cabinet, and the large drawing-room luster was presented to Mrs. Morris. Lear and Dandridge would remain to oversee the cleaning and transfer to the new occupants. Young Lafayette and M. Frestel were coming back to Mount Vernon with the family. Washington Custis was still at school. The party consisted of Martha, Nelly, and the President, the junior Craik and the two young Frenchmen, with their personal servants and luggage, much of the latter being sent round by water. It was quite a cavalcade which set out from Market Street early on the morning of the 9th.

Martha had caught a severe cold sometime during the late festivities, but she refused to delay the departure. Washington wrote back to Lear from their first night's stop at Chester, about all the things they had forgotten: "Thus far we have arrived safe, but found it disagreeably cold," he reported. "To give greater surety to the large looking-glasses, and such other articles as are liable to be injured by the jolting of a dray, be so good as to have [them] taken down by hand and stowed where they will not be trod on, or tossed about in the vessel's hold. . . . Mr. Hill told me he had done something (but what I do not recollect) about the livery clothes; I pray you to inquire and know they are sent round. . . . The newly printed pamphlets pray purchase, and bring with you for me; Mr. Dandridge knows what I already have. . . . P.S. On one side I am called upon to remember the parrot; on the other to remember the dog. For my own part, I would not pine much if both were forgot."

They all knew that it was only a pretended fractiousness to cover an almost unbearable schoolboy elation. He was free. He was going home.

CHAPTER TEN

His Vine and Fig-Tree

1797–1799

MARTHA'S COLD PERSISTED during the journey, and hung on after they had reached Mount Vernon. This time there was no fortuitous absence on George's part during which she might collapse in comfort without his being aware of it, and she kept on her feet with a dogged determination not to spoil his homecoming by being ill. They were of course inundated with neighborly visitors and letters welcoming them home, which was very kind of everyone and they were always glad to see old friends, but they would have been still gladder of a little solitude in which to sort themselves out and draw breath after the bustle and social demands of the final days in Philadelphia.

Mr. Lear saw all the household goods and baggage aboard the sloop and went home by road to Georgetown, having faithfully discharged those small leftover jobs which kept occurring to Washington along the way, and were conveyed in his hasty letters sent back from Chester and Head of Elk—new carpeting for the blue parlor at Mount Vernon, Wilton preferred if not much dearer than the Scotch carpeting; one of those thermometers which told the state of the mercury within twenty-four hours; pocket money ($200) for young Dandridge who was leaving with Washington's blessing after six years of service, for a secretaryship with the diplomatic mission at The Hague; Nelly's bedstead and the trundle under it which, Martha had just informed him, to his surprise, belonged to him and must be sent to Virginia; one-half dozen white silk stockings (without gores and *with* small clocks, as he preferred them); raw silk boot stockings; a new pair of bellows.

They could expect Lear to arrive at Mount Vernon in time to help with the removal of the goods from the river-landing to the house. As he intended to maintain for his boys the little property called Wellington which Washington had given to Fanny as a wedding present, he would be almost a member of the household again, in his frequent visits to and fro. Fanny's Maria was still with her New Kent relatives, who were so concerned about her health, dreading her father's disease, that the idea of the Bethlehem school was abandoned.

It was rather like 1784 all over again, when he came home from the war, and everyone's tongue slipped easily into the old terms—he was the General again, as he had always been to most of them, and the title of President belonged now to a stranger. Again there was for Martha the odd sensation of survival and deliverance; eight more years had been successfully lived through, and sanctuary was achieved without mishap. Nothing more could happen to him now, the burden was at last transferred to other shoulders. By a miracle of endurance and good fortune, which was God's own mercy, George was home safe again, and this time it was forever. From now on it would be her daily task only to see that things went on well for him, that his household was peaceful and happy, and that nothing which it was within her power to prevent caused him anxiety. All her love and devotion closed gently round him, like a spreading of wings over the rest of his life. Now he was hers.

As soon as Washington began to make a thorough inspection of his estate, which he had not had time to do for eight years, he was appalled at the disrepair both inside and out—from a loosening of the parlor mantelpiece and the sag of a main girder which endangered the floor of what they still called the New Room at the north end, to overgrown fields and hedges and weather-worn outbuildings. The need of ready money for workmen and materials again drove him to the sale of some western lands, and within ten days the whole plantation sang like a beehive with the activity of joiners, painters, and glaziers. "I have scarcely a room to put a friend into or set in myself without the music of hammers or the odoriferous smell of paint," he wrote Secretary of War MacHenry, in the course of a serious consideration of the outrageous behavior of the French Directory in refusing to receive the new American Minister, Charles Cotesworth Pinckney, sent to replace Monroe.

He made it quite clear to them in Philadelphia that he had no intention of being drawn back into the maelstrom of public affairs. "For myself," he wrote to Oliver Wolcott at the Treasury, "having turned aside from the broad walks of politics into the narrow paths of private life, I shall leave it to those whose duty it is to consider subjects of this sort; and (as every good citizen ought to do) conform to whatever the ruling powers shall decide. To make and sell a little flour annually; to repair houses (going fast to ruin); to build one for the security of my papers of a public nature, and to amuse myself in agricultural and rural pursuits will constitute employment for the few years I have to remain on this terrestrial globe. If to these I could now and then meet the friends I esteem, it would fill the measure and add to my enjoyments, but if ever this happens it must be under my own vine and fig-tree, as I do not think it probable that I shall go beyond the radius of twenty miles from them. . . ." So he had written to Lafayette and Knox in '84, Martha recalled ruefully. After thirteen years, now it was coming true.

Once more it was spring at Mount Vernon, and neglected though the gardens might have been during their absence, the place was a fairyland of tender green and overnight blossom, as the cherished trees and shrubs and plants, which its owner had been collecting for years, even when he was not there to see them set out and nursed into feeling at home, seemed to respond to his presence. Almost each day something new appeared, and in the intervals between the arrivals and departures of their innumerable guests, he and Martha would walk together across the dipping lawn to stand in front of the latest miracle of leaf or petal and admire. Soon it would be forty years since she had first come to Mount Vernon in the spring, a bride with two unruly little children of her first marriage, and hopes of more by the tall, quiet man at her side. Now her grandchildren were grown and having babies of their own, and George was childless. Nephews were not the same. Except for George Augustine, none of them had really been a success as adopted members of his family, and even little Washington was proving a disappointment, in his father's fashion.

There was an unhappy echo in the letters written to Mount Vernon by the President of Princeton College about Washington Custis, who was exhibiting all the same traits of character which had called forth those long-winded homilies from Dr. Boucher in Jacky's time. Like his father, young Custis always admitted handsomely that he had done wrong, promised to mend his ways, and then pursued his charming, idle, self-indulgent course, just as Jacky had done.

Lund Washington had died at Hayfield in the summer of '96, but his widow still lived in the house. The news of Betty's death at the home of her married daughter in Culpeper County came in a letter from George Lewis, who lived nearby. She was sixty-three, but death was sudden, from a cold caught during the outdoor exercise she loved. Martha knew that George felt the loss of his only sister, next to him in age, more than his usual stoic acceptance of death revealed in his reply to her son. Of his generation, only Charles was left now, father of the late George Augustine, but Charles' affinity for the bottle received scant tolerance from his self-disciplined brother, and Charles' only other son, Samuel, had never won his uncle's heart.

Sometimes she wondered, looking out across the placid silver river from the broad piazza, what would become of Mount Vernon when its master was finally called away from it forever. He loved the house and its green acres as he might have loved a son. She wondered too, thinking of his brother Charles, and the children of his brother Samuel, what George's son might have been like. Better none at all, she thought with something like discovery, than a boy who did not measure up, and it would have been hard, she decided ruefully, very hard indeed, for anyone to be George Washington's son. She had often felt a sense of failure when she remembered the children she might have given him and somehow had not. Now she wondered. His requirements were high. The world's would be higher still, for one of his name. Almost impossible now, for a boy not to fall short of such a father. . . . But it was a compensation she knew better than to offer the proud, lonely man who liked best to think of himself as Farmer Washington.

That he felt a lack she was well aware, for his thoughts often turned backward to young men he had loved; those who had seen the worst of it with him in the war, those who had stood beside him in the bewildering early days of the Presidency. Too many of them were dead, like Tilghman. Most of the rest were married, like Jackson, who on his return from a European tour had won one of the beautiful Willing girls in Philadelphia. David Humphreys was still in the diplomatic service abroad, now as Minister to Spain, and when he sent a pair of handsome shoe buckles and a fine gold chain by a recent traveler, not so much as gifts of value to his friends at Mount Vernon as in remembrance of good times past, Washington wrote with his guard down, of "a desire for a companion in my latter days, in whom I could confide"—in case Humphreys ever chose to return as one of the family. The answer was another disappointment.

Humphreys was about to be married to the daughter of an English banker in Lisbon, which closed the book on those old, easy days of his jolly bachelorhood before the first administration. They both wrote to him, wishing him every possible happiness.

Tobias Lear was of course still at hand, often in the house and always ready to be helpful in any capacity, but he had his own family obligations and preoccupations now. The new manager, Anderson, was a good man in his place, but touchy, opinionated, and hard to handle. George Washington Craik had returned to his father's house in Alexandria, except for frequent visits as one of Nelly's circle. George Washington Lafayette expected any day to receive news of his family's release from imprisonment, and was ready to start for France at a moment's notice.

There was, however, still one unmarried Lewis nephew—Lawrence, whom Betty had most depended on since the death of his father. He was older than Robert and Howell, responsible, certainly, tall, good to look at, self-contained—a Washington, like his mother. They had never seen much of him, it was true, but he was perhaps Betty's favorite among all her boys, and she did not need him any more. George wrote to him: "As both your aunt and I are in the decline of life, and regular in our habits, especially in our hours of rising and going to bed, I require some person (fit and proper) to ease me of the trouble of entertaining company; particularly of nights, as it is my inclination to retire . . . either to bed or to my study soon after candlelight. In taking these duties (which hospitality obliges one to bestow on company) off my hands it would render me a very acceptable service. . . ." Lawrence might not find it quite so dull as it sounded, they told each other hopefully, when George read out the letter to Martha. The house was often full of Nelly's friends and the Stuart young, and the Laws and the Peters and their children from Georgetown, as well as George's own contemporaries, many of whom were distinguished people. Lawrence would have plenty of time to read, and he might help a little with the correspondence, and there was always Nelly's music, and Alexandria was not far away.

Lawrence accepted. They could expect him before the summer was out.

Meanwhile the plantation life with its multitude of small interests went on. There was a new improved threshing-machine; the Hessian fly was in the wheat, and rust invaded the straw; a drought damaged the corn, which in July was not half a leg high; and then it poured rain and ruined the hay. Pearce on his little farm sent a bag of rye grass seed as a present to his former employer; George's body-servant, Christopher, was bitten by Nelly's little dog and was sent to Pennsylvania for treatment by a specialist in such things, returning none the worse. Martha's health was still low, and she fought a perpetual fatigue and frequent colds, while presenting the smiling, cordial front which was so much admired and commented on by the many visitors who taxed it pitilessly. At the end of July, when Nelly and the two French lads were on a visit to the Stuarts at Hope Park, and Washington Custis was away at school, and Lawrence Lewis had not yet arrived, she and George had one of their rare dinners alone together—the first in twenty years, he remarked, but it was not as bad as that. They had dined alone together in '85.

Then everybody came home again, and Lawrence began his duties, and proved to have the happy knack of fitting in and taking hold. Nelly's female friends found him highly eligible, but Lawrence was still a bachelor at thirty, and had got hard to catch. The younger Harewood nephew, Lawrence Augustine Washington, married a Miss Wood in September. George esteemed her grandmother, and approved the match.

Beyond the snug little world of Mount Vernon the national emergency swirled and mounted. President Adams was not giving satisfaction. He had not the dignity nor the prestige with which Washington had held down the venomous party bickerings, and was often taunted with his skimpy three-vote majority. Abigail had not Martha's tact and serenity. Abigail talked back, took sides, and scored points, and was known without affection as Mrs. President. Hamilton had got into a nasty scandal involving a woman and blackmail, and chose to sacrifice his private life to his public reputation, by making a full confession of a very sordid affair. Martha astonished George by remarking that she was not surprised. Betsy forgave him, and defended him, but the Republicans jeered. Monroe arrived at Philadelphia, furious over his recall from France, and demanding explanations. There was yellow fever in the city again.

Washington Custis turned up at Mount Vernon from Princeton in October, with no visible intention of ever resuming his studies at the College. He had been in another scrape, and George sent a letter of regret and thanks to the Princeton president, and allowed himself to be persuaded by his womenfolk that the boy would employ his time if allowed to remain at home. Possibly a tutor or a new school could be determined on after the holidays, which were still a good two months away.

Only a fortnight later young Lafayette and Frestel departed for New York and a ship to France, on what Washington feared was a premature rumor of the safe reunion of the family at Hamburg. He gave them $300 for expenses and accompanied them in his carriage as far as the Federal City, where they were to take the New York stage. In the thirteen years since he had parted with the boy's father on a similar journey, the whole face of Europe had changed, and the repercussions were shaking the foundations of the young Republic which France had helped to found.

Domestically, they were in sudden luck, in the arrival at Mount Vernon before Christmas of Mrs. Forbes, a housekeeper found for them by Bushrod Washington, who was now at thirty-five a sober, successful, but childless lawyer in Richmond, on whom Washington relied for his small legal chores in connection with land rentals, overdue accounts, and so on. Mrs. Forbes was a capable, motherly woman who had once run Governor Brooke's household, and now took the Washington family into her charge. Martha found herself with leisure on her hands for the first time in living memory, and was able to nurse her little ailments and enjoy her guests in unaccustomed freedom from the hundred small cares of a conscientious hostess.

The winter began with severe weather, but the rooms were warm and bright inside the Home House, and at the end of the old year Nelly Custis wrote a cheerful accounting to her friend Mrs. Wolcott in Philadelphia: "We have spent our summer and autumn very happily here, have in general been blessed with health—have had many very agreeable visitors, and are now contentedly seated round our winter fireside, often speaking of and wishing to see again our good friends in Philadelphia, but never regretting its amusements, or a life of ceremony. I stay very much at home, have not been to the city for two or three months. My grandparents, brother, a nephew of the General, and your *humble servant* compose the family at present. I never have a dull or lonesome hour, never find a day too long, indeed time appears to fly, and I sometimes think the years are much shorter for some time past than they ever were before. . . ."

The General's nephew. But among Nelly's many beaux and callers, from earnest George Washington Craik to dashing young Carroll of Carrollton in Maryland, nobody yet was reading between the lines, unless it was the elusive Lawrence himself.

"I am not very industrious," Nelly continued to Mrs. Wolcott, her style a happy blend of her grandmother's homely inconsequence and Washington's rolling sentences, her penmanship a model even to him, "but I work a little, read, play on the harpsichord, write and walk, and find my time fully taken up with the several employments. My mother and her young family are all well, my sister Peter has lately presented us with another little relation, a very fine girl who is thought to be very like her mother . . . I send [you] by my sister Law a cotton cord and tassels which I have made on purpose for you, I learnt last summer to make them. I hope you will like it, and you will gratify me very much by wearing it for remembrance of me. . . . Mr. G. W. Craik is at present very much indisposed from a violent cold, which was occasioned by his going out and exposing himself too much [to] some severe cold weather that we have had lately. Poor young man, I fear he is not long for this world, and his father probably will live to see all his children buried. . . . He is much to be pitied, and Mrs. Craik also, only they can comfort themselves with reflecting that their children were very deserving and have gone to that Being who never fails to reward merit; but I believe when our feelings are so much hurt, by the loss of a worthy object, it is impossible to reason with ourselves, we are wholly occupied with our present affliction and cannot immediately recollect any circumstances to alleviate or remove it.

"Alexandria had been very gay, balls in abundance. . . . When in a city, balls are my favorite amusement, but when in the country I have no inclination for them, and am too indolent in winter to move to any distance from home for any species of amusement. . . . My beloved Grandmamma joins me in love and best wishes to you and your children, with all our compliments to Mr. Wolcott. . . ."

Early in the year they sent Washington Custis to Hope Park for a visit, in the hope that Dr. Stuart might by observation of him make some helpful suggestion, for George was satisfied, as he wrote Stuart, that the boy would soon forget what he did know, "so inert is his mind," he concluded bitterly. It was decided to enter the boy in the College at Annapolis for a fresh start, and Stuart accompanied him there early in March. Within a month, Custis wrote of a Maryland rumor that Charles Carroll, Jr., was courting his sister Nelly, and very kindly gave his approval to the match. George replied at once that the less said on that subject, especially by Nelly's friends, the more prudent it would be.

With the return of spring to the Potomac, the old nostalgia for days and friends that were gone began again, and set them to wondering why it was that Sally Fairfax had never come home. So far as they knew, she was still living at Bath, in poor health, since the death of her husband all of ten years ago. Ironically, now that George William was no longer alive to receive it, the title had recently crossed the Atlantic to his half-brother Bryan Fairfax, who after a somewhat unstable boyhood had wound up in Holy Orders, and was now rector of Christ Church in Alexandria. When as a consequence of his inheritance Bryan announced his intention of visiting England in the spring of '98, the Washingtons sat down to devise a letter to Sally at Bath.

They found it hard to know where to begin, and agreed that George should write about affairs in general, and Martha would add a page of neighborhood news at the end. When he had finished, he read it all out to her, so they need not repeat each other, and she smiled at the recurrence, before he had gone far, of his favorite phrase, from the Book of Micah: "Worn out in a manner by the toils of my past labor," he had written to Sally, "I am again seated under my vine and fig-tree, and I wish I could add that there are none to make us afraid; but those whom we have been accustomed to call our good friends and allies are endeavoring, if not to make us afraid, yet to despoil us of our property; and are provoking us to acts of self-defense which may lead to war. What will be the result of such measures, time . . . must disclose. My wish is to spend the remainder of my days (which cannot be many) in rural amusements; free from those cares [from] which public responsibility is never exempt . . . and it is a matter of sore regret, when I cast my eyes toward Belvoir, which I often do, to reflect that the former inhabitants of it, with whom we lived in such harmony and friendship, no longer reside there. . . . A century hence, if this country keeps united (and it is surely its policy and interest to do so) will produce a city, though not as large as London, yet of a magnitude inferior to few others in Europe, on the banks of the Potomac . . . where elegant buildings are erecting and in forwardness, for the reception of Congress in 1800. . . ."

George had a resident clerk now, young Albin Rawlins from Hanover County, who wrote a beautiful hand and had no objections to keeping accounts and doing some of the travel for the estate work. With Mrs. Forbes in charge of the kitchen and a noticeable improvement in Martha's health, they were able to make a round of summer visits to the Stuarts at Hope Park and to Georgetown, where they praised Patty's new daughter, and recognized unwillingly that her sister Eliza was finding Mr. Law increasingly difficult to live with.

Martha could not quite believe in the growing threat of war with France, even when at Philadelphia an apprehensive Congress insisted that George should accept the command of a new army which as yet had barely begun to materialize. France had one war on her hands already, with Britain, and the idea of building defenses against an invading French fleet in American ports seemed to Martha just more of Hamilton's theatrics, though Secretary of War MacHenry actually came to Mount Vernon in July to bring George's commission as Commander in Chief—again!—and Lear gave up his Georgetown business and returned to full-time employment as secretary to deal with the inevitable flood of applications and advice in the mailbag. Something about the Mississippi, something about Florida—Martha was impatient. They surely didn't expect George at his age to lead an attack on Louisiana. Anyway, he had stipulated that he would not come into the field until they had got an army ready for him, and at the rate they were going about it that would be never. Obstinately, she blamed Hamilton for the whole thing, though he was no longer in the government, except for his wire-pulling with his friends MacHenry and Wolcott, and he had somehow got himself named Inspector-General over people like Knox.

President Adams went home to Braintree and stayed there all summer. In November Congress finally prevailed on George to come to Philadelphia for a conference, partly because MacHenry was proving so inadequate in the War Department. She thought it a pity George had to make the journey in bad weather, but somehow the matter of war with France remained to her remote and unreal, and she refused to get excited about it. When they had had to fight England there were English soldiers already in possession of Boston. France would have to bring her troops through the British blockade and across the Atlantic and land them. It made no sense. Besides, Nelly and Lawrence Lewis were in love, and that was important.

They broke it to George when he got back from Philadelphia in the middle of December, and he at least pretended to be surprised, though Martha assured him she had seen it coming, and had told him so. In her pleasure at the prospect of another wedding, she even consented, as did Nelly Stuart, to the granting of a cornet's commission in Lawrence's proposed troop of Light Dragoons in the still nebulous army to Washington Custis, with the vague expectation that it would give him something to do and divert his mind—at eighteen—from its matrimonial trend. George Washington Craik (happily recovered) and Charles Carroll, Jr., were to be in the same corps.

Nelly chose to be married on the birthday of the man she called Grandpappa, in February, '99, and as his new army uniform had not yet arrived from the Philadelphia tailor, he wore his old blue Continental coat and buff breeches in honor of the day. Not every man of sixty-seven could get into the same waistband he had laid aside more than ten years before. The brief entry in his diary that night was the echo of one he had made in '85. "The Revd. Mr. Davis and Mr. George Calvert came to dinner, and Miss Custis was married about candlelight to Mr. Lawrence Lewis."

For their honeymoon the young Lewises went to Lawrence's married sister Carter's house in the mountains, and on to the Springs. While they were away Martha succumbed to one of her rare collapses, and Dr. Craik was sent for, and the two Custis girls hurried down from Georgetown. She gave them all a thorough fright, and then the ague and fever yielded slowly to doses of the bark, leaving her weakened and low.

The late summer was saddened by two more deaths: Charles Washington's at Happy Retreat in the Valley, which had long been expected, and Patrick Henry's—the last of George's brothers and almost the last of his colleagues in the high, inspired days before the war. Lear fell ill with a rheumatic lameness, and went to Philadelphia to consult a physician there. For several weeks, with Martha still only convalescent, George was left to wrestle almost alone with his many problems, not the least of which was always financial, and he spent some time in drawing up a will. Lawrence had somewhat precipitately given up his military career before it had a chance to begin, and anyway the war scare was petering out and no one really believed now that the French were coming. There was again an odd sensation of having been there before, when George wrote to Lawrence and Nelly of the joint inheritance he had made out for them, some two thousand acres including the Dogue Run Farm, and suggested that while they were building a house on the land they might live at Mount Vernon, as Fanny and George Augustine had done.

Martha was herself again by the time they returned from the Springs, and was delighted to learn that Nelly would have a child before the year was out. A daughter was born at the end of November, in the room where Nelly herself had grown up, and when it was seen that all was going well, Lawrence Lewis and Washington Custis went on a visit to New Kent before Christmas.

As was his custom at the end of each year, George wrote out a detailed plan for the one to come, farm by farm, the arable land to be restored, the succession of crops, the ditching and the hedging, the inventories of cattle and slaves. With a copy of the procedure for the River Farm overseer in his coat pocket he rode out on the 12th of December

as usual, a little belated in starting because of having composed a letter
to Hamilton about the projected military academy. Soon after midday it
began to snow and sleet, and he found fault with a cattle pen shelter,
which delayed him further.

Dinner was kept waiting while he completed his rounds, and contrary
to his usual custom he went straight to the table without changing his
clothes. At the back of Lear's mind an alarm bell rang, and he protested
that snow was still clinging to the General's hair and collar, but Washington answered that his greatcoat had kept him quite dry. Nevertheless,
he considered the weather too bad to send a servant out with letters to
catch the Alexandria post, and spent the evening reading the newspapers
and going through his mail.

The next morning he confessed to a sore throat, and remained in the
house till after dinner, when it stopped snowing and he went down to
the riverside edge of the lawn to mark some trees he wanted taken away.
In the evening he was hoarse, but read aloud to Lear and Martha from
the newly arrived gazettes, and expressed something more than surprise
that Monroe had been elected the next governor of Virginia. When they
parted for the night Lear suggested that he ought to take something for
the cold, and Washington made his habitual exasperating reply: "Let it
go as it came." Nelly was still confined to bed after the birth of her
child, and they looked in on her and the baby together on their way to
their room.

Martha roused in the small hours to find him in great distress, with
labored breathing and a very painful sore throat. The fire had burned
down and he would not allow her to get out of bed to call a servant for
fear she would catch one of her own devastating colds. Yielding to his
feverish insistence, she lay beside him in a growing apprehension, waiting for the slow winter dawn to bring a housemaid to rebuild the fire
—and then sent the girl flying to summon Lear and Rawlins, whom
George thought capable of bleeding him at once.

They found Martha up and dressed, and Washington barely able to
speak. Lear's own servant went galloping for Dr. Craik. While they
waited for him, Rawlins unwillingly bled the sick man, and Lear rubbed
his throat with *sal volatile* and wrapped it. George could not swallow
his usual remedy of onions boiled in molasses, which brought on a spasm
of near suffocation instead of relief.

Craik took one look at him and sent for two consultants, Dr. Brown
and Dr. Dick. After that the day became a nightmare to Martha, while

she tried not to alarm Nelly, and fought a rising panic every time she visited George's bedside. He was not able to gargle, but was made to inhale from a steaming kettle of vinegar and water. She was convinced that bleeding was wrong, but under Craik's advice it was done again, and again.

She could not have told, later, exactly when she first realized that this was not like those other illnesses, which were sufficiently frightening each time, but were bearable because of his well-known ability to rebound. Some time during the afternoon, like a cold draft in the room, the knowledge reached her. Something in his breathing, something in his eyes as they met and passed beyond hers, something in the few difficult words he spoke, told her that this time they were going to lose him. At that moment passionate protest and frantic appeal flared within her, even while she strove for composure, sitting very still, careful to make no move, no sound, to betray the emotion she endured. And it was just then, as though the awareness had passed from him to her, that he asked her to bring the wills.

The request was whispered by him to Lear, who was never out of reach of Washington's hand, kneeling at the bedside to turn and ease him when he could. Lear spoke to her quietly over his shoulder—the wills—two of them—from the writing-desk in the library—bring them here. There was a ringing in her ears as she rose, without replying to him, steadied herself with a hand on the bedpost, and walked out of the room —down their little private stair—over to the writing-desk—she knew where to look, he had shown her more than once. . . .

When the crisp folded papers rustled and wavered under her touch she saw that her hands were shaking, and leaned her weight on them quickly on the desk top, to hold them still, as though she were ashamed of them. Bent above his desk, she made her last rebellious prayer—not yet—once more—*not yet*—and the papers under her hands reminded her that it was no use now. He knew that. He was waiting for her to bring the wills. He would expect her to behave well. She was not a woman who went to pieces.

Leaning on the desk, she waited while from the strong dark wood which knew him so well, some of his own fatalism entered into her. She straightened slowly, and found she could stand—drew a deep breath, and found her hands cold but firm again. Carrying the wills, she made her way back to the bedside.

Their eyes met in a long, still look as she approached. It was enough

to fling her weeping on his pillow—and it was more. Wordless but composed, she held out to him the two documents. He touched one of them
—and the other he discarded. Again Lear spoke for him. She was to burn
the old one—the one he had sent back from Philadelphia in '75. She went
to the fireplace and laid it on the flames. When she turned back to the
bed Lear gave her the will George wanted kept, and she put it away in
her own cabinet across the room.

The slight effort had exhausted him, and he was obscured from her
sight by the physicians, who hovered over him. He gasped, and strangled,
and was quiet, with a long sigh. She clenched her cold hands and sat
down again in her chair at the foot of the bed.

She would have interfered, and begged them not to torment him any
more with futile remedies, but it would have made an unseemly disturbance in the room. He himself could be patient with them, in his unfailing
courtesy, even though he knew their desperate measures were useless.
She must behave as well as he did, matching her endurance to his, while
he could still see her. So she sat quietly, not watching him all the time,
listening to the agonized breathing, and the ticking of the clock—waiting
for the doctors to admit that there was nothing more to do but wait. . . .

Before nightfall she could see that at last they had given up, and Lear
had sent for the Laws and the Peters—too late. Washington Custis and
Lawrence were beyond recall on the Pamunkey. Christopher, who had
been standing beside the bed all day, except when he was given some
small service to do, moved to the door to receive from Mrs. Forbes a cup
of tea she had brought for Martha, who had eaten nothing since morning. The cup jarred in the saucer as he offered it in both his black hands.
Looking up at him, she saw his face wet with silent tears. Out of pity for
him, she accepted the tea, and allowed it to cool in the cup untasted.
When Christopher returned to his place, George noticed that he had
stood there all day, and motioned him to a chair.

The windows darkened and the candles were brought. The clock kept
striking. She had lost all sense of time. She waited. Her self-control was
no longer an effort, it was a permanent condition. There was no hope
left—no prayer—no protest. It was all but over. If only they would leave
him in peace. . . .

Finally the two consultants went out of the room together, and Dr.
Craik sat helplessly beside the bed while his old friend lost his last battle.
She was sorry for Craik, who had been his comrade so long, and could
do nothing for him now; and she was grateful to Lear, who still knelt

beside the bed, ready to lay his arms around the great shoulders and raise or lower them in the hope of finding easement in the struggle for breath. At ten o'clock Washington took his hand from Lear's warm clasp to feel his own pulse, and then without another movement or a sound, he withdrew from life.

When Dr. Craik leaned to lay his hand over the eyes of the man on the bed, Martha spoke, and her voice was calm and steady because she had already taken leave of him, long ago. "Is he gone?" she asked, and Lear's wordless gesture confirmed it. "I shall soon follow him," she said simply.

Even then, prepared as she had thought she was, the room was suddenly emptier. She stayed in her chair, conscious of a decent stirring around the bed, unable herself to rise and do what, if anything, should be required of her. There was no one to come to her, because Nelly was not allowed to move about. She would have to go and tell Nelly soon, nobody else could do that for her with Lawrence away. Poor Mr. Lear had dropped into the chair by the fire with his face hidden in his hands —now and then his shoulders shook. She ought to go to him with some word of comfort—he was a dear, faithful friend to them all—but she sat still, dry-eyed, her hands quiet in her lap, her head a little bent, drained of compassion, of fortitude, of grief itself.

Dr. Craik came and laid his hands on her shoulders, raising her to her feet. Other strong, warm hands reached out to her as he drew her toward the door—Molly her maid, and Mrs. Forbes were both weeping, but they meant to comfort her. She passed them gently and went to Nelly's room. Even when Nelly sobbed in her arms, she did not break down.

Lear sent out all the letters and made the necessary arrangements. Lawrence and young Washington could not even arrive in time for the funeral, but the Laws and the Peters and the Stuarts and half of Alexandria were there to do him the last honors. Sitting silent and composed upstairs with Nelly and the baby, Martha heard the muffled drums and measured tread of the procession as it started down the slope from the piazza where the coffin had last stood, to the vault.

The bedroom she had shared with him was closed, and she chose to sleep in the garret room above it, which had a window looking toward the vault, but no fireplace. Abigail Adams' letter of condolence brought her the gift of tears at last, for it roused the memory of that first hot summer in New York when George had gone to the very threshold of death, and that time he had got well.

Inevitably she asked herself the futile, tormenting questions which always come too late. Was there anything she should have done, or done differently, which might have saved him? Had she been preoccupied with Nelly and the baby, as his cold first came on, and not taken fright soon enough? If she had risen at once that morning, against his wish, so that Dr. Craik could have reached the house by the time he was only sent for, would it have made all the difference? Could she have prevented the repeated bleedings, by setting her woman's will against the doctors, or was the harm already done? George had known that it was no use, that was why he sent her for the wills. George had known from the early morning, she thought now, that it was his last illness. Perhaps a Philadelphia doctor, like Benjamin Rush who, whether you liked him or not, had braved all the yellow fever epidemics there, would have known something to do. . . .

George was a quiet man with a light tread, but the house had always seemed empty and still when he left it. Now, without the promise of his return to solace her, she would wander from room to room rather like a ghost herself, counting up her memories—here he would sit listening to Nelly at the harpsichord—here he had laid down a book and would never pick it up again—here they had sat with Lafayette in '84, and discussed the measures which might be taken to preserve the union of the rival States—here he had given Fanny in marriage, and Nelly too, and here he had held Patsy while she died—here the glittering French had stood on their way to Yorktown and marveled at the hummingbirds—here she had sat with him in the long, peaceful evenings, while they composed letters to absent friends, and remembered the small, close rooms at Newburgh and Valley Forge. . . .

The house was full of helpful young people, solicitous lest she have time to grieve, and she was driven to claiming her old hour of solitude after breakfast, which in recent years had been sacrificed to the demands of public life. Nelly's new house, to be called Woodlawn, was being built of rosy brick nearby, but she and Lawrence and Washington Custis all swore never to leave Martha alone at Mount Vernon. Nelly's baby Frances was often put into her great-grandmother's arms, and there was another child the following year.

General Washington's widow did not hide herself from the many well-meaning people who came, out of kindness, to bring their condolences and keep her company. Gracious and cordial in her black gown and white frilled cap, she dispensed the lavish Mount Vernon refreshments and hospitality which had always been his pride, and listened with lively interest to the visiting Congressmen's talk of President Jefferson's new administration. Sometimes her unofficial comments were carried away and repeated with delight.

Summer came, and went, and came again, and she kept busy and cheerful, while Nelly ran the house and Lawrence and Lear saw to the estate affairs. Patty Peter's marriage was a happy one, but it was very plain that Eliza had made a mistake, as Law's speculations and wild promotion schemes began to dissipate his fortune and his good humor. Washington Custis, handsome and jolly in his precarious bachelorhood, was still her favorite of all the family, and she watched with amusement while all the girls set their caps for him.

As the second anniversary of George's death approached, she was spending more time resting in bed in the little garret room, with a couple of charcoal heaters tempering the cold because there was no fireplace. Nelly brought her novels to read—she enjoyed them guiltily like a schoolgirl, finding herself enthralled with Richardson's romances, and Fielding's *Amelia* and, most enchanting of all, the anonymous *Evelina* and *Cecilia,* which she was convinced could only have been written by a woman. She wished she had had the last two in time for Mr. Lear to read them aloud in the evenings, for she was sure that George would have heard them with many a knowing smile. . . .

Nelly worried about her being alone, and would come up with a bit of sewing or knitting to sit by the window and chat, but the room was chilly unless you were in bed, and Martha sometimes felt obliged to descend to the warm, bright rooms below for fear the children would think she was moping, when she was only a little tired. It was a long way back to her third-floor sanctuary. By the spring of 1802, the stairs had begun to tell on her. Time was running out. And now George was not there to worry if she stayed in bed.

She had one remaining task to make sure of, and knew that she must not put it off too long. She waited for a day when all the others were busy with their own concerns, and took from the little chest at the foot of her bed a packet of letters tied with fading ribbon. These were all that remained of the many George had written her from Headquarters during the war, and since then on their rare separations. They had already had a burning after they returned to Mount Vernon to stay, and all her letters had gone then—those which had not already perished by his discretion when his baggage had always been subject to capture by the enemy. The accident of his having left a few of her later ones forgotten in a drawer of a writing-desk which was sold to Mrs. Powell when they left Philadelphia had brought home to them the necessity to protect their privacy from even friendly curiosity. His official papers would be left to posterity —he had been a public servant. But they winced at the thought of less discreet people than Mrs. Powell having access to their family writings. They believed her when she said she was returning them unread, and yet she had read enough to make that little jest about finding "love letters" to him from a lady—knowing quite well who that lady was. The packet she enclosed was consigned to the library fire that night at Martha's wish, along with all the rest. She had never found letter-writing easy, and was never proud of the result.

Then George began to remember things he had written to her which were better lost to view, and she surrendered page after page to the flames. These few she now held in her hands she had kept back that evening, for one reason or another—the two from Philadelphia as he set out to take command at Cambridge in '75—the one which reached her at Eltham inviting her to join him for the first winter of the war—the one from Keith's house in Pennsylvania before the Trenton gamble, when he thought the game was pretty near up—the one after Princeton, when the tide seemed to have turned against the British—one from West Point, when he was still dizzy with the shock of betrayal by Arnold—a reckless, ardent one after he had seen her off homeward from Middlebrook—the ringing, vital announcement that the army was moving toward Yorktown by way of Mount Vernon—a discreet, unhappy note from Philadelphia in '87, with the Constitution looming—a lonely one from Germantown in '93 while the fever was still raging in Philadelphia—she read them all again, her cheeks shining with tears, and then gathered them tidily together and tiptoed downstairs to the parlor fire.

She had chosen her opportunity, and the room was empty. Kneeling on the hearth, she laid the letters in the flames one by one, and watched them curl into ashes. She had nearly finished when a door closed briskly in the hall—Lawrence, by the footstep. Two letters were still in her hand —the two from Philadelphia in '75. She thrust them quickly into a drawer of a writing-desk and was sitting, apparently idle, in an armchair by the fire when Lawrence entered the room.

The next day she did not come down to breakfast, and there were anxious faces round her door. She lay still in the bed, feeling feverish and unwell, and knew that they had sent for Dr. Craik. Well, let him come. Sometimes doctors were no use, but George had taught her that they must be allowed to try. She kept her eyes on the white blur of the window which looked toward the vault—that way when she went, toward the River. There was no reason to linger. She thought sometimes of the two letters in the desk in the parlor, forever beyond her reach. The desk would be Nelly's soon, and she would find them there. One could trust Nelly. She and Lawrence would go to live at Woodlawn, and Bushrod, childless like George, would have Mount Vernon. Bushrod's brother Corbin had children. . . .

There was nothing to grieve for, nothing to regret, it had turned out the way she had hoped, all through the war, all through the Presidency. George had got home safe at the end, in spite of everything, and they had had two good years together at Mount Vernon, after all. He was not called away to the new army, he had seen the French threat fade, he had seen Nelly married, he had seen her baby. Once more he had left his wife behind, but now that she came to follow him it would be rather like that first adventurous journey to join him at Cambridge in the unknown New England country, a quarter of a century ago. This time she must set out alone, but he had shown her the way, and he would be there waiting when finally she too arrived at Headquarters.

TABLE OF RELATIONSHIPS OF
THE WASHINGTON AND CUSTIS FAMILIES

George Washington's father, Augustine Washington (1694-1743), married as his first wife Jane Butler, by whom he had two surviving children:

(1) Lawrence (1718-1752)

(2) Augustine ("Austin") (1720-1762)

By his second wife, Mary Ball, he had five surviving children:

(3) GEORGE (1732-1799)

(4) Betty (1733-1797)

(5) Samuel (1734-1782)

(6) John Augustine (1736-1787)

(7) Charles (1738-1799)

Lawrence Washington (1) (Mount Vernon) married Anne Fairfax, and their several children all died in infancy.

Augustine Washington (2) (Wakefield) married Anne Aylett, by whom he had several daughters and a son:

(a) William Augustine

GEORGE WASHINGTON (3) married Martha (Dandridge) Custis, (1732-1802) a widow with two children, Jack and Patsy Custis. There were no children of this marriage.

Betty Washington (4) married Fielding Lewis (1725-1781) of Fredericksburg, by whom she had six surviving children:

(a) Fielding, Jr.

(b) George Fielding

(c) Betty

(d) Lawrence

(e) Robert

(f) Howell

Samuel Washington (5) (Harewood) married five times and had four surviving children:

(a) Thornton

(b) George Steptoe

(c) Lawrence Augustine

(d) Harriot Perrin

John Augustine Washington (6) (Bushfield) married Hannah Bushrod, by whom he had four surviving children:

(*a*) Jane

(*b*) Mildred

(*c*) Bushrod

(*d*) Corbin

Charles Washington (7) (Happy Retreat) married Mildred Thornton, by whom he had several children, one of whom was:

(*a*) George Augustine

In the third generation a few personalities stand out among George Washington's numerous nieces and nephews:

William Augustine Washington (2*a*) married his cousin Jane Washington (6*a*).

George Fielding Lewis (4*b*) and his brothers Robert and Howell were all at different times aides or secretaries to General Washington.

Lawrence Lewis (4*d*) married Martha Washington's granddaughter Eleanor Parke Custis.

George Steptoe Washington (5*b*) and his brother Lawrence Augustine and their half-sister Harriot composed the troublesome younger generation at Harewood.

Bushrod Washington (6*c*) married Julia Blackburn. He was named Washington's heir after Martha, in the General's will. Bushrod's marriage was childless.

George Augustine Washington (7*a*) served as aide to General Washington during the war, and as steward at Mount Vernon during the early years of the Presidency. He married Martha's niece Fanny Bassett, by whom he had three children: Maria, Fayette, and Charles Augustine Washington.

On the Custis side, Martha was one of eight children, and remained in close touch with her family after her marriage to Washington; especially with:

(1) Bartholomew Dandridge (1737-1783) whose son:

(*a*) Bartholomew Dandridge II (176?-1802) served as Washington's secretary during the Presidency.

(2) Anne Dandridge ("Nancy") (1739-1777) married Burwell Bassett, by whom she had several children:

(*a*) Fanny Bassett (1767-1796) married Washington's nephew George Augustine Washington (7*a*). After his death she married Tobias Lear, who was Washington's secretary.

Martha's son, John Parke Custis ("Jacky") married Eleanor Calvert, by whom he had four children:

Eliza Parke Custis (1776-1832) married Thomas Law.

Martha Parke Custis ("Patty") (1777-18   ) married Thomas Peter.

Eleanor Parke Custis ("Nelly") (1779-1852) married Lawrence Lewis (4*d*).

George Washington Parke Custis (1781-1857) married Mary Lee Fitzhugh.

After Jacky Custis' death his widow married Dr. David Stuart, by whom she had numerous children.

A Bibliographical Note

A complete bibliography for an informal book of this kind would be superfluous. I am one of the conscientious few who can honestly claim to have read straight through the 39-volume Bicentennial Edition of Washington's *Collected Writings,* edited by John C. Fitzpatrick, and my notes on these alone fill nine closely written indexed note-books—as I found it helpful to get the essential outlines of his correspondence all together within my reach at one time, instead of using the volumes singly on loan from the library as my narrative progressed through the years. This method entailed hours of copying in my own system of longhand-shorthand, some of it verbatim, some key-notes and page-numbers to which I could return in the text weeks later without scuffling through the indexes. The main value of these letters for me lay in the brief paragraphs Washington habitually inserted towards the end of almost any communication to a neighborhood friend or a member of his family or Staff, giving the most recent personal news of Martha and the children, or other members of the family and mutual acquaintances—often providing clues to their whereabouts, health, and current doings which exist nowhere else. For instance, his "Mrs. Washington prays you to accept her sincere thanks for your kind attention to her while she was in the city of Philadelphia—" or "Mrs. Washington left this the day before yesterday for Mount Vernon—" make it possible to fix almost to the day her arrivals and departures from Headquarters during the war, of which there is seldom any other record.

Whenever possible I have secured photostats of Martha's own letters, which nowhere have been quoted in full, and except for those written to George have survived in surprising numbers, scattered through various historical societies and manuscript collections. Photostat copies of Robert Lewis's *Journal* written in 1789 when he acted as escort to Martha and the children on their journey to New York after the first inauguration, and letters to their friends from Tobias Lear, Nelly Custis, and other relatives and visitors, have contributed useful small details of Martha's daily life and surroundings which are not available in print. A particular effort has been made to get plans and descriptions of the many houses she lived in during the course of Washington's duties as Commander in Chief and President, and to visit those which still remain.

Douglas Southall Freeman and John C. Fitzpatrick have recently superseded the standard works on Washington's life which prevailed for years, from John Marshall and Washington Irving on, though much of the older material is still vital and interesting. Even the casual reader need not shy away from Freeman's seven volumes, for they are as entertaining as they are scholarly. Besides the *Collected Writings* prepared under the Bicentennial Commission (1931-44) Dr. Fitzpatrick also edited the *Diaries of George Washington* in 4 volumes (1925) and wrote several other valuable books on the period. Stanislaus Murray Hamilton prepared a 5-volume collection of *Letters to Washington* (1898), written during the period before the Revolution, and Jared Sparks edited 4 volumes of the *Correspondence of the American Revolution* (1853) consisting of letters to Washington throughout the years 1775-83. William S. Baker compiled two unique volumes, *The Itinerary of General Washington* (1892) and *Washington After the Revolution* (1898), which together with the Bicentennial Commission's *Washington Atlas* make it possible to follow in his very footsteps almost from day to day.

More intimate material is to be found in George Washington Parke Custis's *Recollections* (1860), Tobias Lear's *Letters and Recollections of Washington* (1906), Stephen Decatur's *Private Affairs of Washington* (1933), based on the Lear records, and Charles Moore's *The Family Life of George Washington* (1926), along with Welles's *Pedigree and History of the Washington Family* (1879). These are the bare bones, the beams and girders on which any account of his personal life must rest.

When we look for opinions, deductions, controversy, and easier reading, we come again first of all to John C. Fitzpatrick and his volume called *Washington Himself*, published in 1933 during his work for the Bicentennial Commission, and probably the best single-volume estimate of Washington as a man. Moncure Conway, in a publication by the Long Island Historical Society in 1889, gives a valuable account of *Washington and Mount Vernon*, and Benson Lossing (1870) and Paul Wilstach (1916) have both devoted a volume to the gracious life that was lived in Washington's day in his home and neighborhood.

When we come to the Revolution, the source material is vast and varied, led off once more by John C. Fitzpatrick with his *Spirit of the Revolution* (1924), and ranging from Lossing's invaluable *Pictorial Fieldbook of the Revolution* (1858) to the very recent *Rebels and Redcoats* by George Sheer (1957) and David Chidsey's *Valley Forge* (1959). I prefer always to follow the footnotes in a modern publication back to the sources, a trail which leads all the way to Mercy Warren's *History of the Revolution* (1805), the fascinating Adams family letters, Elias Boudinot's *Historical Recollections* (1894), the Chevalier de Chastellux's *Journal of His Travels in North America* (1827), Alexander Graydon's *Memoirs* (1811), Jacob Hiltzheimer's *Diary* (1893), General "Lighthorse Harry" Lee's *Memoirs of the War in the Southern Department*, James Thacher's *Military Journal*, etc.

Amongst the bales of literature devoted to men like Alexander Hamilton and Thomas Jefferson, each reader must sample and choose for himself. And each must discover for himself the more specialized treasures such as Jonathan Boucher's *Reminiscences of an American Loyalist* (1925), Stephen Bonsal's *When the French Were Here* (1945), William Stryker's *Battles of Trenton and Princeton* (1898), John Tebbel's remarkable *Washington's America* (1954), Emily Stone Whiteley's *Washington and His Aides-de-Camp* (1936), and Mabel Ives's *Washington's Headquarters* (1932).

For Martha Washington herself, the list is brief. Anne Hollingsworth Wharton's biography published in 1897 is still the most valuable. Memoirs of Mrs. Washington, Sr., and Martha were compiled by Margaret Conkling in 1859, and by Benson Lossing in 1886, in each case published together in one volume, a closer association than Washington's mother and his wife ever enjoyed during their lifetimes. A somewhat romanticized book about Martha Washington by Anne Curtis Desmond appeared in 1955. But however scarce the material appears to be, it is always possible and sometimes it is best to come at a subject obliquely, through the eyes and lives of contemporaries, and many lively first-hand accounts of Martha are hidden away under other names, notably Abigail Adams and Mercy Warren.

Of the general biographical reference books, Appleton's 6-volume *Cyclopedia of American Biography*, in the revised 1898 edition, remains my standby, while no one has ever rivalled Jared Sparks's *Library of American Biography*, 1st and 2d Series, in some 25 volumes, for memoirs of the more obscure figures of the Revolution such as Pulaski and Benjamin Lincoln.

This is only a sample, however, of the reading which enriched the two years involved in the production of this book, and it still leaves unnoticed many rewarding *Lives* of Washington's contemporaries, like David Humphreys, William Stephens Smith, George Mason, Henry Knox, Gouverneur Morris, Lafayette, Charles Willson Peale, Philip Schuyler—the hard-to-find ones like Francis Drake's *Life of Henry Knox,* and Moncure Conway's *Edmund Randolph,* which are always worth the search—and the necessary background material like Eberlein and Hubbard's *Diary of Independence Hall* (1948), and Carl Becker's *Declaration of Independence* (1922), or Paul Wilstach's *Tidewater Virginia* (1929). Perhaps a better acquaintance with the Washingtons in this volume will lead more people to investigate for themselves the fabulous scene of 18th century America.

Acknowledgments

A book which requires historical research can seldom be accomplished without the patient assistance of experts. I would like to name with gratitude for illuminating correspondence, Miss Susan Armstrong and Mr. Thad W. Tate, Jr., of Colonial Williamsburg; Mr. Charles C. Wall and Mr. Walter Densmore of the Mount Vernon Ladies' Association; Dr. Francis S. Ronalds, Dr. Walter E. Hugins, Mr. Francis Ross Holland, Jr., and Mr. Hans Mayer of Morristown National Historical Park; Dr. Lloyd Eastwood-Seibold of the Valley Forge Historical Society; Dr. R. N. Williams of the Pennsylvania Historical Society; Dr. Whitfield J. Bell of the Yale University Library, and Miss Eleanor Murray of the Fort Ticonderoga Museum. I am also indebted to the Yale University Art Gallery, the Duke University Library, the Harvard University Library, the State Normal School at West Chester, Pa., the Library of Congress, the Pierpont Morgan Library, the Metropolitan Museum of Art, the New York Public Library, the New York Historical Society, the Virginia Historical Society, the Maryland Historical Society, and the Bennington Museum at Bennington, Vermont. My particular thanks go to Mr. Lloyd D. Heflin of Los Angeles, who went so far as to lend rare books from his own library to a stranger; and to Mrs. M. P. Strandberg of Marshfield Hills, who spent time and trouble to secure helpful material at Cambridge and Boston. As always, special mention must be made of the friendly and intelligent service rendered by the staff of the New York Society Library.

Index